AC
COL
PLAIN

PETER J. LEWTY

ACROSS THE COLUMBIA PLAIN

Railroad Expansion in the
Interior Northwest, 1885-1893

WSU
PRESS

Washington State University Press
Pullman, Washington

Washington State University Press, Pullman, Washington 99164-5910
©1995 by the Board of Regents of Washington State University
All rights reserved
First printing 1995

Cover: Tracklaying on east side of Stampede Pass, 1887. Courtesy Eastern Washington State Historical Society, Spokane.

Library of Congress Cataloging-in-Publication Data

Lewty, Peter J., 1934-
    Across the Columbia plain : railroad expansion in the interior Northwest, 1885-1893 / Peter J. Lewty.
      p. cm.
    Sequel to : To the Columbia gateway.
    Includes bibliographical references and index.
    ISBN 0-87422-115-3 (alk. paper). — ISBN 0-87422-114-5 (pbk. : alk. paper)
    1. Northern Pacific Railroad Company—History—19th century.
2. Oregon and Transcontinental Company—History—19th century.
3. Oregon Railway and Navigation Company—History—19th century.
4. Union Pacific Railroad Company—History—19th century.
5. Railroads—United States—History—19th century. I. Title.
HE2791.N855L48 1995
385'.09795'09034—dc20
                         94-39630
                         CIP

Washington State University Press
Pullman, Washington 99164-5910
Phone: (800) 354-7360
Fax: (509) 335-8568

To Beverley,
with love

Contents

Preface

When I first went to live in the mountains of the West Kootenay I was surprised to find that if I followed the Columbia River south into the State of Washington it soon brought me to a wide-open prairie country, a land of broad wheat fields on rolling hills, with small towns nestling in the dry valleys between. This was certainly not what I had expected in the heart of the Cordillera, but there it was, and it extended as far as I could see, from the foothills of the Bitterroot Range in the east all the way to the Cascade Mountains on the far horizon to the west. Southwards it presented a great vista of land and sky.

That first surprise in discovering this country was to be followed by many more, for it is a land of surprises, which it reveals one by one. Looking at maps of the Inland Northwest I was struck by the close mesh of the railway network, and at once began to wonder why such a sparsely populated agricultural area should have been blessed with so many competing lines. Before my questions could be answered, I had much to learn, and not only about railways. Donald W. Meinig's admirable book, *The Great Columbia Plain*, provided me with a wealth of information. Moreover, the threads of regional railroad history, so skillfully woven into it, suggested that someone should make an attempt to assemble a more detailed account of the way in which the railway system developed. Without fully realizing what was involved, I foolhardily decided, in 1978, to write a complete story of railroad construction in the Columbia Interior between 1879 and 1914. Unfortunately, as my research progressed, it soon became clear I was exploring an ever-expanding field. If I was to cope successfully with the wealth of information available from newspapers and periodicals published prior to the financial collapse of 1893, I would have to end the saga at that point. Since any study of later events would have required access to railroad company archives, which I did not have, the decision was easily made. I gladly opted for further exploration of the more forthright world of the 1880s. Even then I found there was far too much material for one book and had to divide the work into two at the construction hiatus of 1885.

This second volume, a sequel to my *To the Columbia Gateway: The Oregon Railway and the Northern Pacific, 1879-1884* (Washington State University Press, 1987), covers the period of adjustment following the collapse of Henry Villard's first empire. It deals with the shifting relationships between the Northern Pacific, Oregon & Transcontinental, Oregon Railway & Navigation, and Union Pacific Railway companies, and traces the effects of company rivalry on the pattern of railroad expansion in the Interior. An account is also given of the advent of the Great Northern Railway. I have taken pains to describe the features of the various lines, examine contemporary methods of construction, and chronicle the contractors' advance. I have also added a chapter to cover railway operations of the time. Wherever possible I have used anecdotal material to add human interest.

Geographically the narrative covers events occurring between the Rocky and Cascade mountains, including the Flathead, Kootenai, and Big Bend countries, the Coeur d'Alene mining region, the Yakima Valley, the wheat lands north and south of the Snake River, and the foothills of the Blue Mountains. Given that events occurring in the Columbia Interior cannot be considered alone, I make occasional excursions to points beyond the Cascade Mountains. In the realm of omission, I have made no reference to Daniel C. Corbin's Spokane Falls & Northern Railway built between 1889 and 1893. That railway, however, seems to be a topic blending in more readily with an account of events occurring on both sides of the Canadian border during the following 20 or more years.

Although I have made every attempt to ensure that the historical data presented in this book are accurate, there may inevitably be some mistakes. For these I undertake complete personal responsibility and offer sincere prior apology.

Before leaving the reader with the text, I would like to acknowledge the help given to me by many kind people during the preparation of this book. Among these I am particularly indebted to the staff of Selkirk College Library at Castlegar, British Columbia, and especially to Mrs. Arlene Ommundsen, who went to great pains to supply me with reference material from elsewhere. Others deserving special mention are Mr. Charles Mutschler of the Archives and Special Collections section of Eastern Washington University Library at Cheney, who searched out material otherwise difficult to find; Mr. Lawrence Shawver of Spokane, Washington, who generously provided information from his extensive collection of railroadiana; Mr. James Reiser of the Union Pacific Railroad Company Division Engineer's Office, Portland, Oregon, who cheerfully complied with my repeated requests for civil engineering data; my friend, the late Mr. Ernest Turner of Ottawa, Ontario, who sought out material held in the National Science Library of Canada; and last, but by no means least, my wife Beverley and son Steven who typed the manuscript several times over. To all of these wonderful people and to the staff of the WSU Press I express my sincere thanks.

PETER J. LEWTY

North Bay, Ontario
January 1995

Prologue

The Interior Plain of the Pacific Northwest is hemmed in by mountains. The Columbia River alone provides an outlet to the Pacific Coast and has always been the most important avenue of commerce. In the days before American settlement, Hudson's Bay Company voyageurs plied its waters to maintain a tenuous transcontinental trade link with Montreal. And when the Oregon Country was overtaken by Manifest Destiny, American prospectors, traders, and farmers passed upriver to the promised land.

In 1860 a group of independent Columbia River steamboatmen and portage owners pooled their resources to form the Oregon Steam Navigation Company, which monopolized the river trade for the next 19 years. Short railways eased freight-handling bottlenecks at the Cascades and Celilo portages, and the sternwheelers provided adequate frontier transportation. Seasonal variations in river level, however, limited their capacity to handle bulk commodities. By 1878 the riverboats could barely cope with the increasing quantities of export grain. The region urgently needed a better system of transport. Fortunately, as the nation emerged from the depression of the 1870s, money again became available for railway construction.

Congress chartered the first American overland railroad, linking Omaha, Nebraska, with Sacramento, California, in July 1862, and the Union Pacific and Central Pacific companies completed that connection in May 1869. To keep California loyal to the Union, Congress not only granted land to the transcontinental railway builders but also loaned them money. No such political imperative, however, furnished funds for the second transcontinental venture. The Northern Pacific Railroad, chartered in 1864 to build and operate a railway on a northern route from the head of Lake Superior to both Puget Sound and Portland received a huge land grant. The legislators, however, withheld financial assistance and refused to guarantee the company's bond issues. Jay Cooke & Co., the well-known wartime financial agents for the United States, attempted to sell Northern Pacific bonds, but without government guarantees their efforts were badly handicapped. Construction nevertheless got underway in 1870, and by June 1873 the track extended west from Duluth to the Missouri River. A separate section of railway, meanwhile, linked Kalama on the lower Columbia River with Tacoma on Puget Sound. By August 1873 Jay Cooke & Co. had committed their entire resources to the Northern Pacific venture and were financially over-extended. In September of that year they failed to meet their obligations and had to declare insolvency, thus precipitating a stock market panic, plunging the nation into a long and severe depression.

Before the Northern Pacific Railroad could resume construction, the company had to pay off bondholders with preferred stock. This process was completed in 1875, but construction of the northern transcontinental line did not get under way again until 1879. In that year the company set out to occupy the Columbia Interior so as to claim and sell good agricultural land. Their plan was to bring up materials and supplies on Oregon Steam Navigation Company steamers and build 200 miles of railway from the mouth of the Snake River northeast to Pend Oreille Lake in Idaho. The money derived from bond issues and land sales would then be used to build the road along the Columbia Valley. Just as the work got under way, however, a syndicate of Eastern financiers and Portland capitalists headed by Henry Villard purchased the Oregon Steam Navigation Company. To the dismay of the Northern Pacific board these intruders immediately formed the Oregon Railway & Navigation Company (OR&N) and occupied the left bank of the Columbia.

Villard, who had been acting as an American representative for German investors, quickly made clear that he intended to funnel all the northern transcontinental railway traffic onto his own line to Portland. He could thus perpetuate the monopoly formerly enjoyed by the Oregon Steam Navigation Company, preserve the established regional influence of Portland, and control the commerce of the entire Pacific Northwest. As the Northern Pacific Railroad Company remained impecunious he believed that his terms would be accepted. In October 1880 Northern Pacific formally recognized the OR&N right of way along the Columbia Valley and agreed to divide the Interior Plain into separate zones of influence north and south of the Snake River. The OR&N for its part undertook to complete a railway from Wallula to Portland within three years and granted Northern Pacific the right to run trains over it. For a few days Villard and his associates "were exultant," but within a month the tables were turned on them. In November 1880 Northern Pacific reached a financial agreement with Eastern bankers for a $40 million bond issue. They thus secured enough money to complete their entire transcontinental road, including a direct line over the Cascade Mountains to Puget Sound.

Villard was thoroughly alarmed, for the Northern Pacific clearly intended to side-step The Columbia Valley and bypass Portland altogether. This would place the value of OR&N securities, upon which his credit depended, in jeopardy. Suddenly he was confronted with selling out to either the Northern Pacific or Union Pacific, or boldly attempting to buy a controlling interest in the Northern Pacific Railroad Company itself. Unwilling to abandon his dreams of a Northwestern empire, he opted for the latter course and began to acquire Northern Pacific stock. When he reached the limit of his own resources he appealed to friends and business associates, asking them to invest $8 million in a potentially profitable venture. As the OR&N had already paid dividends as high as 10 percent, the money came rolling in and by March 1881 he had secured a majority of the outstanding Northern Pacific stock. Northern Pacific president Frederick Billings at first put up a stout resistance by issuing the company's reserve stock to the old proprietors, but then secretly sold out his own large interest to Villard for personal advantage. In May 1881 Villard emerged victorious. Appealing for another $12 million capital from his enthusiastic followers, he set up a holding company named Oregon & Transcontinental (O&T) which took control of the two older concerns.

Under Villard's aegis, railroad construction proceeded apace. The OR&N completed a line along the Columbia Valley from The Dalles to Wallula in April 1881. Converting the existing Walla Walla & Columbia River Railroad to standard gauge they then built a two-pronged extension north to both Dayton and the mouth of the Tucannon River, reaching the latter vicinity in the fall of 1881. Plans had been made to bridge the Snake River at Grange City, and workers had already graded a roadbed for an extension north into the Palouse country. Following the incorporation of the O&T, however, a branch line was built east to Colfax from a connection with the Northern Pacific main line at Palouse Junction, 51 miles north of Wallula. The Villard lines then crossed the Snake River on a single bridge at Ainsworth. In Oregon, meanwhile, OR&N started a line from Umatilla southeast over the Blue Mountains to Baker City to head off the Union Pacific's Oregon Short Line. As a result of Villard's quarrels with Union Pacific about access to mining areas in Montana, this road was eventually extended beyond Baker City to Huntington. Further west, the OR&N main line was pushed down the Columbia Valley toward Portland, and by November 1882 trains were running through to Albina, on the east bank of the Willamette River.

Advancing across the Interior from Ainsworth, the Northern Pacific Railroad reached Spokane Falls in June 1881 and Pend Oreille Lake by the end of the year. During 1882 and 1883 Villard spent most of the available money rushing the northern transcontinental road to completion. Blasting their way east up the Clark Fork Valley, forces directed by OR&N construction superintendent John L. Hallett reached the Flathead River crossing, just east of Paradise, Montana, in March 1883. In the meantime, construction crews working their way west advanced up the Yellowstone, and Mormon contractors, starting out from the Montana end of the Utah & Northern Railway, completed the sections in between. On September 8, 1883 Villard assembled an unlikely host of American and foreign guests at a point just west of Garrison, Montana, and there he drove a ceremonial last spike. Even as he did so, however, his several companies were on the verge of bankruptcy.

The Northern Pacific, like most American railroads of the time, was built with loan capital, the shares being distributed as a bonus to encourage bond sales. The investing public innocently assumed the land grant would yield enough money to pay off the bonded debt and retire the preferred stock, thus allowing earnings to be translated into dividends on common shares. Unfortunately, in June 1883, it became clear that construction costs would greatly exceed the estimate engineers had made. Villard realized that if a second mortgage was placed on the property and another tier of bonds took precedence over the preferred stock, the holders of common shares would sell. Desperately he tried to avert disaster, but the old proprietors of the company, betrayed by Billings in 1881, now seized the opportunity to regain control. As soon as the company announced the construction cost overrun there was a great rush to sell stock, thus forcing down the price of Villard company shares to levels at which it seemed Oregon & Transcontinental could no longer remain solvent. On December 17, 1883 Villard was forced to resign from the presidencies of both the Oregon & Transcontinental and Oregon Railway & Navigation companies, and on January 4, 1884 he withdrew from leadership of the Northern Pacific. During the next week a Philadelphia syndicate, including former Northern Pacific president Charles B. Wright, took advantage of the depressed stock market prices to purchase a large block of Northern Pacific shares previously held in the Oregon & Transcontinental treasury. The old proprietors thus regained control of the railroad. On January 17, 1884 Robert Harris, an experienced railway manager already associated with Wright in the Tacoma Land Company, gained election as Northern Pacific president. The company then placed all emphasis on building the direct line through the Cascade Mountains to Puget Sound.

Despite the debacle, the Oregon & Transcontinental Company retained control of Oregon Railway & Navigation. T. Jefferson Coolidge of Boston, who took over from Villard as president of the Oregon railway, straightened out some of the tangled affairs left by his predecessor and then arranged for a short-term loan to push the Baker City branch through to a connection with the Oregon Short Line. When the Blue Mountain snows melted in the spring of 1884, construction began anew, and on November 25 of that year the OR&N rails were joined to those of the Union Pacific system at Huntington, Oregon. In Washington Territory meanwhile, O&T sold the Columbia & Palouse line to OR&N instead of handing it over to the Northern Pacific, as previously planned. The Oregon Railway & Navigation Company thus gained a disconnected foothold in the Palouse country north of the Snake River.

By January 1884 Charles B. Wright and Robert Harris could largely dictate Northern Pacific policy. Oregon & Transcontinental nevertheless retained a significant residual share in the railroad and tried to use it for the benefit of OR&N, which provided most of the holding-company's income. For the next five years the Northwestern railways remained plagued by the problem of overlapping ownership. A great deal of money and effort were wasted constructing competing lines and carrying out stock raids. When company officials at last arranged a satisfactory separation in 1889, the Northern Pacific and Union Pacific companies found their credit nearly exhausted. They were then in no condition to compete with interlopers or weather the coming financial storm.

Chapter One

Lease and Joint Lease

Following Henry Villard's downfall, Oregon & Transcontinental Co. shareholders sought recompense for recent financial reverses. Retaining control of the Oregon Railway & Navigation Co., they resolved to use it to best advantage. Northern Pacific still lacked an independent outlet to tidewater and had to hand over westbound traffic to the OR&N at Wallula. Held off at the mouth of the Burnt River canyon, Union Pacific would be obliged to exchange the Oregon Short Line traffic at Huntington. The Oregon Railway & Navigation Co. would then be free to charge exorbitant rates, and neither transcontinental would dare retaliate lest eastbound traffic be diverted to the other. This situation was promising for the exaction of tolls, but it was certain to expire as soon as one of the two Pacific companies completed a direct line of its own, either to Portland or Puget Sound. The O&T therefore attempted to discourage such construction, offering as an alternative a lease of the OR&N property.

During the next five years the railway companies discussed a lease by Northern Pacific alone, a lease by Union Pacific alone, and a lease by both companies acting jointly. A first round of negotiations with Northern Pacific continued throughout the spring and summer of 1884.[1] No agreement could be reached, however, for although the Northern Pacific directors proved reluctant to let the OR&N lines fall into other hands, they were neither willing nor able to pay the extortionate rental, which would have amounted to interest on OR&N bonds plus 6 percent dividends on the stock in the first year, 7 percent in the second year, and 8 percent thereafter. As the Portland *Oregonian* pointed out at the time, OR&N earnings would not then have justified guaranteeing more than a 5 percent dividend on the stock. The existing branch lines were unprofitable, the riverboats were run at a loss to exclude competitors, and two new sidewheel steamers for the Puget Sound service were too expensive to operate. There was also a real risk that income from Oregon traffic would be diluted by competition from Central Pacific should that company gain control of the now-orphaned Oregon & California road.[2]

All of these factors, plus the need to protect the Northern Pacific land grant, supported arguments favoring early completion of the Cascade Branch. Charles B. Wright of Philadelphia, who headed the most powerful faction within the Northern Pacific board, enthusiastically espoused that scheme. Wright and company president Robert Harris both had large interests in land on Puget Sound and were therefore anxious to promote Tacoma as the terminus of the northern transcontinental line; a lease of the OR&N could only bolster the fortunes of Portland. Worse still, the rental would be an intolerable burden, weakening Northern Pacific at a time when maximum financial confidence would be needed to attract funds for construction of a railway over the Cascade Mountains. The OR&N lines had not yet been connected with the Oregon Short Line, and observers did not expect the Union Pacific to be financially capable of leasing the OR&N for some time. On September 9, 1884, therefore, Northern Pacific directors passed a resolution recommending rejection of the OR&N offer, and at the annual general meeting, held 10 days later, shareholders accepted their motion.[3] On the Cascade Branch, meanwhile, workers began the second 25-mile section of the Yakima Valley line and the company let a contract for clearing a right of way on the west side of the mountains.

For the OR&N, the winter of 1884-85 proved difficult indeed. The Columbia Valley line remained closed by snow for 23 consecutive days, with the Baker City branch similarly afflicted by a blockade at Pyle's Canyon for 17 days. The company therefore derived little benefit from the newly opened connection with the Oregon Short Line. By spring 1885 the company's financial situation was desperate. At the beginning of March the company ordered layoffs and salary cuts in Portland, and in April it postponed dividend payments.[4] Just as the OR&N position deteriorated, however, that of the Union Pacific, now under new management, began to improve.

Northern Pacific therefore decided not to delay any longer and in February 1885 offered to lease the OR&N for a guarantee of 5 percent dividends on the stock for three years and 6 percent thereafter.[5] It was a fair proposition and OR&N needed the money, but the directors suddenly feared that if they leased the property exclusively to the Northern Pacific, Union Pacific might build its own line to Portland.[6] They consequently demanded 6 percent for three years and 7 percent thereafter, and the talks again broke down. Immediately afterward, however, Boston capitalists proposed that Northern Pacific and Union Pacific lease the OR&N system jointly.

William Endicott, Jr. and the new Union Pacific president Charles Francis Adams were the principal protagonists of the joint lease proposal of March 1885. Northern Pacific people generally were less than enthusiastic, and the powerful Philadelphia group, led by Charles B. Wright, completely opposed it. The interested parties quickly put the lease terms together, based on a rental equivalent to 5 percent dividends on OR&N stock for three years and 6 percent thereafter, the cost being equally shared by the Northern Pacific and Union Pacific companies. The O&T then attempted to expedite ratification.[7] Nothing quickly materialized, however, for although a few Northern Pacific directors were ready to agree to a joint lease, others wanted exclusive control, and Wright and Harris remained determined to concentrate all efforts on the Cascade Branch.

Despite struggles for power within the Northern Pacific Railroad and Oregon Railway & Navigation companies, the status quo remained undisturbed.[8] The Northern Pacific Railroad Co. election of 1885 in fact confirmed the supremacy of the Philadelphia group and enabled Wright and Harris to expedite work on the Cascade Branch.

By December 1885 construction was well under way on 40 miles of the Cascade Branch between Yakima and Ellensburg, and on another 27-mile stretch west of the mountains. When these sections were finished, only 75 miles of the line would remain to be built. This distance, however, included the formidable 40-mile-long mountain section, with almost two miles of tunnels, expected to cost no less than $4,072,000. The developers estimated the total cost of completing the 75-mile gap to be $5,912,000, of which $3,513,000 would become available from the proceeds of first-mortgage bonds and $2,399,000 would have to be found.[9] Harris faced a difficult task, but the OR&N compounded his problems when it refused to bear any share of the losses resulting from a transcontinental railroad rate war which broke out in February 1886. When the freight rate from Chicago to the Pacific coast fell to 65 cents per hundred, the OR&N demanded and obtained 28 cents per hundred for the 213 miles from Wallula to Portland, leaving Northern Pacific only 28 cents for moving the goods 1,699 miles from St. Paul to Wallula. Small wonder, then, that during the fiscal year ending June 30, 1886, Northern Pacific generated a mere $111,200 profit, a poor showing partially offset by the sale of 370,925 acres of land worth $1,376,844.[10]

Ultimately, OR&N's actions proved self-defeating, for they forced the Northern Pacific Railroad to expedite the opening of the Cascade Branch to traffic. The contract for driving the 9,850-foot-long tunnel under Stampede Pass was let on January 21, 1886 and the work was expected to take two years to complete.[11] In the meantime Northern Pacific trains were scheduled to continue using the OR&N line along the Columbia Valley. During the third week of April 1886, however, Harris decided, almost certainly as a result of OR&N extortion, to build a switchback railway over the pass and begin running trains between Pasco and Tacoma well before the tunnel was finished.[12]

By mid-1886 the Oregon & Transcontinental management had to accept that no earthly power would ever dissuade or prevent Harris from pushing the Cascade Branch to completion. Within 12 months Northern Pacific would be running trains directly to Puget Sound on their own line. The only course left open to the OR&N was to lease its property to the Union Pacific. That company was only too anxious to enter into such an agreement, for the California "Big Four" were diverting the "Overland" traffic to the "Sunset Route," and there were already alarming indications that Chicago & North Western intended to build west to Boise and link up with the struggling Oregon Pacific.[13] The UP and OR&N companies began serious lease negotiations in the fall of 1886 and by November 19 had worked out all the main points.[14] Union Pacific directors approved a draft of the agreement in mid-December.[15] The companies then took immediate steps to obtain legislation enabling the OR&N Co., as lessor, to convey the property and the Union Pacific

Railway Co., as lessee, to receive it.[16] An amendment to Oregon law, governing the actions of OR&N, was introduced into the state legislature at the end of January 1887 and senate bills 54 and 55, sanctioning the steps to be taken by the Union Pacific, were submitted almost simultaneously to the United States Congress.[17] The legislators worked quickly, for the Oregon measure passed on February 10, 1887[18] and federal blessing followed soon afterwards. Finally, on April 25, 1887, the agreement was signed, sealed, and delivered.[19] The Oregon Railway & Navigation Co. leased its property for 99 years to the Oregon Short Line Railway Co., the Union Pacific guaranteeing the rental. Oregon Short Line would pay $1,440,000 per annum, in quarterly installments, thus guaranteeing a 6 percent dividend on the $24,000,000 stock outstanding. The arrangement left open a way for Northern Pacific to enter the contract as joint lessee at some later date if so desired.[20]

The Union Pacific lease of the OR&N property in no way improved the acrimonious relationship with Northern Pacific. The rental threatened to be an onerous burden for Union Pacific alone to bear, even if it could have maintained the traffic density on OR&N lines at levels reached in 1885-86. That goal, however, hardly seemed attainable, for the imminent opening of the Northern Pacific's Cascade Branch,[21] and the almost simultaneous Southern Pacific purchase and completion of the Oregon & California road,[22] clearly threatened to dilute earnings. Using borrowed money, Oregon & Transcontinental therefore set out to purchase greater representation on the Northern Pacific board.

However, at the end of July 1887 a minor financial panic overtook the stock market.[23] Money quickly became tight, and the Oregon & Transcontinental Co. floating debt was called. Imminent failure of the Oregon & Transcontinental Co. in turn threatened to bring down the New York financial house of Chase Higginson & Co. and precipitate a more widespread financial collapse. In desperation, O&T president Elijah Smith was forced to appeal for help from the Oregon companies' once-illustrious founder.[24]

Henry Villard had returned to the United States from Germany in October 1886 bearing a commission to act as New York financial agent for the Deutsche Bank of Berlin. On August 27, 1887 Elijah Smith approached him seeking a $5 million loan for the Oregon & Transcontinental. In return he offered Villard the presidencies of the two Oregon companies and total control of the voting rights pertaining to the Oregon & Transcontinental holdings of Northern Pacific stock. Within 36 hours Villard obtained the money Smith required and stood every chance of regaining his former prominence in railroad circles. Remembering, however, that his current responsibility was primarily to European investors, he declined the positions. Philosophically contemplating the sudden "revolution of the wheel of fortune," he decided instead to assume the role of mediator. His object would be to bring the warring factions together and eliminate wasteful competition between railroad companies operating in the far Northwest.[25]

Wright and Harris viewed these events uneasily. They were fully conscious not only of the voting strength placed in Villard's hands but also of the financially exhausted condition of the Northern Pacific. In the fiscal year ending June 30, 1887 the railroad rate war and the OR&N exactions had reduced the annual surplus to a mere $65,707. Moreover, construction of the Cascade Branch had been very expensive. Northern Pacific needed the financial strength at Villard's command. Villard now acted on behalf of Europeans with interests in both the OR&N and Northern Pacific companies. If Northern Pacific was to be forced to a compromise in the Oregon country, Villard might serve to moderate Union Pacific influence. Wright therefore invited him to rejoin the Northern Pacific board.[26]

With some misgivings Villard accepted Wright's offer. He then used the voting power provided by Smith to secure Northern Pacific directorships for himself and three additional Oregon & Transcontinental representatives. Following the annual meeting, held on September 15, 1887, John C. Bullitt, James C. Fargo, John H. Hall, Johnstone Livingston, and J. Lewis Stackpole all stepped down and Villard, Edwin H. Abbott, Charles L. Colby, Colgate Hoyt, and John B. Trevor took their places. In addition to their Oregon & Transcontinental affiliations, Abbott and Colby were officials of the Wisconsin Central Railroad, by which Northern Pacific later gained access to Chicago. Trevor, meanwhile, doubled as a representative of the Union Pacific. Villard thus achieved a partial interlocking of directorships, but this fell far short of his objectives and later proved insufficient to overcome the forces opposing his plans for coordinating railroad policy in the Pacific Northwest.[27]

Thrust once more into a position of strength, Villard immediately set out to impose what he perceived as order upon the regional railroad scene. Forming a committee consisting of himself, Frederick Billings, and August Belmont, he quickly prepared a plan whereby Northern Pacific would join Union Pacific in the OR&N lease, sharing the rental on an equal basis. As expected, he proposed to restore the former territorial division on the Snake River, abandoned when his first empire collapsed in 1884. Under terms of the new agreement Northern Pacific would again have exclusive control over the country to the north of the river, while the OR&N system would be confined to the region further south. The Oregon Railway & Navigation Co. would cede the Columbia & Palouse road to Northern Pacific, which would in turn abandon any projected affiliation with the locally promoted Oregon & Washington Territory Railroad then under construction between Wallula and Pendleton. Shippers offering goods for carriage between Interior points north of the Snake River and either Tacoma or Portland would be free to choose Northern Pacific or OR&N routing in each direction, with the same rates applying.[28] The Northern Pacific board received a draft of the agreement at the end of September 1887 and approved it by a vote of nine to one. Their only proviso was that for the first three years Northern Pacific losses due to the expense of the joint lease must not exceed $250,000.[29]

Having secured the tentative approval of his fellow directors, Villard then approached the other two companies involved. In general the scheme was well received. Union Pacific president Charles Francis Adams was by no means unwilling to have Northern Pacific share the expense of the OR&N lease, and the Boston directors of the OR&N welcomed the greater security offered by a joint agreement and guarantee of rental payment. The negotiations proceeded satisfactorily and during the third week of January 1888 the Northern Pacific, Union Pacific, and eastern members of the OR&N board ratified the agreement.[30] In New York, therefore, the joint lease appeared to be an established fact. Villard, however, failed to take full account of residual hostility between individuals or the extent of opposition likely to arise in the Pacific Northwest.

The joint lease foundered over the issue of division of territory. Well before the two transcontinental roads ratified the agreement it was already quite clear that neither Charles B. Wright nor

Elijah Smith really intended to honor any imposed territorial settlement. Each of these mutual adversaries, moreover, could count on wholehearted public support for plans to penetrate the region assigned to the other.

Farmers and merchants of the Pendleton and Walla Walla areas had long wanted to break the OR&N monopoly in the southern Interior. Now, just as plans for independent connections with Northern Pacific were at last beginning to mature, the joint lease threatened to nullify all their efforts and perpetuate 25 years of bondage. Anxiety, however, was unwarranted, for even as Villard conducted negotiations for the joint lease, Charles B. Wright proceeded with his own subversive scheme for invading the area south of the Snake River. In November 1887 Northern Pacific announced it would make a traffic agreement with the Oregon & Washington Territory Railroad.[31] Then, early in December of that year, the public learned that Charles B. Wright, Jr. and contractor George W. Hunt had become sole owners of the Pendleton road.[32] By December 31, 1887, workers had laid track from Wallula almost to Helix and grading was in progress on a branch to Centerville. At the end of March 1888 Hunt concluded an agreement with local residents to build a line to Walla Walla, and within three weeks his graders were at work in the rich Eureka Flat wheatland.

Portland merchants, meanwhile, had invested heavily in the Coeur d'Alene mines and erected a smelter at East Portland. The mines were said to be "a source of untold wealth" which would "overshadow all other interests" and "do for Portland what the Comstock did for San Francisco."[33] Unfortunately, Northern Pacific had already monopolized access to the mining areas and adjusted the freight rates to favor a long haul over their own road to the Wickes smelter in Montana.[34] The only hope Portland capitalists had of sharing profitably in the mining business therefore lay in the construction of an OR&N line into the Coeur d'Alene camp, preparations for which were duly made.[35] An OR&N subsidiary, named the Washington & Idaho Railroad, was incorporated in Whitman County, Washington Territory in July 1886 and provided a legal vehicle for the advance north from Farmington to the mines.[36] Surveys for such a line, and for another from Farmington to Spokane Falls, were carried out later in the same year.[37] The mining business, meanwhile, expanded rapidly. On July 29, 1887 Simeon

G. Reed of Portland incorporated the Bunker Hill & Sullivan Mining & Concentrating Co. which was to be the Coeur d'Alene's greatest mining venture.[38] All that was then needed to bring the "untold wealth" to Portland was an OR&N extension to Wardner, Idaho. A month later, however, Henry Villard suddenly reappeared and, brandishing his joint lease proposals, stood directly in the way of any such development.

In Portland, news that the railway companies had ratified the joint lease and all its territorial provisions generated vigorous protest. On January 19, 1888 the *Oregonian* came out strongly in favor of extending the OR&N system from the Palouse country to the Coeur d'Alene mines and urged the Union Pacific to withdraw from the agreement.[39] Four days later the same paper questioned the legality of joint tenure, pointing out that recent Oregon legislation forbade leasing of the OR&N property to "any company or corporation which forms a competing or parallel line to its railroad." The *Oregonian* asserted that the Northern Pacific clearly fell into that class and added that learned legal opinion in Salem considered the agreement to be a contravention of the newly enacted interstate commerce law, which also prohibited pooling (collusion between railroad companies for the purposes of sharing traffic and fixing freight rates).[40]

Thus inspired by the press, the Portland Board of Trade launched an energetic campaign to air their grievances against both the Northern Pacific Railroad and Villard's joint lease proposals. Besides exchanging and publishing correspondence with Thomas F. Oakes (who was already Villard's successor elect to Robert Harris) and Daniel C. Corbin, concerning discriminatory rates charged for shipping Coeur d'Alene ore to Portland, they also made issue of the continued isolation of the Columbia & Palouse line from the main part of the OR&N system. Northern Pacific, they pointed out, charged $1 per ton to haul Portland-bound grain from Palouse Junction to Wallula. Since an average of 20 loaded cars was handed over to Northern Pacific daily, the OR&N, they averred, had already paid out 10 times the sum of money required to lay track on the abandoned Texas Ferry to Pampa roadbed. Referring to the proposed common rates between the northern Interior and Portland or Tacoma, they alleged that such tariffs would negate the inherent OR&N advantage of a water-level grade without providing any compensation for the burden of channel dredging and ship towage between Astoria and Portland.[41]

As the Board of Trade campaign continued, Mr. Van B. De Lashmutt, a capitalist interested in both the OR&N and the Coeur d'Alene mines, resorted to litigation on the basis of the existing Oregon State Railway Lease Law. Northern Pacific, he complained, could not, as a parallel and competing railroad, become joint lessee of the OR&N property. On March 2, 1888 Judge Loyal B. Sterns of the Oregon State Circuit Court upheld his contention, issuing an injunction ordering the Oregon directors of the OR&N to refrain from voting to ratify the joint lease agreement.[42]

At the time of the injunction against the joint lease, Henry Villard was about to leave for Germany to consult with his principals. Anxious to bear tidings of harmonious relationships and favorable investment climates, he could ill afford the embarrassment caused by the Oregon litigation. Hoping to resolve the matter quickly, he therefore invited the Portland Board of Trade to send a delegation to New York to discuss the objections to his proposals.[43] Consequently, on March 17, 1888 a group of six influential Oregonians set out for the East.[44] On most issues they found Villard conciliatory. To compensate for the common freight rate between the Interior and both Tacoma and Portland he agreed that OR&N would maintain towage services on the lower river and make charges not exceeding those levied between Tacoma and the open sea. He also undertook to plead with Northern Pacific for the establishment of mileage-based rates for carrying Coeur d'Alene ores. Then, having announced the approval of a $2 million OR&N bond issue for the immediate construction of branch lines to Heppner and Eureka Flat, both of which lay south of the Snake River, he curtly dismissed the crucial territorial issue by stating that it would not at present be financially possible to build an OR&N line to the Coeur d'Alene mines. That point made, he nevertheless expressed the hope that the injunction would be withdrawn as he could not ask his German friends "to put their money in a lawsuit."[45]

The members of the Portland delegation seem to have realized that further discussions with Villard would serve no useful purpose. That they remained skeptical of his policies and solutions is evident from the tone of one member's New York dispatch to the *Oregonian* published on March 28, 1888:

None of the parties to the joint lease suppose it to be a binding and legal contract. It is in the nature of an effort to secure an amicable working relationship between the several roads. It can hardly bear any severe strain or conflict of interests and therefore is not likely to be permanent. To us the various interests appear irreconcilable but Villard thinks they can be harmonized and made to work fairly together. Members of the Portland committee would prefer that the Union and Oregon roads adhere to and pursue their course of action and development, keeping out of combination with the others, but whenever this statement is made it is met by the objection that unless such agreement between the roads is reached there will be a disastrous railroad war which neither the roads nor the country can afford. At present we can see nothing but to await developments

Signed H. W. Scott.[46]

By "developments" Scott probably meant the outcome of the Oregon company elections, to be held in Portland less than three months later. Clearly, there would be a struggle for control of the Oregon & Transcontinental and OR&N companies. Villard and Adams had decided that if the joint lease was ever to be successfully implemented, Smith and the recalcitrant Portlanders would have to be ousted. In the time available before Villard left for Europe, the two men therefore selected all but one of their nominees for the Oregon & Transcontinental board. Leaving Colby and Hoyt in charge of his affairs, Villard then sailed for Germany, where he immediately made arrangements for the money needed to purchase absolute control of the Oregon & Transcontinental Co. This opened the way to enforce the joint lease agreement. As usual, however, everything went wrong.

After Villard's departure, Colby and Hoyt found themselves between the devil and the deep sea. They had difficulty deciding who should fill the vacant seat on the Oregon & Transcontinental Co. board. Adams and Wright each feared that the other's company would secure the balance of power. Villard, moreover, had apparently failed to make clear to Adams that the ticket chosen for the Oregon & Transcontinental election would also be put forward for the OR&N contest. The list included only one wholly committed Union Pacific candidate out of the six proposed. Adams therefore became convinced that his company was about to lose effective influence in OR&N affairs. As the Union Pacific depended upon the OR&N property for its only reliable outlet to the West Coast, this was a serious matter. There was also the question of how well the Union Pacific could function in Oregon if it continued to be a party to policies unacceptable to the general public. Disillusioned, and perhaps influenced by Elijah Smith, Adams decided to withdraw from the joint lease agreement. Together with Ames he now supported Smith.[47] In the company elections held in Portland in June 1888 Villard and his nominees gained control of the Oregon & Transcontinental Co., but the OR&N board remained unchanged. The joint lease, as the *Oregonian* had predicted nearly two months earlier, thus "passed into the limbo of impossibles."

Supported by the Union Pacific Railway and drawing strength from public opinion favoring an extension to the Coeur d'Alene mines, OR&N advanced northeast well before the O&T and OR&N companies held elections. On May 15, 1888 the United States Senate passed a bill granting the Washington & Idaho Railroad right of way through the Coeur d'Alene Indian Reservation.[48] Eleven days later a second OR&N subsidiary, named the Oregon Railway Extension Company, was incorporated to complete the connection between Riparia and the Columbia & Palouse road, and build a new railway from Dutch Flat (Winona) to a point five miles north of Farmington on the Washington & Idaho road at Seltice.[49] The new line, known as the Pleasant Valley Branch, passed entirely north of Colfax, thus allowing heavy trains to avoid the steep gradient just west of that town. It also opened up some of the finest agricultural land in all the Palouse. Once the legal arrangements had been made, railway building began immediately. At the end of May 1888 a general contract was let for lines north of the Snake River and a large construction force, assembled at Prescott to build the branch to Eureka Flat, suddenly moved north. Work began in earnest on June 1, 1888 and progressed so rapidly that by August 26 regular trains were running between Pendleton and Farmington, crossing the Snake River on a temporary bridge. Meanwhile, construction began on those sections of the Washington & Idaho Railroad lying outside the Indian reservation, passage through which was yet to involve a great deal of wrangling with several departments of the federal government. Despite the outstanding problems a certain euphoria prevailed and as the lines advanced towards the north and east, OR&N horizons began to widen. On August 15, 1888 the *Oregonian* announced that although the Washington & Idaho would stop that year at Mullan, it would soon be extended east to Garrison, Montana, where it would link up with J. J. Hill's Montana Central. A month later, Washington & Idaho in fact filed supplementary articles of incorporation for an extension from Mullan to Missoula for that very purpose. The OR&N subsidiary, however, did not reach Mullan until the spring of 1890, and the remainder of the scheme, which included a long tunnel through the Bitterroot Mountains, never came about.[50]

The eastward expansion of the OR&N system and the prospect of a Union Pacific alliance with Hill raised anxiety in the Oregon & Transcontinental camp, causing them to file a lawsuit. Charles L. Colby, Brayton Ives, and Edward Sweets & Company hastened to the superior court of New York to complain that the lines being built north of the Snake River not only violated the joint lease and previous traffic contracts but also wasted OR&N funds. On July 27, 1888 Judge Van Brunt granted a temporary injunction restraining the OR&N from building such railways or completing the bridge at Riparia, and issued an order to show cause on August 2, 1888 why this action should not be made permanent.[51] The hearing, however, was postponed several times, and as New York was a long way from the scene of construction, and notice of the temporary injunction apparently got lost en route, the work proceeded without interruption.[52] The supreme court of New York eventually took up the case, deciding in favor of the plaintiffs on December 4, 1888.[53] Just then, however, Villard was busily putting together yet another scheme for harmonizing relationships between the four companies.

By means of the so-called "Arbitration Contract," made public on February 21, 1889, Villard proposed to create a joint railway system in which the majority ownership of subsidiary railroads would be vested in a trust company account set up for the collective benefit of the Northern Pacific Railroad and Union Pacific Railway companies. Northern Pacific would hand over its holdings in the Spokane & Palouse Railroad, Spokane Falls & Idaho Railroad, and Coeur d'Alene Railway & Navigation companies and Union Pacific and Oregon Short Line would deposit their interests in the Washington & Idaho Railroad and Oregon Railway Extension companies.

Oregon & Transcontinental, meanwhile, would sell its $12 million worth of OR&N stock to the Northern Pacific and Union Pacific companies jointly. As the two railroad companies could not immediately pay for the OR&N stock, it would be deposited with a trust company, and Oregon & Transcontinental would issue 5 percent collateral trust-mortgage bonds against it. Northern Pacific and Union Pacific would share the 6 percent rental charged for the OR&N property, using their payments to guarantee the interest on the Oregon & Transcontinental bonds and build up a sinking fund providing for eventual retirement of the debt. The joint railway system so created would be governed by a board of five managers, or "arbitrators," consisting of the company president and one representative from both Northern Pacific and Union Pacific, and a mutually acceptable fifth member chosen by the other four. Voting rights pertaining to all the stock placed in trust were to be vested in the board of arbitrators, who were to issue beneficiary certificates or debentures enabling the holders to enjoy all the cash and other benefits associated with it. In order to allow for preparatory arrangements, the contract would not take effect until July 1, 1889. In the meantime the railroad companies would suspend rival construction and abandon all litigation against each other.[54]

Villard's arbitration contract was merely a revised and somewhat expanded version of the joint lease, suffering from all the same weaknesses. Once again the prime objective was to rescue the Oregon & Transcontinental Co. from debt, which in November 1888 amounted to $5.8 million.[55] For this reason the rental/purchase fee for the OR&N property was kept at a level equivalent to a 6 percent dividend on the stock. During the year that had elapsed since Northern Pacific and Union Pacific first ratified the joint lease, the flow of traffic on the northwestern railroads had changed completely. With the opening of the Stampede Tunnel on Northern Pacific's Cascade Branch on May 27, 1888, the OR&N suffered a significant and increasing loss of business. By the time the arbitration contract was proposed, Villard and his Oregon & Transcontinental nominees wielded enough influence in Northern Pacific affairs to force that company to pay dearly for a line it no longer needed. Union Pacific, however, suffered from no such subversion. Charles Francis Adams felt strongly that the OR&N rental should be reduced to compensate for the loss of revenue, and said so. Portlanders, meanwhile, regarded restrictions upon OR&N expansion as unjust, especially because the arbitration contract totally ignored the existence of the pseudo-independent Oregon & Washington Territory Railroad which continued to build Northern Pacific feeder lines south of the Snake River.[56]

Villard's efforts to persuade the Union Pacific to come to terms failed. Adams had already concluded that negotiations with the Oregon & Transcontinental Co. offered no promise of relief from the burden imposed by the OR&N rental. In March 1889, moreover, relations with Villard suffered further when the Northern Pacific began to construct a new line to Butte, Montana, one of the Union Pacific's most important sources of traffic.[57] At that point, apparently, Adams decided that if such problems were ever to be solved, the Union Pacific and its allies would have to acquire the Oregon & Transcontinental.

Matters came to a head on April 25, 1889 when the Northern Pacific announced withdrawal from the arbitration contract.[58] A contest then developed for control of the Oregon & Transcontinental, both sides buying up every share available to them. By the second week of May, Villard realized the outcome would be uncomfortably close. On May 13, 1889, therefore, he ordered Oregon & Transcontinental officials in Portland to issue the $10 million reserve stock of the company. This stock was to be held in trust for Villard to vote as he saw fit.[59] Moreover, it was to be given a preferred character with 6 percent dividends guaranteed. The move was a desperate attempt not only to retain control of the O&T but also to ensure that the OR&N dividends, which represented the holding company's most significant earnings, went directly into the pockets of the controlling group. The reaction in Portland was one of outrage. The *Oregonian* produced perhaps the most vitriolic editorial it ever printed. "It is not probable..." the paper said, "...that in the whole history of railroad wrecking a more high handed proceeding was ever attempted. If it could succeed it would virtually destroy the value of the $40 million of O&T stock now outstanding. The proper thing for legitimate stockholders of the OR&N to do is to contest the right of the manager of the O&T to vote the stock held in the name of the piratical corporation, an instrument of jugglery and fraud. It is high time to strike at this robber corporation and strike to kill."[60] The paper urged those interested in the Union Pacific and OR&N companies to seek state legislation negating Oregon & Transcontinental Co. control over the Oregon Railway & Navigation Co.

In New York, meanwhile, Elijah Smith and Edward R. Bell, as stockholders of the OR&N, sought and received an injunction preventing the issue of the O&T reserve shares.[61] The battle on the stock exchange then intensified.[62] The Oregon & Transcontinental Co. transfer books were to close on May 18 for the annual election. In the few remaining days, therefore, Villard and his opponents desperately tried to gain marginal advantage. Some described May 17, 1889 as one of the most exciting days in Wall Street history. Cash stock sales had to be delivered before 2:15 p.m. and 29,000 such shares were traded. The price increased steadily from $37 to $45. It then jumped to $50, moved ahead to $51, and leaped to $60 in a single transaction. Finally it peaked at $64 1/8, the highest point reached in six years. At the end of the day the Villard faction claimed 201,700 of the 400,000 shares not subject to litigation, and thus controlled the company.[63] Henry Villard had prevented the Union Pacific party and their St. Paul Minneapolis & Manitoba Railroad allies from gaining a foothold on the way to full control of the Northern Pacific. His opponents, however, threatened to ask the Oregon courts to delay the OR&N election until the state legislature could pass a law preventing him from voting the O&T holdings of OR&N stock.[64] To that extent, therefore, his victory was Pyrrhic. The contest for control of the Oregon & Transcontinental Co., moreover, had been expensive, and Villard needed money for other more profitable ventures. He therefore decided to seek a compromise.[65]

On June 4, 1889 Charles Francis Adams and Thomas F. Oakes reportedly reached a full understanding concerning the approaching OR&N election. A compromise board of directors was to be selected and agreed upon by Henry Villard and General Grenville Dodge prior to the annual meeting. The OR&N rental would continue at 6 percent dividends on the stock, but the terms of the lease would be modified so that operating revenues would no longer be used to pay for line improvements. The agreement also dropped the territorial provision of the joint lease and arbitration contract and conceded OR&N ownership and responsibility for the Oregon Railway Extension and Washington & Idaho lines. Finally, and most significantly, the two parties agreed to recommend the early dispersal of the Oregon & Transcontinental Co. holdings of Oregon Railway and Navigation Co. stock.[66]

Henry Villard, accompanied by Thomas F. Oakes, Paul Schulze, and four New York lawyers, arrived in Portland early on Wednesday June 12, 1889.[67] During the next five days Villard met with Grenville Dodge and G. M. Lane of the Union Pacific and Elijah Smith of the OR&N, thrashing out final details of the agreement. The meetings went on until 1:00 a.m. on June 17, the very day of the company elections, and resulted at last in an accord whereby Union Pacific undertook to surrender their O&T holdings at cost, and O&T in turn agreed to sell all 120,027 of their OR&N shares to Union Pacific at a price of $90 per share.[68]

Although the company elections were then anti-climactic, Portland was overjoyed. At last the OR&N lay safely in the Union Pacific fold, with access to the Coeur d'Alene mines beyond dispute. The *Oregonian* crowed a great deal about victory and credited the satisfactory outcome primarily to Elijah Smith and his threats of lawsuit and legislation to negate O&T voting power.[69]

That was only partially true, for Villard's lawyers had advised him that Union Pacific's lease of the OR&N Co. property could not be broken. The branches in eastern Washington and northern Idaho, moreover, were an established fact.[70] Most significantly, he proved ready to make concessions enabling him to strengthen his own business matters. Grenville Dodge, in a letter to Charles Francis Adams on June 17, 1889, reported that Villard had been ready "to concede anything to get O&T in shape".[71] By that time Villard's ambitions lay largely in the electrical field. He had been one of Thomas Edison's earliest backers and also knew the German electrical pioneer Werner Siemens. In March 1889 he set out to organize the Edison General Electric Company, a New Jersey corporation with a capital of $12 million, which was to merge all the Edison companies into a single entity and expand their activities. Financial backing would come from an international syndicate of German and American banking houses.[72] Villard needed a financial coup to restore his ability to attract capital. Sale of the Oregon & Transcontinental holdings of OR&N stock to the Union Pacific at $90 per share promised to restore his stature in the financial world. Oregon & Transcontinental ownership of a controlling interest in the OR&N no longer offered any advantages, even in terms of protection for Northern Pacific. Villard therefore sold out, and as time would tell, his was the better part of the bargain.

Thereafter the Oregon & Transcontinental Co. played an important part in financing Edison General Electric, and although it continued to provide Northern Pacific with some capital, the railroad interest took second place.[73] In 1890 it was reorganized as the North American Company.[74] Oregon Railway & Navigation, meanwhile, became one of Union Pacific's most valuable assets, but the manner in which its purchase was financed led to a large increase in floating debt and contributed significantly to that company's later collapse.

The Portland agreement of June 17, 1889 resolved the problems caused by overlapping ownership of the Oregon Railway & Navigation and Northern Pacific Railroad companies. In one important respect, however, it fell short of producing an ideal outcome. At the time of the preliminary agreement between Oakes and Adams, on June 4, 1889, the two presidents were said to be "pledged to the early consummation of a trackage arrangement by which Union Pacific and Northern Pacific will use in common the tracks of the OR&N Co. in the region east of the Cascade Mountains, AND THE NORTHERN PACIFIC IS TO AFFORD THE NAVIGATION COMPANY ACCESS TO PUGET SOUND BY TRACKAGE OVER ITS PACIFIC DIVISION [emphasis added]."[75] This part of the agreement, however, soon fell by the wayside. On June 19, 1889 the *San Francisco Chronicle* noted that the matter "is in doubt and is exercising the Union Pacific considerably."[76] Perhaps Oakes had spoken out of turn. At any rate Northern Pacific very quickly welshed on any such commitment. The terms demanded for the use of the Kalama line were described, on September 28, 1889, as being "so exorbitant as to be out of the question."[77] Union Pacific consequently decided to build its own line from Portland to Seattle. In November 1889 the Portland & Puget Sound Railroad Co. was incorporated for that purpose,[78] and in 1890 construction got underway. After spending about $2 million, however, mounting financial difficulties forced Sidney Dillon, UP president, to shelve the project.[79]

The Portland & Puget Sound Railroad, as originally conceived, was never completed, and the problem of access to Puget Sound remained to plague the successors to the Union Pacific Railway

Co. Just as control of the OR&N line along the Columbia Valley had been the major point of concern of the 1880s, use of the Northern Pacific connection between Portland and Seattle would fuel the railroad controversies of the early 20th century.

Chapter Two

To Moscow, Pomeroy, and Weston

Following the collapse of Henry Villard's empire, the OR&N's first construction priority was to extend the Baker City branch to a meeting with the Union Pacific's Oregon Short Line. Until that link was forged, no further attempts could be made to generate the local traffic and revenues needed to render the company's property more attractive for lease. Branch line construction therefore remained in abeyance until mid-1885. The promise of a bumper harvest then brought renewed public pressure for completion of projected lines into wheat-growing areas north and south of the Snake River.

Work on the extension from Colfax to Moscow had already started as part of the Columbia & Palouse railway scheme originally sponsored by the Oregon & Transcontinental Company. During 1883 arrangements were made to construct grain elevators at both Pullman and Moscow,[1] and 20 miles of the line were graded. Simultaneously, workers used rock material excavated from cuts in the south fork of the Palouse River Valley for rip-rapping at Colfax, and laid six miles of track to bring it down.[2] When construction stopped early in 1884, pile-driving operations were almost complete, bridges had been framed, and the rails and ties lay ready for the steel gang. In May 1885, therefore, company officials thought 60 days' work would be enough to finish the road.[3]

The OR&N exploited the settlers' desperate need for transportation. To induce the company to resume construction of the line to Moscow, farmers had to agree that during the first year of operation they would ship at least 30,000 tons of grain to Portland and pay a freight surcharge of $1 per ton (i.e., $8 per ton instead of $7).[4] With this concession made, work again got underway. The company dispatched a contingent of laborers from Portland to Colfax on July 24, 1885, and by the end of that month the sounds of railway construction once more echoed through the canyon.[5]

The Moscow branch followed the south fork of the Palouse River southeast from Colfax to Pullman and then turned east to Moscow, Idaho. The line was 28 miles long and at first had intermediate stations at Shawnee, Guy, and Pullman.[6] Eastbound trains climbed from an elevation of 1,945 feet at Colfax to 2,560 feet at Moscow, with a maximum 1 percent grade occurring just beyond Pullman.[7] Rock work in the canyon was quite heavy, with Howetruss bridges required at several crossings of the river.[8] The permanent bridges were not completed until after the line opened.[9]

Trains began running to Pullman daily, including Sundays, on September 15, 1885,[10] and track was laid into Moscow on September 23, 1885.[11] The road having been ballasted and surfaced and the bridges completed, the construction force then went to Starbuck to work on the Pataha branch.

Engineer Hale made the first surveys for a railway along the Tucannon River and Pataha Creek in the summer of 1879,[12] but nearly seven years passed before the road was built. For some time, early in the 1880s, the Tucannon-Pataha line was described as being part of a projected OR&N route to Lewiston, Idaho, the total length of which would have been 67 miles.[13] Steamers plying the Snake River from Riparia, however, served Lewiston twice a week and continued to cope with upriver traffic.[14] The company never pursued the railway scheme in its entirety, therefore, and farmers who settled the productive wheat lands along the proposed right of way found themselves lacking convenient year-round transportation.

By 1883 settlers had taken up much of the land in the Pataha country.[15] They produced larger crops each year and soon outstripped the capacity of the Snake River steamboats. From a local point of view the construction of a railroad appeared to be a matter of urgency. In April 1883 a delegation from Pomeroy and Pataha City, consisting of B. B. Day, C. B. Foote, John Hauser, Cyrus Davis, and F. W. D. Mays, went to Walla Walla to meet Henry Villard and ask for his help.[16] Villard consulted civil engineer Hans Thielsen and determined that a railroad could be built up the Pataha Creek for about $18,000 per mile. The matter, however, was obscured by the financial difficulties encountered by the OR&N and Northern Pacific companies later that year, and no further action was taken. In 1884 the area served by the riverboats produced 40,000 tons of grain; by mid-December of that year only about half of the crop had been moved.[17] Local residents therefore made further appeals for a railway. Joseph Jorgensen, the registrar at the Walla Walla land office, and E. H. Morrison went to New York to try to persuade OR&N president Elijah Smith to build a line before the next harvest.[18] These emissaries pointed out that if nothing was done, the next season's grain would lie on the banks of the Snake River until the following spring.[19]

Despite the fact that the branches to Moscow and Pomeroy were certain to carry a heavy grain traffic, Smith wanted to defer the expense of their construction for as long as possible. Moreover, if and when such lines were built, he wanted concessions. Jorgensen and Morrison went home with a preliminary understanding that if the settlers would grade the Pataha line and supply railroad ties, the OR&N might be willing to lay the rails in time to move the next season's crop. The scheme offered farmers an advantage of 10 to 15 cents a bushel, but because of the practical difficulties involved in such work, local residents took no action. In June 1885, Jorgensen and Miles C. Moore went to Portland during the OR&N's annual meeting and tried to obtain a firmer commitment to build.[20] Elijah Smith, however, continued to hedge, saying that although the directors generally favored extending a branch line into the Pataha country, he could not say when construction would begin. He hoped that the company would soon be financially healthy enough to undertake the task. In the meantime, all available riverboats would be put into good order to carry the harvest. The Portland *Oregonian* urged farmers to ship their grain before the river level fell![21]

For the time being, apparently, that was that. The OR&N sent a large force of carpenters to Riparia to overhaul the Snake River steamers,[22] and provided a wharf boat and incline to allow grain to be trans-shipped to railway cars at Martin's Ranch, about 4 miles below Wallula on the Columbia River.[23] These arrangements may well have offered operational advantages. Carrying grain downstream in riverboats was probably cheaper than having a procession of heavy trains struggle over the Alto Summit, south of

Starbuck.[24] Moreover, the shorter railroad haul would undoubtedly have required less cars. As it happened, however, the harvest of 1885 was so bountiful that both the railway and the riverboats were needed to move the great quantity of wheat produced. By late July of that year, more than 60,000 tons of grain awaited shipment down the Snake River. There was no longer any hope that the steamers could move it all in a timely fashion.[25]

Construction of a railroad was clearly essential. Early in August 1885 H. S. Rowe, superintendent of the OR&N railway division, and civil engineer Robert McClellan visited Pomeroy with Joseph Jorgensen and Frank Paine of Walla Walla. All agreed that the Pataha branch should be built without further delay and Rowe promised that if the right of way and depot grounds were provided free of charge, the company would bring the railway into operation by January 1, 1886.[26]

The land required for the railway right of way was purchased from farmers with money subscribed by merchants and others residing in Pomeroy and Pataha City. Individual landowners first pledged the property to a settlers' committee which was to sell it to a Pomeroy merchants' committee at previously agreed prices as soon as the railway was substantially complete. Having raised the necessary funds and purchased the property, the merchants' committee, composed of F. W. D. Mays, W. C. Potter, and David Dixon, were to convey it to the OR&N for railroad use.[27] At first everything went well and by August 15, 1885 most of the right of way had been pledged. It then became clear, however, that the railway company would not be satisfied with free land. Work on the line was again delayed until the settlers also agreed to pay a grain rate surcharge similar to that levied on people served by the Moscow branch.[28]

On October 15, 1885 the OR&N at last announced it would proceed immediately with the extension from Starbuck to Pomeroy.[29] Nine days later a survey party of seven men, directed by C. F. Riffle, left Portland to make a final location of the line.[30] George W. Hunt of Corvallis, Oregon, meanwhile, became the prime grading contractor. Quickly gathering 40 men, 140 horses and mules, and "four carloads of scrapers, carts, etc." he passed through Portland on October 30 and began work in the Tucannon Valley at noon on November 5. Subcontractors had already made a start on the grade, and railway company forces, transferred from the Moscow branch, had put in a "Y" for turning engines at Starbuck and laid the first mile of track.[31]

The Pataha branch extended 29 miles from Starbuck up the Tucannon River and Pataha Creek valleys to Pomeroy.[32] The line climbed steadily at a rate of about 40 feet per mile from 645 feet at Starbuck to just over 1,800 feet at Pomeroy. Rock work was minimal and there were no truss bridges, but 37 trestles were eventually built at various points along the line.[33] Sidings and section houses were put in at the 8th and 14th miles, and water tanks were installed at Starbuck, at the 14th mile, and at Pomeroy.[34] Hope for a three-mile extension to Pataha City was eventually frustrated, for Pomeroy won the Garfield County seat and emerged as the more important center. Moreover, the company obtained better terminal grounds there.[35]

With grading completed on December 12, 1885, Hunt and his entire outfit shipped out in a 12-car train for Portland the following day, whence they took the Willamette River steamer back to Corvallis.[36] Local subcontractors, such as John Gordon and Henry Garred of Walla Walla River, who had provided ten teams, also went home, leaving only the OR&N bridge builders, track layers, and surfacing gang.[37] By December 20, 1885, track had been laid to Costan's, about 12 miles above Starbuck,[38] and there the steel gang halted until another batch of second-hand rails became available from re-laying operations between Portland and The Dalles.[39]

As construction proceeded and the time came to convey the land set aside for right of way, some of the settlers had second thoughts about the prices for which they had agreed to sell their property. An acre of land in the Pataha country produced 35 to 40 bushels of wheat and normally sold for between $8 and $10. Many farmers apparently felt that if they had to accept a freight surcharge, then, to even up the burden, the merchants should pay more for the right of way. Some individuals, therefore, decided to hold out for higher prices, and the Pomeroy citizens who had undertaken to procure land for the railway company suddenly found themselves faced with an extended financial commitment.[40]

The Pataha line was a long time a-finishing. On January 9, 1886, the construction train was reported to be within nine miles of Pomeroy, but track laying again stalled for want of rails. The steel gang laid skeleton track into Pomeroy on January 23, 1886, but the 450 men still laboring on the road were then ordered to Hood River to clear snow from the Columbia Valley main line.[41] On February 6, 1886 the OR&N announced that although a regular train service would not begin for a few weeks, it would accept freight for Pomeroy and intermediate points on the branch at all stations, to be carried by construction trains.[42]

Meanwhile, workmen drove piles and built trestle bridges to replace temporary cribbing. On March 9, 1886 materials were delivered for the Pomeroy depot, and soon afterward the company moved the old wooden turntable from Riparia, recently replaced by an iron one, up to the branch line terminus.[43] Not until the end of March 1886 was the road ready to carry heavier locomotives and through trains, and not until the end of May did the last of the bridge carpenters leave for the extension to Farmington.[44]

Further south, the unfinished line from Walla Walla to Pendleton, begun in 1882, still required work. In July 1886 the OR&N decided to close the gap between Blue Mountain Station and Centerville to facilitate eastbound grain movements over the Oregon Short Line.[45] Work got under way early in October 1886 when 90 Chinese laborers were sent to Blue Mountain Station to clear out the cuts excavated in 1883.[46] As there was a lot of bridge work at the north end of the line, the engineers decided to lay track from Centerville. On the high ground, grading was easily accomplished, and by mid-November the railway was approaching Weston. The bridge work, however, proceeded slowly, for only 40 carpenters were available to build the three big trestles in the Dry and Pine Creek valleys. These bridges totalled 2,000 feet in length and were up to 95 feet high. Not until January 20, 1887, therefore, was the Pine Creek bridge at Weston finished, and only then could the steel gang proceed.[47]

The gap was finally closed on January 28, 1887,[48] and a special train conveying OR&N superintendent H. S. Rowe and his entourage passed over the line on Thursday, February 17, 1887.[49] A regular passenger service, consisting of one train from Pendleton to Walla Walla and back daily, began operating on March 1, 1887.[50]

Chapter Three

Rivals in the Palouse

In 1884 the loss of the Columbia & Palouse road left the Northern Pacific without access to the grain-growing areas of eastern Washington. The surrender of the Colfax line to the OR&N was soon recognized a serious blunder[1] and steps were quickly taken to regain a foothold in the country lying between Spokane Falls and the Snake River. Late in October 1885 an engineering party led by J. W. Edwards set out to locate a preliminary line from Cheney to Rosalia and Farmington.[2] This move not only caused great excitement in Cheney but also provoked immediate reaction in Portland. Within a few days the OR&N sent surveyors into the field between Colfax and Farmington, and a race to that section of the country was on.

On November 15, 1885 a Northern Pacific subsidiary company called the Eastern Washington Railway was incorporated in Washington Territory for the purpose of building a railroad south from the Northern Pacific main line to "some eligible or practicable point in the Territory of Washington on or near the Snake River."[3] Until April 1, 1886, the company's affairs were to be in the hands of seven trustees: Thomas F. Oakes of St. Paul, Minnesota; Nelson Bennett of Deer Lodge, Montana; Charles B. Wright Jr. of Philadelphia, Pennsylvania; Anthony M. Cannon, Paul F. Mohr, and A. A. Newbury, of Spokane Falls, Washington Territory; and Joseph Jorgensen of Walla Walla, Washington Territory. Construction would commence as soon as frost left the ground in the spring. During the winter, however, changes were made. On February 6, 1886, the company filed supplemental articles of incorporation, changing the name to Spokane & Palouse Railway and making provision for the construction of branch lines.[4] To the disappointment of Cheney residents it finally became clear that the new road would diverge from the Northern Pacific main line at Marshall, seven miles east of their town. Worse still, the trains would terminate at Spokane Falls. A shareholders' meeting held in the company's newly occupied premises in the Van Valkenberg Building on Riverside Avenue, Spokane Falls, on March 12, 1886, elected officers, closed stock subscriptions, and adopted resolutions for the construction of the first 50 miles of railway.[5] Officers chosen were A. M. Cannon, then mayor of Spokane Falls, president; Charles B. Wright, Jr. of Philadelphia, vice-president; and Paul F. Mohr, Spokane Falls, chief engineer. Robert Harris and Wright were the largest stockholders.

Line location commenced early in March 1886 and progressed rapidly enough to allow construction to begin about a month later.[6] Early in April, Nelson Bennett won a grading contract and immediately re-deployed forces previously engaged on the Cascade Branch.[7] On April 19, 1886 these were assembled at Marshall. Bennett also let subcontracts, and within two weeks work was in full swing along the entire line.[8]

To maintain steady gradients, the Spokane & Palouse Railway followed a somewhat tortuous course across the undulating uplands of the Interior. From an elevation of just over 2,100 feet at Marshall, the line climbed for about 15 miles to a first summit more than 2,500 feet above sea level about four miles south of Spangle. Proceeding south, it then descended about 300 feet in eight miles to the forks of Pine Creek. Then it followed the southern branch of that stream to a point just above Rosalia. Diverging from the creek the railway climbed southeast to cross the 2,500-foot line again about four miles north of Oakesdale. With only minor variations it then maintained this altitude for the rest of the way to an interim terminus at Belmont, about six miles due west of Farmington.

Grading proceeded rapidly. By May 5, 1886 the whole 43 miles of line was reported to be "covered with men and horses." The most southerly construction camp was located at McCoy Hollow, 18 miles north of Colfax, where the graders excavated the deepest cut on the line.[9] Despite a shortage of labor,[10] work proceeded apace, and by the end of May 1886 earthworks were nearly finished.[11] Two weeks later track had been laid to Spangle,[12] and on June 27, 1886 Northern Pacific president Robert Harris visited that place in his private car.[13]

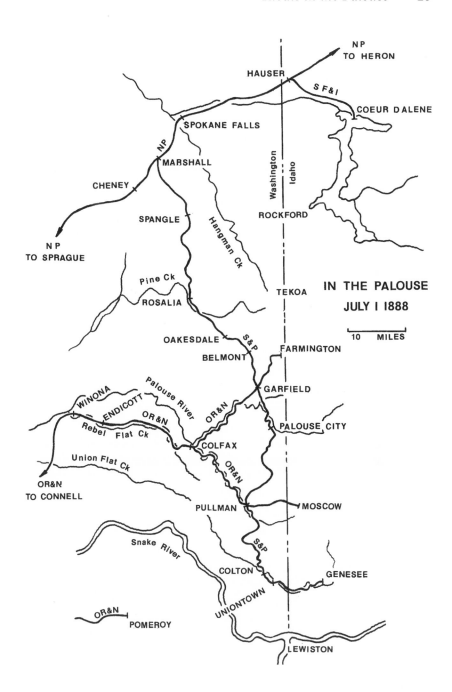

IN THE PALOUSE
JULY 1 1888

10 MILES

As the railroad advanced to the south, Northern Pacific re-
quested land for terminal facilities at Spokane Falls.[14] In return for
several lots to be used as sites for "a roundhouse and a commodi-
ous yard," the railroad company promised that Spokane would become the perpetual terminus of the Palouse line. The city readily
ceded the land, and later in the year it was duly announced that a
roundhouse, repair shops, and car yards for both the Spokane &
Palouse and Spokane Falls & Idaho lines would be accommodated
on a large level block bounded by McClellan, Washington, Railroad Avenue, and Second Streets.[15] Northern Pacific also proposed
to build a new passenger depot on the site of the existing one.

At the southern end of the Spokane & Palouse line, Belmont
lay "in the center of a vast area of the choicest agricultural land." It
was near to an abundance of timber and enjoyed an unlimited supply of good water from flowing springs. Indeed, according to the
NP, the site possessed all the advantages needed to make it "the
most important agricultural and commercial center of the famous
Palouse Country."[16] In June 1886 the railroad announced that it
would immediately build a depot, freight house, roundhouse, and
"all other necessary complements of a terminal point." It then platted a town site, and by July 10, 1886 offered lots for sale.[17]

Grading was completed early in June 1886[18] and the tracklayers
entered Belmont at the end of August.[19] Several weeks then elapsed
before the road was ballasted and surfaced. A regular passenger
service did not begin until October 15, 1886.[20] A single daily train
then began to make the round trip from Belmont to Spokane Falls.[21]

The first indications of a Northern Pacific advance into the
Palouse country immediately brought the OR&N scrambling to
extend their own line northeast.[22] At a meeting held at the Ladd &
Tilton Bank in Portland on November 2, 1885, the directors resolved to commence construction as quickly as possible.[23] First of
all, however, they needed an appearance of local acquiescence, and
for that purpose the company induced George W. Truax and H. F.
Stratton of Farmington, and Thomas Kennedy of Garfield, to raise
a petition asking OR&N manager C. H. Prescott to build the line in
time to move the next season's crops.[24] That done, Truax formed a
committee to procure the right of way, and by November 26, 1885
all the necessary land between Silver Creek and Farmington had
been pledged.[25] To emphasize a commitment to the area, the OR&N

then moved its general land office, headed by T. R. Tannatt, from Portland to Farmington.[26]

Despite the initial haste, six months passed before the construction of the Colfax-to-Farmington line finally commenced. Given the prospect of rock work in the canyon, there was some reluctance to follow the North Palouse River. The company surveyed another route, diverging from the Moscow line at a point about eight miles southeast of Colfax,[27] but eventually took the course originally contemplated. Early in March 1886 Engineer McClellan and a number of surveyors set out to make a final location of the line,[28] and were quickly followed by a second party estimating cross sections.[29] A spring flood and the difficulty of moving around the country so early in the year delayed the survey and held up final land procurement. To expedite matters and discourage people from waiting to see what the Northern Pacific would do, OR&N had to pay liberally for the right of way.[30] Even so, construction did not commence until the third week of May.

The Colfax-to-Farmington extension of the OR&N climbed continuously for the first 23 miles, ascending from a 1,945-foot elevation at Colfax to 2,614 feet at a point about five miles north of Garfield. There was then a dip to 2,558 feet and a recovery to 2,617 feet in the last four miles to Farmington. The total distance was 27 miles.[31]

Surprisingly, Nelson Bennett won the contract for grading the Farmington line, his close relations with Northern Pacific not preventing him from undertaking work for a rival company.[32] Bennett, however, sublet the contract to George W. Hunt, who had recently worked on the OR&N line from Starbuck to Pomeroy. Hunt left Corvallis, Oregon, with 135 men on or about May 18, 1886.[33] Within a month a thousand men and "a corresponding number of teams" were making the dirt fly,[34] and within two months they had finished the entire Colfax to Farmington grade.[35] The bridge carpenters moved up from the Pataha line before the end of May and completed their work well ahead of the steel gang.[36] Tracklaying got under way late in July and by August 4 the railway had reached a point about seven miles from Colfax. An alarming event then overtook the project. The American bark *W. H. Besse*, 160 days out from New York with a cargo of steel rails for the OR&N, was lost on the Columbia Bar.[37] Fortunately a frantic check of inventory produced enough rails to complete the road. The company then concluded the work with all dispatch, but not without incident. At the end of August 1886, 50 or 60 discharged construction workers ran amok in Colfax, defied the sheriff and his deputies, and terrorized the town.[38] The OR&N's Farmington extension nevertheless opened to traffic on the last Sunday of September 1886.[39]

Along the rival Spokane & Palouse, Belmont would not remain a terminus for long. The dust of the 1886 construction season had hardly settled before Northern Pacific prepared to extend the Spokane & Palouse road southward. About a week before Christmas local residents began receiving reports of surveying and land procurement for another 70 miles of railway.[40] The line was to pass through prime wheat land to Garfield, Palouse City, and Pullman, then arc southeast through Colton and Uniontown to Genesee in Idaho. Before the end of the year, Northern Pacific also threatened to descend upon Colfax. Indeed, early in January 1887 a survey party led by Engineer Lewis laid out a reasonably graded line from Oakesdale to Colfax via Conway Gulch and Dry Creek.[41] Eventually, however, the company concentrated all effort on the line to Genesee. On April 5, 1887, two engineering parties were reported to be converging on Pullman from opposite directions.[42] During the following week Paul F. Mohr returned to Spokane Falls from New York with authority to commence construction. Nelson Bennett, meanwhile, undertook to grade an additional 70 miles of line and appointed E. M. Wilson as his local lieutenant. By April 12, 1887, Bennett's forces were on their way from Ellensburg and subcontractors had already started work between Belmont and Garfield.[43]

From Belmont the Spokane & Palouse extension proceeded south to Garfield, where it crossed the OR&N's Colfax-to-Farmington line. It then descended to a crossing of Cedar Creek and joined the North Palouse River, which it crossed and followed upstream as far as Palouse City. Turning south it climbed onto higher ground and pursued an undulating course southwest to Pullman. Intersecting the OR&N's Moscow branch and crossing the South Palouse River, the Northern Pacific subsidiary then picked its way through the hummocky loess hills to Colton, where it joined the headwaters of the Union Flat Creek. It then proceeded southeast to Uniontown, and finally swung eastward to terminate on an extensive flat at Genesee, Idaho.

South of Garfield construction was held up until Paul F. Mohr decided whether to approach Palouse City by Dufield Flat or the North Palouse River.[44] By April 25, apparently, he had chosen the latter route, but the graders could not move earth until the surveyors prepared cross sections.[45] Work, consequently, did not get under way there until about mid-May 1887. Even then, land procurement problems at Palouse City hindered progress, and were resolved only by on-site negotiations personally conducted by president Cannon and company attorney H. E. Houghton.[46] All these setbacks may have been portentous, for construction of the extension to Genesee was to suffer many more delays.

During the first five months of 1887 hostile OR&N reaction to the Spokane & Palouse extension was confined to harassment of survey parties.[47] Toward the end of May, however, the Oregon & Transcontinental Company sought an injunction to prevent Northern Pacific from issuing bonds for the Spokane & Palouse Railway or exercising any kind of control over its operations.[48] As holders of one-sixth of Northern Pacific's stock, Oregon & Transcontinental claimed that such an action would burden the company with debt and thus defraud shareholders. In fact, the move was calculated to protect the much larger O&T interest in the OR&N. Interviewed at Missoula early in June 1887, Robert Harris remarked that he did not think that Oregon & Transcontinental could really prevent the construction of Northern Pacific branch lines. "We, Mr. Wright and the other directors and myself," he said, "... are looking out for the Northern Pacific and no court will ask us to be particularly mindful of the OR&N Co. just because some of our shareholders happen to hold stock in that company."[49] The temporary injunction, however, proved to be a nuisance, for as the hearings dragged on, funds became scarce and work slowed down. Restlessness among the construction laborers then resulted in trouble. In July, Palouse City witnessed a riot and before order could be restored one man was shot dead.[50]

Despite the shortage of funds, grading went on along the Spokane & Palouse line both north and south of Pullman throughout the summer. Track laying, however, did not get under way again until about September 10, 1887 and led, within a week, to a further confrontation with the OR&N. At the intersection with the Oregon company's Farmington line at Garfield, mischievous individuals among the Spokane & Palouse construction force belligerently installed a crossing before official negotiations had resulted in permission to do so. They then defied the OR&N forces to remove it.[51] The net result was that Northern Pacific chief engineer Adna Anderson had to go to Portland to apologize to W. H. Holcomb.[52] Track laying, meanwhile, came to a temporary halt. Consequently the railway did not reach Pullman until early in December 1887.[53] In the meantime Nelson Bennett tired of the repeated and costly delays and instructed his manager, E. L. Cowgill, to work until December 24 and then pull out.[54] With track laid as far as Colton, Northern Pacific was thus left to complete the road to Genesee by itself.

In January 1888, as a result of icy conditions on the Columbia River, eastern Washington was cut off from supplies of Roslyn coal. To save the situation, the Spokane & Palouse construction force withdrew to cut wood for the Idaho Division locomotives.[55] Further work was therefore delayed until the beginning of March and the steel did not reach Genesee until April 17. The line was finally turned over to the operating department on July 1, 1888.[56] Then, at last, Spokane passengers could take advantage of the stage connection at Uniontown and reach Lewiston, Idaho, in one day. Increasing quantities of Palouse wheat, meanwhile, began to flow over the newly completed Northern Pacific line to Puget Sound.

Chapter Four

The Cascade Branch

North of the Columbia River the Cascade Mountains presented the railway builders with an unbroken barrier separating the Interior Plain from Puget Sound. At no point could the range be crossed at an elevation of less than 3,000 feet above sea level. And, without driving long summit tunnels, the ruling grades could not be made easier than 145 feet to the mile.[1]

The United States Army first investigated possible routes through the mountains as part of the Pacific railroad survey of 1853-54. At that time Governor Isaac Stevens of Washington Territory became responsible for exploring the most northerly transcontinental route and Captain George B. McClellan oversaw survey work in the Pacific Northwest. McClellan ascended the Columbia and Yakima rivers and examined Snoqualmie Pass. Despite disagreement with Stevens, who had a direct interest in promoting lines of communication within Washington Territory, McClellan's report stressed, quite properly, that the best route from the Coast to the Interior lay along the Columbia River.[2]

In 1867 Northern Pacific chief engineer Edwin F. Johnson asked General James Tilton, the former surveyor general of Washington Territory, to find and report on passes suitable for a railway through the mountains. Tilton sent out three parties, headed by J. S. Hurd, W. H. Carlton, and A. J. Treadway, who reported on several possible routes, the most feasible of which were Cowlitz Pass, Snoqualmie Pass, and Skagit Pass, the Cowlitz being the most southerly. "This latter pass," said General Tilton, leads from the Tanum branch of the Natchess River, a tributary of the Yakima, to the Cowlitz River and is about 12 miles to the south-east of Mount Ranier [*sic*]. The second pass leads from the Kitchelus branch of the Yakima to the Snoqualmie branch of the Snohomish River and is about 40 miles north of Mount Ranier, and the third pass leads from the Wenatchee, a tributary of the Columbia River, in one direction to the Skykomish branch of the Snohomish River, and in another and northerly direction to the Sawk branch of the Skagit River. Between the Snoqualmie Pass and Mount Ranier are two passes, the Cedar River or Yakima and the Natchess, elevated the former 1060 ft. and the latter 1900 ft. above the Snoqualmie Pass.[3]

Tilton's report, submitted to the Northern Pacific board in April 1869, made quite clear that the construction of a line through the mountains would be very difficult and costly. Chief engineer Johnson therefore advised the company to follow the Columbia River, and W. Milnor Roberts, acting for Jay Cooke & Company, soon endorsed his recommendation.

In December 1873 Northern Pacific completed a railway from Kalama, on the lower Columbia River, to Commencement Bay on Puget Sound, and made a commitment to creating a Pacific Coast terminus at Tacoma. In 1877 a spur line was built east from Tacoma, by way of Puyallup, to collieries at Wilkeson. To protect its land grant the company described this as part of the Cascade Branch. The preferred route across the mountains from the Interior consequently became one which would lead to Puget Sound by either the Green or White river systems. In 1878 W. Milnor Roberts, who was by that time chief engineer of the company, was asked to initiate a search for a better route.[4] After exploring the Cowlitz Pass, his survey parties moved north to reexamine the Naches and Snoqualmie passes. Under Roberts and his successor, General Adna Anderson, the work went on for three years and finally resulted in the discovery of an intermediate location for a relatively short tunnel at an elevation of about 2,800 feet above sea level. This route was called the Green River Pass until, one fine day, a party of men cutting trail ahead of the surveyors west of the divide got fed up with the job and quit. After the mutineers had gone, a sign, written by one of their ringleaders on a piece of board, was found tied to a fir tree. It read, "Stampede camp!" From then on the line became known as Stampede Pass.[5]

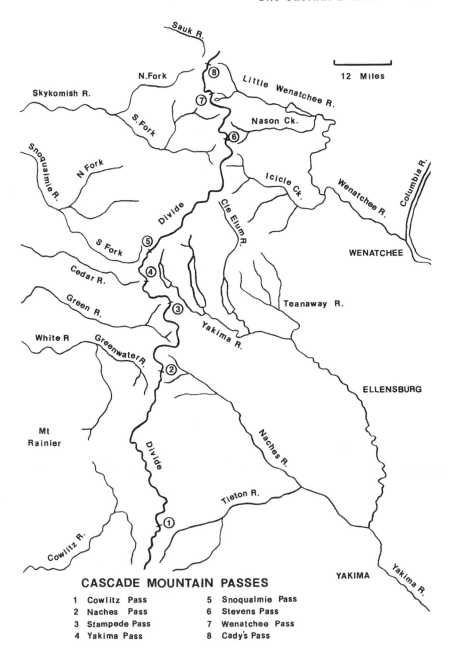

Sauk R.

N.Fork

Skykomish R.

S.Fork

Little Wenatchee R.

Nason Ck.

12 Miles

⑧

⑦

⑥

Snoqualmie R.

N Fork

Icicle Ck.

Wenatchee R.

Columbia R.

Divide

Cle Elum R.

WENATCHEE

S Fork

⑤

Cedar R.

④

Green R.

③

Teanaway R.

White R

Greenwater R.

Yakima R.

②

ELLENSBURG

Mt
Rainier

Divide

Naches R.

Tieton R.

①

Cowlitz R.

YAKIMA

Yakima R.

CASCADE MOUNTAIN PASSES

1	Cowlitz Pass	5	Snoqualmie Pass
2	Naches Pass	6	Stevens Pass
3	Stampede Pass	7	Wenatchee Pass
4	Yakima Pass	8	Cady's Pass

As long as Frederick Billings remained president of the Northern Pacific Railroad, construction of the Cascade Branch was seen as a matter of urgency.[6] Engineers Sheets and Kingsbury spent the winter of 1880-81 running a line through the mountains.[7] The company, meanwhile, invited bids on the supply of 350,000 ties and 10 million feet of timber, and ordered rails. For several months the project appeared likely to go ahead but in June 1881 the Oregon & Transcontinental takeover brought matters to a halt. The annual report published in September 1881 stated evasively that routes over the Cascades were still being studied, and reported that the 250,000 ties already cut had been stockpiled on the Puyallup branch.[8] Of eleven survey parties in the field in December 1881, only one was working in the Cascades.[9]

Villard had no intention of building the Cascade Branch, for his policy was to channel all the northern transcontinental railroad traffic onto the OR&N line along the Columbia Valley. The entire resources of both the Northern Pacific Railroad and Oregon & Transcontinental companies were therefore committed to completing the main line east of Spokane Falls. Speaking at Walla Walla early in May 1883, Villard was discouraging about the Cascade Branch, explaining to his audience that the grades would be too steep to work heavy trains and that a lot of money would be required to drive the tunnel.[10] During the summer of 1883, however, threats to rescind the land grant once more became acute, forcing him to order the construction of a token 25-mile section of the Cascade line.[11] Nelson Bennett's forces went to work on the west side of the Columbia River at Kennewick in August 1883 and by October 26 of that year they had graded a roadbed passing south of Badger Mountain to meet the Yakima River. By the end of November the steel gang had laid nine miles of track, and an engine and several flat cars were forwarding materials brought across the Columbia River by steamboat from the new wharf at the Ainsworth sawmill.[12] The company's intention was to complete 25 miles of railway within the next two months and then suspend all further construction. On January 4, 1884, however, Henry Villard resigned from the Northern Pacific presidency and the company's policy changed abruptly.

In January 1884 chief engineer Adna Anderson invited tenders, to be submitted by February 12, for clearing, grubbing, grading, bridging, and furnishing ties for 60 miles of line from the existing end of track to Yakima.[13] However, due to the land grant again being attacked in Congress[14] and to negotiations for a right of way agreement with the Yakima Indians,[15] the contract was not let until mid summer. In the meantime the company took steps to resolve outstanding questions about the route to the Sound. A line through the Naches Pass would have allowed the company to avoid the Yakima River canyons and all the attendant rock work. In all, it would have been 20 miles shorter and $1.6 million cheaper. The grades, however, would have been steeper.[16] Anderson therefore decided that Stampede Pass offered the better route, and concentrated his engineering effort upon it. On May 9, 1884, W. H. Kennedy, assisted by W. T. Chalk and P. C. Paulson, set out from Tacoma with 18 men "to find an easier route through one of the passes already surveyed." Reexamining the western approach to Stampede Pass, Kennedy found that it was "practicable to reach the tunnel on an easy grade by building... a loop by means of which the railroad doubles on itself and readily gains elevation by so doing."[17] The results of his work were reflected in the Northern Pacific annual report for 1884, which stated that, "That pass known as the Stampede, midway between the Natches and Snoqualmie passes, has been adopted by the company as the place for crossing the range."[18] Company directors finally confirmed this choice on November 21, 1884, when, meeting in Philadelphia, they formally adopted Anderson's recommendation.[19]

The Cascade Branch left the existing main line at Pasco Junction, about three miles east of Ainsworth. It then proceeded southwest to the Columbia River, which was originally crossed by transfer boat. On the Kennewick side of the river the railway set off westward, climbing about 300 feet in 14 miles to a gap between Badger Mountain and the Horse Heaven Hills. The maximum gradient on this section was 45 feet to the mile, and at Badger station the line attained an elevation of almost 700 feet above sea level. Heading in a northwesterly direction the railway then descended about 140 feet in seven miles to meet the Yakima River at Kiona. Turning nearly southwest along the foot of the Horse Heaven escarpment, the railroad followed the Yakima upstream to a point about four miles above Prosser's Falls. Diverging from the river, it then turned northwest onto a 21-mile tangent traversing the broad Simcoe

Valley almost all the way from Satus through Toppenish to the gap between Ahtanum Ridge and the Rattlesnake Hills. Making its way through the narrows, the railway crossed Ahtanum Creek, passed by the existing town of Yakima, and came to a halt in the new town of North Yakima.[20]

In preparation for pushing the Cascade Branch westward to Yakima, the company took immediate steps to expedite the movement of materials and supplies across the Columbia River at Pasco. During the third week of June 1884 the transfer boat *Frederick Billings*, no longer required for the Snake River crossing at Ainsworth, was sent downriver for overhaul and modification. Before she returned, late in August, a spur was built from Pasco Junction to the east bank of the river, and inclines were constructed at both sides.[22] Simultaneously, the first 25 miles of the line, which had apparently lain disused throughout the winter, was put back in shape.[23]

Under the supervision of Northern Pacific engineer H. S. Huson, grading began west of Kiona on July 1, 1884. The work got off to a good start and within three weeks another nine miles of roadbed lay ready for ties.[24] By August 23, 1884, 450 men and a large number of teams were hard at work,[25] and within another month they had graded 25 miles of the line. Track laying then commenced.[26] The construction of minor trestles, of which there were no less than 27 between Kiona and Prosser, however, delayed the advance.[27] The railway, therefore, did not reach Prosser until early in November. The carpenters then built a depot and water tank there and a sizeable town grew up.[28] Meanwhile, on the tangent section of railway across the Yakima Indian reservation, the pace quickened. On December 6, 1884 Nelson Bennett put on a night shift and the rate of advance increased to $1^1/_4$ miles per day. By December 11 steel had been extended to within five miles of the existing town of Yakima, which was then a thriving community of 600 people, the county seat, with three churches, a national bank, a United States land office, hotels, stores, and many fine homes.[29] Local residents prepared to celebrate the railroad's debut, but just as the first locomotive came within whistling distance, Northern Pacific made a startling announcement. Their trains would not stop there! A depot was to be built at a new townsite platted by the railroad company 4.5 miles further west.[30]

The railroad arrived in the vicinity of Old Yakima on December 17, 1884 and was extended to North Yakima during the next two months.[31] In February 1885 Washington Territory brought legal action to compel Northern Pacific to establish a depot at the old town.[32] Many local residents realized, however, that the existing site was limited and would eventually restrict growth. Despite the fact that the courts ruled in their favor,[33] businessmen moved their premises one by one to North Yakima. In mid-April 1885 a force went to work "to put the remainder of the old town on screw jacks and rollers," and within a month Old Yakima was said to be "a thing of the past."[34]

Work, meanwhile, got under way further up the valley.[35] By mid-February 1885 the roadbed was complete to a point 18 miles beyond North Yakima and was advancing steadily.[36] Less than three months later, however, construction came to a halt pending the outcome of negotiations for a joint lease of the OR&N system. The company then discharged all 700 construction workers, who tramped away to look for work elsewhere.[37] Despite mounting pressure to accept the Oregon & Transcontinental Company terms and use the Columbia Valley line to reach coastal areas, the Philadelphia group with interests in the Tacoma Land Company remained determined to push the Cascade Branch to completion. At the end of June 1885 president Robert Harris, accompanied by engineers Anderson and Bogue, journeyed from North Yakima to Ellensburg and, following the route of the railway, crossed the mountains to Puget Sound.[38] Within two weeks of Harris's visit to Yakima, rock work in the canyon had resumed.[39] For the next four months, however, total expenditure on the Cascade Branch was limited to a mere $10,000 a month,[40] and the work proceeded very slowly. Harris's determination nevertheless paid off, for the collapse of the joint-lease negotiations, and the success of the Philadelphia group in the Northern Pacific elections of September 1885, eventually resulted in greater appropriations. In November 1885 the board ordered the rapid completion of the section between North Yakima and Ellensburg.

Leaving North Yakima the railroad crossed the Naches River on a two-span bridge[41] and headed northward through Selah into the lower canyon of the Yakima. Just below the mouth of Wenas Creek it crossed to the left bank of the river and began to follow the meanders deeply incised into the great Umtanum Ridge. Within seven miles it was forced back to the west side of the river, which it then followed for about 19 miles to a third crossing at the upper end of the canyon. Regaining the left bank, and proceeding northwest across the broad and fertile Kittitas Valley, the railway came at length to the flourishing town of Ellensburg.[42]

Work crews finished the Naches River bridge, just west of North Yakima, in the fall of 1885, and laid track to the first crossing of the Yakima River. Thereafter, the advance up the canyon was regulated by progress at the river crossings, all three of which required long, single-span bridges. At the first crossing the company decided to use the 336-foot drawspan originally made for the aborted OR&N bridge at Grange City. The company's intention had been to incorporate this span into the Snake River bridge at Ainsworth, but an unfortunate mistake was made in spacing the piers there and the iron again became surplus.[43] The bridges at the second and third crossings were no less noteworthy, for they provided chief engineer Anderson with an opportunity to experiment with through-truss spans using iron decks and tie bars in combination with timber compression members.[44] The experiment being a success, somewhat shorter spans of the same type were later used for the Columbia River bridge at Pasco.

The erection of the bridges in the Yakima canyon took longer than expected because early in February 1886 the river suddenly rose, and, bearing large quantities of ice, swept away the falsework (a temporary supporting structure used during the erection of a permanent bridge) at both the first and second crossings.[45] Repairs were quickly made but some delay resulted.[46] Not until the second week of March were Hoffman & Bates able to start work on the permanent bridges,[47] and only then could materials be brought up to the third crossing. The completion of 740 feet of approach trestling and the falsework for the bridge at that point took another two weeks. The steel gang rapidly laid track on the remaining seven miles to Ellensburg and the construction train arrived there on April 1, 1886.[48]

The decision to expedite completion of the section between Yakima and Ellensburg marked a turning point in Northern Pacific affairs. Thereafter, construction of the Cascade Branch gathered momentum. On January 21, 1886 Nelson Bennett won the contract for driving the Stampede Tunnel,[49] and by early March his miners had started work.[50] On the west side of the mountains, meanwhile, workmen had already laid track to Eagle Gorge in the Green River Valley, 50 miles from Tacoma.[51] Between that point and Ellensburg there was a gap of 77 miles via the tunnel, or 81 miles by way of the proposed switchbacks over the ridge. The tunnel was to be almost two miles long, leaving 75 miles of main line to be built. The distance between the ends of the switchback line, via the tunnel, was nearly three miles, and the length of that line, not including tail tracks, was to be just over seven miles.[52] The company opened bids on May 15, 1886 and within two weeks contracts were let to Hale, Smith, Burns & Company for the 61 miles from Ellensburg via the switchbacks to a point 70 miles east of Tacoma, and to Nelson Bennett for the remaining 20 miles to Eagle Gorge.[53] Government acceptance of the sections already completed, meanwhile, allowed first mortgage bonds to be sold, and eased the financial situation considerably.[54]

Leaving Ellensburg, the Cascade Branch headed northwest through the Kittitas Valley, crossing and re-crossing the Yakima as it did so. It then followed the river for eight miles through the narrow defile known as the Upper Canyon. Emerging into a broader vale, and crossing the mouth of the Teanaway River, which flows into the Yakima from the north, the railway proceeded onward to Cle Elum. Intersecting the Cle Elum River, which also drains the region to the north, it then crossed the Yakima for the sixth and last time.[55] Advancing northwestward, the line passed through Easton, and in order to remain on the south side of the river, tunneled 385 feet through a high spur of unconsolidated ground just east of Cabin Creek. Thus far the ruling grade had been 42 feet to the mile, but from that point on the road became much steeper. Six miles from the Stampede Tunnel the grade stiffened to 116 feet to the mile. Clinging to the mountainside the railway climbed northwest, passing through the 525-foot-long Dingle Tunnel as it went. Less than two miles further it swung sharply south into the ravine below Mosquito Creek Falls. Crossing the creek directly in front of the cataract, and turning slightly westward, it then plunged headlong into the mountain wall.

Within the 9,844-foot-long tunnel the railway climbed for a mile on a 0.2 percent drainage grade. Passing over a summit about 2,830 feet above sea level just beyond the mid point, it then descended on a 0.74 percent grade to the west portal.[56] Emerging into the open air, the road began a steep and tortuous eight mile descent into the Green River Valley. On a falling gradient of 115 feet to the mile it headed west, tunneled 620 feet through an intervening ridge, and swung northwestward. Then, turning south onto a long 10-degree curve and passing through two more short tunnels,[57] it almost completely circumnavigated a prominent outlying hill. After pursuing an eastward course for a mile or so, it again about-faced to take up an alignment high on the southeast side of the Sunday Creek Valley. Descending southwest for several miles, it then swung sharply southeast through Weston to meet the Green River head-on. Describing a 10 degree hairpin bend in the valley bottom, and crossing the river as it did so, the line followed the rushing waters downstream.[58] Temporarily taking up position on the north side of the Green River the railway passed over the mouth of Sunday Creek and headed west towards Eagle Gorge, South Prairie, Puyallup, and Tacoma.

The first problem facing the contractors working in the Cascade Mountains was to find enough men.[59] On August 3, 1886, George W. Hunt, who had taken subcontracts for work on both sides of the divide, stated there was then "room and work with good fare" for a thousand men. He added that about half of those they hired were "good men who want to work and are not to be blamed for the conduct of the other half who will not work."[60] Two weeks later the Portland *Oregonian* reported that laborers would no longer be taken from Portland to the front free of charge, as the company was fed up with them quitting after the first pay day. Despite growing hostility to the use of Chinese labor, the lack of a reliable white work force led to the employment of a large number of the despised "Celestials." In July 1886 Hale, Smith, Burns & Company made an agreement with Chinese agents for the provision of 1,500 men to work between Ellensburg and the summit,[61] and took elaborate precautions to prevent trouble with the whites.

Prior to the arrival of the first contingent of Chinese, Pinkerton detectives went ahead to Ellensburg and points beyond. In a widely circulated press report, this security force was said to consist entirely of "large and able bodied men, who have seen hot service, and are well equipped with Winchester rifles and heavy duty Colt

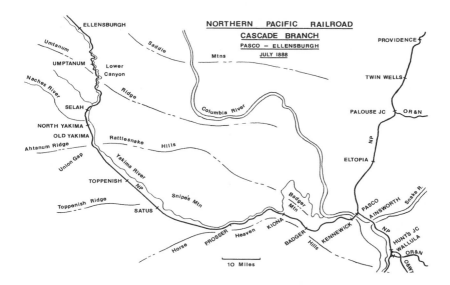

double action revolvers." Commissioned as deputy U. S. marshals and led by Captain Swain, "a shrewd and trusty chief," they were said to be "ready to move upon a moment's notice" and "thoroughly prepared to quell any disturbance or resistance to the advent of the Chinese upon the grade." To avoid trouble en route, Swain and his men shepherded the first 38 Chinese cross country from Palouse Junction to Ellensburg by wagon train.[62] By the end of September 1886, however, such extreme theatrics had been dropped. Thereafter the Chinese were brought to the front by rail. The movement, however, was not entirely without incident, for just as one train of ten cars, drawn by two locomotives, approached North Yakima, some malicious person threw a switch diverting it toward the roundhouse. Fortunately it stopped before running into the turntable pit.[63]

Apart from the rock work in the Upper Canyon of the Yakima River, grading between Ellensburg and Cle Elum was largely a matter of scraping up alluvial material from the flood plains of the river.[64] Below the mouth of the canyon, bridge construction governed the rate of advance. The bridges at the fourth and fifth crossings of the Yakima were to consist respectively of two 150-foot spans and 1,300 feet of approach trestle, and a single 200-foot span with 700 feet of approach trestle. Mr. Taylor, the foreman carpenter, was therefore hard-pressed to complete the falsework and trestling before the arrival of the steel gang.[65] Tracklaying began at Ellensburg about August 20, 1886, using a patent tracklaying machine designed by a Mr. Holman, who personally supervised its use. Despite his ministrations, the initial advance amounted to no more than 1,600 feet per day.[66] It is not clear whether subsequent rapid progress was due to the machine, or to its early abandonment.

The rock work in the Upper Canyon went on for three months and was not completed without loss of life. Early in September 1886 a premature blast killed four men: John Viavonia, an Italian; Andrew Krupp, a Bavarian; H. J. Jorndorf, a German; and John Rutts, from Switzerland.[67] The work nevertheless continued. By the end of the month, with the way through the canyon clear, tracklaying, whether manual or mechanized, moved into high gear. On October 8, 1886, no less than 12,500 feet was laid in 9 hours and 20 minutes.[68] Three days later the railway reached the crossing of the Teanaway River, where a 100-foot, single-span bridge with 700 feet of approach trestle was still under construction. After several days' delay the construction train moved on westward over the falsework to Cle Elum, where it arrived on October 19, 1886.[69]

At Cle Elum the company diverted construction forces and materials to build an important branch. During the location of the main line, showings of coal had been noticed in the hills just to the north. Upon investigation these proved to be major deposits of high grade, non-clinkering steam coal, of a type ideal for locomotives. This was a find that could not be passed by, for South Prairie and other coals found on the west side of the mountains were of inferior quality and occurred in deposits difficult to mine. In May 1886 the Northern Pacific coal agent, Mr. Bullitt, visited Cle Elum and declared the townships in which the coal lay to be mineral reserves.[70] By June 19, 1886 the company had brought up a diamond drill and intersected seams of coal five to nine feet thick. A hundred men immediately went to work to develop the mines and make preparations to build a railway.[71] Clearing the heavy growth and undergrowth for the steeply graded, three-mile-long Roslyn branch began before the main line reached Cle Elum,[72] but grading remained uncompleted until Hunt could release men from the main line. Nevertheless, the roadbed was ready on December 8, 1886,[73] track was laid by December 13,[74] and the railway was opened on December 21. The mines then began to ship coal, and their business expanded rapidly. Despite the destruction of Roslyn by fire in July 1888 and bitter labor strife thereafter, the output increased steadily. By early 1890 the mines employed 900 men and produced more than 800 tons of coal daily.[75]

Between Cle Elum and Cabin Creek the only major rock work was a deep cut at the sixth crossing of the Yakima. The most significant bridges consisted of a 200-foot, single-span and 1,200-foot approach trestle at the Cle Elum River, and another 200-foot span and 150 feet of trestling at the sixth crossing.[76] Work progressed satisfactorily and by the end of November 1886 crews had the temporary bridges in place and track laid. Beyond Cabin Creek, however, matters were not quite so far advanced. The tunnel at that point, being in earth, proved difficult to drive and required timbering throughout.[77] Dingle Tunnel, excavated in rock, took time. When it was finished the grade was almost ready for steel, not only to the east portal of Stampede Tunnel but also to the summit of the high line over the pass.

On April 15, 1886 the company decided to build a railway over the top of the Stampede Pass and operate it until the long tunnel was opened.[78] Due to deep snow pack in the mountains, however, location work could not begin for another two months. The work then had to be pushed. On June 14, 1886 a party under the direction of a young engineer named J. Q. Barlow began work above the tunnel. By July 12 they had finalized the location of the switchback line, and staked out 4.5 miles of the route. Construction then commenced. On the east side the line climbed 850 feet in 3.7 miles to a summit 3,660 feet above sea level. The maximum grade on tangent track was 5.6 percent or 296 feet to the mile. The grade, however, was compensated .04 percent per degree of curvature, so that the average inclination was 4.95 percent. On the west side the difference in elevation was 945 feet, achieved in 3.5 miles on a maximum gradient of 5.2 percent or 275 feet to the mile. Compensation for curvature reduced the average grade on that side to 4.06 percent. There were two switchbacks on each side of the ridge, each one having 575 feet of tail track. The tail tracks were laid on 2.5 percent upgrades and connected to adjacent ascending and descending sections by vertical curves. At the summit there was a cutting 40 feet deep accommodating 500 feet of level grade, and a 1,300-foot spur extending northward along the west side of the ridge to allow cars to be set out.[79]

The east end of the switchback route diverged from the main line on the sharp curve at the mouth of Mosquito Creek Gulch. Heading west and crossing the creek on a high trestle bridge, it ran almost immediately onto the tail track of the first switchback. Setting off in the opposite direction, the high line climbed out of the gulch and turned away northwestward up the mountainside. Climbing steeply and crossing three deep ravines as it did so, the railway reached the second switchback about a mile further on. Reversing again, it climbed southeastward for about half a mile, negotiated a full horseshoe curve, and finally struggled north and west to the summit, which lay nearly a mile northwest of the tunnel alignment.

On the west side the road descended southwest in a more or less straight line for more than a mile. At a point high on the mountainside north of the tunnel's west portal it entered a loop consisting of two consecutive 15 degree horseshoe curves, which enabled it to reapproach the main line. Emerging from the lower end of the loop it proceeded in a westerly direction for nearly a mile to the second west-side switchback, the tail track of which was laid on a high dead-ended fill. Doubling back eastward toward the tunnel mouth, the line dropped down to the first switchback on the west side and reversed again. It then descended westward to rejoin the main line at a point nearly three-quarters of a mile beyond the west portal of the tunnel.[80]

The switchback line had no less than 31 trestle bridges up to 150 feet high.[81] Local timber being unsuitable for structural purposes, material for these bridges was cut at lower elevations and sawn at the Johnson and Leonhardt sawmills below Easton. It was then hauled up on the summit wagon road and dropped off at points where the trestles were to be built. By the second week of December 1886 crews had graded the high line and nearly completed the trestle work. The only thing needed to finish the job was rails.[82] Tracklaying resumed at Cabin Creek on Tuesday December 14, 1886.[83] Four days later, however, winter set in with a vengeance. Snow fell continuously for weeks on end, and despite the efforts of more than 500 Chinese, the line could hardly be kept clear for the steel gang.[84] The company nevertheless ordered the work to proceed. On December 24, 1886 the railway was within 2.5 miles of Stampede Tunnel, and by January 18, 1887 nearly another mile of track had been laid. A further week's work, however, produced only 1,000 feet of advance, and by

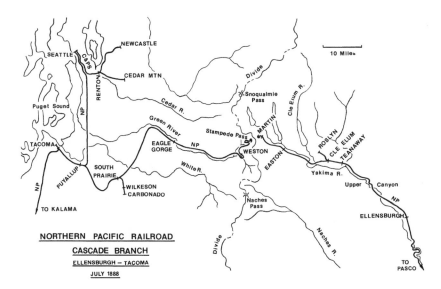

NORTHERN PACIFIC RAILROAD
CASCADE BRANCH
ELLENSBURGH – TACOMA
JULY 1888

January 27 everything was at a standstill. By that time 15 feet of snow lay on the switchbacks.[85]

On the west side of the mountains construction work was more difficult and progress slower. By December 15, 1886 the railroad had been completed to Sunday Creek and graded five miles further. Engineer Huson, who crossed the mountains from Tacoma to Ellensburg during the second week of December, thought that the roadbed could be finished to the 75th mile from Tacoma within another 30 days. Beyond that point, however, there were three tunnels to drive and a great deal of other rock work to complete.[86] Hunt's forces were only then arriving from Cle Elum. Their supplies, moreover, had been lost in a fire that consumed a warehouse tent set up on the switchbacks.[87] Given the added probability of snow, Huson doubted that the two ends of the railway would meet before May 1, 1887, and events proved him more than right.

At the end of January 1887 the weather did its worst. For several days, howling winds swept relentlessly up the mountain valleys from Puget Sound, and early on January 30 they reached a crescendo. Near Sunday Creek the winds ripped immense fir and cedar trees from their roots and sent them flying in all directions. About 1:00 a. m. a huge tree fell across a tent occupied by sleeping Chinese laborers, killing nine and injuring four others.[88] The survivors apparently regarded the storm as an ill omen, and many demanded to leave.[89] Although Chinese agents induced them to stay, their grievances nevertheless festered. During the second week of April, 1887 matters came to a head. The trouble began when a white foreman ordered some Chinese laborers to camp higher up on the mountainside, where the only shelter was an old log cabin. At this they again threatened to leave, and the company once more sent in the agents to persuade them to stay. On the morning of April 11 a commotion broke out in the Chinese camp, when the workers tied one of the hated labor procurers to a tree and thrust a large knife into his back. The white security guards protecting the camp then intervened and a full-scale riot broke out. Forced onto the defensive, the guards opened fire, killing one laborer and wounding five others.[90] The rest of the Chinese dispersed, but 300 of them quit and made their way south to work on the still-uncompleted Oregon & California road.[91]

February at last brought improved weather conditions and allowed the shovelers to make some headway.[92] Ten feet of snow was removed from the eastern approach to the Stampede Tunnel and on Thursday March 4, 1887 track finally reached Martin.[93] Daily trains then began running between there and Ellensburg. On the west side of the mountains, meanwhile, the railway reached mile 71 from Tacoma in mid-February and mile 73.5 on March 16. Eight more bridges then had to be built before the line could be completed to the west end of the long tunnel. On March 28, 1887, 500 whites and 300 Chinese were reported to be at work, and rails had been extended to mile $74^3/4$. As soon as the steel gang laid the track the railway was ballasted and surfaced, so that whenever the east and west ends were connected, through trains could begin running immediately.[94] As the spring advanced, work again got under way on the switchbacks. High up on the east side of Stampede Pass 500 Chinese shovelers, working in eight tiers, cleared out the cuts and chopped their way through the deep snow drifts.[95] Closely following them, 200 whites completed the trestle bridges and laid track as they went. Passing onward and upward between vertical walls of snow, they eventually arrived at the summit on April 18, 1887.[96]

Almost as soon as rails went down on the east side switchbacks the dangers of operating the high line were amply demonstrated. On March 30, 1887 a relatively small locomotive, which had struggled almost a mile up the steep grade with one car, became incapable of going any further. Worse still, its brakes proved to be inadequate. As it began to run away downhill the crew jumped off, leaving it to accelerate to an estimated speed of 100 miles an hour. Further down the line three carpenters working on a curved trestle suddenly found the engine upon them. One man was killed outright and another had both his legs chopped off. The third, however, was more fortunate, for he threw himself flat on the timbers and as the train took off into mid air it passed over him. The engine fell 100 feet into the canyon below, and was smashed to pieces on the rocks.[97]

That runaway was not the only railway accident before the line was handed over to the operating department. On Thursday, April 21, 1887 a disastrous head-on collision occurred just east of the sixth crossing of the Yakima River. Engine No. 486, which only functioned reliably in reverse, was running tender-first eastbound toward Cle Elum when it met a westbound work train pushing a flatcar loaded with Irish laborers. The flatcar was driven half-way through 486's tender and then crushed against the pilot of the other locomotive, upon which two more men were sitting. The impact was so great that it sent No. 486 rebounding 80 feet back up the line, killed seven men, and seriously injured twelve others.[98]

By the beginning of May 1887, with the switchback line almost finished, supply trains were making daily trips over the pass.[99] The main line from Tacoma, meanwhile, was extended to the foot of the switchbacks, three-quarters of a mile west of the tunnel.[100] Two hundred car loads of gravel were brought up every day, and ballasting and surfacing operations progressed rapidly.[101] By the end of the month, therefore, the railway was practically finished.

At 6:00 o'clock in the evening on June 1, 1887 Northern Pacific officials, engineers, trainmen, employees, and guests gathered at the summit of the Stampede Pass to celebrate completion. Mrs. Huson and other ladies present tapped a ceremonial last spike into the appropriate tie, missing it several times in the process. Assistant General Manager J. M. Buckley then seized the hammer, and remarking jovially, "It is evident that you are not railroaders," drove the spike vigorously home. At precisely 6:02 p.m. the last of his well-directed blows fell, and for the second time the Northern Pacific Railroad was declared complete.[102]

Once the last spike had been driven the company made final preparations to open the line. On July 1, 1887, 23 telegraph offices between Pasco and Tacoma commenced day and night operations,[103] and two days later regular passenger service began. At first this consisted of one through transcontinental and one local train each way daily. At Stampede Pass, where a switchback trainmaster directed operations, only one train was allowed on the high line at any given time. Train crews were required to take positions at the brakes, one brakeman being assigned to every two cars. The men were instructed not to rely on the air brakes but to be prepared to use the hand brakes at all times. Passenger trains were to utilize the automatic air brake when ascending, and the automatic air brake and pressure-retaining valves when descending. Since retaining valves were not considered sufficient to safeguard freight trains on the downgrades, and resetting valves occupied too much time, freight trains were to use automatic air brakes ascending and the straight air brake, for which the cars were also fitted, when descending.

Locomotives were not permitted to come down the steep grades with any more cars than they could take up. Trains passing over the switchbacks were normally to have an engine at each end. The instructions, however, provided that in cases where trains were to be worked by one engine alone, it was always to be on the downgrade end of the train, both ascending and descending. To conform with this regulation trains had to be pushed uphill onto the tail track of the first switchback, where the hand brakes of the cars were set. The locomotive then backed down the hill to clear the switch, the switch was thrown, and the cars were allowed to run by gravity onto the lower part of the next uphill section, where the brakes were again set. The engine then ran onto the vacated tail track, the switch was once more thrown, and the train was propelled to the next switchback, where the operation was repeated.

At the summit there was a false switchback allowing locomotives to be transferred to the opposite ends of their trains. Every switch on the entire line was manned by a switch tender who responded to whistle signals from approaching trains. Conductors had to leave a clearance ticket with each switch tender, and he in turn had to telephone the trainmaster's office to report that the train had safely passed by.[104]

For the switchback line Northern Pacific purchased two noteworthy locomotives of the 2-10-0 wheel arrangement. Always called the "Decapods," these engines, Nos. 501 and 502, delivered in November 1886, were the first ten-coupled locomotives built by the Baldwin Locomotive Works for standard gauge. The philosophy behind the "Decapod" design was to obtain a large and powerful locomotive with a low axle loading, one that could take as many cars as possible over the switchbacks without damaging the trestle bridges. To develop as much tractive effort as one of the latest "Consolidation" type locomotives required about 130,000 pounds of adhesion weight. But to prevent damage to the bridges that weight had to be spread over five driving axles instead of four. This increased the length of the rigid wheel base and adversely affected the locomotives' ability to negotiate curves. To offset this effect the designers reduced the diameter of the driving wheels to a minimum compatible with a reasonable piston stroke and crank length. They also removed the flanges from one pair of driving wheels. In common with other contemporary locomotives built for working on steep grades, the engines were equipped for counter-pressure braking. A comparison of the dimensions and particulars of the "Decapod" locomotives with those of the improved "Consolidation" type engines built for Northern Pacific shortly afterwards emphasizes these points:

	"Decapod"	Large "Consolidation"
Built	1886	1888
Driving Wheel Diameter	48 ins.	50 ins.
Cylinder diameter	22 ins.	22 ins.
Piston stroke	26 ins.	28 ins.
Boiler pressure	150 lbs./sq. in.	150 lbs./sq. in.
Tractive effort at		
85% boiler pressure	34,800 lbs.	34,557 lbs.
Adhesion weight	128,000 lbs.	135,000 lbs.
Factor of adhesion	3.67	3.91
Driving axle load	25,600 lbs.	33,750 lbs.
Coupled wheelbase	18 ft.	14 ft.
Weight of locomotive		
in working order	144,000 lbs.	150,000 lbs.
Weight of tender	80,000 lbs.	75,000 lbs.
Total weight of		
locomotive & tender	224,000 lbs.	225,000 lbs.

In service, the "Decapods" could pull only about 80 percent of the trailing load handled by the new "Consolidations." This deficiency was attributed to the extra frictional resistance of the fifth driving axle. Another reason might have been the high cylinder back pressure required to draw combustion gases through the longer boiler. On the switchback line, the two "Decapods," working together, could handle five twelve-wheeled sleeping cars or seven eight-wheeled passenger cars. With a freight train the two engines could take 10 loaded 20-ton freight cars. The normal locomotive combination used on the high line, however, seems to have been one "Decapod" and one of the existing smaller "Consolidation" locomotives. Running speeds were limited to 10 miles an hour and the journey, one way, took about an hour and a quarter.[105]

Technical details of the switchback line and its locomotives hardly portray the atmosphere of that incredible piece of railway. A better idea of what it was really like is conveyed in contemporary accounts, such as that published in *Walla Walla Union* on August 27, 1887, which described an east bound journey as follows:

> At Weston, the engine, which is about the same dimensions as those which haul trains through Walla Walla, gives way to one weighing twice as much and having eight drive wheels, that in railroad parlance is called a "Hog." The "Hog" goes snorting up the steep inclines, around the sharp curves, and over the high trestles, along hillsides, through tunnels, to the first part of the switchback, where a huge "Decapod" engine with 10 wheels and a firebox large enough to hold one of the little blanket engines which ran on Dr. Baker's road in the early days hitches onto the other end of the train. The switchback crew take their stations under Nick Lawson, an experienced and careful railroader, and the "Decapod," giving a preliminary scream which is answered by the "Hog," starts up the great marvel of modern railroad engineering. The "Decapod" and "Hog" puff and snort in concert, and send great masses of black smoke from the stacks, the numerous wheels turn, the fronts of the cars rise like a ship mounting a wave. Passengers poke their heads out of the window and marvel at the steepness of the road, or shudder at the depth of the canyon below, or point out the gleaming tracks in the valley or the newly dug earth on the mountain sides above, or go stand up on the platform only to re-enter the car upon hearing the alert brakeman "Must ride in the car, please," until the mountains reverberate the hoarse whistle of the engines as the first switchback

is reached. A moment the train stands still, the brakemen jump to the ground, peer under the cars, wave a signal, the monster at the switch screams, the one at the other end of the train answers, and the snorting and puffing and smoke throwing is again resumed as the train backs up to the next switch, and the other engine goes forward to the summit, where the whole train is carefully examined and the air brake apparatus and the hand brakes are all tested preparatory to plunging down the mountain. Three times [actually there were only two switchbacks does the train change ends before the base of the switchback is reached. The "Decapod" lets go its hold and the train speeds on down the mountain under the sole control of the "Hog." …The grades are the greatest yet essayed in railroading… The motion is like that felt in an elevator, but the track is solid, the trestles look strong, the engines are so powerful, the switchback crew so earnest, quiet, attentive, and determined in appearance that the most timid feel no fear, while the courageous revel in the delights of the visible dangers.[106]

Summer railroading was all very well, but winter lay ahead and required preparations. Late in July 1887 the company let contracts to Hugh Glenn & Company and Hoffman & Bates for the construction of snow sheds on the mountain grades and on the switchbacks.[107] Eventually the line had snow sheds totalling 13,612 feet in length, all robustly constructed of the best red fir.[108] Before the sheds could be completed, the United States government accused the company of excessive timber cutting.[109] A Seattle court decision of November 12, 1887[110] allowed Northern Pacific to cut timber adjacent to the Cascade Branch for building snow sheds and lining tunnels on those sections of the railway not already inspected and accepted by the government. The company, however, was forbidden to take out material for the Columbia River bridge at Pasco, or for bridge timbers and ties required on the Oregon & Washington Territory Railroad. The legal proceedings appear to have delayed construction of the snow sheds from late August to early October 1887. By the end of October, however, the sheds on the switchback line were reported nearly complete[111] and a month later those at the eastern approach to the tunnel had also been finished.

The government's action nevertheless seems to have curtailed the company's snow-shed building program and left many critical parts of the line exposed to winter weather. By December 31, 1887 the railway was again blocked by snow.[112] Just at that

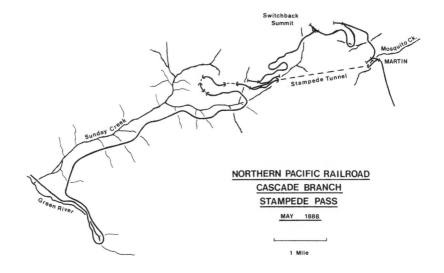

time, however, a new weapon became available for use in the battle against the weather. On January 2, 1888 two Leslie steam rotary snow shovels, built by the Cooke Locomotive Works in Paterson, New Jersey, went to work on the switchback line.[113] These machines, propelled by four locomotives marshalled between them, cleared the whole line in one day. Manual snow clearing suddenly became a thing of the past, and the company henceforth erected snow sheds only in areas subject to avalanches.

The rotary snowplows solved the snow-clearance problem but did nothing to remove other hazards plaguing winter operations on the switchbacks. Hoarfrost and ice reduced adhesion to levels below which trains could no longer safely work over such a steeply graded line. On January 19, 1888 a "Decapod" locomotive, descending the east side of the pass, began to slide on the rails and immediately became unmanageable. Like a great toboggan, it slid to the end of one of the tail tracks and turned over on its side, seriously injuring locomotive engineer R. A. Bellinger and his fireman, John Paulsen.[114] Covered in snow and ice, the re-railed "Decapod" joined seven other locomotives and the two rotary snowplows in the Ellensburg repair shops. Such was the cost of keeping the switchbacks open in the winter.[115]

Construction of the switchback line was reported to have cost $350,000.[116] It allowed traffic to move over the Cascade Branch for perhaps 290 days prior to the opening of the Stampede Tunnel. At the peak of operations on the high line, 1,900 cars went over the pass in 30 days, a rate of 63 cars per day.[117] The switchbacks allowed Northern Pacific to evade the extortionate charges levied by the OR&N for use of the Columbia Valley line and enabled the company to realize net cash earnings more than equal to the cost of construction. Robert Harris and his allies may therefore have been quite justified in claiming the line as a success.[118]

The company did not have to use the high line for very long, for as trains shuffled precariously backward and forward over the top of the pass, miners working in the tunnel, 800 feet below, were slowly advancing the headings towards each other. At midday on May 4, 1888 they broke through, and on May 27, 1888 trains began to use the tunnel. Less than two months later crews finished the permanent bridge across the Columbia River and the Northern Pacific Railroad at long last was complete.

Chapter Five

The Stampede Tunnel

The driving of the Cascade Tunnel at Stampede Pass was to have started early in 1885 but the feud between Northern Pacific and Oregon & Transcontinental delayed matters for almost a year.[1] When the political roadblock was at last removed, the company lost no further time. In mid-December 1885 an engineering party was sent to Stampede Pass to carry out preparatory work, and contractors were again asked to submit tenders. The tunnel was to be 9,850 feet long, 16 feet wide, and 22 feet high, penetrating the mountain wall more than 800 feet below the summit ridge. Since intermediate shafts would have been too deep to offer any advantage, excavation was to proceed from the ends alone.[2] Nelson Bennett won the contract on January 21, 1886,[3] and despite winter weather, work quickly got under way.

Recent experience in tunnel work had demonstrated that pneumatic equipment offered the best means of drilling rock. The air compressor plant previously used at the Mullan Tunnel in Montana had been stored at Ainsworth since that time, and immediately became available for use at Stampede Pass.[4] Nelson Bennett, meanwhile, purchased additional machinery in the East. Transportation to the tunnel site proved to be an onerous, time-consuming task. Bennett's men hauled the machinery up to the McGinnis place, 12 miles below the east end of the tunnel, by wagon train. At that point they transferred it to sleds and took it to Georgetown, a mile and a half from the tunnel. The deep snow then demanded the use of horse-drawn toboggans and yet another transfer.[5] Bennett's brother, "Captain" S. J. Bennett, who acted as resident superintendent, kept 11 teams on the road and, piece by piece, brought up the ponderous apparatus.[6] At Mosquito Creek Falls, meanwhile, carpenters built two bunkhouses and a mess hall to accommodate the men working in the east end of the tunnel.[7] Workmen then cut a trail over the pass to the west portal, shovelling snow away to ground level to give the pack animals a foothold.

The tunnel drive got under way at the east end on February 13, 1886 and work began at the more inaccessible west end on March 18.[8] Within the tunnel, miners carried out the excavations in two stages. A pilot "heading," opening up the arch-backed upper part of the tunnel to a height sufficient for men to stand in, was maintained about 25 feet ahead of the remainder of the cross section, known as the "breast." A large carriage borne "on wheels, running on rails near the edges of the tunnel" provided an elevated platform behind the breast, allowing broken rock from the heading to be wheeled to the rear in barrows and tipped through holes into narrow-gauge cars standing below. The breast, meanwhile, was worked in benches, from which the spoil was laboriously shovelled or thrown into the same cars.[9] For the first three months the rock was drilled off by hand, 18 men being employed simultaneously in each end of the tunnel for that purpose.[10] Good rock men received $2.25 a day for eight-hour shifts and the small army of muckers, who were still wheeling the spoil out of the tunnel in barrows, received $1.75 for ten-hour shifts. The men had to pay $5.25 a week for board.[11] By the end of April 1886 the east-end heading had been advanced 279 feet into the mountainside. The west-end heading, meanwhile, was extended 67 feet.[12] Despite the laborious nature of "John Henry" style mining operations, the first 200 feet at the east end of the tunnel was drilled off to full cross section by hand so that blasting could be accomplished before the air compressor foundations were laid at the portal.

From the beginning of the drive there were strong indications that the ground would be poor. The first 150 feet at the east end of the tunnel crossed 65 feet of "decomposed coal indications" that promptly collapsed into the workings.[13] The contractors therefore had to start installing closely spaced 12 x 12 timber support frames almost immediately. By the end of April the east-end heading had entered a rock resembling soapstone, which peeled off in large slabs soon after exposure to air and water. On May 4, 1886 falling rock killed a man, and on the following day another had both arms crushed.[14] In the west end, meanwhile, the drillers encountered what was at first termed "blue granite"[15] and later referred to as "metamorphosed conglomerate."[16] This material, which seems to have been an altered volcanic tuff, likewise tended to decompose and lose its structural integrity. In both ends of the tunnel, therefore, timbering became virtually a standard procedure for which Nelson Bennett received additional payment over and above the $85 per-foot contract price.[17]

The air compressor plant was finally brought into operation in June 1886, by which time the east-end heading had advanced 410 feet and the breast had been taken out for 333 feet.[18] The original plan had been to install air compressors at the east portal only, the air required at the west end being piped three miles over the ridge.[19] Early in July 1886, however, the Bennetts abandoned this plan, and as soon as a road could be completed over the ridge, they installed one set of air compression machinery at the west end.[20] In addition to the steam-driven air compressors, the stationary plant included ventilation fans and electric lighting generators. The fan equipment drew out foul air and blasting fumes through wooden ducting extending from the mouth of the tunnel almost to the face of the heading.[21] The lighting plant supplied power not only for arc lamps but also for the electric detonation of explosives. J. B. Dougherty, a skilled mechanic sent out from New York by the Ingersoll Rock Drill Company, supervised the installation of the machinery.[22]

The establishment of Nelson Bennett's camp at the east portal was paralleled by the growth of Tunnel City, which occupied an elevated plateau overlooking Mosquito Creek Gulch. By late August 1886 the population there, not including those working on the tunnel, amounted to 150. Among these were about 20 women and some children. The *Kittitas Localizer* noted of the women that "A portion are wives of men working there." The town already had two stores, two eating and lodging houses, a butchery and slaughter house, and three saloons. Local business was said to consist "mostly of gambling and whiskey selling." Whenever matters got out of hand the saloons were paid to close, and for a while life would be orderly and quiet.[23] The liquor problem, however, recurred again and again until eventually, in March 1887, Northern Pacific bought up the whole townsite and imposed its own rigid controls.[24] At about the same time the place was renamed Martin.

Once the air compressor plant had been commissioned, Bennett brought pneumatic rock drills into operation and the tunnel drive picked up speed. Some weak ground was encountered in October 1886, causing minor delay, but in general the work proceeded fairly steadily.[25] By November 29, 1886 the headings were in 1,292 feet at the east end and 1,189 feet at the west end. The tunnel had by then been opened up to full cross section for 1,266 feet in the east end and 1,152 feet in the west.[26] On December 16, 1886, however, a serious setback occurred when a night-shift workman in the west end drilled a misfired hole. In the resulting explosion three men were instantly killed and eight more were badly hurt. With the equipment shattered, work came to a temporary halt.[27] Rock falls also continued to be a hazard. In mid-February 1887 a large piece of rock fell directly onto a timbering crew of 11 men, killing Charles Humphrey and seriously injuring four of his workmates.[28] Fortunately, by the time these accidents occurred a hospital had been established at the east portal, and Dr. Morisey was able to treat the surviving victims.[29]

By the end of March 1887, 4,100 feet of tunnel had been bored and, with 300 men employed, the headings were advancing at a combined rate of more than 16 feet a day. At about that time a visitor to the east end of the tunnel related that, "The traversing of this giant cavern carries with it a feeling of awe, which is not lessened by the din of the machinery, the rushing of the waters, and the uncanny light of the electric candles." He noted that there were "about twenty-five candles in each end of the tunnel, the cost of which is only 6 cents to the light per day." At the face, the drillers were using four Burleigh pneumatic rock drills, two each in both the pilot heading and the breast. The broken rock was being hauled away in dump cars, each drawn over a tram road by a single mule.[30]

As the two headings of the tunnel grew longer the tramming distance became too great for animals to haul out the spoil. The Bennetts therefore ordered two diminutive locomotives, which arrived on site at the end of May 1887. Named *Sadie* and *Celia*, after Nelson Bennett's young daughters, these 10-ton, narrow-gauge, 0-4-0 saddle-tank engines were built by the H. K. Porter Company of Pittsburgh, Pennsylvania. They were said to be "about 12 feet in length, cab and all," with an "engine…of the upright pattern…in the cab."[31] *Sadie* was used in the east end of the tunnel and *Celia* went to the west end.[32] By May 31, 1887 both were in service and Nelson

Bennett was reported to be "doing good business with the baby engines."[33] They were able to haul trains of six loaded muck cars out of the tunnel and thus displaced at least as many mules and handlers.

At the end of July 1887 ground conditions again became poor and on the last day of the month another rock fall killed three more men and injured two others.[34] Thereafter, whenever the miners encountered bad ground they installed arch timbers almost up to the face of the pilot heading. The breast then had to be extracted without disturbing them. Despite this inconvenience, the crews driving the tunnel through the first such "wall plate" still succeeded in advancing 217 feet during the month of August.[35] Keeping the timbering closer to the face of the heading seems to have reduced the number of casualties, for in November 1887 the construction hospital reportedly contained "only three persons."[36] Exercising greater caution also reduced labor turnover, for whenever accidents occurred men took fright and quit. Despite the fact that wages had already been increased to $3.00 per day for drillers and $2.50 for muckers, labor had been so short in June 1887 that "Captain" Bennett had contemplated using Chinese workers.[37]

Beyond the two-thirds mark, the headings were consistently advanced 14 feet or more each day. On January 21, 1888 the crews made 18 feet headway, bringing the east end to 4,103 feet and the west end to 3,891.[38] In February 1888 the men pulled out all the stops and, despite wall plates in both ends, drove 263 feet in the east end and 262 in the west, thus averaging a total advance of 18 feet per day.[39] By mid-March 1888, shots fired in one end of the tunnel could be heard in the other,[40] and by mid-April crews were tapping on the rock to warn each other of impending blasts.[41]

The shot that broke through the pilot headings was fired at 12:10 p.m. on Thursday May 3, 1888.[42] The news quickly was relayed to all parts of the Northern Pacific system and at 3:00 p.m. Robert Harris telegraphed Nelson Bennett as follows:

Helena, Montana
May 3, 1888 3 p.m.

In behalf of the company and for myself I desire to thank and congratulate you on the successful and speedy manner in which you have driven the Cascade Tunnel. Your good judgement and self reliance indicated by your proposal two years ago have been justified today by the meeting of the two headings. Let us all rejoice.

At Tacoma, May 5, 1888 was declared a gala day of celebrations, with a grand parade, bonfires and illuminations, a civic banquet and speeches, music, and the firing of cannon.[43] At the tunnel, meanwhile, the remaining rock was removed. Nelson Bennett then treated all his men to a turkey dinner and a box of cigars. Those who had worked in the tunnel for more than three months also received a new suit of clothes and a pass to any point on the Northern Pacific Railroad.[44] Once the contractors had finished work and removed their narrow gauge tramway, railway company forces put down 18 inches of the best Cle Elum gravel and laid the permanent track.[45] The tunnel opened to main line traffic on May 27, 1888.[46]

Having fulfilled his contract, Nelson Bennett dismantled the compressor plant and shipped it off to a tunnel site on the Siskiyou section of the Oregon & California Railroad.[47] Items of equipment left behind for Northern Pacific included a Leffell water turbine, for which Mosquito Creek Falls provided 160 feet of head. The turbine drove a new 1,200-volt, 300-light Edison direct-current municipal dynamo supplying 300 incandescent lamps of 30-candle power each. The lamps were set three every 200 feet on each side of the tunnel and staggered to give a lamp for every 33 feet of tunnel length. Six lighting circuits could be connected at will with a common return wire, thus allowing any or all parts of the tunnel to be illuminated. Water discharged from the turbine passed into the old six-inch compressed air line, which, used in conjunction with hydrants, provided protection against fires in the tunnel timbering. A "Ball" 50-horsepower, high-speed steam engine drove the electric lighting generator during the dry season.[48]

The completed Stampede Tunnel was 9,844 feet long,[49] with the point of intersection being 300 feet closer to the west end.[50] The cost as of June 30, 1888 was reported to have been $1,141,311.[51] Even before track was laid, the bed of the tunnel was said to be heaving wherever there were inflows of water. The rock walls continued to decompose and exfoliate, so that within four months the company considered a continuous lining to be essential.[52] The tunnel, however, was such a smoke trap that few men could be induced to work in it.[53] By the end of June 1889 the deterioration had progressed to such an extent that trains were again diverted to the switchbacks to allow the worst places to be repaired with concrete.[54] The tunnel was later lined with brickwork and equipped with ventilation fans. Over the years, however, it remained a maintenance liability, and since the formation of Burlington Northern in 1970, has been little used. At Martin the tracks remain, but the only sound heard today is that of Mosquito Creek cascading over the falls.[55]

Chapter Six

The Columbia River Bridge

The Columbia River crossing at Pasco presented an engineering task of similar magnitude to the Stampede Tunnel. At high water the river, almost half a mile wide and up to 45 feet deep, flowed with a mid-channel velocity of seven miles per hour, the difference between high and low water levels being about 28 feet. The river bottom at that point consisted of between 5 and 14 feet of coarse gravel, underlain by stiff, hard clay.

Given Northern Pacific's impecunious condition, cost proved a significant factor in determining the means adopted for crossing the river. A bridge consisting of solid masonry piers and an all-iron superstructure would clearly be much more expensive than a large transfer boat and permanent landings. The latter solution, however, would have limited the capacity of the railway. Based on the advice of consulting engineers and the results of experiments conducted at the second and third crossings of the Yakima River, Adna Anderson therefore opted for a compromise bridge with a combined timber-and-iron superstructure resting on stone-filled crib piers with nested-pile foundations. Consulting engineer Lefferts L. Buck then undertook the detailed design. Since Pasco was remote from any iron bridge construction plant, yet good quality fir was readily available on the Cascade Branch, trusses using timber compression members offered significant cost savings. Moreover, because the local climate was quite dry, such a structure was expected to last for 15 or 20 years. The bridge was to have nine such through-truss spans of 250 feet each. Plate girder spans 50 feet long at each abutment then brought the total length of the bridge to 2,587 feet.[1] The drawspan was to rest on pier number seven, with five of the combination spans on the Pasco side and four on the Kennewick side of the river.

The contractors constructed the piers using a method commonly employed where bedrock lay far below the river bottom. As a first stage, workers sank an elongated frame, pointed at the upstream and downstream ends, which served as an enclosure for a tight cluster of foundation piles. When fully driven, these piles were sawn off flush with the top of the frame, which was positioned to remain submerged by about three feet at low water. A great solid timber "grillage," consisting of multiple layers of 12 x 12 timbers laid across each other and firmly bolted together, was then sunk and secured to the frame. Finally the timber crib pier was mounted on top of the grillage, filled with stones, and capped with concrete to carry the superstructure. In the case of the pivot pier the grillage was much larger, being about 35 feet square by 35 feet deep. This pier, moreover, was of masonry construction, the stonework being laid on the floating grillage as it gradually sank into position on top of the piles.[2]

A decision to build a bridge rather than a permanent ferry and landings appears to have been postponed until December 1886.[3] By that time the two combination iron and timber spans on the Yakima River had been erected and found satisfactory. Planning therefore proceeded on that basis. Construction, however, could not commence until after high water in June 1887.[4] The contract for erection of the bridge was let to Hoffman & Bates early in May 1887.[5] Meanwhile, to obtain material for the compression members of the trusses, the company engaged L. C. Seaton to cut the choicest fir timber to be found on the Teanaway.[6] Pile driving began late in July 1887[7] and the erection of falsework proceeded concurrently. The company urged the contractors to complete a temporary bridge before icy conditions prevented operation of the transfer boat *Frederick Billings*. The government, however, demanded that interference with navigation be minimized. Since trestlework of the temporary bridge obstructed the passage of river vessels, the company therefore took immediate steps to erect the pivot pier and place the drawspan.

Late in October 1887 the grillage for the pivot pier was floated out into the river between two scows interconnected by heavy spars. The whole assembly was moored in mid-stream above the foundation piling and masons were brought out to erect the stone work of the pier. The idea was that as the pier grew higher and heavier, the supporting grillage would gradually sink onto the piles. Unfortunately, the great mass of timber proved to be more buoyant than expected, and instead of sinking it merely became top heavy. Early in November the wash from a passing steamer upset the equilibrium and the entire mass overturned toward the east shore. As the restraining tackle snapped, the workmen sprang for safety on the scow to the west. All escaped except 45-year-old Charles Ericson, whose leg had been injured in a recent accident. Unable to jump, he was carried away with the pier and drowned.[8]

The upset of the pivot pier delayed erection of the drawspan and dictated the closure of the river to navigation.[9] Herbert Huson pushed construction of the falsework and at 4:00 p.m. on December 3, 1887 the temporary bridge was declared ready for railroad traffic.[10] The transfer boat was then laid up and trains began to run through to Tacoma. Shortly afterwards, however, winter intervened. Early in January 1888 floating ice swept away part of the falsework.[11] Workers attempted to bring the *Billings* back into service, but as fast as a channel could be cleared the water froze over again. As the temperature dropped, the ice became thicker, and at some places it piled up as much as 20 feet high. Finally, in desperation, the river crew resorted to the use of explosives. On or about January 18, 1888 a blast fired on the Kennewick side of the river freed a massive ice jam of about an acre in extent. As the men stood helplessly watching it, this enormous ice flow swept majestically downstream toward the bridge, gathering speed as it went. Reports of the ensuing damage varied. An eyewitness to the disaster stated that the piers on each side of the drawspan were "cut through as cleanly as if they were made of cheese" and that after they had gone, "the bridge, for a distance of about 300 feet sagged down but hung together until the workmen could remove the rails, when the roadbed broke and falling into the stream was a total loss."[12] A letter written on January 20, 1888 reported that "over 600 feet of the piling of the bridge" had been swept away.[13] Hoffman & Bates, the contractors, stated afterwards that the successive onslaught by ice took out the falsework under no less than seven spans.[14]

With the bridge down and the transfer boats at both Kennewick and Kalama ice bound, the railroad lost all connection with Tacoma.[15] Deprived of Roslyn coal, the Interior suddenly faced a serious fuel shortage. As the engine fires went out and Idaho division trains came to a halt, Northern Pacific tried to lay rails across the ice in hope of transferring a few carloads of coal from Kennewick to Pasco.[16] This scheme apparently failed, but by January 21, 1888 the Kalama ferry once more came into operation and limited quantities of coal again became available. The company, meanwhile, brought the Spokane & Palouse construction force north from Colton to cut wood near Marshall, saving the situation. The temporary bridge across the Columbia, however, was not repaired and ready for trains again until April 27, 1888.[17]

The permanent spans across the deep channel of the river were all placed by May 5, 1888 so that no harm could result from high water.[18] But before the bridge was finished the river claimed two more lives. On June 12, 1888 two men working on the superstructure fell into the water and drowned.[19] The last span was swung into position on July 14, 1888[20] and the bridge was completed shortly afterwards.[21]

Chapter Seven

The Hunt System

In the mid-eighties the OR&N monopoly south of the Snake River became an increasingly contentious issue. Farmers and merchants believed that if only the Pendleton and Walla Walla areas could be linked with the Northern Pacific, the resulting competition would lead to lower freight rates. The Northern Pacific Railroad Company, however, could hardly find enough money to complete the Cascade Branch, let alone build feeder lines into agricultural areas. Local residents therefore had to act on their own initiative.

Early in March 1886 a group of enterprising Umatilla County citizens formed the Oregon & Washington Territory Railroad to build and operate a railway between Wallula and Pendleton. The company had an authorized capital stock of $200,000, divided into $100 shares. The promoters were Jacob Frazer, W. S. Byers, H. L. Marston, W. W. Cavness, H. W. Wheeler, W. T. Chalk, R. Alexander, and John J. Balleray.[1] When officers were elected, Frazer became president; Byers, vice president and treasurer; Marston, second vice-president; Wheeler, secretary; and Chalk, chief engineer.[2] In May and June 1886 the company carried out preliminary surveys and located a line from Wallula up Vansycle Canyon onto the high ground north of Helix.[3] Money then ran out and the company did nothing more until March 1887, when it held meetings in schoolhouses at Kendall's, Helix, Norwegian, Juniper, and Vansycle, to solicit stock subscriptions.[4] The response, however, was disappointing, for farmers either feared a sell-out to the OR&N, or, knowing the promoters, doubted their ability to raise the remainder of the money needed to build the line.[5] On March 15, 1887 the Pendleton *East Oregonian* lamented that:

The hard working farmer will groan and squirm under the iron heel of monopoly, but when chance is offered to better his condition by extending a helping hand to a competing railroad he shows his ignoble spirit by holding back and letting others more enterprising do the work.

Clearly, if the railroad was to be built, it would have to be financed by other means. Changes came late in April 1887. F. W. Griffith suddenly replaced W. S. Byers as O&WT vice president, and an auxiliary "construction company" was formed to facilitate financial maneuvers.[6]

Construction company financing was a fairly common but somewhat disreputable practice. In its classic form a group of promoters, acting as individuals, borrowed enough money to undertake preliminary work. They then set up two independent but closely associated companies, the one to own and operate the railroad, and the other to handle financial affairs during construction. The railroad company handed over its stock and bonds to the construction company as successive sections of the line were completed. Acting as an intermediary, the construction company then let out the physical work to sub-contractors and used railroad securities to obtain short-term loans. Funds raised on one section of the line were used to build the next section, the process being repeated until the railway was finished. The stock and bonds issued against the last section were then sold to the public, with the proceeds used to pay off the loan on the preceding section. Successive sets of securities were thus redeemed and sold, and one by one all the loans were paid off. Sale of the last set of stocks and bonds then provided the promoters with enough money to pay off their personal loans. Having made a handsome profit from building the railway, they dissolved the construction company and divided its assets among themselves, leaving the railroad saddled with long-term debt. Compared with conventional methods of raising share and loan capital, construction company financing allowed impecunious promoters, taking maximum advantage of short-term credit, to realize rapid returns on very limited investment. It also provided them with a legal avenue avoiding the liability risks associated with selling stock at a discount.[7]

In the case of the Oregon & Washington Territory Railroad the promoters first filed supplemental articles of incorporation

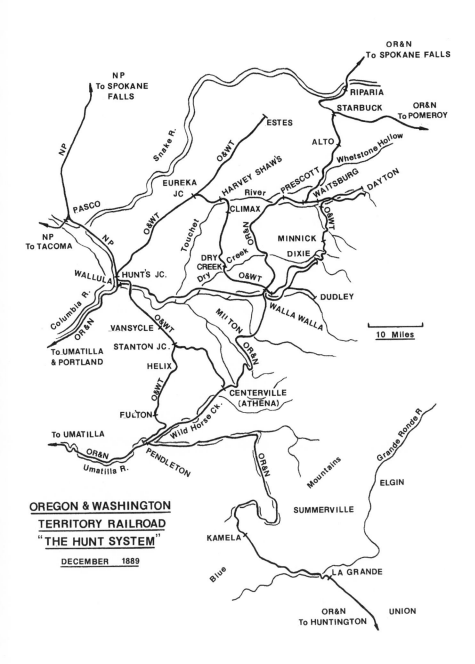

OR&N
To SPOKANE FALLS

NP
To SPOKANE
FALLS

RIPARIA

STARBUCK

OR&N
To POMEROY

NP

ESTES

Snake R.

O&WT

ALTO

Whetstone Hollow

EUREKA
JC

HARVEY SHAW'S

River

PRESCOTT

WAITSBURG

DAYTON

PASCO

NP

Touchet

CLIMAX

OR&N

MINNICK

O&WT

NP
To TACOMA

O&WT

Creek

DRY
CREEK

DIXIE

WALLULA

HUNT'S JC.

Dry

O&WT

DUDLEY

Columbia R.

OR&N

WALLA WALLA

10 Miles

VANSYCLE

O&WT

MILTON

STANTON JC.

OR&N

To UMATILLA
& PORTLAND

HELIX

O&WT

CENTERVILLE
(ATHENA)

Grande Ronde R.

FULTON

Wild Horse Ck.

To UMATILLA

OR&N

PENDLETON

OR&N

Mountains

ELGIN

Umatilla R.

**OREGON & WASHINGTON
TERRITORY RAILROAD
"THE HUNT SYSTEM"**

DECEMBER   1889

SUMMERVILLE

KAMELA

Blue

LA GRANDE

OR&N
To HUNTINGTON

UNION

authorizing the construction of a branch line to Centerville and increasing the capital stock to $750,000. That done, they formed a construction company that agreed to build the road for a sum of $1,350,000. Early in May 1887, F. W. Griffith, acting as eastern agent, concluded an agreement with Charles B. Wright and his Philadelphia business associates concerning placement of the O&WT bonds. Within a few days the construction company then sub-contracted the actual railway building to George W. Hunt. The 50 miles of railroad were expected to cost $850,000 to build, with Hunt allowed a profit of $100,000. The railway was bonded to the extent of $16,000 per mile, and the company set aside $150,000 to compensate for selling the $800,000 worth of bonds at a discount. The construction company thus stood to make a profit of about $200,000, to be shared among the promoters. These gentlemen, as officials of the railroad, agreed to accept stock in lieu of their self-awarded $5,000 per year salaries, and thus preempted a significant part of any future dividends.[8] Despite protests from minor shareholders, the company duly implemented these arrangements and on Saturday, May 28, 1887 Hunt's men started work at Wallula.[9] The Oregon & Washington Territory Railroad thus became established as an independent means of diverting OR&N traffic to the Northern Pacific, and soon enabled the Philadelphia group to undermine Henry Villard's plans for rationalizing railroad relationships in the Pacific Northwest.

From a junction with the Northern Pacific near Wallula, the O&WT line set out east up a dry valley some distance north of the Walla Walla River. Reaching the head of this gulch the road turned south through a deep cut at Watson's Ranch[10] and ran out onto a 60-foot-high, 700-foot-long bridge[11] carrying it over both the OR&N Wallula-to-Walla Walla line and the Walla Walla River. Thence it headed directly into the mouth of Vansycle Canyon and began to climb southeast on a gradient of 116 feet to the mile.[12] Struggling uphill from Henry Adams's sheep camp through Killian's and Vansycle to a summit cut just beyond Stanton's, the line ascended 1,500 feet in 14 miles. From the summit, almost 2,000 feet above sea level, the road descended to the town of Helix, which lies in the heart of a prosperous wheat growing area. Leaving Helix in a southwesterly direction, the O&WT line climbed for about two miles and then began a seven mile descent down the south facing slope of the hills between Wild Horse Creek and the Cold Springs canyons. At Fulton the railway turned east into a gulch leading down to Wild Horse Creek. On a falling gradient of 73 feet to the mile,[13] the road swung sharply around to the southwest to parallel the last two miles of the OR&N's line from Walla Walla to Pendleton. It then crossed the Umatilla River on a bridge immediately downstream from that of the Oregon company[14] and ran through city streets to the new Pendleton depot.

The Centerville branch left the main line just north of the summit cut at Stanton's and wended its way east. Reaching a summit about 2,200 feet above sea level near the halfway point it then descended to an elevation of just over 1,700 feet at Centerville.

The company lost no time getting the grading started. By June 7, 1887, 270 teams were at work between Wallula and the head of Vansycle Canyon.[15] About a month later Hunt's men began to excavate the deep cut above Stanton's and others moved on toward Helix. Although there was little rock work, other difficulties arose. On the high ground a shortage of water caused suffering among the animals. At harvest time, moreover, many of the men deserted and the company had to increase wages to $2.25 per day to attract replacements.[16] By the second week of August depot grounds had been levelled at Helix, but work was still going on at the summit cut and at the bridge across the Walla Walla River.[17] The plans and specifications for the bridge were drawn up in the O&WT office at Pendleton by Mr. G. Sayles.[18] The structure, which required 200,000 feet of lumber from the upper Yakima, was built under sub-contract by J. Taylor. Ninety men began work on the bridge during the second week of July 1887 and completed it in mid September.[19]

The steel gang began to lay side tracks and connections at Wallula on Monday, August 29, 1887 and commenced work on the main line 10 days later.[20] By the time they reached the Walla Walla River the bridge had been completed and they were immediately able to lay track for another two miles.[21] The supply of rails then ran out, halting the advance. The delay, however, allowed the carpenters to finish the minor trestles in Vansycle Canyon, so that by October 24, 1887 the grade lay ready for track all the way to the summit.[22] Unfortunately, rails and fastenings were only delivered spasmodically, and no great quantity again became available until about November 10.[23] Nevertheless, before the end of the year,

steel had been laid to N. R. Atkinson's place about two miles beyond Stanton Junction.[24] By January 10, 1888, crews had ballasted
and surfaced the first 20 miles of the line, and the railroad had
shipped 330 carloads of grain to Tacoma. In the meantime the railroad passed into other hands.

In the latter part of August 1887 Hunt was reported to be buying up the stock.[25] The story was that, having advanced the money
needed to begin construction, he sought to protect his own interest. During the next two months he bought out one shareholder
after another and secured a large stake in the road. On November
9, 1887 he set out for Philadelphia to conclude his own financial
agreement with Charles B. Wright. Returning to Pendleton early
in December, he paid off the remaining shareholders and took
charge of the whole enterprise.[26] Details of the agreement between
George Hunt and the railroad's backers were not made public. Hunt
apparently took over the functions of the Pendleton promoters, while
the Philadelphia group continued to guarantee long-term financing. The contractor from Corvallis would reap the profits of construction, while the Wright family and their associates bought the
railroad's bonds at a discount and sold them at or above par. The
difference between Hunt and his predecessors was that, by a process akin to extortion, Hunt persuaded local people to promise subsidies for the construction of his lines. He then used the subsidy
agreements as collateral to borrow the money needed to get the
work started.

At the end of October 1887 Hunt suggested that if the people of
Pendleton wanted to enjoy the benefits of an O&WT connection they
should provide his company with free right of way and depot grounds,
along with a bonus of $30,000[27]–concessions costing, in all, about
$85,000.[28] The Pendleton merchants associated with the road from
the outset were indignant and refused to pay.[29] In the spring of 1888
Hunt therefore completed the branch to Centerville and began to
build a line to Walla Walla, since both places had agreed to provide
him with attractive subsidies. Interviewed at Portland late in June
1888, Hunt stated that the question of the road going to Pendleton
rested with the people of that town. He had made his offer, which he
considered liberal, and if they saw fit to accept it, well and good.
Walla Walla had given him a bonus of $100,000. Committees from
Dayton and Waitsburg were waiting on him, offering him bonuses in

proportion to that of Walla Walla to build his railroad to their towns, and were now anxiously awaiting his decision. He would, of course, favor those places which offered him liberal inducements in preference to Pendleton, where he was offered nothing![30]

The Centerville line was graded in September 1887,[31] but the slow delivery of rails and the effects of winter weather held up track laying until the following spring. At the end of January 1888 a sudden thaw caused serious flooding, damaging the Walla Walla River bridge and washing away a considerable part of the road bed in Vansycle Canyon.[32] Thirty thousand sacks of grain awaiting shipment on the branch line could not be moved.[33] At length, on March 17, 1888, the new O&WT locomotive No. 1, just delivered from the Cooke Locomotive Works at Paterson, New Jersey, brought up a heavy load of ties and rails,[34] and on the following Monday the steel gang went to work.[35] The 60 men engaged laid the 14 miles of branch line in just one month.[36] At Centerville, where workers had staked out depot grounds on the Knowlton farm during the previous September,[37] a well was dug and preparations made for erecting a windmill pump and water tank.[38] By the end of July 1888 carpenters had completed a warehouse and platform, and materials were arriving for a two-story depot.[39] A month later another trainload of lumber arrived for the construction of a large grain elevator, and more was expected for a three-stall roundhouse.[40] Grain traffic, meanwhile, flourished, for Miller & Robley were reported to be shipping 10 carloads from Centerville daily. As a local correspondent of the *East Oregonian* observed early in September 1888, "Next to mines, nothing booms a town like a railroad."[41]

During the summer of 1888 Hunt extended the railway southward to Helix, where it halted to await a change of heart in Pendleton.[42] On August 29, 1888 the Pendleton board of trade capitulated,[43] and within two weeks local residents had raised enough of the subsidy to induce him to resume work.[44] After an initial surge of enthusiasm, however, the subscriptions ceased, and when the line reached Fulton, construction was again suspended.[45] With O&WT trains virtually within whistling distance of Pendleton, the public demanded that the line be completed. At a mass meeting held at the end of December 1888, the citizens collectively resolved to raise the subsidy and secure the right of way and depot grounds.[46] By January 19, 1889 they had subscribed $15,720 and were making efforts to raise another $35,000.[47] Hunt then relented. At another meeting on February 11, 1889 he agreed to advance the money needed to purchase the depot grounds and expressed willingness to accept the subsidy in three installments, the first to be due in October 1889.[48] The deferred payments were to bear interest at 6 percent. He also undertook to move freight to and from Puget Sound at the same rates as those charged by the OR&N between Pendleton and Portland. By the end of April 1889 all the details of the agreement had been thrashed out, and on May 6, 1889 grading was resumed.[49]

Work on the last six miles of the O&WT line to Pendleton went slowly, progress being delayed both by rock work on Wild Horse Creek[50] and the construction of a temporary bridge across the Umatilla River. By July 13, 1889 track had been laid to "the point where the curve is made into Wild Horse" and OR&N engines hauling trains to Walla Walla were reported to have been "saluted by a Hunt locomotive on the hill."[51] The construction train crossed the Umatilla River on or about August 22, 1889 and by the end of the month tracklayers were ready to proceed through the city streets.[52] Property owners, however, threatened litigation that might have delayed the advance, forcing Hunt to present them with a *fait accompli*. On the morning of Sunday, September 1, 1889 he ordered his men into action. All day long "the Sabbath peace and quiet of pious Pendleton echoed to the thud of falling ties and the sharp ringing of the steel rails." By nightfall the O&WT ran through town from one end of Webb Street to the other.[53] The first passenger train arrived at the new Pendleton depot ground opposite the MES church on Thursday September 12, 1889.[54] Hunt, meanwhile, had completed his line from Wallula to Walla Walla and was extending it by way of Dixie to Waitsburg and Dayton.[55]

In southeastern Washington the lack of railroad competition had been a burning question since the fall of 1885. As part of an "On to Ainsworth" campaign, launched in October of that year, the Walla Walla board of trade solicited donations of money and land to induce others to build a railway "from the City of Walla Walla to some point on the road of the NPRR Co. and the Columbia River."[56] The organizers were even prepared to grade the line themselves if any railroad could be persuaded to lay the track. They aimed their scheme primarily at the Northern Pacific, but that company was not immediately prepared to build a line to Walla Walla. In the spring of 1886 the committee persuaded the venerable Dr. Dorsey S. Baker to advance some money for surveys.[57] The old man, however, kept his own interest in mind, for while engineer H. D. Chapman ran a line from south Ainsworth to Walla Walla, the former OR&N location engineer P. Zahner was also asked to explore the possibility of extending the Mill Creek railroad from Dixie by way of Coppei Creek to Waitsburg.[58]

Dr. Baker was hardly the most popular person in Walla Walla, many people resenting his oppressive influence upon local affairs. It was no surprise, therefore, that on July 28, 1886 an apparently dissident group, emulating the example set by the citizens of Pendleton, formed a Walla Walla & Ainsworth Railroad Company.[59] The enterprise, however, was stillborn, for the promoters found themselves unable to raise even the funds required for preliminary work. Later in the year the board of trade committee, dominated by Baker's business partner John F. Boyer, offered Northern Pacific a subsidy of $75,000 and urged farmers to pledge all their grain, for a period of two years, to a pool dedicated to shipment over the new line.[60] In January 1887 Northern Pacific responded by sending in surveyors to look for likely routes. Significantly, they examined Eureka Flat and ran a line from Walla Walla via Dixie to Waitsburg. By March 8, 1887 no less than 300 Walla Walla County farmers had promised to ship 50,000 tons of grain a year if Northern Pacific would undertake construction. Still impecunious, however, the railroad company again declined.

In desperation, Boyer and his fellow pool trustees then formed another company named the Walla Walla & Puget Sound Railroad.[61] In the spring of 1887 they sent Colonel T. F. Gilbertson to secure free right of way, and as of May 7 no one along the line had denied his request.[62] The promoters were prepared to press the project, but just at that juncture they received clear indications that the Philadelphia group controlling the Northern Pacific had decided to use the Oregon & Washington Territory Railroad as an independent means of reaching both Pendleton and Walla Walla.[63] The Walla Walla & Puget Sound company was therefore allowed to lapse, and any plans to include the Mill Creek line in the wider scheme of railway development were finally abandoned. In a last fit of pique, Dr. Baker sold the narrow gauge line to the OR&N in September 1887.[64] Nothing then happened until mid-March 1888 when George W. Hunt advised

the Walla Walla board of trade that he would visit the city the following week "for the purpose of consulting the people as to the advis-
ability of extending his road, the O&WT, to this place."[65]

To build the line to Walla Walla, Hunt demanded free right of
way and depot grounds and a subsidy of $100,000,[66] of which
$40,000 was to be raised by the Eureka Flat farmers.[67] Local resi-
dents promptly pledged the subsidy and by April 10, 1888, had
subscribed $95,000.[68] The subscriptions were drawn up as legal
contracts, to be withheld until Hunt had fulfilled his part of the
bargain,[69] thus encouraging him to start work at the earliest possible moment. On March 24, 1888 he ordered his engineers into
the field and during the second week of April the graders went to
work.[70] By May 5, 1888 nine miles of roadbed were ready and five
miles of track had been laid, the intention being to reach Smith's
ranch at the lower end of Eureka Flat and there to establish a
forward supply base.[71]

The O&WT line to Walla Walla left Hunt's Junction in a northerly direction but soon turned northeast to climb for 10 miles by
way of Columbia Hollow to the southern edge of Eureka Flat. Having attained an elevation of 900 feet, the line continued to ascend
more gently to Eureka Junction, from which point a branch line
followed the same general course to the head of the Flat. The main
line, meanwhile, swung away to the east, descended more than 200
feet into the Touchet Valley, and followed the river upstream to
Harvey Shaw's place, eight miles west of Prescott. Turning south
across the river, the road climbed sharply for nearly three miles to
reach a second summit almost 1,150 feet above sea level at Climax
siding. It then threaded its way downgrade through a maze of hills
to the valley of Dry Creek, which was crossed at an elevation of
less than 700 feet. Finally, to regain lost height it made a sharp
climb to higher ground in the vicinity of Walla Walla.[72] Proceeding
through the lower part of the penitentiary grounds, Hunt's railway
entered the northwest sector of the city. Swinging southeast across
the OR&N line to Prescott it ran along Palouse Street, past the
Weber tannery, to the foot of East Second Street. The line then
curved northeast to cross Main Street at Boyer Avenue, where, for
the time being, construction ended.[73] Between Hunt's Junction and
Walla Walla maximum grades did not exceed 1 percent and curves
were no sharper than eight degrees.

By the end of June 1888 workers had graded the line as far as Eureka Junction and laid 12 miles of track.[74] The focus of construction activity then shifted to the section between Eureka and Climax, where "armies of workmen" were assembled to carry out extensive rock work and build the bridge across the Touchet River.[75] The rock work, which went on until mid-October, was accompanied by a serious blasting accident. Early in September, a 32-year-old Englishman named Edward Jackson was blown to pieces when loading a drilled hole with explosive.[76] Prior to this unfortunate event track reached a point about two miles beyond Eureka Junction.[77] The scraper teams, meanwhile, went to work on the easier ground beyond Climax and by September 15, 1888 they were working all the way to the Walla Walla city limit.[78] A month later other forces finished both the 40-foot-high temporary deck bridge over the Touchet River and the long, deep cut near Climax.[79] The construction train then proceeded south to a point within four miles of Dry Creek. With the main line roadbed substantially ready for ties and rails, the graders transferred to the Eureka Flat branch. On the uplands the soil was easy to handle and with 1,000 men engaged, a roadbed was rapidly thrown up.[80] At the end of November the whole line was opened through to the vicinity of Estes[81] and the railway hauled out the first shipments of wheat. As an added benefit the incoming trains brought up water for farmers who had not yet been able to secure an adequate supply.

Early in December 1888 the steel gang resumed work on the main line, and on Wednesday December 19 the construction train reached the Walla Walla municipal boundary.[82] Establishing a temporary terminus at the foot of East 2nd Street, workers also installed a turning wye just east of Main Street. Railway construction within the city limits gave people a chance to see Hunt's men at work and resulted in the following classic description of tracklaying as practiced at the time, noted in the *Walla Walla Union* January 12, 1889:

Track Laying. How Hunt's Men Make a Railroad Track—Rapid, Accurate, Noiseless Work.

On Monday forenoon the report came down Main Street, "Hunt's men are laying track in front of Baker Schoolhouse." In company with others the editor of the "Union" went up to see what was going on. He found nearly a hundred men swinging picks and shovels, making grade on Palouse Street, moving houses and doing other things to make a track for the iron horse. Back of the graders, almost on their heels, was a force of almost fifty men, a locomotive, several cars bearing steel rails, headed by a sort of derrick, mounted on a flat car. On one side of the car is a series of heavy iron rollers set in a very heavy frame; over these rollers the steel rails 30 feet long, weighing 56 pounds to the yard, or 560 pounds each, are shoved by men armed with iron rods bent at the ends, like a letter L, which they put in the bolt holes, and pull onto the outcome at the forward end of the car, where three brawny men, wearing heavy leather mittens and gunny bag aprons, seize each rail and trot to the front. As the rail comes off the rollers two of them grab it and take two or three steps to the front until one of them sings out a loud guttural "now," which sounds more like a grunt than anything else, when all five stop, and swinging the rail back drop it on the ties laid to receive it. So skillful have the railhandlers become that they seldom fail to throw the rail they carry so that it will strike the end of the rail already laid. On the other side of the car is a framework provided with rollers which is adjusted to the sides of two or more cars, over which ties are rolled by the hands on the cars. As the ties come off the end of the roller frame, which extends in front of the car thirty or more feet, they are seized by the handlers, eight in number, and laid on the ground as near as maybe 2 feet apart from center to center. The first tie taken from the rollers is laid 30 feet from the last tie off the ground, the distance being determined by a large wooden measure which is moved to the front as each set of sixteen ties is laid. A rope stretched along the route gives the direction of the track and forms the line to which the ends of the ties is adjusted. As the ties are laid a man puts four bolts on each of three ties, one near the end, one near the middle, and one near the car. As the rails are laid on the ties, two men on the side next [to] the guide rope quickly drive the first two spikes, with double headed sledges, which fastens the rail in line with the one previously laid. An iron gauge measure holds the rails 4 feet 8-1/2 inches apart until they are spiked to three ties. As the drivers hit the spikes, the man with the crowbar and blocks of wood holds up the end of the tie into which they are driving them to prevent jars. Two of the men, supplied with fishplates, bolts, and nuts, fasten the ends of the rails together. As the last spikes are driven the man upon the derrick grabs a lever and waves a red flag, upon which the engine snorts and the machine moves on about 30 feet, and [is] stopped by the man on the derrick lowering his red flag and turning a brake. The rapidity and accuracy with which the drivers swing their heavy sledges and hit the spikes is marvelous, as is the celerity with which the men work their wrenches and screw the nuts on the bolts. They are under the direction of Peter Tulley, a young man in looks but an old man in experience, who makes no fuss or noise of his duty. The quiet lack of noisy orders was noticed and remarked upon by all visitors. The same lack of noise and yelling of orders was noticed in the operation of the seventy-five graders under William Costello, a well know Walla-Wallan. The construction train is in charge of George Kimball as conductor. Locomotive engineer was Oakley Johnson. Of course all know that the track is spiked to more than three ties, that all the bolts in the fish plates are screwed up, that the track is aligned, levelled up, and if possible, ballasted before it is put in charge of the operating department. These operations take time and labor, but while they are being done the road is usually operated irregularly. When the work ceased Monday evening the road had been graded and track laid from a point beyond the tannery to across Main Street. At the invitation of Conductor Kimball, the editor and several others went with the train to the camp pitched at the station named Cecil's about 5 miles from the city, and took dinner with the railroad workers.[83]

A regular O&WT passenger train service between Hunt's Junction and Walla Walla commenced on Tuesday March 19, 1889, operating on the following schedule:[84]

| 11:50 a.m. Depart | Walla Walla | Arrive 11:00 p.m. |
| 3:30 p.m. Arrive | Hunt's Jc. | Depart 7:30 p.m. |

On March 31 the company added a second daily train, running through to Pasco to connect with Northern Pacific's Cascade Branch train bound for Tacoma.[85] By mid-May local trains also left Walla Walla at 6:00 a.m. Tuesdays and Fridays for Eureka Flat.[86] Until a site could be acquired for a permanent Walla Walla depot, trains used the temporary depot, where a "very nice waiting room and office" had been set up in one of the company's new caboose cars.[87] As a site for a future depot Hunt chose a location at the corner of East Main and Spokane streets but had trouble obtaining the property at a reasonable price. The owner, Dr. J. M. Boyd, demanded $60 per foot of Main Street frontage, but Hunt refused to pay that much and brought suit to condemn. The appraiser appointed by the court awarded Boyd the price he asked, but Hunt again declined to complete the purchase. The matter was not resolved until May 1889 when O&WT

bought the 120-foot square lot between Spokane and Palouse streets for $5,000. Only then could Hunt finalize his plans for a 40-foot by 100-foot two-story brick depot building.[88]

During 1888 the O&WT obtained at least five and perhaps six new locomotives, including two 55-ton Mason ten-wheelers, a 50-ton eight-wheeler, and two 80-ton "Consolidations" for use in Vansycle Canyon. At the same time they also acquired a full complement of baggage, flat, box, and caboose cars, all of which were fitted with Janney couplers and Westinghouse air brakes "of the latest device."[89]

As the O&WT approached Walla Walla, people further up-country also began to agitate for a second railroad.[90] In April 1888 the newly organized Dayton board of trade formed a railway committee consisting of Jesse N. Day, John Brining, W. H. H. Fouts, and J. C. Van Patten.[91] These gentlemen opened negotiations with Hunt, offering him a bonus proportional to the $100,000 put forward by Walla Walla if he would extend the O&WT to their town.[92] Hunt made no commitment until early in December 1888 when Jesse Day and J. E. Edmison finally cornered him at Waitsburg and travelled with him to Walla Walla. Hunt then agreed, in return for a subsidy of $75,000 and free right of way and depot grounds, to extend the O&WT from Walla Walla to Dayton by way of Coppei Creek and Waitsburg. He thought Waitsburg should contribute $35,000 and Dayton $40,000. The two communities would provide depot grounds in their own towns and each bear half the cost of the right of way.[93] He received an enthusiastic response, for as the *Dayton Chronicle* pointed out, the next season's Columbia County wheat crop could reach 1.5 million bushels. If Hunt and the Northern Pacific would carry the grain to Puget Sound for the same rate that OR&N charged to take it to Portland, then the lower Columbia River towage and pilotage fees could be translated into a net gain of $2 per ton and farmers might save $90,000 in a single year.[94] The subsidy therefore appeared to be an excellent investment.

During the month of January 1889 representatives of the Waitsburg board of trade met with Hunt and, in cooperation with their neighbors in Dayton, agreed to subsidize the railway.[95] At about the same time Hunt suggested that the Dayton line be extended to Whetstone Hollow, just north of both Dayton and Waitsburg, and for that purpose he asked the people of Columbia County for an additional $20,000 and the necessary land.[96] His agreement with them specified that the O&WT would be completed to Dayton by December 1, 1889 and extended to Whetstone Hollow by September 1, 1890. Columbia County would pay half of the $60,000 subsidy when the line reached Dayton, provided that it did so by the agreed date. The other half would be held back for a year as a guarantee that the road would indeed be pushed through to its ultimate destination.

In February 1889 Hunt and the citizens of both Walla Walla and Columbia counties agreed that it would be a more equitable way of raising subsidies if voters petitioned their respective county commissioners to issue warrants for the appropriate amounts. Hunt proposed to return all the subsidies already raised for building the Eureka Flat and Walla Walla lines and asked the citizens of Walla Walla County to raise a petition for the issue of $300,000 worth of county scrip. This was to be held in escrow at the First National Bank of Walla Walla and paid out to him in installments as follows: $140,000 when he had repaid the original subscriptions; $50,000 upon completion of the Walla Walla-Dixie-Waitsburg line, on or before December 1, 1889; $40,000 when the road connected to the town of Prescott, on or before September 1, 1890; and $70,000 when a railway was completed "along the foot towards Milton in Umatilla County, Oregon, over and across the Blue Mountains to Grande Ronde valley" on or before May 1, 1891.[97] This proposal soon evolved a step further. At a meeting held in Walla Walla on Monday, May 6, 1889 the taxpayers were also asked to petition the Washington legislature to ratify the action of the county commissioners in issuing the scrip and to create a debt sufficient in amount to redeem these warrants.[98] After further negotiations the amount of the subsidy was reduced to $250,000,[99] and on May 15, 1889 the agreement between Hunt and Walla Walla County was signed.[100] Similar negotiations took place in connection with the $60,000 Columbia County subsidy, and that proposition also carried. On June 24, 1889, therefore, Hunt's graders resumed work.[101]

The Dayton extension of the O&WT left Walla Walla in a northeasterly direction and passed over higher ground to Sapolil. Taking up an alignment on the east side of the Dry Creek Valley it then climbed into the foothills of the Blue Mountains. Just beyond Dixie the railway crossed the two forks of the creek and climbed steeply north to reach a summit more than 1,900 feet above sea level at Minnick. From that point the line made a sharp descent to meet and cross Coppei Creek. It then followed the right bank of that stream down to a confluence with the Touchet at Waitsburg. Due to the enclosed nature of the Touchet Valley, the Hunt road immediately crossed the river and took up an alignment on the north or west side. Between Waitsburg and Dayton the new railway intersected the OR&N branch and made two more crossings of the river.[102] The steepest grades on the extension were 85 feet to the mile, and the sharpest curves 10 degrees. Apart from the Touchet River bridges the only major structures were three trestles up to 80 feet high built at the points where the line crossed Dry, Mud, and Coppei creeks.[103]

Hunt had five months to complete the Dayton line and needed almost every day of it.[104] Although the loose earthworks were completed quite rapidly, rock excavations and bridge building caused delay. On August 24, 1889 the roadbed was reported complete to the big Dry Creek trestle just above Dixie and the steel gang had laid track to the Gilliam place a mile below.[105] It then took more than two months to excavate the summit cut and complete the big trestles in the hills.[106] Meanwhile, further delay was caused by a woman whose garden had been divided in two by the railway. Mr. and Mrs. B. F. Royce, who lived near Minnick, demanded that the railroad cross their property on a trestle bridge, but the graders put in a fill. Mrs. Royce, incensed, began to remove the offending earth, defying Hunt's men to stop her. The *Walla Walla Union* recounted that "she warned them away in a very forcible manner, brandishing an old tin pan and an ancient butcher knife," and that they in turn "insulted her with vile names."[107] To make the way safe for his men, Hunt had to press charges of armed resistance. Once this matter had been cleared up and the other more serious obstacles removed, Hunt pushed the railway to completion. The track reached Waitsburg on November 12, 1889, and on the following day a special train carried "a large number of prominent people" to Walla Walla, free of charge, to attend Liberate's concert.[108] The last 10 miles of the road were completed during the next eight days, and at 2:18 p.m. on Thursday, November 21, 1889 the construction train rolled into Dayton.[109] Crews then quickly ballasted and surfaced the track, and at 1:20 p.m. on November 28, the first regular O&WT passenger train left for Walla Walla.[110]

The inauguration of the Hunt road to Dayton was achieved without the kind of calamity that marred the opening of the OR&N line. The O&WT, however, came close to matching the events of eight years before. On the afternoon of Wednesday, December 18, 1889, the passenger train from Dayton became derailed near the construction supply yard just east of Walla Walla. The locomotive suddenly jumped the track and ran for about a train length on the ballast before turning on its side and plunging into the ditch, dragging the tender and baggage car with it. Fortunately, the passenger car, full of people, remained on the track and no one was injured. Although the engine cab was demolished, Oakley Johnson and his mate crawled out of the wreckage with no more than a few bruises. The accident apparently was caused by a switch rod contracting in the cold weather.[111]

While George W. Hunt worked out the details of subsidies for his lines to Walla Walla and Dayton, he opened negotiations with communities in the Grande Ronde Valley. First hints that the O&WT might be extended over the Blue Mountains into Union County came in September 1888,[112] but firm steps were not taken until January 23, 1889, when Hunt and Frank W. Paine, the chairman of the Walla Walla board of trade, visited Union.[113] They were received there with overwhelming enthusiasm, for in 1884 the OR&N had bypassed the town and established division facilities at La Grande. Other communities, such as Summerville and Elgin—which still lacked transportation—likewise welcomed the prospect of a link with the outside world. Although Hunt demanded a subsidy of no less than $180,000 for the extension over the mountains to the Grande Ronde, the people remained undaunted. Within a few days they had raised $40,000 and Hunt had to make immediate arrangements for preliminary surveys.[114] On March 12, 1889 Engineer M. C. Shaw left Walla Walla on reconnaissance.[115] Less than two weeks later he returned to town reporting the mountains to be "full of snow,"[116] but claiming nevertheless to have found a suitable route. On April 1, 1889 he set out again with a larger party to locate a line "to the Grande Ronde via Linkton Mountain."[117]

By that time the citizens of Union County had raised no less than $132,000 and were approaching the limit of their resources. To raise another $40,000 therefore, a delegation was sent to the ports on Puget Sound.[118] On April 8, 1889, I. B. Rinchart, W. T. Carroll, E. P.

McDonnell, and L. F. McKenzie appeared before the Seattle Chamber of Commerce to plead for help, asking Seattle and Tacoma each to contribute $20,000. Interviewed at Walla Walla on their return journey the members of the delegation stated that they were "highly gratified" by their visit to the Sound.[119] Raising the remainder of the money, however, proved to be a long, drawn-out affair, for not until December 3, 1889 was the subsidy fully subscribed.[120]

At the end of April 1889 engineer Shaw announced the discovery of a practical but expensive route through the mountains from Centerville.[121] Hunt's men carried out more surveys in August, running several lines between Walla Walla and Milton,[122] but matters were then held up until Union County residents had raised the remainder of the subsidy. The terms of the agreement with the citizens of Union County called for 20 miles of the line to be graded by August 1, 1890 and the entire railway to be ready for operation by December 1, 1891.[123] The easiest way to meet the first deadline was to throw up a roadbed across the Grande Ronde plain. In December 1889, therefore, surveyors located a line from Union to Summerville,[124] and on February 26, 1890 a first contingent of graders left Pendleton to begin work beyond the mountains.[125] On April 25 the *Union Scout* reported that 60 men and 35 teams were at work. They had graded seven miles of the line and were diverting Catherine Creek to avoid constructing two bridges.[126] The 20-mile stretch of road between Union and Summerville was for the most part straight and level, requiring the movement of only 8,000 cubic yards of earth per mile.[127] The graders, therefore, easily met the July 31 deadline and fulfilled the first proviso of the subsidy agreement. In the meantime, the survey crews located another nine miles of line between Summerville and Elgin, but accomplished nothing more in the Blue Mountains. Hunt, it seemed, was playing for time.

The O&WT route from Walla Walla to the Grande Ronde was never very clearly defined. The earliest rumors had it going up Mill Creek and through a short tunnel to the valley of the Looking Glass.[128] In February 1889 *Railroad Gazette* suggested that the connection would be made from Pendleton via the Upper Umatilla and the Taylor & Ruckel road to Summerville.[129] This may well have been Hunt's original intention, for early in March 1889 he visited Washington, D. C.,[130] perhaps seeking United States government permission to cross the Umatilla Indian Reservation. If indeed that was the object of his visit, then his request must have been denied. Thereafter, all the indications were that the engineers would take the road south to the vicinity of Weston or Centerville.[131] From there the line would follow either the Pine or Wild Horse creeks into the mountains and reach a summit near that of the existing Linkton toll road from Weston to Elgin. The railway might then have followed that route down into the Grande Ronde Valley. The total distance from Walla Walla to Union was said to be 86 miles, and Shaw asserted that the summit could have been reached on grades no steeper than 64 feet to the mile. But the railroad was never built.

Early in 1890, as a result of changed conditions, Hunt curtailed construction in eastern Washington and Oregon and embarked upon a new policy. After Henry Villard regained control of the Northern Pacific Railroad in September 1888, the Philadelphia group could no longer guarantee freight rates allowing the O&WT to compete advantageously with the OR&N. Hunt's position then became uncertain. He had promised his supporters that he would carry grain to Puget Sound at rates equal to those charged by the OR&N for carrying it to Portland. This promise had been written into the subsidy agreements. If he failed to honor it, he might lose the subsidies and his whole financial house of cards could topple. The only avenue of escape was to extend the O&WT through to the coast as an independent railway. Abandoning his other projects, Hunt boldly set out to confound Villard's Northern Pacific.

Events unfolded rapidly. In February 1890 Hunt approached the Portland board of trade with a proposal to extend the O&WT from Wallula to Portland or Albina, with construction to commence on or before May 1, 1890 and be completed by December 15, 1891. To help finance the venture he asked the merchants of the Oregon metropolis to take $2,000,000 worth of O&WT 6-percent 40-year bonds.[132] Early in the following month it became clear that Portland would not be the terminus. Instead, Hunt evidently aimed to reach Gray's Harbor, in western Washington, where efforts were already under way to establish a deep-water seaport. Residents of the newly platted town of Gray's Harbor City, as well as those in nearby Hoquiam, Aberdeen, and Montesano, had already pledged $750,000 for the construction of a railroad to Centralia, and Hunt had promised that it would soon be extended south to Portland.[133] People in the Interior were spellbound! In mid-March 1890 the

Waitsburg Times averred that, "Truly G. W. Hunt is destined to speedily become a great railroad king, a Jay Gould of the West, as it were, unless all signs fail."[134]

In a more sober editorial the *Portland Oregonian* expressed the opinion that:

> Mr. Hunt has more plainly shown his hand with regard to his designs in the way of securing a seaport terminus for his as yet disjointed eastern line of road than he has ever done before. His line to the sea, once opened, would prove a formidable competitor to the Northern Pacific.[135]

Reaction came swiftly. In April 1890 Northern Pacific announced it would build a branch line from Tacoma to Gray's Harbor by way of Olympia. It then purchased the Port Blakeley Mill Company's 40-mile-long Puget Sound & Gray's Harbor Railroad, which had just been completed between Kamilche on Little Skookum Bay and Montesano on the Chehalis River.[136] They thus obtained nine miles of railway in the Chehalis Valley and attempted to block Hunt's advance. Their efforts, however, scarcely slowed the other company down. In June 1890 grading was in full swing along the entire line from Centralia to Gray's Harbor City, with surveys being undertaken between Wallula and Portland.[137] By January 1891, when Hunt's trains began running between Centralia and Montesano, the Northern Pacific Branch had barely reached Olympia. Having failed to contain the O&WT expansion, Northern Pacific then resorted to desperate measures. Claiming that Hunt owed their company $135,000, Villard's henchmen suddenly served out an attachment against the Centralia & Gray's Harbor line.[138]

Following the stock market panic of November 1890, Hunt's precarious financial position became untenable. In December of that year his creditors seized much of his personal property.[139] The Northern Pacific attachment of the Gray's Harbor line was the final blow. In a suit for damages brought against the larger company in 1894, Hunt claimed that as a result of Northern Pacific's actions, all his plans had been frustrated and his subsidies lost. He testified that at the time of the attachment he had been in New York City, negotiating financial backing for his extensive construction projects. Northern Pacific, he said, had falsely alleged that he had absconded from his usual place of business and was trying to sell his properties to defraud creditors. At Northern Pacific's instigation, the attachment proceedings had been advertised throughout the country, discouraging investors from buying his bonds. As a result he had been unable to continue construction or earn his subsidies, and his credit had been destroyed. Hunt maintained that his debt to Northern Pacific had been fully secured.[140]

Whatever the rights and wrongs of the case, the result was the same. Hunt had to sell the O&WT and Charles B. Wright Jr. had to step in to protect Philadelphia financial interests. Early in March 1891 the O&WT property was conveyed to Wright, and although Hunt remained president of the company, the new owner assumed the position of vice president and general manager.[141] Wright then tried to sell the O&WT system to Northern Pacific. By December 1891 he had worked out a deal whereby Northern Pacific would pay for the Hunt lines with their own securities and guarantee principal and 6 percent interest on the O&WT bonds.[142] Northern Pacific's financial position, however, was deteriorating rapidly. As a result of an 1891 tour of western lines, Villard suddenly and belatedly became alarmed by "the weight of the load that had been put on the Company by the purchase and construction of the longer branch lines in Montana and Washington."[143] At that point, apparently, he decided not to acquire any more such lines, and the purchase of the Hunt system fell through. Realizing that O&WT could not, by itself, meet its financial obligations, Wright then allowed the road to pass into receivership.

In August 1892 Levi Ankeny, Frank W. Paine, and W. D. Tyler of Walla Walla, working in conjunction with Wright, formed the Washington & Columbia River Railroad Company, with a capital stock of $3 million, declaring their intention to build new roads and purchase the Hunt lines. On November 14, 1892 the W&CR bought the O&WT property at foreclosure.[144] The deteriorating economic climate, however, soon forced the new corporation to declare insolvency. Financial reorganization and a general improvement in trade allowed the W&CR to emerge from receivership again in May 1895.[145] Thereafter it became an attractive property, and in March 1898 the Northwestern Improvement Company acquired a controlling interest on behalf of the new Northern Pacific Railway. Due perhaps to Hunt's continuing litigation to recover his subsidies, W&CR did not formally merge with Northern Pacific until 1907.

Despite the unfortunate circumstances attending its early years, the Hunt system achieved long-term success and became a valuable adjunct to the Northern Pacific. In fiscal year 1903-04, for example, the W&CR lines carried 59,223 passengers an average distance of 35.68 miles and moved 253,424 tons of freight a mean 44.30 miles. In 1903 it loaded no less than 181,000 tons of grain, and even in poor crop years, such as 1904, the railway carried away at least 90,000 tons.[146] Today, despite continuing competition from the Union Pacific Railroad and the growth of heavily subsidized road transport, Burlington Northern's way-freights still run to Pendleton, Walla Walla, and Dayton six times a week. Only the Eureka Flat branch has gone, and that but recently.[147] The little trains, as they amble through the countryside, still remind us of the promises made and kept by a man named Hunt.

Chapter Eight

Lexington, Heppner, and the Coal Mines

Even when the OR&N completed its Columbia Valley line, Oregon Interior communities further to the south remained without railway service. For more than five years people living on Willow Creek complained of their isolation, but the railroad declined to build a branch into such sparsely settled country. In 1888, however, Henry Villard's efforts to implement the territorial provisions of the joint lease agreement, and the OR&N's desire to keep out new competitors and monopolize access to prospective coal mines, combined to bring about construction of a railway to Lexington and Heppner.

Theron E. Fell, a Heppner wool broker, spearheaded the Morrow County campaign for the Willow Creek branch.[1] Fell hailed from Illinois, and when negotiations with the OR&N failed he turned to the railroad he knew best. Chicago & North Western cherished ambitions for an extension to the Pacific coast, and in 1887 had surveyors already at work between Casper, Wyoming, and Boise, Idaho. Approached by Fell, C&NW representatives agreed that, if provided with a subsidy of $100,000, they would build a railroad from Heppner to the Columbia River.[2] Returning to Morrow County, Fell therefore set out to raise the necessary money. Just as he achieved his goal, however, the OR&N suddenly recognized this potential threat: a Chicago & North Western invasion of the Columbia Valley was unthinkable. Moreover, with coal deposits recently found in the hills south of Heppner, large-scale mining operations appeared a distinct possibility. Urged on by the Union Pacific Railway Company, OR&N moved quickly to head off the intruders. Before the end of

September 1887 their surveyors were camped at the horseshoe bend on Willow Creek, just below Redford's.[3] A month later, a party of the Oregon company's elite, including superintendent William H. Holcomb, assistant superintendent C. W. Johnson, freight agent B. Campbell, chief engineer W. H. Kennedy, and Union Pacific assistant general manager Cameron, paid a surprise visit to Heppner.[4]

Financing the construction of a 45-mile branch line into the hills posed something of a problem. The OR&N lease was onerous for Union Pacific; OR&N, moreover, was losing traffic to the Northern Pacific and faced the threat of competition from the Southern Pacific. In March 1888 Henry Villard came to the rescue. In an attempt to induce Portlanders to accept the territorial provisions of the joint lease agreement, he suddenly made $2 million available for the construction of OR&N branch lines south of the Snake River. Financial barriers thus removed, W. H. Holcomb invited a delegation from Morrow County to discuss the terms under which the OR&N would build the Willow Creek branch. On Saturday March 31, 1888 Thomas Ayers (Theron Fells's business partner), Henry Blackman (the mayor of Heppner), J. O. Morrow (a pioneer Heppner merchant), C. A. Rhea, Frank Kellogg, and William Penland (founder of Lexington) met with Holcomb in Portland.[5] The OR&N, the superintendent said, stood ready to build the road to Heppner, provided that local residents gave a right of way and depot grounds free of charge. Presented with a savings of at least $70,000, the committee readily agreed to accept OR&N's terms, and the Oregon company thus averted the Chicago & North Western threat. Theron Fell hastened to help the OR&N agent procure the right of way. Considerable lengths of the surveyed line passed through public commons and unclaimed (Northern Pacific) railroad land. With one notable exception, therefore, the ground was easily procured at reasonable cost.[6] On April 14, 1888 Kilpatrick Brothers & Collins of Beatrice, Nebraska, won the grading contract,[7] and within a month subcontractors J. H. Smith of Portland and Thomas Jessop of Utah had the work well under way.[8]

The 45-mile-long Heppner branch left the OR&N main line at Willows Junction 151 miles from Portland and followed the Willow Creek Valley into the hills. Crossing and recrossing the creek the railway climbed steadily all the way to Heppner, where it reached an elevation of just over 1,900 feet. The steepest grade was 1.5 percent.

Grading proceeded apace. By mid-May 1888, 200 men and 300 teams were hard at work on the first 18 miles of the line, with further forces on their way.[9] The weather being dry, dust conditions rendered the job unpleasant, but by mid-August the roadbed was 80 percent complete.[10] Timber arrived early in August and bridge building went on well into October. The track, meanwhile, was laid with second-hand iron rails taken out of the Baker City branch between Umatilla and Pendleton.[11] The construction train followed the carpenters up the line, arriving at Lexington on or about October 19.[12] No further progress was then made until November 14, when more old rails were brought down from Pendleton.[13] The steel gang then made haste to finish the job.

At 2:15 in the afternoon on Monday, November 26, 1888 the mayor of Heppner and the city council, preceded by the Heppner band, Company E of the Oregon National Guard, and 200 school children carrying flags, marched down to the depot grounds. There, on the site of the old race course, they joined a thousand other people who had assembled to greet the arrival of the first train. Mayor Henry Blackman made a "short address, yet to the point," the crowd cheered, and pioneer merchants Jackson L. Morrow and Henry Heppner drove the last spike. Company E then fired

> three ringing salutes, echoing and re-echoing over the hills, which, with the sparks of the locomotives, the rumbling of the cars, and the cheers of the assemblage, proclaimed that Heppner is no longer an isolated town, but is in direct communication with the outside world by that van of progress, a railroad.

That night huge bonfires lit Main Street, anvils were fired, and the city entertained the railroaders to a free ball at Garrigues & Rogers Opera House.[14]

Morrow County welcomed the railway, but some local residents questioned the $22,958 bill for land, the principal bone of contention being the provision of right of way "to and through" Heppner. Despite allegations to the contrary, the railroad committee pointed out that both the agreement with the OR&N and the receipts given to subscribers had stipulated that land would be procured on that basis.[15] The problem was therefore cleared up quite easily. A dispute with a disgruntled farmer, however, caused more trouble. Rasmus Larsen, who owned a ranch about four miles above

Willows, had been in the East when the OR&N land agent was settling right of way claims. He returned home in July 1888 to find the roadbed graded across his property and the track about to be laid. Outraged, he immediately posted signs forbidding any further work. When the contractors paid no heed, Larsen had 40 of their men arrested and fined $5 each for trespassing. Thereafter, matters got worse. When the railroad company laid the track and began to run trains, Larsen greased the rails with bacon fat and stood laughing on the lineside as the locomotives slipped to a standstill. The train crews suffered this mischief for some time, but there came a day when Larsen greased an entire mile of track, causing a great deal of delay. The *Oregonian* of March 29, 1889 related that:

> It happened shortly after that, as a train was going by his place with a gang of Italian laborers on board, and as Larsen was looking on, a cartridge of Giant Powder fell near him with a burning fuse attached. Before he could get out of range the powder exploded and shook up Larsen so badly that he hardly knew what he was doing. He ran this way and that, as one who saw it says "...like a hen with her head off...", and kept on going till he disappeared.[16]

Two weeks later he had the train crew arrested at Heppner on charges of attempted murder. When the railroaders came up for trial, however, no one could say who had fired the bomb and Larsen himself could not rightly tell where it had come from. The case, therefore, was dismissed, and Larsen, it was said, never greased the railroad track again. Inevitably Larsen came out of the whole affair rather badly, for the OR&N appealed an Arlington court decision to award him $600 damages, and his lawyers appropriated nearly all of the $641.44 paid him for right of way. Finally, to make matters worse, he was convicted and fined $75 for obstructing the United States mail.[17]

For more than two years after the Heppner branch opened, it seemed likely it might be extended south to the coal regions and perhaps beyond. In Morrow County locally mined coal had been used in a small way since 1880. In that year the Matteson brothers, Bob, Edgar, Albert, and Ben, began a long search for a commercially viable deposit. Working on the slopes of Black Butte (now Madison Butte) 18 miles south of Heppner, they sank shafts to intersect the coal and then followed a promising-looking seam into the mountainside.[18] Outcroppings of the same coal occurred at several points along an axis extending 20 miles northeastward from the Matteson property. Others, therefore, soon made additional discoveries.

In 1882 Sid Brown of Pendleton found a 36-inch seam exposed on the mountainside above the head of Butter Creek, and he and two associates drove a short drift into it.[19] In 1888 the same general area came under the control of W. D. Fletcher and C. J. Carlson, who formed the Umatilla County Coal Company and secured a three-year option of the surrounding half section of land.[20] At about the same time these partners reached a general understanding with the OR&N concerning railway facilities for any successful mining operation. During the next year they sank a shaft into the underlying rock and found a second bed of coal 54 inches thick. Further to the west, on Johnson Creek, the Blue Mountain Coal Company intersected the same sedimentary sequence and reported similar results. In September 1889 OR&N surveyors were reportedly in the area "taking notes for the benefit of their company."[21] Then, in March 1890, the *Heppner Gazette* reported, "on authentic authority," that Union Pacific contemplated an extension of the Heppner branch, passing within a quarter of a mile of the Umatilla Coal Company Mine and proceeding by way of Camas Prairie and the most practicable route to the Grande Ronde Valley.[22] As the year went on, nothing happened. Becoming impatient, the mine owners therefore took matters into their own hands. In September 1890, W. D. Fletcher, J. H. Roby, T. Rourke, and J. R. Dickson formed the Eastern Oregon Railroad Company to build a railway from Heppner to the coal mines and thence to Sumpter, where it would have met the simultaneously incorporated Sumpter Valley Railroad.[23] The resulting threat of an independent route through the Blue Mountains, vulnerable to acquisition by competitors, however, forced Omaha to assess the feasibility of large-scale exploitation of the eastern Oregon coal deposits.

In the spring of 1891 Union Pacific set up a drilling rig at the head of Johnson Creek and sent in their coal expert E. G. Locke to interpret the results.[24] Eventually Locke found, as others did several times over, that although there was some good coal within the seams, most of it was inferior material. The seams, moreover, tended to pinch out suddenly and could not be followed for any great distance.[25] In the light of these conclusions, Union Pacific, the only potential large-scale buyer of the coal, abandoned all interest in the eastern Oregon deposits. The incipient mining industry collapsed and the Heppner branch was never extended.

Chapter Nine

Coeur d'Alene

The construction and opening of the Northern Pacific Railroad brought a host of fortune seekers to the far Interior. Beyond Coeur d'Alene Lake in northern Idaho, the high peaks of the Bitterroot Mountains lured prospectors into the narrow valleys and guided a fortunate few to great mineral wealth. In 1883 Andrew Pritchard's discovery of alluvial gold triggered a rush to Eagle Creek on the north fork of the Coeur d'Alene River. Although the excitement was short-lived, the influx of miners soon led to the discovery of rich base-metal deposits on the south fork of the Coeur d'Alene. During 1884 the Tiger and Poorman claims were staked on Canyon Creek, with the Gold Hunter, Morning, and Evening being located near Mullan.[1] Then, just a year later, came the greatest strike of all! Early in September 1885 prospectors Noah Kellogg and Phil O'Rourke stumbled upon a huge lead-silver orebody outcropping on Milo Creek, a northward flowing stream joining the south fork river less than 15 miles above the head of navigation. Named Bunker Hill & Sullivan, the two claims formed the nucleus of what later became the single largest and most productive mining property in the American Northwest.[2]

Before the mines could be developed, transportation had to be provided. Access to the Coeur d'Alene Valley was difficult, but lake and river navigation eased the approach. Shallow-draft vessels plied the waters between Fort Coeur d'Alene and the old mission on the Coeur d'Alene River. Travelers at first used the United States government steamer *Amelia Wheaton*, which carried hay and other supplies to the garrison at Fort Coeur d'Alene.[3] With the rush of 1883, however, Portland steamboat man Z. J. Hatch, sensing the greatest opportunity since the Clearwater excitement of 1862, "concluded to build a small sternwheel steamer to ply between Fort Coeur d'Alene and the Mission."[4] Under the supervision of Hatch's associate, Captain I. B. Sanborn, the vessel *Coeur d'Alene* was built during the winter of 1883-84 and launched at Coeur d'Alene early in the following spring.[5] Wagon roads from Rathdrum on the Northern Pacific Railroad to Coeur d'Alene City, and from the old mission to the boom town of Murray, soon linked the mining region with the outside world. In the meantime, others made plans to construct a railway.

Until 1887 Idaho Territory had no statute under which a railroad could be incorporated.[6] Consequently, promoters either had to risk forming a company in a neighboring state or territory, or apply for a charter from the United States government. In February 1884 a group of Spokane Falls businessmen, headed by J. J. Browne, submitted a memorial to Congress praying that they might be incorporated as the Spokane Falls & Coeur d'Alene Railroad Company, empowered to build a railway from Spokane Falls via Coeur d'Alene Lake to the mines. The negotiation in Washington D. C. cost them dearly. Not until January 3, 1886 did they incorporate a company called the Spokane & Coeur d'Alene Railway, and even then they did so without final congressional approval.[7] By that time, however, Montana interests had already gained a foothold in the Coeur d'Alene Valley.

Soon after the discovery of the Bunker Hill & Sullivan, a Murray, Idaho, merchant named James F. Wardner secured an option to market the ore. Since most of the material was not of a grade high enough for direct smelting, Wardner needed to build a concentrator. His search for the required capital led him to Helena, where he met Sam T. Hauser, governor of Montana Territory, a successful banker and president of the Helena Mining & Reduction Company.[8] Hauser sent his mining expert, Anton Esler, to examine the Bunker Hill & Sullivan property and soon received a favorable report. In return for a guarantee of 50,000 tons of ore and a processing fee of $5 a ton, Montana capitalists then agreed to form the Helena Concentrating Company and build a 100-ton-a-day concentrator at the mine site.[9]

In April 1886 Hauser's associate, Daniel C. Corbin, visited the Coeur d'Alene camp to investigate the feasibility of building a

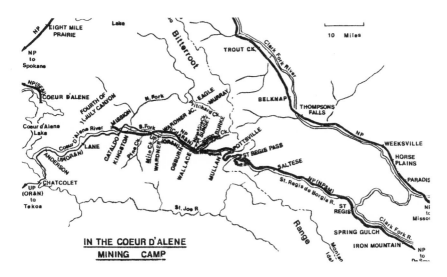

IN THE COEUR D'ALENE
MINING CAMP

railroad and quickly concluded that "a transportation line connecting the district with the Northern Pacific... would pay."[10] Corbin wasted no time getting started on the line. Before the end of that month he had incorporated the Coeur d'Alene Railway & Navigation Company in Montana Territory. The purpose of the new company, which had a capital stock of $500,000, was to build a railroad from Rathdrum, on the Northern Pacific main line, 15 miles to the shore of Lake Coeur d'Alene, where it would connect with steamboats for the old mission on the Coeur d'Alene River. From the mission another railroad would be built to the site of the Helena Concentrating works in Milo Gulch, and to Murray and other towns in the Coeur d'Alene district. The promoters were D. C. Corbin, Governor S. T. Hauser, A. M. Holter (a prominent Helena merchant), A. M. Esler, James F. Wardner, Stephen S. Glidden (owner of the Tiger Mine), and James Monaghan (founder of Coeur d'Alene City and partner in the Coeur d'Alene Steam Navigation & Transportation Company).[11] Construction would be undertaken that year. Before the work could begin, however, Corbin and his colleagues had to make an interchange arrangement with the Northern Pacific Railroad and strike a compromise with the promoters in Spokane Falls.

Northern Pacific officials found themselves in a difficult position. In order to procure land in Spokane Falls they had already formed a close relationship with several prominent local business-men, including Mayor Anthony M. Cannon. An alliance with the Montana group threatened to disrupt this arrangement, but the movement of mineral concentrates to the Helena Mining & Reduc-tion Company smelter offered lucrative long-haul freight potential. Harris and Oakes could ill-afford to alienate either group, and sev-eral months of delicate maneuvering were needed to resolve the dilemma. To placate the Spokanites,[12] and perhaps to counter the OR&N threat to advance north from Farmington, the company made surveys for a Spokane & Palouse Railway branch line from Spangle to the Coeur d'Alene Valley by way of Waverley, Latah, and the south end of Coeur d'Alene Lake.[13] Any decision to build a rail-road on that route, however, depended upon securing United States government permission to cross the Coeur d'Alene Indian Reser-vation, and could not be made immediately. In the meantime Esler set up the Helena Concentrating Company plant on Milo Creek[14] and Corbin began work on the railway from Wardner to the old mission.[15] Northern Pacific then threw in its lot with Hauser. As a concession to the Spokane group, however, the northern section of the Coeur d'Alene Railway & Navigation Company system, link-ing Coeur d'Alene City with the Northern Pacific main line, be-came a separate entity, known at first as the Spokane & Idaho Railroad. On October 23, 1886 this section of the line was re-incor-porated in Washington Territory as the Spokane Falls & Idaho Railroad with representatives of both the Northern Pacific Railroad and the Spokane Falls business community taking seats on the board. The officers were: D. C. Corbin, president; Governor S. T. Hauser, vice-president; A. A. Newbury, secretary; and A. M. Can-non, treasurer.[16]

The Spokane Falls & Idaho Railroad diverged from the North-ern Pacific main line at a point called Hauser Junction, 2.5 miles east of the Idaho-Washington boundary. The line ran southeast to Post Falls and east on the north bank of the Spokane River to the lake front at Coeur d'Alene City, a total distance of 13.5 miles. Much of the line went across open, gravel-surfaced prairie. Excavations amounted to only about 5,000 cubic yards to the mile.[17] Work be-gan under Paul Mohr's supervision at the end of August 1886, and proceeded rapidly.[18] By October 5 the right of way had been cleared and most of the grading and bridge building was completed.[19]

Tracklaying commenced on October 8 and the last spike was driven on October 24.[20] With the railway ballasted and surfaced, construction crews turned the line over to the operating department on November 9, 1886.[21]

Beyond the lake the Coeur d'Alene Railway & Navigation Company's narrow-gauge line set out eastward from a point near the Cataldo Mission church. After about a mile it crossed the Coeur d'Alene River and remained on the south side of the valley for most of the way to Wardner Junction (not a railway junction), which lay opposite the mouth of Milo Creek. This first section of the line, as built in 1886, totaled approximately 13 miles. In that distance it climbed about 160 feet. The profile, however, was undulating, so that both up and down trains had to climb over hills at Kingston and Pine Creek. Consequently, none of the three original engines could haul more than seven loaded ore cars down from Wardner Junction to the wharf at the old mission.[22]

Early in July 1886 Corbin advertised for bids for clearing, grubbing, and tie cutting on the line from the old mission to Wardner.[23] On August 4, W. L. Spaulding of Spokane Falls won a contract for grading and track laying, and Corbin chose J. L. Bayley to furnish lumber and build bridges.[24] By the end of August, 700 men were at work in the Coeur d'Alene Valley, and Kingston was said to look "like an army encampment."[25] Rails arrived at Hauser Junction in October but could not be forwarded to the mission until the Spokane Falls & Idaho Railroad had been completed. Throughout November the steamers made two round trips on Coeur d'Alene Lake each day, and in the clear, cold weather workers hastily laid track on frozen fill. By November 25, 1886 the railway was complete between the mission and Pine Prairie, and a bridge across the river at the old Small & Colby sawmill was said to be progressing rapidly.[26] Two "Mogul" locomotives, purchased second hand from the Texas & St. Louis Railroad, along with several cars, had already arrived.[27] One of the engines (No. 2) had been pressed into service on a supply train, and completion of the railway appeared imminent. But just as the work was finished the weather turned warmer, bringing torrential rains. The embankments, built of soft black loam, quickly thawed out and slumped into the surrounding marshland, leaving the track without support. On December 22, 1886 the *Spokane Falls Review* reported the road was "ironed to

Milo, but as it stands is a useless piece of property. One engine is on the track between Pine Flat and Mud Prairie, and another between Kingston and Mission, unable to move."[28] Corbin was learning about railroad building the hard way![29]

Throughout the winter of 1886-87 the Coeur d'Alene Railway & Navigation Company remained largely ineffective. The Company attempted to run one train a day, but even when cold weather stiffened the roadbed, locomotives or cars derailed on every trip. Icy conditions on the lake, meanwhile, hindered navigation, and by mid-February 1887 nearly 2,000 tons of Bunker Hill & Sullivan ore lay at Wardner Junction awaiting shipment.[30] At that point Corbin purchased the Coeur d'Alene Steam Navigation & Transportation Company and brought its vessels under his control.[31] However, he could do nothing about the railway until after the spring floods. Navigation re-opened on March 10, but two weeks later high water halted the trains.[32] Throughout the spring the line was repeatedly inundated, and even as late as June 7 the tracks still lay submerged. At that time the *Spokane Falls Review* reported that:

> The whole of the narrow valley through which the Coeur d'Alene River winds its crooked, placid, way twixt banks of rush and meadows had been turned into a shallow lake from the Mission to the lake proper, by backwater, the tops of the brush and the trees standing out of the water as a careful Captain guides the boat up the one and only proper course amongst the waste of woods and water. At the Mission the one lone hotel sits... in the middle of a little lake, and the cars slushingly slide around on water covered rails. But the boat runs up close to the coach and transfer is made on a gangplank without any inconvenience. After everybody and their baggage was aboard the train started on her watery way east with Dell Manchester, an old NP runner at the throttle...By carefully creeping over a few bad spots, and lighting out over anyways runable track, the 15 miles to Wardner was made on fair time without any mishaps.[33]

Not until July 1887 could workers repair and finish the line from the mission to Wardner. In the meantime, plans were made for an extension to Wallace.

Corbin's advance to the heart of the Coeur d'Alene camp brought him into continuous struggle with the Oregon Railway & Navigation Company. Portland capitalists became interested in the northern Idaho mines during the summer of 1886, and by the fall of that year they had begun to build a smelter at East Portland to treat Coeur d'Alene ore. In July 1886 an OR&N subsidiary called the Washington & Idaho Railroad was incorporated in Whitman County, Washington Territory. The company, headquartered at Farmington, had a capital stock of $1 million and was to build a railway northeast from Farmington by way of Coeur d'Alene Lake "to some point on the Northern Pacific Railroad."[34] The Washington & Idaho directors, several of whom resided in the Farmington area, were: George W. Truax (president), H. F. Stratton, I. Cooper, Julius Galland (secretary-treasurer), and W. A. Walker.[35] Engineer P. Zahner made a preliminary survey between Farmington and Wardner in the fall of 1886, and by the end of that year engineer E. H. Mix had completed the estimates for grading.[36]

Given the narrowness of the mountain valleys it was clear that one or both companies would be compelled to adopt desperate measures to secure right of way. Corbin appears to have been unsure what privileges the Montana charter of the CdAR&N would afford him in Idaho, especially concerning branch lines. In October 1886, therefore, he formed the Wallace & Northern Railroad Company, incorporated in Washington Territory, to build feeder lines up the valleys of Canyon and Nine Mile creeks to the various mines. His associates in this venture were: W. R. Wallace, E. D. Carter, J. N. Glover, F. R. Moore, and H. M. McCartney.[37] Conspicuously absent was S. S. Glidden, owner of the Tiger Mine at the head of Canyon Creek, who wanted to preserve the option of dealing directly with the OR&N. In July 1887 Glidden set out to build his own railroad down Canyon Creek to Wallace, but soon ran into opposition. On August 17, 1887 the *Spokane Falls Review* quoted him as saying that the task would be accomplished "just as soon as a few parties along the line will permit it by granting the right of way across their premises at a figure somewhere within the bounds of reason."[38]

Apparently Corbin's Montana associates, Holter and Esler, part owners of the Helena & San Francisco (the 'Frisco) mining property half-way along Canyon Creek, had blocked his advance. Glidden held out for another two weeks and then came to terms. During the following year the CdAR&N purchased his Canyon Creek railroad interests and assets.[39] Between Wallace and Mullan, meanwhile, Corbin tackled the OR&N directly. In July 1887 both companies had men at work on that section of the road, and the W&I, which by that time was preparing to advance into Montana, had forces working above Mullan.[40] In the confines of the south fork canyon the two groups increasingly hindered each other's progress. During the second week of August 1887, therefore, Corbin secured a temporary injunction restraining his rivals from working at several points along the line.[41] By August 20, 1887 the Farmington crowd had withdrawn and Corbin expressed confidence that the injunction would be permanent. The OR&N, however, would soon retaliate.

Construction of the 11-mile CdAR&N extension from Wardner Junction to Wallace went on throughout the summer of 1887.[42] By early July contractors had cleared the line, grubbed it, and finished two-thirds of the grading. Bridge building caused some delay, but by the end of the first week in August workers had laid track six miles to Osborn.[43] The graders, meanwhile, concentrated on the north side of the river nearer to Wallace and especially at the mouth of Canyon Creek, where a turning wye was to be installed. Trains began to run through to Osborn on Monday August 22, 1887 and within a few days the railway had been extended another three miles to Swinging Door Cabin.[44] The tracklayers reached Wallace during the week ending September 10, 1887, and the line was then ballasted and surfaced. A last spike ceremony held at Wallace on September 30, 1887, was overshadowed by a Washington & Idaho application for a counter injunction.[45] The OR&N subsidiary claimed that for a mile and a half east and west of Wallace the location of the CdAR&N line did not coincide with that shown on survey documents filed in the land office. The company alleged, moreover, that Corbin had built his railroad upon their right of way.[46] Work on the depot building and the various side tracks came to a halt, suspending the newly inaugurated train service.

When investigators looked into the matter they found that the CdAR&N track was indeed on W&I ground and not in the position shown on the survey. Corbin maintained, however, that this was the result of an error and offered to hand the grade over to its owners as soon as they were in a position to use it. The offer seemed reasonable enough, but Truax and his associates rejected it, leaving the decision to the courts. The railway lay idle until October 29, 1887 when Judge Buck, recognizing the public interest, dissolved the W&I injunction.[47] The legal roadblock having been removed, regular trains began running through to Wallace on Wednesday, November 2, 1887, operating to the following schedule:[48]

10:00 am	Wallace	3:15 pm
10:30 am	Osborn	2:45 pm
11:15 am	Wardner Jc.	2:00 pm
11:50 am	Kingston	1:25 pm
12:15 pm	Mission	1:00 pm
7:20 pm	Coeur d'Alene	7:30 am

Passenger fares from Wallace were: Osborn 50 cents, Wardner Junction $1.00, Kingston $2.00, Mission $2.50, and Coeur d'Alene $5.50. Freight rates on hardware, groceries, and general merchandise were 70 cents per hundred from Coeur d'Alene City to Wardner Junction and 80 cents to Wallace.[49]

As 1887 drew to a close, Corbin set out to complete the steeply graded Canyon Creek railroad from Wallace to Burke. By December 1, 80 men were grading and laying track, and on December 15 a silver spike, driven at Burke, marked completion of the line.[50] A simultaneous attempt to rename the terminus Bayard, after nationally prominent politician Thomas F. Bayard, failed miserably.[51] At Burke the branch passed between the Tiger and Poorman mines, both of which had large quantities of ore ready to go out on the first trains. By early January 1888, therefore, conductor Gray and his overworked crew were making two trips to Burke daily.[52]

In an attempt to maintain a service throughout the winter, Corbin had a single-screw steamer with a specially reinforced hull built for use on Coeur d'Alene Lake. The *Kootenai*, launched near Coeur d'Alene City on Sunday, December 4, 1887, was 110 feet long, 25 feet at the beam, and drew 9 feet of water when fully loaded with 125 tons of cargo. A 480 horsepower engine built by the Willamette Iron Works drove the propeller.[53] Even this formidable vessel hardly proved a match for winter conditions on the lake, for early in January 1888 she blew a cylinder head while trying to break ice.[54] Nor could she be used to full advantage until the railway had been extended about a mile downriver from the mission to a new berth in deeper water, a task not accomplished until February 1888.[55]

The Corbin narrow gauge railroad opened up the Coeur d'Alene camp but could hardly cope with the rapid expansion of mine production. In September 1888 James F. Wardner estimated that the output of lead-silver ore from all the mines in the area amounted to 19,400 tons a month, yielding 6,470 tons of concentrate for shipment to the smelters.[56] On the basis of other figures available for the Bunker Hill & Sullivan, these tonnages and grades appear to have been exaggerated. Nevertheless, the mines may well have been able to produce 5,000 tons of concentrate a month and offer the railway 17 10-ton carloads a day. Of the three small narrow gauge locomotives owned by the CdAR&N, however, one was needed for the passenger train, and another was usually either under repair or employed on work trains.[57] Consequently only one engine was normally available to handle the mineral traffic, and the railroad brought a mere 10 carloads a day down to the mission.[58] Transshipment on and off the lake steamers demanded that the mineral products be carried in sacks instead of in bulk.[59] The CdAR&N route clearly lacked required capacity and was both inconvenient and expensive to operate. Moreover, due to icy conditions on the lake, it was hardly a year-round proposition. These disadvantages, plus the fact that Northern Pacific adjusted freight rates to favor a long haul over their own lines to the smelter at Wickes, Montana, increased the clamor for a direct OR&N standard gauge link with the Coeur d'Alene mines.

The principal impediment to the OR&N advance was the need to obtain United States government permission to pass through the Coeur d'Alene Indian Reservation.[60] The Washington & Idaho first tackled this problem in July 1887 when officers of the company met with Indian leaders and secured permission for the railway to cross tribal land.[61] That done, Truax immediately ordered a special train, and taking Chief Seltice and several elders with him, set out for Washington D. C.[62] There they met with President Grover Cleveland and gained executive approval in principle for a line across the reservation. For a while matters proceeded in an orderly fashion. Senator Joseph Dolph introduced a right of way bill into Congress on February 2, 1888[63] and it became law on May 18, 1888.[64] The OR&N then moved rapidly to begin construction, not only on the Washington & Idaho line, but also on the Snake River bridge at Riparia and the uncompleted link between Texas Ferry and Pampa. On June 1, 1888 Corey Brothers broke ground at Farmington and began to grade a roadbed northward toward the forks of Hangman

Creek.[65] It soon became evident, however, that the passage of the right of way bill only marked the beginning of a long process of wrangling with government officials.

Before the railroad could do any work on the reservation the department of interior intervened, insisting that the Indians formally approve the right of way agreement.[66] Bewildered by such bureaucracy, the Indians protested that they saw no reason why they should hold council to sanction what they had already promised both the railroad and President Cleveland. In answer to rumors that they might welsh on the agreement, Andrew Seltice and Pierre Wyilsho signed a letter to the press reiterating their willingness to have the railway cross the reservation.[67] The secretary of the interior, however, insisted that formalities be observed and sent out the inspector of Indian agencies, General Armstrong, to supervise the proceedings.[68] At a council held at the mission on October 22, 1888 the Indians formally ratified the right of way agreement. Moreover, to ensure that the unanimity of their decision could not be questioned, every one of them signed the articles.[69] General Armstrong then returned to Washington to prepare his report and issue final permission for the work to proceed. Again the contractors assembled their forces and prepared to begin construction on the 53-mile section of line through the reservation.[70] Once again, however, there was a hitch. The attorney general now ruled that the secretary of the interior had no authority to allow the railroad to be built until the amount of compensation had been fixed and formally approved by both the Indians and the government.[71] At that juncture the contractor gave up in despair and dismissed a thousand men who had been standing by for orders. In due course payment was fixed at a sum giving each individual Indian $14.[72] Another council having been held, more papers were sent to Washington and finally, on January 26, 1889, the Washington & Idaho Railroad received the go-ahead.[73]

There was no evidence that the Northern Pacific Railroad Company had stage-managed the difficulties in the nation's capital. Locally, however, they did their utmost to obstruct the Washington & Idaho advance. Northern Pacific officials were well aware that if the OR&N succeeded in opening a continuous standard gauge railway into the Coeur d'Alene camp, Corbin's narrow gauge line would be unable to compete with it. They therefore carried out surveys for a Spokane Falls & Idaho Railroad extension from

Coeur d'Alene City through Fourth of July Canyon to the mission[74] and made plans to purchase the CdAR&N system and convert it to standard gauge.[75] In July 1888 came a bitter exchange of injunctions, followed by condemnation proceedings, as W&I sought to secure right of way across Northern Pacific land near Kingston. During the following month, as W&I set out to clear and grade its line eastward from the Indian reservation, Northern Pacific crews began blasting operations right alongside.[76] Local residents had little doubt that the main object of these activities was harassment of the Oregon company's forces. On August 4, 1888 the *Wallace Free Press* noted:

> The impression gained is that the W&I is in earnest. It has let contracts from Kingston clear through to Mullan and has established a large commissariat at Kingston for supplying the men. On the other hand the Northern Pacific seems to have taken the part of an obstructionist. It is plain that it is in no hurry to come into this country as long as the narrow gauge controls the traffic.[77]

In fact Northern Pacific sought to consolidate its position in the Coeur d'Alene country. Even as negotiations went on with Corbin for the purchase of the CdAR&N system, plans were therefore made to extend the narrow gauge from Wallace to Mullan.

The narrow canyon above Wallace hardly provided enough room for two railways. The right of way had already been contested, and as the railroad companies could not reach a compromise, the courts appointed a commission to investigate the matter and suggest a solution. This body, consisting of engineers W. H. Kennedy (for the OR&N), John F. Stevens (for the CdAR&N), and J. J. Donovan (a mutually acceptable third party), arrived in Wallace on July 26, 1888 and quickly concluded that a joint survey should be undertaken to lay out two railways having separate tracks but sharing common roadbed at the most constricted parts of the route.[78] On August 17, 1888 CdAR&N engineer Jaynes and a dozen men therefore began to lay out just such a line.[79] Northern Pacific took over the CdAR&N property from Corbin on October 1, 1888.[80] It then let a grading contract to J. H. Smith of Portland (who was already working for the W&I),[81] and by mid-November 250 men were hard at work.[82] For once the winter weather favored construction and by mid-January 1889 individual sections of the roadbed were rapidly being merged to form a continuous line.[83] On March 9, 1889 track had been laid more than half way, and on Sunday March 24, 1889 Conductor Tom Cosgrove's construction train, hauled by engine No. 3, drew into Mullan.[84]

Northern Pacific inaugurated a regular train service over the new extension on Monday, April 22, 1889. Wallace then became the hub of narrow gauge railway operations in the Coeur d'Alene camp. Each morning, when the trains came in from Mullan and Burke and crews made up the one for the mission, the depot became a scene of intense activity. And each afternoon the whole process repeated itself in reverse. At these periods the confusion among passengers was so great that the *Wallace Free Press* suggested that "To prevent people getting on the wrong train... the plan [to] be adopted here that is in vogue at other great railroad centers, that is, to place large [destination] placards on each train."[85]

The passenger service was, of course, only one facet of CdAR&N operations. To cope with the expected increase in mineral traffic, Northern Pacific ordered a powerful new narrow gauge locomotive from the Baldwin works at Philadelphia. Engine no. 4, or "the Big Four" as it was locally called, arrived in March 1889. She was of the "Mogul" (2-6-0) type, having 16 x 24 cylinders and 48-inch driving wheels. Without her tender she weighed 37 tons, of which 32 tons was available for adhesion. She was well able to haul 10 loaded ore cars over the Kingston and Pine Creek hills, but her advent demanded that many bridges be strengthened and heavier rails be laid between Wardner Junction and Wallace.[86] Unfortunately the mineral traffic for which she was built failed to materialize, for early in 1889 the price of lead dropped to less than 4 cents a pound. The Bunker Hill & Sullivan mine, which Simeon G. Reed of Portland had purchased in 1887, then shut down to await the opening of the OR&N's standard gauge Washington and Idaho road.[87]

Leaving Farmington, the Washington & Idaho line followed a branch of the Pine Creek downstream in a northwesterly direction to Seltice. It then turned northeast over slightly higher ground to Tekoa, at the forks of Hangman Creek. Following the north branch of that stream across the Idaho boundary and into the Coeur d'Alene Indian Reservation, the railway ascended gently to Lowell. It then made a sharp climb of nearly 370 feet in five miles to Watt Hill summit on the divide between Hangman Creek and the St. Joe River.

Reaching an elevation of more than 2,900 feet above sea level, the line then descended 800 feet in 10 miles to reach the south end of Coeur d'Alene Lake at Chatcolet. Crossing the mouth of the St. Joe River on a long timber-trestle bridge with a central swinging drawspan, the road followed the shore of the lake northward to Harrison. At that point it swung sharply east into the Coeur d'Alene Valley and set off on a water-level grade across the river's marshy flood plain. The W&I line intersected the narrow gauge railway just east of the mission, crossed the river, and bridged the mouth of the North Fork Coeur d'Alene River at Enaville. Crossing the south fork and recrossing the narrow gauge, it then climbed steadily along the south side of the valley to Wallace and eventually to Mullan. The most severe gradient was six miles of 1.8 percent on the westbound climb from Chatcolet to the Watt Hill summit.[88]

Due to the difficulties with the federal government the Washington & Idaho Railroad took almost two years to complete. Kilpatrick Brothers & Collins of Beatrice, Nebraska, won the main contract at the end of May 1888, and Corey Brothers, subcontractors, commenced work at Farmington early in June.[89] They made fair progress and by mid-July 1888 the first 15 miles of roadbed lay ready for track.[90] Despite the right of way dispute at Kingston and the attendant harassment by Northern Pacific forces, work also got under way in the Coeur d'Alene Valley. By mid-August 1888 J. H. Smith of Portland had more than 700 men busily engaged between Mission and Wallace. Supplied with more than 1,500 pounds of beef a day, this force also made satisfactory headway.[91] Work on the up-country section, indeed, proceeded so well that by early November 1888 many of the laborers and teams had completed their tasks and were waiting to grade the line across the reservation.[92] But most of these men were laid off at the end of November.[93] When construction resumed in March 1889 an acute shortage of manpower consequently arose, and the company had to bring workers from as far away as San Francisco.[94] In the meantime the Farmington to Tekoa section of the railway was completed and extended to Rockford as part of the Spokane Falls branch.

When track-laying commenced, early in July 1889, the steel gang could therefore start work at Tekoa.[95] Within six weeks the railway extended across the reservation to the St. Joe River, where a temporary bridge had to be erected to allow the construction and supply trains to proceed.[96] Meanwhile, as the graders approached the disputed right of way near Wallace, a last skirmish with Northern Pacific occurred. On the morning of October 3, 1889 a "small army" of men employed by Burnham & Aldridge, the Northern Pacific contractors, suddenly scaled a high bluff overlooking the scene of work and began rolling boulders down onto the unfortunate laborers below. For a few minutes pandemonium prevailed as the victors cheered and the vanquished fled.[97] The matter was quickly referred to the courts and on October 19, 1889 Judge Logan handed down a compromise decision requiring the two roads to co-exist peaceably alongside each other. Efforts were then made to finish the W&I line before the onset of winter. On December 9, 1889, as the first snow began to fall, the construction train at last pulled into Wallace.[98] Crews then ballasted and surfaced the line and on December 23, 1889 an inaugural passenger train made the round trip from the heart of the Coeur d'Alene camp to Spokane Falls and back.[99]

In March 1890 the Washington & Idaho Railroad was extended another eight miles from Wallace to an ultimate terminus at the Gold Hunter concentrator near Mullan.[100] For more than three years OR&N had toyed with the idea of pushing its road through the Bitterroot Mountains into Montana. In February 1887 rumors surfaced that the line would be extended to Butte to link up with J. J. Hill's Montana Central Railway.[101] Indeed, soon after Union Pacific leased the OR&N property it made positive moves to achieve that end. During the summer and fall of 1887 Union Pacific location engineer C. C. Van Arsdol and a party of 16 men carried out a preliminary survey for a line crossing the mountains and descending the St. Regis Valley to Missoula.[102] On July 12, 1888 the Montana Central Railway reached Butte. Rumors of an alliance between Hill and the Union Pacific then gave rise to further speculation that St. Paul, Minneapolis & Manitoba trains would run through to Portland on OR&N tracks.[103] When contractor Joseph Hansen, who had been working on the Montana Central, arrived in Wallace to take a subcontract on the W&I, the debut of his outfit was cited as clear evidence that Hill was encouraging the OR&N advance.[104] Whether that was the case or not, the Union Pacific sent a location party, led by engineer W. P. Watson, eastward over the height of land,[105] and W&I filed revised articles of incorporation making legal provision for an extension to Missoula.[106] The results of the second survey, however, were sobering, for Watson found that the length of the summit tunnel, which Van Arsdol had roughly estimated to be 5,200 feet, would in fact exceed 7,000 feet.[107]

Faced with two years of costly excavation the directors then entertained second thoughts. Despite Hill's financial assistance in the struggle against Villard, Union Pacific let the summer of 1889 pass by without physically attempting to link up with the St. Paul, Minneapolis & Manitoba/Montana Central system. In October of that year "the Manitoba" underwent financial metamorphosis, emerging as the Great Northern Railway.[108] Hill's immediate intention, it seemed, was to reach Spokane Falls and link up with the Seattle, Lakeshore, & Eastern, thus securing access to Puget Sound. The only benefit OR&N could hope to gain was an agreement to carry Great Northern traffic between Spokane Falls and Portland. Clearly there remained no reason to extend the W&I line east into Montana. For Union Pacific the time had come to quit dallying with Hill and forge a strong partnership with a Midwestern company willing to exchange long-haul traffic at Omaha. Early in November 1889 Charles Francis Adams therefore made a traffic agreement with Chicago & North Western[109] and cancelled all tariffs providing for interchange between Montana Central and Utah & Northern at Butte.[110] On November 11, 1889 Hill retaliated by diverting all his west coast business to Canadian Pacific.[111] The erstwhile entente between the Manitoba and the Union Pacific thus came to an abrupt end, and officials abandoned plans to extend the W&I line beyond Mullan. Oregon Railway & Navigation construction in the Coeur d'Alene mining camp was then anti-climactically completed by building a seven-mile-long branch line closely paralleling the narrow gauge from Wallace to Burke.[112] This line, which was laid on a 3 percent grade and reached an ultimate elevation of 3,734 feet, opened to traffic on November 18, 1890.[113]

The opening of the Washington & Idaho Railroad, and the OR&N threat to advance into Montana, at last brought railway competition to the Coeur d'Alene camp. Northern Pacific's annual report, issued in September 1889, stated that the company intended to convert the former CdAR&N lines to standard gauge and extend the Mullan branch to the Montana boundary. The report also announced that a separate subsidiary, called the Northern Pacific

& Montana Railroad, would build a new railway west from Missoula to meet the extension from Mullan on the height of land.[114] Surveys having been completed during the summer, Woods Larsen & Company of Minneapolis won a contract for the first 40 miles of the Montana section and began work immediately.[115]

The Northern Pacific Wallace branch diverged from the existing main line at De Smet Junction, seven miles west of Missoula, Montana, and followed the Clark Fork River downstream for 71 miles to St. Regis. The railway then commenced a long climb up the St. Regis de Borgia Valley into the Bitterroot Mountains. In the 37 miles between St. Regis and the Idaho line the rails gained 2,091 feet of elevation. More than half of the total climb, however, came in the last nine miles where the gradient steepened to 4 percent. From a summit 4,738 feet above sea level at St. Regis Pass (later called Lookout Pass) the line dropped just as steeply to Dorsey, Idaho. It then doubled back upon itself, descending eastward to meet the South Fork Coeur d'Alene River at Pottsville. Performing a second abrupt about-face, the railway then followed the right bank of the river down to Mullan. Although the excavation of a summit tunnel was deferred, there was one shorter tunnel and a great deal of other rock work.[116] The line also boasted many impressive timber structures, including a three-span bridge over the Clark Fork River just west of Huson, several crossings of the St. Regis River, and a succession of great, curved, multiple-tier trestles in the mountains. Of the latter the most celebrated was the 840-foot-long, 100-foot-high "S" trestle, just west of Dorsey.[117]

Completion of the 120 miles of railway from De Smet Junction to the Hunter concentrator took almost two years. The first 25 miles were relatively easy and the line opened to Petty Creek, just beyond Huson, by February 1890.[118] Six months later track stretched only another 20 miles to Quartz Creek, where the carpenters had to build a high bridge over a deep lateral ravine. The roadbed, however, lay complete to Spring Gulch with graders working all the way to the summit.[119] In the meantime work commenced on the Idaho side of the mountains. By early October 1890 crews had laid track east to Pottsville,[120] and two months later McLain & Jansen completed the section between Mullan and the divide.[121] Racing against the onset of winter, Woods Larsen & Company's men then laid a skeleton track west to the summit, and on December 22, 1890 drove a last spike.[122]

Heavy snowfall then put an end to work in the high country and for many months trains from Missoula terminated at St. Regis.[123] Construction got under way again late in the spring and the first standard gauge locomotive steamed into Mullan on July 29, 1891.[124] The operating department finally took control of the whole railway from De Smet Junction to Wallace, including the section upon which the gauge had been widened, on August 25, 1891.[125]

In the fall of 1891 the former Canyon Creek line from Wallace to Burke was also converted to standard gauge.[126] Other moves, meanwhile, were made to extend a spur up Nine Mile Creek to mines in the Sunset area. The Northern Pacific had made surveys in August 1888 for a steeply graded 13.5 mile railway from Wallace northward over the 4,200 foot Dobson Pass to Beaver Creek, but had done no further work.[127] In April 1890 impatient mine owners formed a Wallace & Sunset Railroad Company to build and operate a steam railroad from Wallace up Nine Mile Creek to a point at or near the west fork of that creek. The promoters were Patrick Clark, Charles S. Warren, Carey D. Porter, John A. Finch, George McCauley, and Charles Sweeney, all mining men, and George W. Dickenson, Northern Pacific assistant general manager at Helena.[128] Grading began in April 1891.[129] Track, however, was apparently not laid to Sunset (later Bradyville) until after the great depression of the 1890s.[130] The Northern Pacific Railway then took over and operated the line. An OR&N plan to build a rival spur up Nine Mile Creek, meanwhile, lapsed completely.

The Coeur d'Alene mining camp was opened up at an inopportune time, for the price of silver, which briefly reached $1.05 per ounce when the Sherman Silver Purchase Act passed in 1890, fell to 87 cents in 1892 and to 63 cents in 1893. Thereafter it dropped to 52 cents and hardly recovered until the United States entered the European war in 1917. Lead, meanwhile, declined to 3.3 cents per pound in 1894 and did not again reach a profitable level until 1899.[131] The opening of the OR&N standard gauge line brought a reduction in freight rates and facilitated ore shipments to other smelters, thus saving about 25 percent in combined shipping and smelting charges.[132]

The mine owners, however, faced mounting problems. In August 1891 the unions staged a successful strike for wages of $3.50 per day for all underground workers. As metal prices continued to decline, mine owners sought further concessions from the railways. To put pressure on the railroad companies, in January 1892 all the mines closed. During the following month the railways again reduced freight rates. As mining profits dwindled, however, the capitalists grew more desperate. When production resumed in April 1892 mine owners cut the wages of many underground workers to $3.00 per day, resulting in an eruption of labor strife that led to an outbreak of violence and the imposition of martial law. Before the industry could recover from these events, metal prices declined to disastrous levels. Even though the railroads offered another $2 per ton of freight relief, the Bunker Hill & Sullivan discontinued operations in March 1893 and the other mines followed suit four months later.[133] Throughout this period the financial condition of the Northern Pacific Railroad deteriorated steadily. The proposed railway from Coeur d'Alene City through Fourth of July Canyon to the mission, therefore, was never built. Nor was Corbin's line from the mission to Wallace ever converted to standard gauge. As the clouds of a great depression gathered, the company also shelved plans to drive a tunnel under St. Regis Pass, and the prospect of Wallace being placed on a through route receded into the distant future.[134]

The enormous cost of building the railway over the Bitterroot Mountains was later cited as a significant factor in the 1893 collapse of the Northern Pacific Railroad Company.[135] Henry Villard wrote in his memoirs that when he made his last official tour of inspection in 1891, the most alarming impression of all

> was the revelation of the weight of the load that had been put upon the company by the purchase and construction of the longer branch lines in Montana and Washington,... representing a total investment in cash and bonds not far from $30,000,000 which together hardly earned operating expenses. The acquisition and building of these disappointing lines had in a few years absorbed the large amount of consolidated bonds set aside for construction purposes, which had been assumed to be sufficient for all needs in that direction for a long time.[136]

The advance into the Coeur d'Alene mining camp cost the old railroad companies dearly. One entrepreneur, however, emerged with an enhanced image and capital enough to propel himself into other ventures. Having sold the Coeur d'Alene Railway & Navigation Company to the Northern Pacific, Daniel C. Corbin settled in

Spokane Falls and formed an alliance with local capitalists. He then set out to extend that city's commercial influence far into the northern hinterland, thus founding what he and his fellow promoters were ever wont to call their "Inland Empire."

Chapter Ten

Oregon Railway Extensions

The OR&N advance to the north and east began with a retreat from Eureka Flat and postponement of plans to reach Lewiston. The stage was first set for these events in the summer of 1886 when surveys were made for a branch westward from Prescott down the Touchet Valley to Winnett Canyon to serve the upper Eureka Flat.[1] In December of that year OR&N right of way agent A. S. Watt promised farmers that the line would be built during the next season.[2] But before any work could be done, circumstances changed.

In April 1887 the Union Pacific Railway Company leased the OR&N system. Union Pacific president Charles Francis Adams, interested in land near Lewiston, Idaho, wanted to build a railroad to serve that area.[3] Indeed he may well have wished to place his development at Concord (Clarkston, Washington) upon an entirely new main line, by-passing the Blue Mountains altogether. Even before the OR&N lease was signed, Union Pacific survey parties went out to examine the Snake River Valley. In mid-April 1887 location engineer A. W. Nutting started downstream from Lewiston to Ainsworth, while T. C. Clark and C. C. Van Arsdol, setting out respectively from Weiser and Lewiston, reconnoitered routes through the deep canyons further south.[4] Simultaneously, an OR&N party, led by John F. Stevens, attempted to find a low-cost line from Pomeroy to Lewiston by way of Alpowai Ridge.[5]

These surveys demonstrated that a railway down Hells Canyon of the Snake River, or along the Weiser and Little Salmon rivers, would be prohibitively expensive. To the west of Lewiston a line following the Snake River to Ainsworth would avoid the steep climb over Alpowai Ridge, but it too would cost a lot of money.

However, a compromise solution was available. A low-cost railroad could be built from Wallula, by way of Eureka Flat, to a crossing of the Snake River at Riparia, thus reducing the length and cost of the line along the river.[6] This road, moreover, could tap the enormous grain-growing potential of Eureka Flat and make good on Watt's promises to local farmers. It was an admirable solution, but financial difficulties encountered in August 1887 forced the company to defer construction. Adams nevertheless made sure, when negotiating the terms of the joint lease agreement with Northern Pacific, that its territorial provisions would allow the OR&N to use the north bank of the Snake River to reach Lewiston.[7]

The joint lease was ratified in January 1888 but was very soon ruptured. In March 1888 George W. Hunt, aided and abetted by the Wright family, set out to extend the pseudo-independent Oregon & Washington Territory Railroad from Wallula to Walla Walla by way of Eureka Flat, thus building on the very line Union Pacific intended to use for the railway to Lewiston. To make matters worse the Eureka Flat farmers, upset by the OR&N failure to complete a railroad in time to move the 1887 crop, welcomed Hunt with open arms. Jubilantly they gave him all the land he wanted and refused to sell any to the Oregon company.[8]

Although Portland advocates of a railway to the Coeur d'Alene mines pressed Adams hard, he had nevertheless been quite willing to abide by the negotiated terms of the joint lease. Now he began to have second thoughts! If Henry Villard could not prevent Northern Pacific from violating the agreement, why should OR&N continue to respect it? One more outrage proved enough to drive him into the Portland camp. On April 19, 1888 the Northern Pacific board adopted a resolution by Thomas F. Oakes objecting to construction of the proposed OR&N line along the north bank of the Snake River, noting that it would closely parallel not only the Columbia & Palouse line, due to revert to Northern Pacific as part of the joint lease agreement, but also the new Genesee extension of the Spokane & Palouse.[9]

Adams was thunderstruck, for on September 28, 1887 both Oakes and Robert Harris had specifically agreed to the Lewiston line. Determined to retaliate for this unwarranted attack upon his own cherished scheme, the Union Pacific president angrily threw in his lot with Elijah Smith and the Portlanders. As soon as the

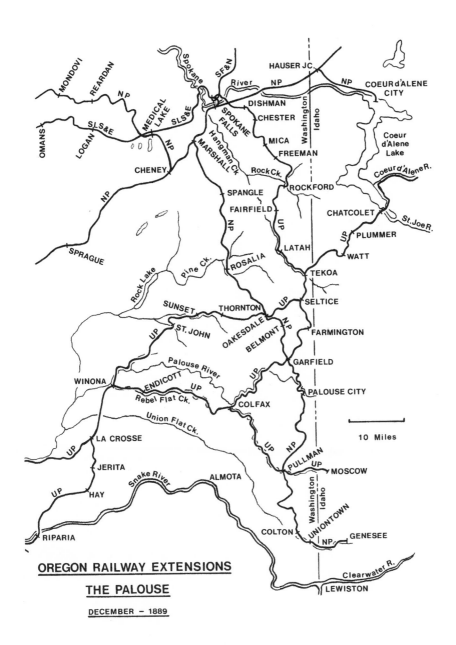

OREGON RAILWAY EXTENSIONS

THE PALOUSE

DECEMBER — 1889

United States Congress passed the bill granting the Washington & Idaho Railroad right of way across the Coeur d'Alene Indian Reservation, Adams shelved the Lewiston project, and forces assembled at Prescott to work on Eureka Flat were suddenly ordered north.[10] During the last week of May 1888 a new OR&N subsidiary, named the Oregon Railway Extension Company, was formed to complete the previously abandoned link between Texas Ferry and the Columbia & Palouse road and build a new railway from Dutch Flat, 63 miles east of Palouse Junction, to a point five miles north of Farmington on the Washington & Idaho Railroad. Men and teams quickly went to work to repair the old roadbed along the Alkali Flat Creek and thrust the W&I line northward from Farmington.

The connecting link with the Columbia & Palouse road was 24 miles long.[11] Starting from an elevation of 550 feet on the north bank of the Snake River opposite Riparia,[12] the railway ascended about 1,050 feet in 19.5 miles to a summit over 1,600 feet above sea level just north of Jerita. It then gradually descended to an elevation of less than 1,500 feet at La Crosse. The most difficult part of the northbound climb was three miles at 1.7 percent between Hay and Jerita.[13]

By mid-June 1888, 30 teams were at work repairing the old Alkali Flat Creek grade.[14] Early in July the force was increased to "several hundred men,"[15] and during the next month more were brought up. Track laying began before the end of July and by August 18 all but six miles of the railway were finished.[16] During the next week carpenters completed several trestles and the line was made ready for use.[17] In the meantime a temporary bridge was thrown across the Snake River at Riparia.

Work on the Snake River crossing began in April 1888 when OR&N engineers carried out a series of trial borings on the river bottom.[18] Early in May a large quantity of heavy timber was brought up,[19] and a month later a construction contract was let. The temporary piling bridge was erected so rapidly that the construction train was able to cross over to the north bank on July 28.[20] The bridge was ready for all traffic by August 23[21] and a regular train service between Pendleton and Farmington was inaugurated on Wednesday September 5, 1888.[22] In the meantime, work began on the permanent bridge, which was to consist of three iron spans, including a swinging drawspan at the south end, all resting on masonry piers

downtown area.[53] Building materials were in great demand and for the time being the railroad had to make do with temporary premises. Nevertheless, the Union Depot Company of Spokane Falls,[54] formed on July 9, 1889, made grandiose plans that blossomed magnificently in the spring of 1890. Situated on the north bank of the Spokane River, just above the falls, the new passenger depot, built to serve both the OR&N and the Seattle, Lake Shore, & Eastern, consisted of an ornate two-story wooden building 111 feet long and 55 feet wide. Elaborately finished in Oregon fir and cedar with cut shingles in belt-court courses, it was embellished with "fine large bay windows" and "a handsome tower" offering "a fine view of the surrounding country." At the railway side of the building a full-length porch, or awning, extended out to the track. Horse-drawn carriages reached the depot by a ramp leading down from the Normandy Street bridge, and did not have to cross the railway at grade. A freight shed 47 feet wide by 247 feet long stood on the opposite side of the tracks from the passenger depot in an area blasted out of solid rock.[55]

By mid-May 1890 the Union Depot handled two OR&N trains daily each way between Spokane Falls and Pendleton. Spokane passengers could then take advantage of through reclining-chair and sleeping-car service to Portland, and connect at Pendleton with trains bound for Omaha and Chicago by "The Short Route."[56]

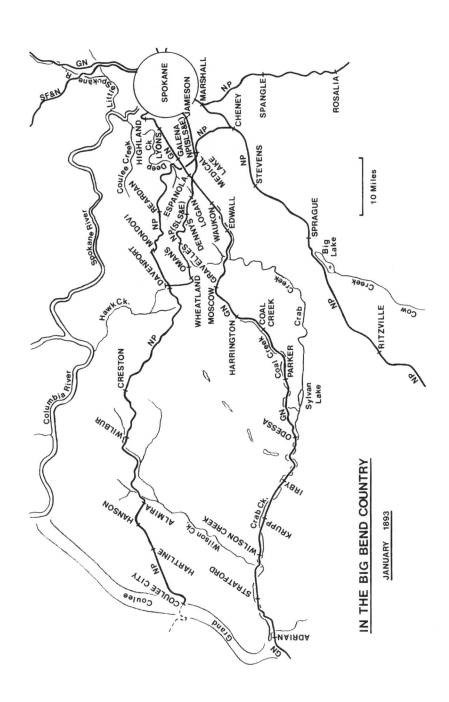

IN THE BIG BEND COUNTRY

JANUARY 1893

Chapter Eleven

In the Big Bend

During the 1880s the agricultural settlement of the country west of Spokane Falls was delayed by the lack of a branch line railway serving Lincoln and Douglas counties. Not until the construction of a rival trunk railroad appeared imminent did Northern Pacific make any attempt to open up the area. Local promoters, meanwhile, failed to translate their own limited ambitions into roadbed and track. Neither the Farmington, Cheney & Big Bend proposal[1] of 1882, or the Sprague & Big Bend scheme[2] of 1886 reached the construction stage. Eventually, however, an alliance between Seattle residents and Eastern financiers presented Northern Pacific with a serious challenge. Early in the summer of 1888 the Seattle, Lake Shore & Eastern Railway Company set out to build a railroad west from Spokane Falls to Davenport, and Northern Pacific quickly followed suit with a line from Cheney.

In 1872 the Northern Pacific decision to establish a western terminus at Tacoma threatened other Puget Sound communities. The advent of the Oregon Improvement Company, however, brought Seattle a share of regional development and fostered that city's continued growth. In October 1881 Henry Villard promised to build a railroad linking Seattle with Tacoma and Portland. Construction, however, proceeded slowly. During the following year Northern Pacific built seven miles of railway from Meeker Junction, on the Wilkeson branch, to Stuck. An Oregon & Transcontinental subsidiary named Puget Sound Shore Railroad then undertook the remainder of the work. Puget Sound Shore extended the line 14 miles from Stuck to Black River Junction in 1883 and built a final 10 miles paralleling the narrow gauge Columbia & Puget

Sound Railway into Seattle early in 1884. The dissolution of Henry Villard's empire then left the sections north and south of Stuck in separate hands. Throughout the summer of 1884 the NPRR and O&T companies bickered over ownership, and for some time the trains were halted altogether. A group of local businessmen in Seattle wishing to develop coal and iron prospects in the vicinity of Snoqualmie Pass put this dissatisfaction to good advantage. Headed by Judge Thomas Burke, these gentlemen deliberately nourished local ill feeling toward the Northern Pacific, attempting to create a climate favorable to the promotion of an independent railway serving their own interests. In September 1884 a Northern Pacific subsidiary, ponderously named Northern Pacific & Puget Sound Shore Railroad, was formed to own and operate the Meeker to Seattle line, and a train service of sorts resumed. Seattle nevertheless remained at a disadvantage. Trains on the branch line failed to connect with those to Portland, and consignments of freight were deliberately delayed. Consequently, just as soon as Burke and his associates promoted an independent railway, Seattle residents backed it to the limit of their resources.[3]

The Seattle, Lake Shore & Eastern Railway Company was incorporated with an authorized capital stock of $5 million at Seattle on April 15, 1885. The company proposed to build and operate a railroad from Seattle to Walla Walla, with a branch line to Spokane Falls. Provision was also made for subsequent railway extensions, for the operation of riverboat and telegraph lines, and for land development. The promoters included Thomas Burke, Daniel H. Gilman, John Leary, David Denny, J. R. McDonald, Dr. T. T. Minor, G. Morris Haller, and Frank Osgood, all of Seattle. McDonald, a local lumberman, became president, Minor vice president, Burke secretary and legal counsel, and Gilman general manager.[4]

When the SLS&E was first formed, the population of Seattle hardly exceeded 7,000. Given the limited number of local bankers and the fact that money for railroad construction was then in great demand, the promoters had to seek the support of wealthy capitalists. Gilman, a New Yorker and a graduate of Columbia University Law School, went east to establish the appropriate connections. Early in 1886 he aroused the interest of Jameson, Smith & Cotting, New York bankers, and persuaded them to form a syndicate to finance the Seattle railway.[5]

The Seattle, Lake Shore & Eastern Railway Company was to issue $15,000 stock and $25,000 six-percent first-mortgage bonds per mile of railroad, most of which were to be handed over to the auxiliary Puget Sound Construction Company as successive sections of the line were completed. Puget Sound Construction was to use the railway company securities as collateral to obtain short-term loans furnishing the cash needed to pay subcontractors who would build the railway. In accordance with classic "construction company" financing, the securities were to be redeemed and sold as the loans were paid off, thus guaranteeing the promoters a short-term profit. The railway company would then be left to service the bonded debt and provide shareholders with future dividends. For the first 40 miles between Seattle and the Squak coal mines, Puget Sound Construction was to receive $10,000 stock and $20,000 bonds per mile. Thereafter the "price" would increase to $12,000 stock and $25,000 bonds per mile. Puget Sound Construction, meanwhile, called for subscriptions to its own stock, offering shareholders SLS&E securities to the extent of $8,000 stock and $15,000 bonds for every $10,000 cash paid in.[6] At the end of December 1886 Gilman announced that as soon as land transactions had been finalized work would begin, and that $100,000 would be spent every month for the next eight months.[7] The railway, he rashly claimed, would be completed to Spokane Falls in two years.[8]

Starting out from Mill Street in Seattle, the railway skirted the harbor to Smith's Cove in North Seattle, where the company secured 300 acres of land and planned to build a roundhouse, shops, and yards. Crossing the outlet of Lake Union the line followed the north shore of Lake Washington to a large lumber camp at Windsor (at or near present day Bothell). It then turned south through the hopyards of the Squak (Sammamish) Valley to the colliery town of Gilman (now Issaquah), where the Seattle Coal & Iron Company was preparing to work four seams of coal. Beyond Gilman the line crossed the divide between the Squak and Snoqualmie rivers and descended to Falls City.

The projected route then lay through Snoqualmie Pass to Ellensburg and southeast to a crossing of the Columbia River at Priest Rapids, where it would connect with steamboats plying the river in each direction. Thence the line followed a largely undefined route north and east to Spokane Falls. The total distance from Seattle was estimated to be about 326 miles.[9]

Construction began on March 21, 1887[10] and by the end of October that same year 42 miles of line had been opened between Seattle and the Gilman mines.[11] Nothing then happened until the following spring when the company's surveyors suddenly appeared in eastern Washington. On March 23, 1888 the *Davenport Times* noted that a party of 16 men "with fine camp and travelling equipment" were on John Hogan's farm south of town, working westward. A right of way agent, moreover, was accompanying the engineers and buying land as the survey progressed.[12] An explanation for this activity was not long delayed. On Saturday, April 7, 1888, SLS&E president J. R. McDonald, attorney Thomas Burke, and newly appointed chief engineer Paul F. Mohr arrived in Spokane Falls to present the board of trade with a proposition. They would build their road west from the city and start work within 30 days, provided local residents purchased $175,000 worth of the company's stock.[13] Responding enthusiastically, Spokane merchants immediately formed a subscription committee to raise a subsidy for building 40 miles of railway, to be brought into operation on or before December 1, 1888. Ten percent of the money would be paid at the commencement of construction and the remainder in four installments as grading and track laying progressed. The board of trade committee began an active canvas of the city on April 12 and within six days had garnered pledges for all the money.[14] The company then let a contract to Burns & Chapman[15] for the construction of 60 miles of railway, and on Thursday May 3, 1888 subcontractors began work on the west side of Hangman Creek.[16]

The Spokane to Davenport section of the SLS&E set out northeastward from a junction with the Northern Pacific Railroad a quarter of a mile east of the existing Spokane Falls depot. Swinging around immediately to the northwest the line crossed the Spokane River just above Division Street and headed west to the Seattle company's own depot grounds on the north side. Leaving the city, the railway ran northwest across Monroe and Boone streets to a point overlooking the canyon and then descended precariously northwards to a second crossing of the river near the big bend. Traversing a huge timber bridge and turning south, it climbed circuitously out of the canyon by way of Greenwood

Cemetery and Garden Springs. Attaining higher ground near Windsor Prairie it then pursued a westerly course to Medical Lake. Passing to the north of the lakes the railway wended its way through the hills to a point named Wheatdale, five miles south of Davenport. Turning abruptly north it then made a beeline for the Big Bend metropolis, entering the municipal precincts near the existing schoolhouse.[17]

As soon as Burns & Chapman had begun work at the Spokane end of the line, the Eastern firm of Ryan & McDonald was awarded a much larger contract for the construction of 225 miles of railway between a point 51 miles from Seattle and the end of the Spokane Division near Davenport.[18] The line was to include a tunnel under the summit of Snoqualmie Pass and an iron bridge across the Columbia River. The total cost was estimated to be $5 million and the contractors were to have the road finished by May 17, 1890. Plans, meanwhile, were made to exploit "the rich anthracite and iron resources of the Cascades" which, it was hoped, would provide raw materials for a steel works, to be set up near Falls City by the Moss Bay Iron & Steel Company of Cumberland, England.[19]

Northern Pacific, meanwhile, had already laid out a line across the Big Bend country. In December 1887 Major J. I. Jamieson and two survey parties made a thorough examination of the terrain between Cheney and Davenport[20] and selected a route locally described as follows:

> It runs from Cheney to Medical Lake, thence to old town of Fairweather, thence passing Mr. Buckman's farm to Charlie Nelson's, following the draw into Potman Flat, thence on a nearly level road passing through Davenport south of the school building and south of City Hotel.[21]

On March 25, 1888 a speculative announcement from Cheney gave notice of Northern Pacific's imminent reaction to the Seattle, Lake Shore & Eastern threat, averring that: "The iron horse, the great leveller of all solid advancement, will soon go shrieking out from the confines of this town over the boundless stretches of agricultural lands reaching away towards the Grand Coulee of the Columbia."[22]

The line, it was said, had already been located, with construction expected to commence within 30 days. In fact, Northern Pacific only began to purchase the right of way in mid-May, and work did not get under way at Cheney until July 10, 1888. In the meantime NP crossed swords with SLS&E elsewhere.

Fifty miles west of Davenport the Interior plain is bisected by a great dry valley called the Grand Coulee, extending all the way southward from the Columbia River to the Quincy flatlands. Towards its northern end the coulee is flanked on its west side by high lava cliffs, while to the south, below Dry Falls, it becomes a deep bilateral trench. Any east-west route must therefore cross it at the one place, just above the Dry Falls, where an easy approach from the east faces a partial break in the rock wall to the west.

In June 1888 this remote and desolate location, then called McEntee's Crossing of the Grand Coulee, was suddenly invaded by rival railway construction forces and became the scene of a boisterous contest for right of way. The trouble first arose on the east side of the coulee, where the two lines intersected. At that point the SLS&E roadbed was graded at a six-foot higher elevation, leaving Northern Pacific without either a crossing or an underpass. As fast as the Seattle company's contractors threw up an embankment, therefore, Northern Pacific forces removed it. Tempers wore thin, and when both outfits tried to seize a narrow gap in a rocky ridge a mile and a half further west, a more serious confrontation ensued. The SLS&E forces at first secured the right of way, but those working for the NP dislodged them "by putting in blasts about four feet from where they were working and firing them off every few minutes." As soon as the flying debris from each explosion fell to the ground the rival gangs of men scrambled for advantage, and the Northern Pacific crowd eventually gained the day. Both sides then rushed up reinforcements and hired every man and team that came along. Northern Pacific boosted wages to $2.25 for day work and $3.25 for nights, and as they offered a firmer guarantee of payment, many SLS&E men deserted and crossed the lines. Altogether, about 360 men were involved in the goings-on at Grand Coulee, and the NP eventually employed a hundred of them, day and night, merely to guard the recaptured section of roadbed.[23]

At Spokane Falls, meanwhile, Northern Pacific secured a temporary injunction preventing SLS&E from completing the connecting link south of the Spokane River. Without waiting for a second court hearing they laid a spur track from their main line down the river bank, thus blocking SLS&E passage and holding up delivery of that company's rails and rolling stock. On July 30, 1888 the Seattle company obtained a counter-injunction ordering Northern Pacific to cooperate, and by the end of August both disputes had been settled out of court. At the Grand Coulee, SLS&E changed its grade to facilitate an intersection, and Northern Pacific allowed it an 18 feet right of way through the constricted zone further west. And at Spokane Falls, NP allowed the Seattle company to link up with the main line, provided NP could use the connection to reach the SLS&E depot.[24] These differences being settled, construction of the rival roads to Davenport proceeded apace.

By the end of June 1888 work on the east end of the SLS&E was well underway. In the Spokane River canyon, to the west of the city, rock work was quite heavy; it took most of the summer to grade the first 10 miles of the line. On the uplands further west the going became easier, and by early August workers had completed the roadbed through Medical Lake to Wheatdale.[25] Construction of the bridge at the lower crossing of the Spokane River began late in June and went on until the end of October. The bridge was 2,000 feet long and up to 150 feet high, consisting of two 156-foot, Howe-truss spans and multiple-tier approach trestles. Every sawmill in Spokane and vicinity, and others on the coast, worked to supply the three million board feet of lumber required to build it.[26]

As the SLS&E roadbed took shape and the big bridge grew, Eastern manufacturers delivered rails and rolling stock. A first shipment of iron arrived in Spokane early in August 1888 aboard 30 flat and 20 box cars built by the Peninsula Box Car Company of Detroit, Michigan. More rails came during the following month, and on September 20, 1888 engine bells with a distinctive tone alerted the local populace to the arrival of two new 43-ton Rhode Island locomotives. At Chicago, Illinois, meanwhile, the Pullman Car Company outshopped a pair of passenger coaches and a combination car similar to those already in use between Seattle and Squak Valley.[27]

The SLS&E began to lay track west from Spokane Falls late in September 1888. One steel gang started out from the junction with the Northern Pacific and another, suppled by wagon train, laid rails on the west side of the canyon. As soon as the big bridge was opened, on November 2, 1888, the supply trains began to run all the way through to Windsor Prairie and the advance across the plateau proceeded rapidly. On November 20 railroad officials and

Spokane Falls dignitaries, who traveled west in the magnificent business car *Snoqualmie*, found that the railroad had been completed to Willow Springs. For the remainder of that month track was laid at a rate of two miles a day, and on December 3, 1888 the construction train reached Wheatdale.[28] The company then suspended construction and Davenport residents had to commute five miles to the railhead. Many suspected that SLS&E planned to create a new town at Wheatdale, and they may well have been right. Other events, however, precluded any such outcome.

Even before the railway reached Wheatdale there were indications that the Seattle company's plans were in a state of flux. In August 1888 Ryan & McDonald withdrew from their contract.[29] Then, on October 5, *Railroad Gazette* reported that instead of going through Snoqualmie Pass the main line to the east would follow the Snohomish River to Cady's Pass and reach the Columbia by way of the Wenatchee River. The existing road west of the mountains would then be used to develop the Cascade coal and iron deposits.[30] Whatever the directors' intentions, it soon became evident that the company was short of money. On January 19, 1889 a gang of 40 men, working on the depot grounds at Spokane Falls, laid down their tools and demanded two months unpaid wages. Their protest, however, gained them no more than superintendent Theo Reid's sympathy and an assurance that the company was trying hard to float another bond issue.[31] The financial negotiations to which Reid referred went on for another three months and were less than wholly successful. As a last resort the auxiliary Seattle & Eastern Construction Company, successor to Puget Sound Construction, increased its capital stock from $1 million to $3 million and offered its own shares to the public as a bonus for subscribing to the railroad company's bonds.[32] At that point it became clear that any money so raised would be used, not to finish the main line through the Cascades, but rather to provide a coastal link with Canadian Pacific.

In March 1888 the Seattle, Lake Shore & Eastern acquired the uncompleted Seattle & West Coast Railway extending 14 miles from Snohomish Junction (Woodinville), on the SLS&E line, northward to Snohomish.[33] This spur, opened to traffic on July 16, 1888,[34] provided the "Lake Shore" with the first part of a hundred-mile-long extension to the international boundary at Sumas. For an impecunious company with lingering ambitions, a connection with

Canadian Pacific was an attractive proposition. On May 20, 1889, therefore, orders were given to begin work north of Snohomish. The company then concentrated what effort it could afford on the northern route and all activity in the Interior came to a complete halt.[35]

Northern Pacific's Central Washington branch left the main line in a northeasterly direction at Cheney. Turning immediately north it passed over slightly higher ground to Medical Lake, where it swung westward and intersected the SLS&E line. Resuming a northerly course it climbed briefly to another height of land and then descended northeastward into the valley of Deep Creek, a tributary of the Spokane River. Crossing the creek on a timber trestle bridge 700 feet long and up to 40 feet high, the line swung around to the west and climbed out of the gulch onto the highest part of the plateau. It then pursued a roller coaster course northwestward through Reardan, Mondovi, and Davenport, to Creston. From that point it made a long descent to the Grand Coulee. Between Creston and Almira, on the headwaters of Wilson Creek, the railway dropped 531 feet in 23 miles. Then there was a steep four-mile climb to an intervening height of land at Hanson's Siding, followed by a sharp descent to flatter ground at Hartline. Reaching the edge of the Grand Coulee the road finally fell rapidly southward to an interim terminus at McEntee's Crossing, where a town named Coulee City was platted.

The Central Washington branch, as built on the above route, deviated widely from Major Jamieson's original survey. The deviations, moreover, appear to have been neither necessary nor beneficial, being made merely for the purposes of land speculation by railroad company officials. There was, for example, no need for the line to pursue a northerly course to elevations of more than 2,500 feet between Deep Creek and Reardan, and certainly no need for the steep climb northwest from Almira to Hanson. So blatant, indeed, was the dishonesty of the persons involved that some of the changes were made after part of the original line had been graded.[36]

The company let the contract for the first 40 miles of the Central Washington branch to George W. Hunt, whose men began to assemble at Cheney late in August 1888. Work was slow getting under way but they completed the roadbed to Davenport before the end of the year. Tracklaying began at Cheney on October 26, 1888 and proceeded at such a leisurely pace that the construction train did not reach Davenport until February 14, 1889. Workmen resumed grading in July 1889, and during that season H. Kirkendall extended the railway through Wilbur to Almira. The final section between Almira and Coulee City was built in the summer of 1890 and completed in October of that year.[37] Several miles of previously graded roadbed crossing the coulee and ascending its west flank were then left to await a further extension to Waterville and the Okanogan mines.[38]

Davenport residents, determined not to allow the Northern Pacific a free hand in Lincoln County, decided that if need be they would subsidize construction of the last five miles of the SLS&E line. On July 21, 1889 a deputation from Davenport met with Paul Mohr at Spokane Falls. He told them that if they would provide $15,000 and free right of way from Wheatdale, the road would be completed in 30 days. After several weeks of animated discussion the townspeople came up with a counter proposal. If the railway company would supply the materials and lay the track, the community would furnish the land and prepare the roadbed. The company accepted this proposition, and on August 11, 1889 Davenport launched a fundraising campaign.[39] Work resumed early in September 1889 and by October 8 track had been laid to an intersection with the Northern Pacific line just south of town.[40] At that point the steel gang found the crossing blocked by a locomotive, which was not removed until the NP maintenance-of-way department recovered track hardware allegedly stolen by the Seattle company from the yard at Medical Lake.[41] The railway was then completed, and on Thursday, October 17, 1889 the SLS&E began to run regular passenger trains between Davenport and Spokane Falls[42] on the following schedule:[43]

7:30 a.m.	Davenport	5:45 p.m.
7:45	Wheatdale	5:31
7:52	Oman's	5:23
8:05	Gravelles	5:10
8:25	Denny's	4:50
8:35	Logan	4:40
9:10	Medical Lake	4:15
9:30	Jameson	3:50
10:02	Greenwood	3:20
10:10	Alta Vista	3:10
10:20 a.m.	Spokane	3:00 p.m.

After completing the line to Davenport, the Seattle, Lake Shore & Eastern Railway retained its independence for less than a year. During that period, moreover, the Spokane Division was blockaded by snow for nearly three months. Train service was suspended on December 31, 1889,[44] and by the end of January 1890 the road was reported as "buried out of sight." The only activity was that manifested by the engine stationed at Davenport, which was said to emerge from its shed occasionally "and run up and down the track for exercise."[45] On March 9, 1890 the *Spokane Falls Review* reported that frozen snow drifts would keep the railway closed until the spring thaw.[46] Fortunately, during the next two weeks the weather moderated and on March 22, 1890 train service was resumed.[47] By that time, however, the company's days were numbered.

Robert C. Nesbit has ably demonstrated in his biography of Judge Thomas Burke that the Eastern financiers' willingness to put up money failed to keep pace with the Seattle promoters' spendthrift ambitions. When the bankers insisted upon restraint the construction company could not generate enough profit to support ancillary ventures. Burke and Gilman, who had spent too much money on real estate promotion and not enough on railway construction, then found themselves financially embarrassed. Debts went unpaid, credit dried up, and work came to a halt.[48] During the summer of 1889 the principal Seattle participants quietly withdrew, leaving the New York bankers to dispose of the property as best they could.[49] In October 1889 the St. Paul, Minneapolis & Manitoba Railroad burst into full flower as the Great Northern Railway and announced plans for a Puget Sound extension. From the outset it was widely assumed that James J. Hill would buy up the SLS&E and use it to reach Seattle. In March 1890 he formed a west coast subsidiary called Seattle & Montana Railroad, with Burke and Gilman as officers, and ordered his engineers to carry out a careful examination of the SLS&E property.[50] Thoroughly alarmed, Northern Pacific then hastened to secure a controlling interest in the Seattle company. A deal was worked out early in June 1890[51] and on July 21 of that year Thomas F. Oakes announced that the Northern Pacific Railroad Company had agreed to purchase $3 million worth of the $5 million total stock of the Seattle, Lake Shore & Eastern Railway Company.[52] They had also agreed to lease the property on the basis of a guarantee of 6 ³/₄ percent interest not only on the outstanding bonds but also on those still to be issued for the Canadian extension. The annual rental, he said, would amount to about $800,000. H. O. Armour, Thomas Logan, and Edward D. Chester signed the contract on behalf of the Seattle company.

For the time being the coastal sections of the SLS&E retained separate identity. The Northern Pacific, however, took over the Spokane Division on September 23, 1890 and operated it as the Spokane Branch of the NPRR Idaho Division.[53] Within a short time train service was reduced to three round trips a week between Medical Lake and Davenport, and the first 22 miles of the line went unused. Northern Pacific completed the stock purchase and gained full control of the SLS&E on March 14, 1892. Northern Pacific officers were then appointed, but the coastal section between Seattle and the Canadian border, opened on April 10, 1891, continued to retain its old name.[54] In 1893 Northern Pacific Railroad found itself unable to meet the obligations on the bonds and had to relinquish control. In March 1896 the former SLS&E property as a whole was ordered sold at foreclosure, and in July of that year it was conveyed to a committee of former bond holders. Two separate companies were then set up. The coastal section was resurrected as the Seattle & International Railroad and the Spokane Division became the Spokane & Seattle Railroad. In January 1898 the new Northern Pacific Railway Company gained control of the Seattle & International, thus preventing its sale to Canadian Pacific. The disgruntled members of the reorganization committee then tore up the track on the Spokane & Seattle line and sold the rails. Northern Pacific acquired the Medical Lake to Davenport section in March 1899 and secured the remainder in October 1900.[55] Four years later, however, the roadbed of the Spokane to Medical Lake section was sold to the Washington Water Power Company, which operated 13¹/₂ miles of it as an electric interurban railway,[56] functioning until 1922. The last operating remnant of the Spokane Division was 18 miles of line between Davenport and a point named Eleanor, which Northern Pacific relaid with track at some date unknown.[57] This section was occasionally used for box car grain traffic until 1982. Burlington Northern finally lifted the track in 1983.[58]

Other railway extensions in the Big Bend country, projected between 1888 and 1891, failed to produce more than a few isolated earthworks. Northern Pacific made surveys for a line from Coulee City by way of Waterville to the Columbia River, and considered pushing it through to the Conconully mines.[59] In July 1890 Chief Engineer J. W. Kendrick reportedly announced that the Central Washington branch would be extended to the Columbia River that year. Nothing, however, happened, and the last heard of the project was a statement of March 1891 declaring the surveys to have been "entirely preliminary."[60]

Pseudo-independent activity, meanwhile, centered upon Ellensburg. In the spring of 1888, Tacoma promoters, including L. E. Post and J. C. Nixon, who may have been secretly sponsored by Northern Pacific with a view to harassing the SLS&E, incorporated the Tacoma, Ellensburg & Conconully Railway & Navigation Company, with the declared object of building a railroad 32 miles from Ellensburg to Port Eaton and operating steamboats on the Columbia River.[61] During the next year the promoters developed more grandiose plans for a cross-country connection east of the Columbia, linking Ellensburg with Lind and forming a cutoff shortening the Northern Pacific mainline by no less than 80 miles. In May 1889 they announced that they had secured financial backing and that the railway west of the river would be built immediately. The firm was then re-incorporated as the Ellensburg & North Eastern Railway. Contractor John Clifden of Ellensburg graded the first 10 miles of the road, extending from Ellensburg across the Kittitas Valley towards Johnson's Creek Pass, in the fall of 1889. In October of that year rails and ties were reported to have been ordered, and early in 1890 work on the bridges was to have been started immediately.[62] What then happened remains a mystery. It may not be unreasonable to suppose, however, that the Northern Pacific takeover of the SLS&E removed any further necessity for occupying the ground. As a point of interest, the Ellensburg & North Eastern Railway route, referred to in 1889-1890 as "the Hypotenuse Railroad," was later used by the Puget Sound extension of the Chicago, Milwaukee & St. Paul Railroad.

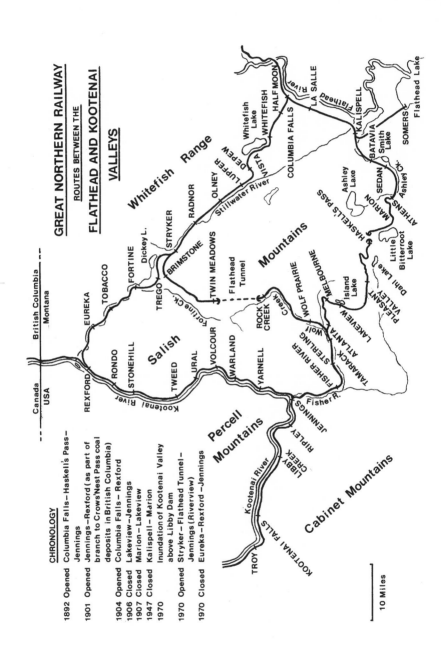

GREAT NORTHERN RAILWAY
ROUTES BETWEEN THE
FLATHEAD AND KOOTENAI
VALLEYS

CHRONOLOGY

1892 Opened Columbia Falls – Haskell's Pass –
Jennings

1901 Opened Jennings – Rexford (as part of
branch to Crows'Nest Pass coal
deposits in British Columbia)

1904 Opened Columbia Falls – Rexford
1906 Closed Lakeview – Jennings
1907 Closed Marion – Lakeview
1947 Closed Kalispell – Marion
1970 Inundation of Kootenai Valley
above Libby Dam

1970 Opened Stryker – Flathead Tunnel –
Jennings (Riverview)

1970 Closed Eureka – Rexford – Jennings

10 Miles

The "Big Four" 2-6-0 locomotive built by the Baldwin Locomotive Works, Philadelphia, for the three-foot gauge Coeur d'Alene Railway & Navigation Company after the Northern Pacific takeover in 1888. *Courtesy Washington State University Library, Pullman, #70-0076.*

Northern Pacific Railroad "Decapod" locomotive No. 500 at Ellensburg, Washington, in 1886 or 1887. This engine was the first of two built specifically for the Stampede Pass switchback line. *Courtesy Oregon Historical Society, Portland, Neg. #49225.*

Saltese, chief of the Coeur d'Alene Indians at the time the Union Pacific Railway built across the reservation to Wallace and Mullan, Idaho, 1888-1890. Photo taken in 1900. *Courtesy Eastern Washington State Historical Society, Spokane, #L93-72.33.*

George W. Hunt of Corvallis, Oregon, was contractor during the construction of the Northern Pacific and the Oregon Railway & Navigation lines in the interior Northwest, 1884-1887. He served as president of the Oregon & Washington Railway, 1887-1891. *Courtesy Oregon Historical Society, Portland, Neg. #88153.*

The bridge at the second crossing of the Yakima River, Northern Pacific Railroad, looking south. *Courtesy Oregon Historical Society, Portland, Neg. #73893.*

The Snake River bridge at Riparia, Washington, Union Pacific Railroad, looking north, *c.* 1915. *Courtesy Washington State University Library, Pullman, Hutchison #119-55.*

An excursion train on the Spokane Falls & Idaho Railroad between Hauser Junction and Coeur d'Alene, Idaho. The locomotive is lettered "Spokane & Palouse." *Courtesy Eastern Washington State Historical Society, Spokane, #4053.*

Head-on collision at Pullman, Washington, Northern Pacific Railroad, December 1891. Both trains were freight and there were no injuries. The view is northward with the OR&N depot faintly visible in the background. *Courtesy Washington State University Library, Pullman, #78-361.*

Bridge collapse, just west of Spokane, Northern Pacific Railroad, July 13, 1891. The train was a livestock extra. The locomotive fireman was killed. *Courtesy Eastern Washington State Historical Society, Spokane, #4150.*

At Hope, Idaho, Northern Pacific Railroad, looking west, in 1891. *Courtesy Haynes Foundation Collection, Montana Historical Society, Helena, #H-2632.*

The arrival of a Union Pacific train at Spokane Union Depot during the 1890s. This is the original Union Depot, looking east. *Courtesy Washington State University Library, Pullman.*

Northern Pacific Train waiting to leave Coulee City, Washington, on March 13, 1892. *Courtesy Haynes Foundation Collection, Montana Historical Society, Helena, #H-2693.*

The incline tramway at Juliaetta, Idaho, in 1892. *Courtesy Latah County Historical Society, Moscow, Idaho, #9-3-1.*

Chapter Twelve

The Great Northern Railway

Much has already been made of James J. Hill's career.[1] There is consequently little need to elaborate upon it here. Born at Rockwood in Upper Canada on September 16, 1838, Hill migrated to St. Paul, Minnesota, where, at the age of 18, he obtained work as a shipping clerk. In 1865 he became a freight and passenger agent and then branched out into the fuel business, accumulated money, and joined Canadian capitalists in a scheme to acquire control of the bankrupt St. Paul & Pacific Railroad. This concern was purchased at foreclosure in 1878 and reorganized as the St. Paul, Minneapolis & Manitoba Railroad in 1879. Under Hill's direction the Manitoba Road prospered and grew. Within four years almost a thousand miles of new line were opened to serve agricultural areas between St. Paul and the Canadian boundary. By 1883 the most westerly of these lines had reached Devil's Lake in Dakota Territory, and Hill stood at the threshold of greater things.

Hill and his partners hoped that the St. Paul & Pacific Railroad might be used to provide the first Canadian transcontinental railway with a means of avoiding difficult and expensive construction work north of Lake Superior. The Dominion government, however, insisted, for political reasons, that the line be located entirely within British territory. When Hill's partners won the franchise for the Canadian Pacific Railway he took an active interest in the company, hoping all the while that the trade of the Canadian Northwest might still be allowed to flow naturally to St. Paul. Again, however, he was disappointed, for under William C. Van Horne's able direction the railway itself became the cornerstone of Canadian nationalism. The community of interest evaporated and the ambitious Hill, retaining firm control of the Manitoba Road, went his own way.

In the mid-1880s certain prominent citizens of Montana, disenchanted with the Northern Pacific Railroad Company, invited Hill to provide them with a second railway. Federal government indecision about opening Indian lands to settlement held up matters, but in 1886 Hill made his first move. During that summer a roadbed was graded for the 87-mile-long Montana Central Railway, linking Helena with Butte. Surveys were also carried out for an extension of the Manitoba Road westward to Fort Bufort and then south to Great Falls and Helena. Early in 1887 the contractors thrust Hill's road forward, laying five miles of track a day. The Manitoba reached Great Falls in September and was immediately pushed through to Helena, arriving there before the end of November. Almost 800 miles of railway were thus opened in a single season. Once workers completed the Wickes tunnel on the Montana Central, Hill seized the lion's share of the Montana mining company traffic. Unfortunately for Northern Pacific worse was yet to come, for Hill's ambitions extended all the way to the Western seaboard.

In May 1886 Hill asked Major A. B. Rogers, who had recently located the line of the Canadian Pacific Railway, to undertake preliminary surveys for a further extension of the Manitoba Road to Puget Sound. Hill instructed Rogers to proceed westward from Fort Bufort to Fort Assinaboine, "thence to Marias River, thence through the mountains by Marias Pass to the Pacific Coast."[2] Rogers, however, stubbornly selected his own route. Ascending the Dearborn River to the continental divide, he followed the Big Blackfoot downstream to Missoula. He then took the Shoshone Pass through the Bitterroot Mountains and reached Spokane Falls by way of Fourth of July Canyon and Coeur d'Alene City. Continuing west he reconnoitered a route crossing the Big Bend country to Waterville and descending Corbaley Canyon to the Columbia River. In the Cascade Mountains he explored both Cady's Pass on the headwaters of the Wenatchee River and Skagit Pass above Lake Chelan. According to E. H. Beckler, then chief engineer of the Montana Central, Hill regarded Rogers's routes as having too many steep gradients and tunnels.[3] Hill, moreover, was interested in the coal deposits of the Flathead country in Montana, on either side of the

British line.[4] Consequently, when the decision was made to build the Pacific extension, it took nearly another year of reconnaissance to find a satisfactory route further to the north.

Late in the summer of 1889 Hill made a now-or-never decision to push the Manitoba Road through to Puget Sound. For that purpose he carried out a series of appropriate but complicated legal and financial maneuvers. To obtain ample powers he formed a new company, called the Great Northern Railway, to lease the Manitoba's assets, operate the railroad, and guarantee the parent company's bonds. He then used the established financial reputation of the St. Paul, Minneapolis, & Manitoba Railroad to borrow the money needed for construction. The Great Northern Railway Company was organized under the laws of Minnesota in September 1889, the founding directors being James J. Hill, George Stephen, Donald Smith, Samuel Hill (Hill's son-in-law), George Bliss, J. Kennedy Tod, William P. Clough, and Edgar Sawyer. The new company had an authorized capital stock of $40 million, of which half was preferred stock entitled to a 6 percent dividend ahead of all other shares. To maintain common ownership of the old and new companies, the Manitoba shareholders were allowed to buy Great Northern preferred stock at par for $50, on a share-for-share basis. The other $50 per share was made up by transfer to the Great Northern of Manitoba holdings in subsidiary companies such as the Eastern Railway of Minnesota. To pay for these assets Great Northern issued $8 million worth of collateral trust bonds, which were to be paid off with the money brought in by the sale of preferred stock. The common stock, meanwhile, was "retained by the Great Northern Railway Company subject to further disposition for its benefit."[5] Construction was initially financed by a bond issue of £2 million sterling (at that time $10 million) raised in London in June 1890.[6] Despite the financial crisis in November of that year, another £1 million worth of St. Paul, Minneapolis, & Manitoba 4 percent bonds were sold at a price of 81 by Glynn Mills & Company in the following July.[7]

On October 21, 1889 chief engineer E. H. Beckler of the Montana Central returned to Great Falls from St. Paul with authority to carry out surveys for the Pacific extension. Hill demanded that as much of the preliminary work as possible be accomplished that winter, so as to allow construction to commence in the summer of

1890.[8] Despite the lateness of the season, Beckler therefore sent out two small reconnaissance parties to determine whether or not Marias Pass would provide a feasible route through the Rocky Mountains to the Flathead Valley. The eastern approach to the pass was to be examined by John F. Stevens, while the much more difficult task of reaching the summit from the west was assigned to Charles F. B. Haskell.

Stevens's "discovery" of the Marias Pass was later portrayed, not least by Stevens himself, as a heroic one-man feat of 19th-century pathfinding. Worse still, his *Recollections*, published in 1935 when he was 82 years old, belittled the equally important part played by Haskell in locating the Great Northern line.[9] Fortunately, family letters written by Haskell during the exploration period[10] and reports appearing in the *Interlake* newspaper in 1890, enable us to assemble a better-balanced account of the Flathead and Kootenai reconnaissance.

The existence of Marias Pass, and the possibility of it providing a suitable route for a railway, were already well enough known.[11] Even had that not been so, the eastern approach to the pass would have been quite easy to find. Anyone traveling west across the plains from Cut Bank can see the gap in the mountains from 40 miles away.[12] As Stevens himself said when he returned to Fort Assinaboine on December 21, 1889, "it is a low, open pass, from one to six miles wide." Nor was the terrain particularly difficult, for he told the press that little solid-rock work would be needed and that the cost of building a railway through the pass would not exceed $16,000 per mile.[13]

Of Haskell's reconnaissance on the west side of Marias Pass, Stevens wrote in 1935 as follows:

> Mr. Haskell's attempt at exploration resulted in nothing of value in the solution of the problem. He left Kalispell with one man late in the winter of '89-90, long after I had been in the pass. They made their way up the Flathead River and followed up the South Fork or turned up a branch coming in from the southeast, about 14 miles west of Marias Pass, reaching no summit whatever. They ran out of food, and nearly starved and froze made their way back and reached one of the engineering parties that had been moved there from the southern passes. Mr. Haskell gave me this information in person, when he was reporting to me the next year, west of Spokane.[14]

Thus did the great engineer dismiss his colleague's work. Poor Haskell, who drowned in the Columbia River in 1895, never had a chance to refute Stevens's distorted account.

In fact, Haskell and two companions, Ed. Boyle and Ed. O'Brien, set out from Demersville in the Flathead Valley on December 16, 1889, reached the summit on January 5, 1890, and returned to base on Tuesday, January 14, 1890. In spite of a longer and more difficult journey, they nevertheless reached the summit of the pass only 25 days after Stevens. Moreover, they met no other forces on the return trip, for the party sent in from the south did not arrive at Demersville from Missoula until February 4, 1890.[15] By that time Haskell was out in the bush again working his way west towards the Kootenai. The remarks made by Stevens 45 years later are clearly at odds with the immediate account rendered by the *Interlake* on January 17, 1890, which reads as follows:

The Manitoba Railroad. C. F. B. Haskell and party returned from their trip to Marias Pass. A feasible and easy route for the Manitoba Railroad, via the pass, to the Pacific Coast.

Tuesday, C. F. Haskell, Ed. Boyle, and Ed. O'Brien came into town. They left here the 16th of last December to examine the country between Marias Pass and Whitefish Lake in the interest of the Manitoba Railroad. They reached the summit of the Rockies January 5th. We understand that they found things more favorable to building a railroad than they expected, both as regards grades and costs. The heaviest grades will not exceed, and may fall under, the maximum which the company is willing to adopt. This heavy grade will all be within 15 miles of the summit and will be about 100 ft. to the mile. After reaching the summit fork the grade will not be over 50 ft. to the mile. There will be no tunnel at the summit. Even the most expensive of the work will not be especially bad for mountain work. A large part of the line will be very cheaply built. The personal experiences of the party were as might be expected on such a trip, at such a time of the year. The snow was five feet deep on the mountains. All their food had to be carried on their backs, and, as is customary on such trips was insufficient for their growing appetites. On the return trip they were four days on half rations and finally had to scrape the flour sack. The last day before reaching the provisions they had left on the way up they only had a quarter of a pint of flour for three. On the upper part of the journey there was no game.[16]

Haskell rightly deserved as much credit as Stevens for the exploration of Marias Pass. Beckler in fact said as much in March 1892.[17] The remaining question then is what, apart from gross egotism, prompted Stevens to say, much later, that Haskell had admitted to him that he had not reached the summit? The answer is that in writing his *Recollections,* Stevens evidently became confused between Haskell and another location engineer named Hamilton!

On June 27, 1890, after the final location of the line had started, the *Interlake* published the following:

Lost in the mountains.

Engineer Hamilton of the Great Northern started out from their main line on the east side of the range with a corps of surveyors to meet Engineer Kennedy from the west side at Marias Pass, and while trying to find Engineer Haskell's imprint, made last January, got lost, and instead of being gone ten days as he anticipated was gone over twenty days, and three days of that time they were out of provisions. They finally struck Kennedy's camp where they were furnished with nourishment and a messenger was sent to Demersville... Hamilton claims he has found a much lower pass than was reported by Haskell last winter. However, he has secured the services of one of Haskell's guides to pilot him through Engineer Haskell's terminal point on the summit.[18]

Ed Boyle in fact was sent back into the mountains to straighten Hamilton out, and on July 18, 1890 the *Interlake* reported his return as follows:

He knows his business!

Ed Boyle came in this week from Marias Pass where he has been to guide Engineer Hamilton over the east side of the range to the pass located last winter by Engineer Haskell. It has been reported by several smart? men that Haskell had not found the right pass and that the surveyors from the east side of the range had found a different and much lower pass, which has proved to be the same and only pass found by Engineer Haskell... Haskell's mark was found without difficulty by Ed. Boyle, and the other knowing ones will be obliged to crawl into their holes and admit that Engineer Haskell understands his business as well as many fossilized wiseacres.[19]

In August 1892 Engineer P. F. Byrne, who had been E. C. Hamilton's assistant, told the *Spokane Review* that Hamilton had laid out the railway on the east side of Marias Pass and deserved credit for the final route.[20] Byrne's comments to the press may have been discussed by Stevens and Haskell, who were then working together. Such discussion may have caused the aging Stevens to mix up his memories of Haskell and Hamilton.

At the end of January 1890 Haskell set out again from Demersville to find a suitable route from the Middle Fork of the Flathead to the Kootenai Valley. With him were Ed Boyle and two assistants, Al. Thompson and Harvey Fitzsimmons. After reconnoitering a few days near the mouth of the Middle Fork they passed along the south side of Whitefish Lake and up the Stillwater River to the height of land between Fortine and Wolf Creeks. They then crossed the divide and descended along Wolf Creek and Fisher River to join the Kootenai at Jennings, thus following the route now used by Burlington Northern. From Jennings the party ascended the Kootenai River to Tobacco Plains where they replenished their supplies.[21] At that point Thompson was sent back to Demersville with a dispatch for Beckler, and the other three men followed the river downstream again as far as Kootenai Falls, where Engineer E. L. Preston's territory began. Returning to Jennings the explorers took a southerly route back to Demersville, where they arrived "forlorn, hungry, and cadaverous" on March 21, 1890. They had spent 52 days in the mountains in the middle of winter, sleeping in the open with "cut spruce or fir boughs for bedding" and but one blanket each![22]

Just what conclusion Haskell reached and what he recommended is not known. When the railway was built, however, it followed the route taken by his party on their return journey to Demersville. Between Ashley Creek and Pleasant Valley the road climbed to a somewhat higher elevation than the divide between Fortine and Wolf Creeks. The southern route, however, was almost the same length as the present line, and 17 miles shorter than the more gently graded Tobacco Plains-Kootenai River route used between 1904 and 1970.

While Haskell and his men plodded through the Salish Mountains on snow shoes, Beckler went west with Hill's principal legal advisor, Colonel W. P. Clough, to establish a Great Northern presence on Puget Sound.[23] In order to secure terminal facilities in Seattle, they quickly made an alliance with Judge Thomas Burke and Daniel H. Gilman, both of whom had by that time withdrawn from the moribund Seattle, Lake Shore & Eastern project. On March 7, 1890 a Great Northern subsidiary, named the Seattle & Montana Railroad Company, was incorporated in King County, with an authorized capital stock of $10 million. The promoters were D. H. Gilman (president), Thomas Burke, Edward O. Graves (vice president), W. E. Bailey, and W. R. Thornhill (secretary). Burke immediately secured a franchise from the city council giving the new company right of way along the entire Seattle waterfront.[24] Clough then made arrangements to purchase Nelson Bennett's Fairhaven & Southern Railway[25] and acquire the Canadian charter of the New Westminster Southern Railway. Arranged end to end, Seattle & Montana, Fairhaven & Southern, and New Westminster Southern were to give Hill a continuous line from Seattle to Vancouver, British Columbia, and allow construction materials to be brought in from the east over the Canadian Pacific.[26] These acquisitions paved the way for building the far western part of the Great Northern Railway eastward toward the summit of the Cascade Mountains.

In April 1890 final location work began at various points along the Pacific extension. Engineers Ellison and Hamilton laid out the line east of the Rockies, while Kennedy and Loraine covered the ground between Marias Pass and Kootenai Falls.[27] Engineer Preston and 15 men, meanwhile, set out from Spokane to work their way east from Chattaroy to the confluence of the Yaak and Kootenai rivers.[28] A first main contract, for the construction of 185 miles of railway from Pacific Junction just west of Havre, Montana, to the summit of Marias Pass went to Shepard Siems & Company of St. Paul on August 1, 1890. On the open prairie workers used large scrapers to throw up a three-foot-high roadbed, and rapidly accomplished the grading. Tracklaying began on October 20, 1890, and 125 miles of railway was completed by January 20, 1891. The advance was then held up by the construction of a 142-foot-high, 1,200-foot-long timber bridge over the Cut Bank River. The steel gang went to work again on April 25, 1891, laying another 48 miles of track to Two Medicine Creek, 13 miles east of Marias Pass. There they were again brought to a halt for two months awaiting completion of a timber bridge 212 feet high and 800 feet long.[29] Meanwhile, a second main contract went to Shepard Siems & Company for work between Marias Pass and Chattaroy, Washington.[30]

The Great Northern Railway crossed the continental divide at an elevation of 5,213 feet. From Marias Pass, 1,153 miles from St. Paul, the line descended southwest for about 12 miles on gradients as steep as 1.8 percent. Meeting the Middle Fork Flathead River and crossing to its left bank, the railway turned northwest along the deep trench between the Rocky Mountains and the Flathead Range. Thirty miles downstream it swung south and then west, crossing the Flathead River just below the confluence of the Middle and North Forks. Following the right bank of the river through Badrock Canyon it reached the broad Flathead Valley at Columbia Falls, 1,213 miles from St. Paul and 3,098 feet above sea level. The road then followed a nearly level tangent alignment across the plain to the newly platted townsite of Kalispell, about three miles north of the existing settlement of Demersville.

From Kalispell, 1,228 miles from St. Paul and 2,946 feet above sea level, the new line set out southwest up the valley of Ashley Creek. At a point named Athens, 18 miles from Kalispell, it diverged from the creek, looped sharply north to limit the grade, and then struggled up the hillside east of Little Bitterroot Lake. Swinging westward it crossed Herrig Creek on a great curved trestle and made its way into a dry, dead-end gulch near the rock-strewn height of land. Turning slightly southwestward the railway passed through a tunnel 1,425 feet long[31] and emerged high on the hillside northeast of Dahl Lake. This was Haskell's Pass, 1,258 miles from St. Paul and 4,135 feet above sea level.[32]

Beyond the west portal of the tunnel the line descended 620 feet in nine miles to Pleasant Valley, the gradient being eased to a mean 1.3 percent (maximum 1.6 percent) by a northward loop into Elbow Creek. Reaching the floor of the valley the railway strode west and north 10 miles on a series of long tangents and easy curves, maintaining an altitude of about 3,500 feet. Passing along the west side of Island Lake it then climbed to a high shoulder of land, 3,622 feet above sea level, overlooking the valley of Little Wolf Creek. At that point, named Melbourne, 1,279 miles from St. Paul, the line swung around to the west again and began a steep descent along the north-facing slope of the mountain. The original railway joined Wolf Creek near Burlington Northern's present Tamarack Siding, about nine miles above the confluence with Fisher River. It then followed both of those streams west and north to meet the Kootenai River at Jennings, 1,309 miles from St. Paul and 2,113 feet above sea level.

Hill's road followed the left bank of the Kootenai River 62 miles downstream from Jennings northwestward through the deep canyons to Bonner's Ferry, Idaho, 1,366 miles from St. Paul and 1,761 feet above sea level. At that point the swiftly flowing waters spilled out onto a broad flood plain and meandered away northward into British Columbia. The railway, consequently, had to turn south over higher ground. After skirting the Mirror Lake marshes, the line wended its way through the hills between Moravia and Naples and climbed with Deep Creek to Elmira, 1,390 miles from St. Paul and 2,162 feet above sea level. Beyond that point it gradually descended into the Pend d'Oreille Valley. Passing within two miles of the Northern Pacific main line near Sandpoint, the Great Northern Railway turned west along the right bank of the Pend d'Oreille River, following it downstream to a good bridge site at Albany Falls. Less than two miles below the bridge the Pend d'Oreille also flowed away to the north and the railway again had to pass southward over higher ground. Since the divide between the Pend d'Oreille and Little Spokane Rivers was very low, just beyond Newport the line was able to resume its descent toward Chattaroy, the route beyond that point remaining a matter of conjecture.

Preparations for construction work west of the Rockies began in October 1890 when contractor Peter Siems visited Demersville. Siems made arrangements for the erection of a "mammoth storehouse" to receive supplies sent to Ravalli by rail and brought north on steamers plying Flathead Lake. To get a head start on the heaviest rock work he also ordered that wagon roads be built along the right of way to tunnel sites east and west of the Flathead Valley.[33] By mid-November 1890 the road to the east had reached Seven Mile Canyon,[34] and by January 1, 1891 a large construction camp, named McCarthysville, had been established within 12 miles of Marias Pass. Welch and Nugent then began to excavate a 900-foot-long tunnel at a point seven miles below the first crossing of the Middle Fork.[35] The wagon road to the west of Demersville, meanwhile, enabled Twohy Brothers to start work on the tunnel at Haskell's Pass. On December 5, 1890 this road was reported to be so well built that "a light rig can be driven clear to the tunnel at a rapid gait."[36]

As the preliminary work got underway in the Flathead country the residents of Demersville prepared to receive increasing numbers of construction laborers. On February 6, 1891 the *Interlake* announced:

> Allen and Hatton will give a grand opening next Monday night February 9th at their saloon, the "Great Northern." They expect their piano, which should have been here some time ago, this week, and will on that night open up in grand style.[37]

Demersville was lively, but its days were numbered. In March 1891 A. A. White and S. G. Comstock, acting for the Great Northern Railway, purchased a thousand acres of land on a level plateau overlooking the Stillwater River, three miles further to the north. Within 30 days a new town was platted and given the name Kalispell, which was said to be "the liquid Indian synonym for Flathead."[38] Great excitement prevailed, and by April 10, 1891 "thousands of men, both laborers and capitalists of moderate means" had "flocked to the new Eldorado seeking opportunities to better their fortunes." By that time the railway contractors had 6,000 men employed and were looking for 4,000 more![39]

The rest of the year 1891 was needed to push the railway through the Rockies to Kalispell. By early September, due to the delay at Two Medicine bridge, the end of track still lay seven miles east of the summit. At that point the steel gang went on strike, demanding a pay increase from $2.00 to $2.25 per day. Low wages and poor food, meanwhile, led to large-scale desertion among the common laborers, who moved on to seek work at camps further west. There they caused a surplus of labor and forced the remuneration down to even lower levels.[40] The contractors nevertheless claimed that the prices paid by the Great Northern would not allow them "to pay any more and save themselves."[41] Still, the steel gang got its raise and track laying quickly resumed. Bridge building, however, remained the critical factor limiting the rate of advance.

The biggest bridge between Marias Pass and Kalispell, a two-span, through-truss structure, crossed the Flathead River at the head of Badrock Canyon, about seven miles east of Columbia Falls. Porter Brothers, which had the contract for all timber bridges on the Pacific extension, began work on the bridge early in September 1891, confidently expecting to have it completed in 90 days. Just as they were erecting the west span, however, misfortune intervened. At 8:00 a. m. on November 24, 1891 a workman operating the lifting tackle dropped an iron rod weighing half a ton, knocking the falsework out from under the span. One man ran 30 feet after the bridge began to fall and saved himself, but nine of his workmates were thrown a hundred feet into the river below. Three were killed instantly with three more mortally injured. The dead were Hugh Donelly, Patrick Lane, John Pooley, Leonard Heininger, Neil Stewart, and Martin Whalen. Their remains were interred in the Columbia Falls cemetery on the following Monday afternoon.[42]

The disaster at the Flathead River bridge held up the advance for less than two weeks. On December 10, 1891 the Columbia Falls *Columbian* reported that the Great Northern Mill Company's forces were busy getting out 40-foot timbers for a replacement span and that Porter Brothers crews were making strenuous efforts to get the structure into shape. The steel gang arrived at the bridge on Saturday, December 5, 1891 and was forced to put in time bringing material up to the front.[43] The bridge was made ready for traffic on or about December 16. The track was extended to Columbia Falls on December 19 and the first consignment of through freight for the Flathead Valley was unloaded on December 24.[44] The railway, meanwhile, was pushed quickly on to Kalispell, arriving there amid great rejoicing at noon on January 1, 1892. In the presence of 3,500 people, an unnamed elderly pioneer drove a ceremonial last spike made from silver dollars donated by local ladies. The contractors and their men, numbering over 200, were then, "escorted by the citizens, headed by a band, to a hotel, where a banquet awaited them."[45]

Between Kalispell and Chattaroy grading work was divided into six sections and let out to a bewildering combination of contractors and subcontractors. As far as one can tell from contemporary newspaper reports overall responsibility was awarded to Shepard Siems & Company of St. Paul, who sublet the work as follows:

Section	*Main Sub-Contractor*
Kalispell-Jennings	Corey Brothers[46]
Jennings-Kootenai Falls	Halverson & Company[47]
Kootenai Falls-Pack R.	Burns & Chapman[48]
Pack River-Sandpoint	P. Welch & Company[49]
Sand Point-Diamond L.	The San Francisco Bridge Company[50]
Diamond Lake-Chattaroy	George W. Hughes[51]

Burns & Chapman themselves only completed the roadbed between Bonner's Ferry and the Half Way House, at or near Pack River. The section between Kootenai Falls and Bonner's Ferry, which involved a lot of rock work, was let out in five subsections (from east to west) to C. A. Mitchell, H. Kirkendall, Jack O'Leary, Olsen & Company, and Williams & Jordan.[52] To complicate matters still further Halverson & Company performed some of the rock work on Corey Brothers contract,[53] Twohy Brothers drove Haskell's Pass tunnel,[54] and a contractor named McMartin pierced a high shoulder of rock rising from Kootenai River near the Montana line.[55] Not all of the tunnels were separately contracted, however. Olsen & Company drove a short one on their own section east of Crossport,[56] and Georges W. Hughes likewise completed the two on Chain Lakes.[57]

Many of these contractors could not start work until the snow was off the ground in the spring of 1891. On P. Welch's contract, for example, Campbell & Brown of Sandpoint did not begin to clear and grub the right of way until the first week of April.[58] As midsummer approached, however, the pace quickened. At the end of May, Burns & Chapman claimed that 2,000 men were engaged on their subcontracts in the Kootenai Canyon.[59] Headquarters for this work was Crossport, five miles east of Bonner's Ferry, where a sizeable temporary town grew up. Crossport and camps upriver to Kootenai Falls were at least partly supplied by steamboat from Nelson, British Columbia, a small vessel named *Spokane* being built for that purpose.[60] The difficulty of provisioning the camps in the canyon soon combined with other factors to produce labor unrest. In June 1891 2,500 Italians went on strike and attempted to drive other workers from the grade. Joel F. Warren and nine special peace officers, hurriedly sent up from Spokane, saved the situation. Warren and his men quickly disarmed the Italians, expelled the ring leaders, and brought about a return to work. Although greatly exaggerated in the press, the strike was unusual in having at least some European-style political overtones. It was applauded, if not supported, by the labor movement at large, and the radical journal *Industrial World* loudly condemned Warren's actions."[61]

Such difficulties were not the only factors delaying work on the Burns & Chapman contract. Grading between Bonner's Ferry and Naples was held up for several months because James J. Hill could not make up his mind which of two surveyed routes the railway should follow.[62] The alternatives apparently were to proceed west across the flood plain from Bonner's Ferry and ascend the Deep Creek valley, or pursue an easterly course through Moravia and reach Naples by way of Brown Creek. Both routes had disadvantages. Thousands of feet of piled trestlework would have been needed to cross Mirror Lake, but a tunnel had to be driven to breach a high spur of unconsolidated ground just beyond Moravia. Hill eventually chose the higher and drier easterly route, but the Brown Creek section of it was only used until about 1904 when both it and the original grade between Naples and Elmira were superseded by extensive line relocation.[63]

The holdup between Bonner's Ferry and Naples shaped the course of events for many months afterwards, the more so because other sections were completed with commendable rapidity. Along the Pend d'Oreille River rock work was expedited by a combination of novel methods and favorable circumstances. Slackwater allowed barges equipped with dynamos to moor near the heaviest cuts, thus facilitating the supply of power to electric rock drills.[64] By early November 1891, therefore, the roadbed between Sandpoint and Albany Falls was practically complete. The section between the Montana line and Eatonville (i. e. Bonner's Ferry), meanwhile, needed only another three weeks' work, with Pat Welch hoping to be finished between Pack River and Sandpoint before the end of the year. Burns & Chapman's work between Bonner's Ferry and the Half Way House, unfortunately, was expected to go on all winter.[65]

With this situation in mind, and in order to avoid any delay in building the Pend d'Oreille River bridge, Hill ordered Beckler to make a connection with the Northern Pacific at Sandpoint and lay track westward.[66] Having reached Albany Falls, the same forces were to return to Sandpoint and extend the steel east to a point 32 miles above Bonner's Ferry (i. e. to Troy.) By December 11, 1891 a large force of men were at work clearing and grading the mile-and-a-half long connecting line at Sandpoint. The San Francisco Bridge Company, meanwhile, brought up its pile driver and set to work on foundations for a three-span timber bridge across Mill Creek.[67] Great Northern locomotive No. 333 arrived at Sandpoint over the Northern Pacific on Wednesday, December 30, 1891 and tracklaying began on the same day.[68] On January 11, 1892 an excited Sandpoint

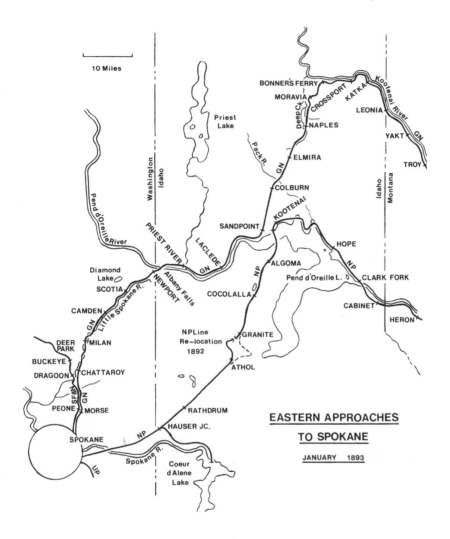

EASTERN APPROACHES

TO SPOKANE

JANUARY   1893

correspondent of the *Spokane Review* reported that he had just rid-
den a Great Northern construction train over the spur line. Nor was
that all, for Great Northern had already cleared a storage yard, laid a
side track, and set up a water tank at the east end of the bridge.[69]

The steel gang set out westward from the end of the Sandpoint
spur on or about January 20, 1892[70] and reached Albany Falls on
February 20, 1892.[71] They then returned to Sandpoint and began
to extend the steel eastward. After laying eight miles of track in six

days they were obliged to return to the Pend d'Oreille Valley to relay a section of line just washed out.[72] The holdup, however, gave Burns & Chapman enough time to finish the grading and thus avoided any further delay. With the advance resumed, the construction train reached Bonner's Ferry at 11:00 a. m. on March 22, 1892.[73] "The Iron Horse" the *Kootenai Herald* remarked, was "in the Garden of Eden."[74]

In January 1892 the steel gang slowly laid track west from Kalispell up Smith Valley. The going was difficult, for three to four feet of snow had to be shovelled from the grade.[75] At the end of the month tracklaying was stalled at Athens by uncompleted rock work in the next 12 miles[76] and did not get under way again until mid-March. By that time Corey Brothers had completed the rock cuts near its camp at Island Lake, and the way to the Kootenai Valley lay clear. By the time the San Francisco Bridge Company's steel gang reached Troy, on or about April 10, the east-end forces had again moved into high gear, putting down three miles a day.[77] On April 25, 1892 the gap in Montana was closed, thus bringing the end of track to a point less than 50 miles from Spokane.[78]

The Great Northern Railway did not finalize its route across Washington State from Chattaroy to Puget Sound until early in 1892. The first step in the decision-making process was to select a route through the Cascade Mountains. That done, efforts were concentrated upon finding the best route across the Big Bend Country. Then, at last, Hill confronted the problem of whether or not to enter Spokane.

In May 1890 John F. Stevens took charge of reconnaissance work in the Cascades.[79] That summer three six-man engineering parties explored all the passes north of the Stampede. Engineer Sterritt examined the Lake Chelan, Methow, and Entiat routes. Engineer Haskell inspected Snoqualmie Pass and six passes on the headwaters of the Wenatchee, and Engineer Thompson assessed the corresponding approaches on the west side of the mountains.[80] Walking the summit ridge by himself, Stevens noticed a very low notch above what he thought must be a particular tributary of the Wenatchee. Subsequently he sent Haskell upstream to confirm his hunch.[81] As a result, a way was found to cross the divide at an altitude of just over 4,000 feet between Nason Creek on the east and the South Fork Skykomish River on the west.[82] Haskell generously named this route Stevens Pass. John Stevens himself conveyed the good news to Beckler, and by the end of September 1890 a force of 48 men had been put together for detailed location work.

Once the line through the Cascade Mountains had been established the engineers had to find an acceptable route into and out of the Spokane River Valley, a means of avoiding the steep westward climb out of the Grand Coulee, and a way of descending from the plateau to the Columbia River. The first of these requirements was met in May 1891 when Engineer Thompson ran a line down to the vicinity of Mondovi. To everyone's surprise Thompson found that the westward climb out of the Spokane Valley would be no steeper than 45 feet to the mile.[83] The line passed 10 miles north of Spokane, but Hill's immediate purposes were admirably served by having a viable route which could be used to bypass the city. Colonel Clough, indeed, had already announced that nothing short of extra inducements would lead the company to place Spokane on its main line![84] The first proposed Great Northern route across the Big Bend Country, outlined in the press on May 16, 1891, fitted in well with both the Spokane bypass and the Wenatchee River route. Reaching the high land at the head of Coulee Creek, the line was to go west from Mondovi to Davenport and Creston, pass three miles north of Almira, and head for Coulee City. Having crossed the Grand Coulee it was to climb 500 feet in nine miles and then turn south down Moses Coulee to Rattlesnake Springs and the Columbia River, which it would bridge at or near Rock Island. It was then to follow the right bank of the Columbia north to the mouth of the Wenatchee.[85] Unfortunately, the gradient on the west flank of the Grand Coulee was much steeper than the mean suggested above, reaching 2.2 percent on tangent track.[86]

Hill, not satisfied, told his engineers to keep on looking. As the year 1891 passed by, however, they appeared unable to come up with any better solution. A clue to what happened next is given in *History of the Big Bend Country*, published in 1904. This work, quoting articles previously appearing in the *Big Bend Chief* newspaper, related that Crab Creek stockman Donald Urquhart, who had taken an interest in the movements of the Great Northern survey parties, wrote to Mr. Hill offering to show him a way of reaching the Columbia River without "toboggan slides." A few weeks later an engineering party drove up to Mr. Urquhart's Ranch and recruited his aid in finding the Crab Creek-Lynch Coulee route eventually adopted. The account went on to say that when the Crab Creek party eventually reached Rock Island it encountered the engineer who had surveyed the more northerly route and he "could hardly believe the evidence of the field notes. More especially was he hard to convince as he had made several investments along the northern route for himself and friends."[87] The Great Northern engineers, it seems, were no less susceptible to the temptations of the real estate business than their Northern Pacific counterparts.

Early in December 1891 all engineering effort was concentrated on the Crab Creek line and the northerly route was abandoned. Going through Spokane no longer involved a lengthy detour to the south. Hill consequently came to grips with the problem of securing a right of way through the city. On February 11, 1892 he addressed a meeting in the Spokane auditorium, stating that the million dollar extra cost of routing the railway through the city would have to be at least partly offset by free right of way within the municipal boundary. He asked of Spokane:

> that from the time we come to the city limits, till we go out, that the right of way upon the building of the road will not cost us anything. We must be at work on one line or the other within a few days. I am going to the coast, to be gone five or six days, when I return home by way of Spokane. I hope that the matter can be arranged so that we can go to work at once.[88]

The citizens of Spokane thus had one week to provide the Great Northern Railway Company with a right of way worth $500,000. Rising to the occasion, Mayor David B. Fotheringham quickly appointed a committee charged with interviewing over 100 individual property owners and securing donations of land and money.[89] By February 19, 1892 more than $70,000 in cash and $50,000 worth of property had been raised "to indemnify such as were unable to, or would not, donate the right of way."[90] When Hill returned, therefore, Anthony M. Cannon presented him with a deed for nearly all the property required.

Once the Spokane right of way problem had been solved, Hill lost no time extending the Great Northern to the city. The steel bridge over the Pend d'Oreille River at Albany Falls, consisting of an arch span of 300 feet and a through-truss span of 180 feet was erected by the Wisconsin Bridge Company[91] and completed on or about May 10, 1892.[92] Track was then laid rapidly southwest through Chattaroy to the height of land overlooking the Spokane Valley at Hillyard. A first through-train from St. Paul, consisting of engine No. 335, a baggage car, and a passenger coach arrived at the outer end of the Ross Park street railway line at about 10:30 p. m. on May 28, 1892. Conductor H. Van Allen was in charge and locomotive engineer Ed Depew held the throttle. Three passengers who had traveled all the way from St. Paul and several others from intermediate points entered town on one of the electric cars.[93]

On June 1, 1892 workers laid GN track to a junction with the Union Pacific Railway at the eastern approach to Spokane Union Depot.[94] Until their own line could be built through the city the Great Northern elected to use the Union Depot and proceed westward over the former Seattle, Lake Shore & Eastern Railway. Unfortunately, they did not reach agreement with Northern Pacific for the use of that line until July 18, 1892 and then only after Hill himself had made a special trip to Spokane to settle the matter.[95] By that time the roadbed across the eastern part of the Big Bend country was largely ready for track and enormous quantities of rails and ties were stockpiled at Hillyard. Tracklaying resumed at the SLS&E connection west of the Spokane River Canyon on July 23, 1892 and proceeded apace.[96]

The decision to pass through Spokane added another peak to the profile of the Great Northern Railway. From a low point less than 1,800 feet above sea level between Milan and Chattaroy the line climbed to a summit 2,026 feet above sea level at Hillyard, five miles northeast of Spokane. It then descended on a 1 percent grade to the north bank of the Spokane River, joining the Union Pacific Railway just west of that company's bridge. The eventual Great Northern line crossed the river above Division Street and ran west past the hospital. It then swung northwest into depot grounds on Havermale's Island, 1,479 miles from St. Paul and 1,876 feet above sea level. Setting out for the west the railway crossed over to the north bank of the river at the end of the Washington Street bridge. It then proceeded due west on Sinto Avenue to a point just west of Pine Street, where it again turned briefly northwest. Resuming a westerly course it then ran out onto a high steel bridge carrying it across the Spokane River Canyon to Twickenham.[97]

From an elevation of 1,847 feet above sea level at what was later Fort Wright Junction, the Great Northern Railway climbed northwest along the flank of the Spokane River canyon. Near the top of the hill, at Highland, it made a complete reversal of direction and headed southwest across the plateau. Leaving the thinning pine forest behind, it briefly encountered the upper reaches of Crab Creek near Edwall, but did not immediately follow that stream. Passing northwestward over an intervening height of land, the line met and followed the seasonal water course of Coal Creek, which offered 20 miles of straighter alignment. From the established settlement of Harrington the railway descended gently southwest to a point just east of Nemo Siding. It then climbed briefly over a spur of higher ground and dropped more sharply into the lower coulee of Crab Creek. Beyond Odessa the line followed the wanderings of the coulee in a generally west-northwest direction to Wilson Creek. Reaching what was known as the sinks of Crab Creek, near Adrian, and passing by the south end of the Grand Coulee at Soap Lake, it ran southwest and then west along the foot of the Beezly Hills, north of the Quincy flatland. Beyond Quincy the railway made a spectacular descent of 700 feet in 16 miles, best described in the words of a passenger who traveled over the line soon after it was opened:

> The road at length begins to descend to the Columbia River by following a shallow draw which leads down to the edge of the canyon. Passing through a long rock cut the view suddenly opens up a chasm, or deep coulee, several hundred feet sheer below the track, with stupendous cliffs rising on the opposite side [of the river]. Then one notices that the roadbed is winding northwards, cutting its way along the rocky bluffs near the summit on a steadily descending grade. Trestle after trestle is crossed, as successive coulees are passed, until the head of the main gulch, called Lynch Coulee is reached. This is crossed on a gigantic tower trestle 135 ft. high and 1,200 ft. long. As one's eyes are lifted from measuring the depth below, the grand vista opens down the length of the coulee revealing a glimpse of the Canyons of the Columbia. The train winds down the western side of Lynch Coulee until a point is reached directly opposite where the descent was begun on the cliffs above. It is a complete horseshoe of far greater dimensions than the celebrated curve of that name on the Pennsylvania road. A turn is made and we are in the [Columbia] canyon. The river is flowing 500 ft. below. The gaze is distracted from these attractions above by the roar of the great river as it foams down the Rock Island Rapids.[98]

At Columbia River Siding, 1,637 miles from St. Paul, the railway reached a low point of 598 feet above sea level. Crossing the river on a huge steel bridge just above Rock Island Rapids it then followed the right bank north to the mouth of the Wenatchee.

Diverging from the Columbia River at a point about three miles above the nascent town of Wenatchee, the Great Northern Railway followed the Wenatchee Valley northwestward into the hills. At Leavenworth, 1,676 miles from St. Paul and 1,165 feet above sea level, it began to climb in earnest. The line proceeded north through the narrow Tumwater Canyon, turned west across the swiftly flowing Wenatchee River, and wended its way through the hills to meet Nason Creek. A break in the steep gradient then allowed the locomotives a short respite. Beyond Merritt, however, the trains had to struggle up another 12 miles of 2.2 percent grade to Cascade Tunnel station, 1,709 miles from St. Paul and 3,382 feet in elevation.

At the summit the line curved southwest and plunged into the 2.63-mile-long Cascade Tunnel, which was driven on 1.7 percent westbound downgrade. Emerging at Wellington, the road descended a 2.2 percent grade cut into the steep south-facing flank of Windy Mountain. After about six miles it turned northwest to meet and cross Martin Creek. Describing a circular path, the line then passed through a horseshoe tunnel, recrossed the creek on a high timber bridge, and headed southeast and then east, paralleling itself at a lower elevation. At a point originally named Madison, and later called Scenic, it performed another abrupt about-face and descended westward to Foss Creek at the foot of the 2.2 percent mountain grade, 1,732 miles from St. Paul (via the tunnel) and 918 feet above sea level. The rest of the way was downhill and the trains rolled on easily to meet the waters of Puget Sound at Everett, 1,785 miles from St. Paul (via the tunnel) and 33 miles north of Seattle.[99]

Until the tunnel was completed in 1900 trains went over the top of Stevens Pass, 4,025 feet above sea level, on a 12-mile-long high line having multiple switchbacks, with 3.5 percent grades on the east side and 4 percent on the west side. There were, in all, eight tail tracks, each 1,000 feet long, laid on 6 percent upgrades, three on the east side and five on the west.[100] When the tunnel finally opened, distances from St. Paul to Wellington and beyond were reduced by nine miles. In 1929 a new 7.79-mile-long Cascade Tunnel was opened, superseding the original. Driven directly from Berne to Scenic on a more southerly alignment, the new tunnel reduced the summit elevation to 2,883 feet and saved another seven miles. At the same time the railroad abandoned the Tumwater Canyon route in favor of a new line bypassing Leavenworth and following Chumstick Creek.[101] These changes finally removed the terrible snow-slide hazard to which parts of the old line were badly exposed.

On the coastal side of the Cascade Mountains the 87-mile-long Seattle & Montana road was completed to a connection with the Fairhaven & Southern Railway at Janin's Prairie in Skagit County on October 12, 1891[102] and opened to traffic on November 27, 1891.[103] Materials for the far west end of the Great Northern were then brought by Canadian Pacific to the international boundary at Sumas, handed over to Bellingham Bay & British Columbia Railroad, and delivered to the Fairhaven & Southern at Bellingham.[104] A contract for construction of 73 miles of the Great Northern line between Everett and the west end of the Cascade Tunnel went to Shepard, Henry, & Company in November 1891 and preparatory work began immediately.[105] By June 24, 1892, 2,600 men were at work west of the Cascade Mountains and had completed the roadbed almost to the foot of the mountain grade.[106] A few days later work got under way in the high country, and when Hill himself crossed the mountains a month later he found the graders only four miles apart at the summit.[107]

Between Spokane and the Columbia River grading began in March 1892[108] and was completed early in August.[109] Tracklaying finally got under way on July 23 and progressed at a rate of three-and-a-half to four miles a day. By September 2, 1892, therefore, the end of the track was already 100 miles west of Spokane.[110] Since the big steel bridge at Rock Island could not be erected until the materials were delivered by rail, interim arrangements were made to ferry trains across the Columbia River. For that purpose Great Northern purchased the steamer *Thomas L. Nixon* and had her brought upriver from Pasco to Wenatchee, removing her upper deck to receive track.[111] During the third week of August, Engineer W. C. Armstrong arrived to direct the construction of landing slips located above the bridge site "at Rev. Mr. Mack's place." The transfer was equipped with 100-foot-wide pontoons at each side of the river.[112]

As the summer drew to a close, pressure to complete the railway increased. On September 21, 1892 the bridges on Lynch Coulee were reported to be nearly all finished, and graders were said to be finishing off the roadbed along the Columbia River below Rock Island.[113] At that time there were 4,000 men at work east of the mountains and another 3,000 on the west side, the crews making every effort to complete the railway to the summit before the snow flew. By October 5, 1892 they had laid track to the mouth of Moses Coulee on the east side and to "the Index" on the west side.[114] Three weeks after that the inland steel gang had crossed the Columbia and were well on their way up the Wenatchee. Unfortunately, another disastrous bridge accident then occurred.

The construction train reached the second crossing of the Wenatchee late on Sunday, October 23, 1892. A temporary bridge, resting on piling, had been built there at a period of low water earlier in the year. When the river rose, apparently, it pushed some of the piles out of line, thus twisting and weakening the upperworks. At 8:00 a. m. on October 24 the steel gang began to lay track across the bridge. The construction train crossed the approach trestle and the first span, then halted to allow the crew to place and spike the rails on the second span. At that moment the bridge "began to totter" and before the men could run to the other end of it the entire structure collapsed, sending them all into the river 60 feet below. The track laying machine and several flat cars loaded with ties and rails then rolled in on top of them, killing seven men outright and badly injuring another five. Fortunately the locomotive was not coupled to the cars and remained on the track. The dead were listed as J. Brodie, J. Johnson, John Leonard, N. Nelson, A. Olsen, Daniel Watkins, and James Wright. Within an hour the hospital car, "which follows the construction party," arrived from Wenatchee and the injured were placed in it, to be cared for by four physicians and a priest. All efforts, however, failed to save James Campbell and James Gilman, who died soon afterward.[115]

On the mountain grades and the switchback line, work was pushed day and night. At the end of October 1892 John F. Stevens reported 2,000 men employed on the west side and 1,500 on the east and added that "About fifty men a day leave, for I never saw such a restless class of labor as there is on the coast, but we are sending up three-hundred men a week, just about enough to keep the ranks full."[116]

On December 4, 1892 only 30 miles of track remained to be laid to complete the entire railway. The east side steel gang was then only eight miles from Cascade Tunnel.[117] A few days afterwards snow began to fall in earnest and 300 men went to work to clear the roadbed.[118] On December 17, 1892, despite this inconvenience, the inland steel gang was still laying 2,000-4,000 feet a day and had already passed over the summit. The two engines propelling the construction train were stated to have "a tank car attached for there is no going back for water once the day's work is begun. It is steadily pushing to the front through all the short daylight hours."[119]

On January 3, 1893 there remained a gap of only two miles,[120] and on January 6, 1893 the last spike was driven.

The rails met at a point "13 miles below the summit of Stevens Pass on the western slope of the Cascades," presumably at or near mile 1,726 from St. Paul measured by way of the switchbacks, or about five miles below Wellington and one mile above Martin Creek. The contemporary account read as follows:

> The only officials present were superintendents Shields and Farrell. As the last rail was brought forward by the workmen and laid in position, Messrs. Shields and Farrell took the spiking mauls from the spikers' hands, and with alternate blows, drove the last spike home. It was not golden, but only iron. So unpretentiously was it done that the laborers on the right of way were not aware of it until the group on the spot set up a wild hurrah. Foreman Benson relaxed his usual gravity and grasping Superintendent Shields by the right hand with the left, emptied into the air his six shooter. The engineers took a cue and the hoarse whistles of the great Moguls sounded and reverberated through the canyons of the Skykomish, accompanied by such a yell as only two hundred emancipated men can make. This occasion was Thanksgiving, Christmas, and New Year combined, for there has been no time for these festivities during the past six weeks.[121]

The tracks had been joined, creating a continuous line from St. Paul to the Pacific. But much work remained to put the railway into operating condition. On the west slope of the Cascade Mountains a temporary switchback at Martin Creek bypassed the horseshoe tunnel which remained unfinished for several months afterwards. At Rock Island, meanwhile, work got underway on the Columbia River bridge. This enormous structure was to have a main cantilever span 420 feet long between the east side and a natural rock in the river, and a through-truss span of 170 feet on the west side.[122] Early in January 1893 the masonry was still not quite finished but all the steel was on the ground, and the Edgemoor Bridge Company's men were waiting to erect the superstructure.[123] The main span was built entirely from the ends without having a vessel moored in the river. As the work progressed, each overhanging part supported itself until at last the mid-span connection was made. The bridge was completed and opened for traffic on Tuesday, May 2, 1893, the first train being an extra westbound which passed over at 5:00 p. m.[124]

Before train services could be established on the Pacific extension the track had to be ballasted and surfaced and minimal infrastructural requirements met. Even before the gap in Montana had been closed, the surfacing gang set out eastward from Sandpoint to bring the railway up to a reasonable operating standard. By April 20, 1892 they were working above Bonner's Ferry,[125] accompanied by a crew of telegraph linemen. As the job progressed, the four double-deck boarding cars in which the men slept were slowly moved up the valley. At 10:00 a. m. on April 29, 1892 the train had reached a point just west of the long tunnel near the most northerly point in Kootenai Canyon. Engine No. 330 was pulling the cars very slowly around a curve on the outside of a bend in the river and many of the men were walking alongside. The brakes on the rear car were still set, thus inducing a considerable tension in the couplers and drawing the train inward on the curve. The super-elevated track and the abnormal height of the vehicles contributed to the centripetal force. Suddenly, without warning, the cars toppled over into the river, killing three men and seriously injuring nineteen others.[126] Ironically, those engaged in making the line safe for fast running lost their lives in a very low-speed accident. The work, however, went on, and by the beginning of July the road was in fair enough condition to begin running the twice-weekly mixed trains between Pacific Junction and Spokane. These trains covered the 512 miles in 39 hours at an average speed of 13 miles per hour.[127]

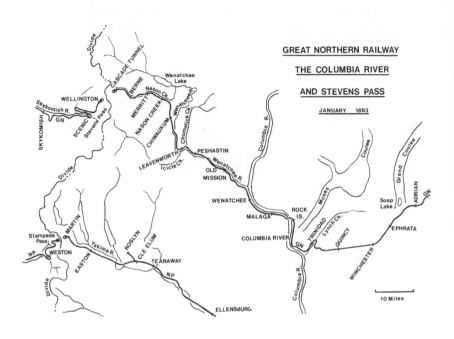

A complete mail and passenger service, with through sleeping cars between St. Paul and Spokane, began on August 14, 1892, when daily trains began to operate on the following schedule:[128]

Westbound			Station		Eastbound	
Day 1	Dep.	7:40 p.m.	St. Paul	6:55 a.m.	Arr.	Day 4
Day 2		8:35 a.m.	Grand Forks	6:20 p.m.		Day 3
		3:25 p.m.	Minot	10:50 a.m.		
		6:30 a.m.	Havre	6:35 p.m.		
		10:48 a.m.	Shelby Jc.	2:32 p.m.		
Day 3		6:06 p.m.	Columbia Falls	8:03 a.m.		Day 2
		7:00 p.m.	Kalispell	7:30 a.m.		
		11:30 p.m.	Jennings	3:30 a.m.		
		12:01 a.m.	Libby Creek	2:59 a.m.		
Day 4		1:15 a.m.	Bonner's Ferry	11:45 p.m.		
		3:55 a.m.	Newport	9:20 p.m.		Day 1
	Arr.	6:00 a.m.	Spokane	7:40 p.m.	Dep.	

The average speed was thus a very creditable 25 miles per hour over the whole journey in each direction. The first train, consisting of a combined mail and baggage car, a colonist sleeper, a day coach, and the first-class sleeper *Seattle* arrived at Spokane Union Depot at 7:43 a. m. on August 17, 1892 and departed eastbound on schedule the same day. The cars were reported to be painted a deep red or maroon color, decorated with gold lettering.[129]

Beyond Spokane, twice-weekly accommodation trains began to run to Wenatchee on November 13, 1892.[130] A through freight train service between St. Paul and Seattle was inaugurated on February 1, 1893, passengers being carried between Spokane and Wenatchee, and Everett and Sultan.[131] The accommodation trains were extended from Wenatchee to Leavenworth at the beginning of May.[132] Then, on June 18, 1893 through trains carrying mail and passengers began to run over the entire Pacific extension.[133] The Great Northern Railway had at last taken its place among the transcontinentals.

Chapter Thirteen

Down to Juliaetta

There was ever an element of mystique about Lewiston's supposedly strategic position at the meeting of the Snake and Clearwater rivers. Perhaps because Lewis and Clark had crossed the Bitterroot Mountains by way of Lolo Pass and followed those waters, transcontinental railroads were expected to do likewise. But none ever did.

In the vicinity of Lewiston the Snake and the Clearwater run in canyons 1,500 to 2,000 feet deep, cut into the high volcanic plateau. Further upstream these rivers pass through deeper and more forbidding defiles, impassable for roads and railways alike. For a long time the Lewiston area remained remote and inaccessible. The town was born of a placer gold rush in the early 1860s and established in violation of the original boundary of the Nez Perce Indian reservation. Once the mining boom ended, however, Lewiston languished. Throughout the 1880s it remained a somewhat vague objective for the Oregon Railway & Navigation Company's tracks. Even Union Pacific President Charles Frances Adams's personal interest in land development there failed to justify the high cost of building a railroad through the canyons. Riparia remained the railhead, and Snake River steamers continued to function as the only link with the world downstream. In 1889 circumstances at last began to change. The bonds of common ownership uniting OR&N and Northern Pacific in unholy matrimony were finally broken, and Henry Villard's unpopular territorial restrictions were abandoned. Passage of the Dawes Act, meanwhile, made provision for white settlement on Indian lands. The fertile Camas Prairie highlands to the southeast thus became available to provide Lewiston with an extensive agricultural hinterland. The merchants at the confluence of the rivers sensed that their moment of opportunity had arrived.

On Wednesday, February 19, 1890 local citizens, meeting at Vollmer's Hall, voted to offer the Northern Pacific Railroad Company a subsidy of $100,000 to extend the Spokane & Palouse Railway to Lewiston.[1] In mid-March the board of trade went to Spokane to confer with Northern Pacific chief engineer J. W. Kendrick[2] and asked Spokane businessmen to subscribe to the Lewiston subsidy. Matters appear to have progressed favorably, for Dr. Kelly of Lewiston had another "encouraging" meeting with Kendrick on April 8, and before the end of the month surveyors went into the field. The only unresolved issue was "the absence of right of way across the Nez Perces Indian Reservation."[3]

In order to make adequate legal provision for an extension to Lewiston and the Camas Prairie plateau, a new company, named Northern Pacific & Idaho Railroad, was formed at Tacoma, Washington, on June 2, 1890 with a capital stock of $2 million. The promoters were listed as John H. Mitchell, Jr., William O. Chapman, and Herbert Huson, all of Tacoma; James B. Williams of Stamford, Connecticut; and Henry Stanton of New York City. The company was empowered to build, equip, and run a railroad from a junction with the Spokane & Palouse Railway in Whitman County, Washington, across the Idaho line to Moscow and Cornwall, thence via the West Fork of Bear Creek and Big Potlatch River to Juliaetta and down the Clearwater River to its confluence with the Snake at Lewiston. Beyond that point the railway was to follow the right bank of the Snake River upstream to the mouth of Tammany Creek and ascend Tammany and More's creeks to Lake Waha. The total distance was estimated to be 91 miles. The company was also authorized to build branch roads to other points in Washington, Idaho, or Montana.[4]

The Lewiston extension diverged from the existing Spokane & Palouse Railway at a point a mile-and-a-half south of Pullman and passed east over higher ground to Moscow. Having crossed the South Fork Palouse River, it proceeded directly to Cornwall, at the head of Middle Fork Potlatch Creek. From that point the line climbed northward to a summit over 2,700 feet above sea level near Howell and commenced a steep descent east and southeast along the West Fork of Bear Creek. In the 14.4 miles between Howell and Kendrick (formerly Latah) the railway dropped 1,525 feet. At Kendrick it swung sharply southwest into the canyon of the Big Potlatch River and descended at a gentler rate through Juliaetta to the north bank of the Clearwater. Three miles below Arrow the railway crossed the Clearwater River and followed its left bank downstream to Lewiston. For a distance of about 12 miles, between points two-and-a-half miles south of Juliaetta and three miles west of Spalding the line was located within the Nez Perce Indian reservation.

Contractors Donald, Smith, & Howell of North Yakima began grading between Pullman and Moscow on or about May 19, 1890 and soon had 500 men engaged.[5] By mid-August work had also commenced at Lewiston and several intermediate points.[6] The steel gang then began to lay track, but proceeded at a very leisurely pace. At Pullman the coming and going of the construction trains nevertheless supplemented the eight regularly scheduled runs on two railways and made the city "more than ever conscious of its importance as a commercial center."[7] Tracklaying was held up at Moscow by land procurement problems and not resumed until October, by which time the roadbed on the West Fork of Bear Creek had been completed.[8] Progress was evidently quite slow, for the railway did not reach Kendrick until the end of January 1891.[9] There was little point in hurrying, however, for the Northern Pacific Railroad Company had encountered difficulty in obtaining United States government permission to cross the Nez Perce Indian reservation.[10]

Wrangling with the federal government went on for another two years. The process closely paralleled that previously undergone by the Washington & Idaho Railroad in crossing the Coeur d'Alene reservation, but was greatly complicated by the simultaneous opening of the Indian lands to settlement. The contractors completed the roadbed west of the reservation and built a substantial embankment to protect the Lewiston terminal from flooding.[11] Workers laid track to the northern boundary of the reservation in June 1891 and train service was extended to Juliaetta soon afterwards. Twelve miles of roadbed, however, remained uncompleted, and 18 miles of track were not laid.[12] The plan to extend the Lewiston line to Tammany Creek and Lake Waha, moreover, was completely abandoned.[13]

When most of the grading had been finished on the Lewiston line, Donald, Smith, & Howell moved their forces north to build a six-mile-long Northern Pacific branch in Washington from Belmont to Farmington. Local residents had agreed in July 1890 to provide the railroad with free right of way and a subsidy of $10,000.[14] Track entered Farmington on or about November 20, 1890[15] and the railway was turned over to the operating department on January 2, 1891.[16]

The federal government did not grant final permission to cross the Nez Perce Indian reservation until March 1893. By that time, however, the Northern Pacific Railroad Company was in financial difficulties. Receivership followed in August, and for five years the company suspended all further railway construction. Consequently the first train did not arrive at Lewiston until September 15, 1898, and another 10 years passed by before a railway opened up the Camas Prairie.

Juliaetta, the interim terminus of the Lewiston line, became an important railhead for shipping grain grown on the tableland towering above the Big Potlatch Canyon. To save many miles of tedious haulage over rough wagon roads, farmers on Potlatch Ridge agreed to hand their grain over to the Juliaetta Tramway Company, which lowered it down the escarpment on an inclined railway with rope haulage. Built in 1892, the tramway was 2,800 feet long on slope, with about 2,000 feet difference in elevation between upper and lower stations. The track was laid with three rails, except at the mid point, where four rails allowed the cars to pass each other. Normally a loaded car going down drew an empty one up. Motive power in the form of a 30-horsepower Lidgerwood engine, built by Holley, Mason, Marks, & Company of Spokane, handled upcoming loads as required. The haulage rope, three-quarters of an inch in diameter, had a breaking strength of 33 tons and was subjected to a maximum pull of seven tons. The cars, made of steel, were said to be twenty feet long. At the top of the incline was an engine house, a small warehouse, and a dwelling for the operator. Another warehouse, 80 feet by 200 feet, provided grain storage adjacent to the NPRR at the foot of the hill.

The Juliaetta Tramway, built and owned by J. L. Hallett & Sons, charged $1.25 per ton for combined lowering and storage. As the customary warehousing fee was 50 cents, the haulage amounted to 75 cents per ton. The agreements with farmers were contingent upon crops averaging 25 or more bushels per acre in any given year.[17] Hallett (who had been Villard's hotshot construction boss during the building of the OR&N and Northern Pacific main lines in the early 1880s) was said, in 1892, to be contemplating the construction of a narrow gauge railway "through the heart of the Big Potlatch Country to the edge of the white pine timber region."[18] This more ambitious scheme was never translated into roadbed and track.

Chapter Fourteen

To Keep the Wheels Turning

This book has been concerned largely with the expansion of the railway system in the Columbia Interior between 1885 and 1893. Notice should also be taken of ongoing improvements and day-to-day railway operations.

The upgrading of existing lines soon became a necessity. Bridges built between 1879 and 1884 deteriorated rapidly and soon had to be replaced with more durable structures. Larger locomotives and cars required heavier rails, and more traffic demanded bigger passenger stations and freight terminals.

In October 1885 OR&N decided to replace the timber-truss and crib-pier bridges over the Deschutes, John Day, Umatilla, and Walla Walla rivers, using iron structures resting on masonry piers. Stone was brought from Rocky Butte quarry, nine miles east of Portland, Oregon, and the ironwork was purchased in the east.[1] All four new bridges were completed by the end of February 1887.[2]

The Northern Pacific Railroad gave first priority to replacing the huge timber bridges across the O'Keefe and Marent gulches, in the Coriacan defile between De Smet and Evaro, Montana. This work was commenced in 1886 and completed in 1889.[3] Further west, the original bridge across the Spokane River at Trent, Washington, was replaced early in 1887 by a new bridge with a 160-foot iron through-truss main span and plate girder subsidiary spans, resting on solid granite piers and abutments.[4] Three years later, the company rebuilt the multiple-span bridge at the first crossing of the Clark Fork River, between Clark Fork and Cabinet, Idaho, in a similar manner.[5]

At least one major new bridge remained to be built. At Portland, Oregon, the construction of a railway bridge across the

Willamette River had been long delayed. In September 1882 the company announced plans for a double-track bridge with two drawspans, to be built just above Swan Island.[6] A year later, despite litigation concerning rights of navigation,[7] another scheme was put forward for a double-track bridge located on a line extending from a point on Front Street north of the intersection with 16th Street, to a point on the Albina side 32 feet north of the Northern Pacific Terminal Company dock. The bridge was to consist of three fixed spans of 264 feet each and one swinging drawspan of 394 feet, the latter being placed the third span from the Portland end.[8] This scheme was left in abeyance when Villard's empire collapsed.

Nothing more happened until July 1886 when Elijah Smith of the OR&N asked consulting engineer George R. Morrison to prepare plans for a less costly structure. On August 14, 1886 Smith and Morrison selected a site near the south end of Ainsworth wharf, at the narrowest part of the river.[9] The eventual design of the bridge[10] was more modest than that proposed in Villard's time. The steel super-structure, manufactured by the Union Bridge Company of Buffalo, New York, consisted of a 340-foot, centrally pivoted swinging drawspan at the Portland end, and a 320-foot, through-truss, fixed span at the east end. The two spans, each 40 feet deep, carried a single railway track on the lower chord and a wagon road on an intermediate deck above the railway. The superstructure was supported at an elevation allowing trains to pass on and off the bridge at river bank grade. The steelwork was thus only 27 feet, 6 inches above low-water level, and barely above high water in times of flood. The designer's justification for this arrangement was that the highest river levels were due to backwater from the Columbia, and thus involved little velocity of flow. Nor in the Willamette was there ever much ice or floating debris.

The two main spans of the Willamette River bridge rested on three piers. The masonry pivot pier was built on a timber grillage resting on piles cut off below water level. The piers at the outer ends of the drawspan each consisted of two 14-foot diameter cast-iron cylinders filled with concrete and stone. Each cylinder rested on 19 piles extending upward into the concrete. Steam machinery rotated the drawspan while hydraulic rams lifted and latched each end after closing. The bridge could be opened to navigation in less than one minute. Corrugated steel plate covering the lower chords of the bridge spans formed a continuous stiffening "skin" giving protection against damage by collisions from ships.

At each end of the bridge the elevated wagon road was carried clear of the railway tracks on a series of 150-foot-long steel approach spans with timber-trestle access ramps. Road vehicles reached the bridge from Holladay Avenue in east Portland and the intersection of Third and G streets on the west side. The railway curved away sharply northward at the Portland end, crossing the west side O&C tracks and Front Street at grade before making an end-on junction with the NP Kalama line.

A bill to grant the OR&N a franchise for the Willamette River bridge was placed before the Oregon legislature in January 1887[11] and passed early in February.[12] However, Governor Sylvester Penoyer of Oregon, acting on the advice of U. S. Army engineers, vetoed the bill[13] and the legislature had to pass it again two weeks later to overrule his veto.[14] On or about May 20, 1887 the OR&N directors accepted the franchise, clearing the way for construction.[15]

The bridge was built under the supervision of civil engineer George A. Lederle,[16] who had previously directed work on the Snake River bridge at Ainsworth, Washington Territory. Pile driving for the pier foundations began on July 26, 1887.[17] The grillage for the pivot pier was sunk early in November,[18] and by year's end the masonry was well advanced.[19] High water then delayed work until February 1888.[20] By March 13, however, the pivot pier was finished and the cast iron cylinders forming the subsidiary piers were already in place.[21] The falsework was then put up, and before the end of March 1888 ironworkers began to erect the superstructure.[22] The last panel of the drawspan was riveted together early in June[23] and on July 10 the bridge was tested and declared ready for use.[24]

The first eastbound OR&N train to leave Portland proper departed from a temporary ticket office on the west bank of the Willamette at 2:15 p. m. on July 11, 1888. The train consisted of mail and express car No. 84; a baggage car; coaches Nos. 958, 7, and 18; and the Pullman sleepers *Bonita* and *Walla Walla*—all drawn by engine No. 54. Members of the inaugural train crew were conductor E. M. Stevens, locomotive engineer W. J. Sherman, fireman H. P. Smith, brakeman W. Gray, sleeping car conductor W. S. Whitman, and sleeping car porters G. W. Sampson and W. Clipper.[25]

The OR&N had at last arrived in Portland, but still had a lot of work to do. For the time being the passenger business was carried on at a wooden temporary depot on the west side of Couch Lake at Fifth and I streets.[26] These premises were opened on September 26, 1888,[27] the understanding being that they would soon be replaced by the long-awaited Union Depot.[28] Changed circumstances for both OR&N and Northern Pacific, however, dictated that further work at Portland be given a low priority. The task of filling Couch Lake began in 1888,[29] but the "great depot" built on that site was not completed until 1896.[30]

In 1891 the Northern Pacific Railroad had to undertake line improvements enabling it to compete with the Great Northern Railway. As part of this upgrading program new alignments totalling 14 miles in length[31] were built between Algoma and Athol, Idaho.[32] A five-mile section at the Algoma end involved moving the railway to the west side of Cocolalla Creek to eliminate trestles. West of Granite, a new nine-mile-long cut-off crossed the end of Lake Prescott on a 1,400-foot-long, 100-foot-high steel viaduct[33] and passed through a tunnel 440 feet long.[34] It then followed a pronounced westward detour, designed to ease the grade from 52 feet to the mile to 20 feet to the mile on the westbound climb to the height of land near Athol. The main contractor, Thomas Olsen & Company of Spokane,[35] began work in October 1891.[36] When the new alignment was completed in the summer of 1892[37] the company abandoned the original easterly loop.[38]

Throughout the late 1880s and early 1890s, heavier rails were laid on all main lines. In 1888 OR&N relaid the Mountain Division between Pendleton and La Grande, Oregon, with 70-pound rails of English manufacture,[39] and used the old 56-pound iron rails for the Heppner branch.[40] In 1890 upgrading of parts of the Pendleton-Spokane route similarly produced enough old rails to lay track on the new branch line from La Grande to Elgin. At the same time, Northern Pacific spent over $1 million, system wide, for new rails enabling its trains to run faster in competition with the Great Northern.[41]

Increases in passenger traffic placed a considerable strain on existing depot facilities. Spokane, with a population of nearly 12,000 in July 1888,[42] soon required a bigger station.[43] A new Northern Pacific passenger depot was opened on the site of the original building on Railroad Avenue between Post and Mill streets in April 1887.[44] Unfortunately, it burned to the ground in the great fire of August 4, 1889.[45] The company then built an entirely new passenger station several blocks further east, on the south side of Sprague Street, a short distance east of Bernard.[46] This new two-storey brick building, 150 feet by 70 feet, was opened in January 1891[47] and is still used by Amtrak (albeit with the railroad tracks elevated to first floor level as part of downtown grade separation works completed in 1917). In 1890 a start was also made on railway yards at the east end of Riverside Avenue in Spokane. The new NP yard facilities included a freight house 360 feet by 60 feet, and cost, in all, $250,000.[48] This investment, however, was probably justified, for in the fiscal year 1888-1889 the combined passenger and freight revenues collected by Northern Pacific at Spokane reached $1,579,882, a figure that compared well with $2,082,504 at Tacoma and only $925,642 at Seattle.[49]

Until 1891, passenger train schedules were frequently augmented to keep pace with the expansion of the railway system and meet competition from rival lines. When the old companies subsequently encountered financial difficulty, however, the same services were curtailed to reduce operating expenses.

The most significant schedule changes were caused by the divorce of the Northern Pacific and OR&N companies in 1889. Shortly afterward[50] Northern Pacific ceased to use the Columbia Valley line, routing all through-trains from Portland to Spokane via Tacoma and the Stampede Tunnel. Union Pacific trains from Portland, meanwhile, reached Spokane via Pendleton, Walla Walla, Riparia, and Colfax. As a result of this corporate upheaval, the distance and journey time between Portland and Spokane increased from 375 miles in 15 hours and 20 minutes on the Villard route via Wallula, to 481 miles in 23 hours and 45 minutes over the Union Pacific via Pendleton, and 544 miles in 21 hours and 55 minutes over the Northern Pacific via Tacoma. Such were the benefits of competition!

Perusal of the *Traveller's Official Guide*[51] for June 1893 indicates that in January 1893, Northern Pacific was running one through train each way, each day between St. Paul, Tacoma, and Portland (trains Nos. 1 and 4). West of Spokane this service was supplemented by one additional fast train each way, each day (Nos.

2 and 3).[52] Further east, a pair of daily trains between Helena, Montana, and Wallace, Idaho (Nos. 5 and 6), supplemented Nos. 1 and 4 on the main line between Helena and De Smet.

On the Northern Pacific branch lines, train services were designed primarily to link the country areas with regional centers. The Spokane & Idaho and Spokane & Palouse branches, therefore, were served from Spokane without special effort being made to provide connections with main line trains. Each of these branches enjoyed one train each way daily except Sunday. The former SLS&E line from Spokane to Davenport, meanwhile, only saw trains on Tuesdays, Thursdays, and Saturdays. In contrast, the two daily (except Sundays) Central Washington branch trains that did not run through to Spokane were scheduled to make close connections at Cheney with main line trains Nos. 1 and 4. Good connections were also available at Pasco for the Hunt system, and at Puyallup for the Northern Pacific & Puget Sound Shore line to Seattle. In the Coeur d'Alene mining camp, meanwhile, the narrow gauge Mission-Wallace-Burke line continued to operate as a separate entity, without providing connections at Wallace with standard gauge trains on the Northern Pacific & Montana branch.[53]

On the Hunt system, W&CR trains No. 1, from Dayton to Pendleton, and No. 2 in the opposite direction, were both timed to arrive at Hunt's Junction at 10:00 a. m. and depart at 12:35 p. m., thus allowing time for an intervening round trip to Pasco to connect with Northern Pacific trains Nos. 1 and 4. Between Hunt's Junction and Walla Walla there was an additional round trip (trains No. 4 eastbound and No. 3 westbound) daily except Sundays. On Mondays, Wednesdays, and Fridays, No. 1 took a side trip from Killian's Junction[54] to Athena (Centerville) and back before completing its journey to Pendleton. And on Sundays only there was a round trip (trains No. 6 outward and No. 5 return) from Hunt's Junction to Pleasant View (Estes) and back.

Meanwhile, Union Pacific's subsidiary Oregon Short Line & Utah Northern Railway ran two through-trains each way daily over the former OR&N lines between Huntington and Portland, Oregon. Of these trains, No. 1 (westbound) and No. 2 (eastbound) were the Omaha/Kansas City expresses. West of Umatilla, train No. 7 from Huntington was merged with No. 3 from Walla Walla and proceeded to Portland as No. 3. In the opposite direction No. 4 from Portland to Walla Walla was divided at Umatilla, leaving Huntington section to go southeast as No. 8.[55] Spokane was served from Pendleton, Oregon, by train No. 5 (northbound) and No. 6 (southbound). Train No. 6, leaving Spokane at 7:00 a. m., connected at Pendleton in the evening with No. 8 for Huntington and No. 1 for Portland. Train No. 5, leaving Pendleton at 7:00 a. m., took on passengers arriving from Portland on No. 2, but made no connection with any train from the East. Spokane-bound passengers on No. 1, therefore, had to stay overnight at Pendleton.[56] Numbers 5 and 6, however, made excellent connections with trains on the Dayton, Pomeroy, Pleasant Valley, and Moscow branches. On Mondays, Wednesdays, and Fridays there was also a connection with the westbound train from La Crosse to Connell.

The former OR&N route to the Coeur d'Alene mining camp was operated from Tekoa in a manner allowing passengers to proceed directly from Spokane to Wallace on trains Nos. 6 and 92 in the morning, and return on Nos. 91 and 5 in the afternoon.[57] The Heppner branch, meanwhile, was worked from Heppner by No. 10 (northbound) in the morning and No. 9 (southbound) in the afternoon, good connections for Portland passengers being made at Arlington with trains Nos. 3 and 4.[58]

The above account of train services in 1893 fails to take into account the fact that for many years passengers could travel in the caboose cars of regular freight trains. On November 27, 1888 the *Pendleton East Oregonian* advised its readers that the full complement of OR&N trains leaving Portland each day was:

Train No.	Type	Leaves at:	From	To
2	Express	8:00 a.m.	Portland West Side	Walla Walla
10	Freight	8:45 a.m.	E. Portland	Wallula
12	Freight	11:00 a.m.	E. Portland	The Dalles
4	Express	2:40 p.m.	Portland West Side	Huntington
8	Freight	8:30 p.m.	E. Portland	Umatilla
14	Freight	10:45 p.m.	E. Portland	Wallula

Anyone missing express No. 4 was advised to take freight No. 8, allowing him to reach Pendleton at 5:20 p. m., almost eight hours ahead of the next regular passenger train. Westbound freights were reported to leave Umatilla at 9:15 a. m., 2:20 p. m., and 12:45 a. m., thus supplementing passenger train No. 1 (from Walla Walla) and No. 3 (from Huntington) leaving Umatilla respectively at 8:55 a. m. and 8:10 p. m.[59]

Main line passenger trains were scheduled to cross the Columbia Interior at overall average speeds (including stops) of about 24 mph. Higher speeds were called for only on the relatively few sections of straight and level track. The tightest Northern Pacific timings pertained to the long, easily graded tangents in the lower Yakima Valley. Over the 66 miles between Kiona and Yakima, the mean timetable speed of all four daily passenger trains was 32.8 mph. Similar speeds were called for on the newly upgraded 20-mile section of main line between Algoma and Granite, Idaho. On the Union Pacific, the fastest timings were for the 20 straight miles between Baker City and North Powder, Oregon, where the mean passenger train speed was again 32.8 mph.[60]

On the mountain grades speed fell to less than 20 mph. Between De Smet and Arlee, Montana, the 10-mile climb to Evaro in each direction slowed down Northern Pacific Nos. 1 and 4 respectively to 17.1 and 16.5 mph. The ascent to the Stampede Tunnel produced similar speeds in the Cascade Mountains. Union Pacific main line trains likewise were scheduled to run at about 16 mph when climbing from Hilgard or Huron to Kamela in the Blue Mountains. On the Alto hill, meanwhile, train No. 6 from Spokane to Pendleton was allowed 23 minutes to struggle up the last five miles of 3 percent grade from Relief to the summit, thus attaining a mean velocity of 13 mph. On all of the above-mentioned grades, helper engines would almost certainly have been required.

Branch line operations generally proceeded at a leisurely pace. Between Marshall and Genesee, trains on Northern Pacific's Spokane & Palouse branch ran at an overall average speed of 15 mph. Similar speeds also prevailed on Union Pacific branch lines into agricultural areas. Dayton passengers thus sped to their destination at 15.6 mph, while those bound for Pomeroy had to be content with only 13.3 mph. Train No. 9 on the Heppner branch was scheduled to complete its 55.7-mile homeward trajectory in 3 hours 18 minutes at a mean velocity of 16.9 mph. Complaints voiced in the press, however, tell us that the elderly and decrepit engines successively based at Heppner often failed to accomplish even this modest task. On November 14, 1889 the Heppner *Gazette* reported that:

> The OR&N people have put an old tub of an engine on the Willow Creek branch and as a result the train comes in late almost every evening. This antiquated piece of railroad furniture should be relegated to a pile of scrap iron, and an engine put on in its place that will pull its own weight at least. We are informed that it is not uncommon for the train to stop between stations coming up, to allow the tub to get up steam.[61]

A few favored branches were better served. Between Cheney and Coulee City the Central Washington branch trains were scheduled to run at an average speed of 22.7 mph, and on the W&CR Railroad, trains between Walla Walla and Hunt's Junction were booked to achieve a mean 23.5 mph. The Coeur d'Alene mining camp, meanwhile, was particularly well served, OSL&UN train No. 92 was scheduled to cover the 80 miles from Tekoa to Wallace in 3 hours 5 minutes at a mean speed of no less than 25.9 mph. The return journey on No. 91, moreover, was accomplished in only 3 hours at 26.7 mph, a performance better than that achieved by the same company on its main lines. Mining men evidently were afforded better service.

In addition to regularly scheduled trains there were many "specials" of various kinds. In those days before the advent of the automobile, Spokane residents could enjoy Northern Pacific summer Sunday excursions to both Medical Lake and Coeur d'Alene City. In 1892 these outings were so well patronized that the excursion season was extended for several weeks into the month of September.[62] Railroads often put on specials to convey people to musical and theatrical performances, or to other unusual and spectacular events. As an example of the latter, on May 18, 1890, Heppner residents, paying only $2.50, were taken to Cascade Locks to see the steamer *Harvest Queen* shoot the rapids on her way down the Columbia River.[63] Some special excursions also ran for the exclusive benefit of railroad employees. Early in August 1886 the entire staff of the Northern Pacific shops at Sprague, and many other railroaders from Cheney and Spokane Falls, were taken with their families to Hope, Idaho, for an annual picnic. The elaborately decorated train left Sprague at 6:00 a. m. and arrived at Hope at 10:30 a. m. with 700 people and two bands aboard. The party-goers spent the day in "various amusements and excursions on the lake," dancing being one of the principal features. Everything was said to have "passed off with the most perfect harmony."[64]

Not all the passengers traveling on special trains made their journeys by choice. On May 10, 1887 a "tough looking crowd" of 93 convicts, chained together in pairs, were transferred under heavily armed guard from Seatco, Washington Territory, via Portland to the newly built penitentiary at Walla Walla.[65]

Other involuntary passengers included circus animals. The coming of a circus was heralded two weeks before any engagement by the arrival of an advertising car, bearing men charged with the task of decorating each town with "flaming gorgeous posters." The circus trains themselves caused severe headaches for railway operating departments, for they were heavy and had to be run in several sections. The poor condition of the rolling stock, moreover, brought delays. For example, the Sells Brothers' circus train, visiting the Pacific Northwest in 1888, consisted of 48 cars and ran in two sections, the second being composed of the menagerie and the sleeping quarters for the performers. The train left Dayton (OR&N) for La Grande, Oregon, on an early August day in 1888 with the running gear of most of the cars in "badly dilapidated condition, causing hot boxes, slowness in travel, and profanity on the part of the trainmen." After a late start and trouble with the cars, engine No. 69, hauling the first section, failed "because of the severe strain placed upon it." This breakdown held up the departure of the regular morning passenger train from Pendleton to Walla Walla and disrupted railway operations for the whole day.[66]

When "specials" were not available, companies offered reduced fares for excursion travel on regular trains. For example, in the fall of 1888 OR&N advertised excursions from Pendleton to the Mechanics' Fair at Portland for $11.00. On Mondays only, the fare was further reduced to $9.75. Outings were simultaneously available to the Walla Walla Fair for $2.00 and to the Whitman County Fair at Colfax for $9.60.[67]

Long hours spent in trains obliged passengers either to bring their own food or obtain meals en route. Meal stops remained the order of the day throughout the 1880s. On the OR&N, trains continued to pause at "Grandma and Grandpa" Munra's famous establishment at Bonneville, Oregon, where there was always a variety of well-prepared food on the tables.[68] Further east, the meal stop in the Blue Mountains was moved in 1886 from Meacham to Kamela, where a new dining room 20 feet by 36 feet had just opened.[69] The days of the line-side restaurants, however, were numbered. In August 1889 Union Pacific introduced dining cars on the Portland to Omaha service, offering elegant meals at a cost of 75 cents. The first such car to arrive in Portland, on August 22, 1889, was the *Coronado*, with conductor F. H. Duncan supervising "attentive and courteous" black waiters.[70]

When passengers desired to stop overnight at intermediate points, or had to do so because of poor connections between trains, some railway hotels were available. The Northern Pacific Railroad intended the handsome *Lakeside*, built on a high bench overlooking Lake Pend d'Oreille at Hope, Idaho, to be a tourist attraction. Opened late in the summer of 1886,[71] this establishment gave sightseers the opportunity to pause long enough in north Idaho to take a lake cruise aboard the Pend d'Oreille & Northern Pacific Steam Navigation Company vessels *Bluebell* and *Antelope*. After March 1889 guests were also able to enjoy outings on the handsome new 70-foot-long *C. H. Prescott*.[72]

Wallula was hardly a place to attract tourists. The modest OR&N hotel there catered more to those obliged by the railway timetable to stop over. The original hotel was destroyed by fire on January 10, 1886. The building, however, was insured for $26,000 with the Liverpool, London & Globe Insurance Company,[73] and was replaced later in the same year by a new hotel[74] with 27 rooms. Newburger & Oline, lessees of the original building, took out the franchise on the new one and opened its doors to the public on December 1, 1886.[75]

Completion of the largest railway hotel in the Pacific Northwest was delayed for almost a decade. Villard's grandiose project for the Hotel Portland was first announced in March 1883.[76] Situated on a city block bounded by 6th, 7th, Morrison, and Yamhill streets in Portland, the building was laid out in plan as a great "H," with a courtyard on 6th Street, and 225 rooms, all facing outward. Work began in 1883 but was brought to a halt by Villard's downfall.

The architects, McKim, Mead, & White of New York, were left unpaid for their services and in March 1885 brought suit under the mechanics lien law for the recovery of $17,544.99 owed to them.[77] The partly constructed hotel, meanwhile, was left derelict.[78] In December 1887 prominent citizens of Portland offered a $50,000 bonus for the completion of "Villard's Hotel," as it was called in the city.[79] In response, the Portland Hotel Company was formed on April 26, 1888 to finish the work.[80] Construction resumed later in 1888 and continued throughout 1889. The hotel was finally opened on April 7, 1890 at an estimated cost of $1 million.[81]

Freight carried on the railroads of the Columbia Interior prior to 1893 reflected the primarily agricultural nature of the economy. Grain, livestock, and other farm products took first place. Mineral traffic failed in the short run to justify the high cost of extending railways into mountainous mining areas, while the lumber trade had not yet reached transcontinental proportions.

The increasing output of grain from the Columbia Interior presented the railroads with perennial difficulty. The situation first became serious in the fall of 1885 when the OR&N faced the task of moving nearly 300,000 tons of grain and flour[82] to Portland. On May 22, 1886, 50,000 tons still remained to be moved,[83] and some people expressed doubts about the railroad's ability to handle the larger crops expected in future. In 1886 the construction of rival branches in the Palouse added to the OR&N burden west of Wallula. Grain traffic originating on the Northern Pacific lines in the Interior provided 1,823 carloads, all shipped to Portland.[84] Oakesdale alone loaded over 200 cars.[85] In 1887, Northern Pacific opened the Stampede Pass switchbacks and offered to ship Palouse-grown wheat to Puget Sound for $5.00 per ton. Given that NP charged $1.00 per ton for moving grain from Palouse Junction to Wallula, OR&N had to charge $6.00 per ton to break even on carrying the same grain to Portland.[86] The Northern Pacific inducement succeeded in diverting 1,622 carloads to Tacoma. However, because the capacity of the switchback line was very limited, 2,763 cars originating on NP lines still had to be sent to Portland over the OR&N.[87]

The Oregon company, meanwhile, had great difficulty moving all the grain loaded on its own lines. Although it blamed its problems on a shortage of cars,[88] there were other factors. The OR&N still employed a large number of obsolete, 12-ton capacity cars.[89] Press reports of unusually long trains, moreover, indicate that there may also have been a shortage of serviceable locomotives. On September 30, 1887, a train of 61 cars, loaded with 915 tons of wheat, left Walla Walla for Portland;[90] and again on November 5, 1887 a 68-car train was dispatched with 1,020 tons.[91] Returning trains of empties, meanwhile, had as many as 90 cars.[92] The 1887 harvest took almost a year to move. In the following spring grain trains were still leaving Pomeroy, while the riverboats continued to service areas without railway access. On April 19, 1888 the *John Gates* was reported to be moving Eureka Flat grain down the Snake River from Jim Fort's Landing to Wallula. The *D. S. Baker*, meanwhile, went upstream to a point 25 miles above Lewiston to take on grain from Montgomery Ridge.[93]

The crux of the problem was that the railroads could not reasonably be expected to handle the entire Columbia Interior grain crop in 30 days each season.[94] Farmers complained bitterly about delays in shipment but waited for the railroad companies or their nominees to build most of the grain elevators needed for interim storage. In February 1889, OR&N announced that elevators would be built that same year at 29 points on their lines. Company officials had also selected sites for the future construction of another seven elevators.[95] At Portland, meanwhile, a one-million-bushel terminal elevator[96] was completed in October 1889.[97] All of these storage facilities were built by Peavey & Company, the Minneapolis flour merchants.[98]

In 1888 Northern Pacific set out to divert a large proportion of the Interior grain traffic to the Port of Tacoma. Some 3,775 carloads originating on NP lines were sent over the mountains to Puget Sound, 900 were dispatched to the East, and only 312 were ceded to the OR&N for shipment to Portland.[99]

Less grain was produced in 1889, but in 1890 there was another bountiful harvest, and Northern Pacific found itself overwhelmed. Pasco especially became a bottleneck in the system, for although the locomotives could easily bring large incoming trains downhill from the grain-growing areas, they could only draw small ones away uphill to the Stampede Tunnel. On December 23, 1890 the *Spokane Review* reported the Pasco yards choked with cars. During the previous week there had not been a day when less than 600 loaded cars stood there, unable to move "for lack of motive power."[100] Until larger and more powerful engines became available, the capacity of the Cascade Branch was quite limited. In the fiscal year ending June 30, 1891, some 7,121 carloads of wheat were moved over the Stampede Pass to Puget Sound. Another 206 were handed over to Union Pacific at Wallula, and no less than 6,000 went east, apparently to relieve the congestion.[101]

For the time being, Northern Pacific proved incapable of handling all the grain offered to it, and OR&N, despite efforts to provide better service, remained the farmers' *bête noir*. Consequently, several schemes, both public and private, were advanced for the revival of water transportation on the Columbia River.

The "Open River" movement, as it was called, brought pressure to bear on the United States government to complete the canal at Cascade Locks and build another at Celilo. Work at the Cascades began in 1877 but the canal was not opened until November 6, 1896.[102] Meanwhile, in 1891 the newly organized The Dalles, Portland, & Astoria Navigation Company placed the sternwheelers *Regulator* and *The Dalles City* respectively on the Middle and Lower rivers.[103] At the same time, as an interim measure, the Oregon State Board of Portage Commissioners opened a narrow gauge portage railway on the south side of the river at the Cascades,[104] a railway phased out when the canal was opened.

The obstructions to navigation between The Dalles and Celilo took much longer to overcome. Due to the slowness of government decision making, private interests at first seized the initiative. Early in October 1890, Spokane capitalists formed the Columbia Railway & Navigation Company to operate steamboats on the Columbia and Snake rivers and build a 21-mile portage railway between Columbus and Crates Point in Klickitat County, Washington.[105] The officers of this company were A. M. Cannon (former Mayor of Spokane), president; Paul F. Mohr (of the SLS&E), vice-president; J. R. Allen, secretary; and W. Lair Hill, general counsel. In 1891 these promoters invited citizens of Portland to purchase $500,000 worth of 6 percent, 40-year bonds,[106] claiming, at that time, to have graded half of the roadbed and laid four miles of track. In January 1893 the company let a contract to McKenzie & Glynn for the remainder of the construction work and purchased rails.[107] However, the project soon encountered difficulties, both financial and political.

The United States was slow to formulate a policy for improving navigation at The Dalles-Celilo. For several years prior to 1890 senators from Oregon had actively promoted what was known as "the Boat Railway," a means by which vessels could be berthed on huge rail-mounted carriages and moved between different river levels on two inclined planes with stationary winding engines and rope haulage.[108] The Boat Railway was extensively studied, and bills for its construction were introduced into Congress. The U. S. Army Engineers, however, opposed the scheme and it was finally abandoned. In September 1893 the Board of Engineers recommended that a canal eventually be built on the Oregon side of the river. It further recommended that, in the interim, a portage railway, also on the south side, be built to satisfy the urgent demands of wheat growers and facilitate construction of the canal.[109]

This pronouncement dealt the Spokane promoters of the Columbia Railway & Navigation Company a blow from which they never fully recovered. In a last spasm of activity in 1899-1900 they purchased and refitted the former Northern Pacific transfer boat *Frederick K. Billings* and once more attempted to complete the Columbus-to-Crates Point railway,[110] but without success. Construction of the eight-mile-long Oregon State Portage Railway between Celilo and Big Eddy, Oregon, started in 1903.[111] Despite legal harassment by Union Pacific, the work proceeded satisfactorily, and the line was opened on June 3, 1905.[112] It took another nine years, however, to complete the Celilo Canal. Consequently, between 1882 and 1914 water transportation on the Columbia River remained an insignificant factor in the economy of the Pacific Northwest.

Although grain was the single largest commodity handled by the railroads in the Interior, movements of livestock and wool represented seasonally important sources of revenue. Cattle were carried each spring from the Willamette Valley in Oregon to pastures beyond the mountains in Idaho and Montana, there to be fattened for the Chicago market. Empty trains were sent south from Portland on the Oregon & California Railroad to pick up the cattle and take them directly eastward over the Northern Pacific without change of cars.[113] Horses from the Yakima and Umatilla valleys were also shipped east in large numbers.[114] On September 20, 1886, for example, Northern Pacific ran a special train of 33 cars bearing 760 horses eastbound from Prosser, Washington Territory.[115] The horse traffic, however, collapsed when Eastern cities adopted electric streetcars in the early 1890s. Thereafter, only a brief revival took place in 1899 to meet British army requirements for the South African War.[116]

Eastern Oregon raised large numbers of sheep for both meat and wool. On May 10, 1887 some 22,000 mutton sheep were reported to have been dispatched from Pendleton, both east to Chicago and west to Puget Sound and Victoria, B. C.[117] Other sheep, however, continued to walk to their destinations. Even after OR&N opened the Heppner branch, flocks of many thousands were still driven overland each year from Morrow County to points as far away as Nebraska.[118] Wool produced in eastern Oregon was first sent to Portland for sorting, grading, and bailing before being shipped east. Thus, on May 27, 1886, no less than 125 carloads arrived at Albina for such treatment.[119]

Before 1893 the forests of the Great Lakes region were not yet wholly depleted, and the transcontinental lumber trade remained in its infancy.[120] Nevertheless, by 1888 OR&N was already shipping lumber, laths, and shingles from Portland to Denver, Colorado, the latter city being described by the *Oregonian* as "the largest and most profitable market Oregon has east of the Cascades." In April 1888 the rate charged for carrying lumber to Denver was reduced from 55 cents per hundred to 40 cents to compete in that market with an inferior product brought north from Texas over the newly opened Denver, Texas, & Gulf Railroad.[121] The OR&N, however, continued to charge 15 cents per hundred for the much shorter haul from Portland to the treeless agricultural areas of the Columbia Interior.[122]

Lumbering operations, meanwhile, were rapidly established in the Grande Ronde and Powder River basins of eastern Oregon. In 1888, Spencer, Ramsey, & Hall and other smaller producers shipped 1,300 carloads of lumber eastward from North Powder.[123] During the following year lumbermen from Chippewa and Eau Claire, Wisconsin, formed the Grande Ronde Lumber Company and built extensive mills three miles west of La Grande.[124] These gentlemen changed the course of the Grande Ronde River and created a mill pond capable of holding seven million board feet of sawlogs. They then established flood dams on tributary streams to facilitate log drives at all seasons of the year. Drawing timber from as far as 25 miles away, they estimated their reserves at 800 million board feet and aimed to produce 200,000 feet daily, all to be dressed and seasoned before shipment.[125]

Other timber barons soon followed. In April 1890 residents of Baker City were asked for a $50,000 subscription to the stock of a company proposing to build a logging railway to Sumpter Valley and open a sash and door factory at Baker.[126] The request was well received, and later that year the Sumpter Valley Railroad was incorporated in Oregon to build a narrow gauge road from Baker westward up the South Fork Powder River 25 miles to Fort Sumpter. The promoters were John Stoddard, C. W. Nibley, David Eccles, T. D. Lee, and J. C. West.[127] Work began immediately and the railway was opened to Sumpter in the fall of 1891.[128]

Besides grain, livestock, wool, lumber, coal, and other minerals, the railroads carried everything else offered to them, from live black bass for stocking Western lakes[129] to watermelons for the manufacture of Jamaica ginger.[130] Innovations were welcomed and challenges met. The hop traffic provides a good example. In the fall of 1888, E. Meeker & Company of Puyallup, Washington, sent an experimental shipment of hops to London, England. In 1889 Northern Pacific offered to run a special train of 16 or more cars to the Atlantic seaboard, leaving Puyallup on September 18 and reaching New York on October 2. The hops would thus be available on the London market when prices peaked about October 20.[131] It is unclear whether or not the offer was taken up that year. On September 23, 1890, however, a solid train of 24 cars, loaded with hops from the Puyallup and White River valleys, went east, each car loaded with seven and a half tons of hops valued at 30 cents per pound. The whole consignment was expected to sell for $108,000 when it reached London 32 days later.[132] The hop growers and the railroads spared no effort to develop the trade. Within 10 years a large traffic in hops had developed. In the long run, however, sudden and unpredictable fluctuations in world hop prices mitigated against the export trade in that commodity.[133]

In order to handle increasing railway traffic, the railroads purchased larger locomotives and cars. The Northern Pacific used large 2-8-0 locomotives in the Cascade Mountains.[134] Five heavy freight engines of the same wheel arrangement were built for use on the steeply graded parts of the OR&N system by Rome Locomotive Works, Rome, New York in 1888.[135] The press extensively heralded the arrival of these engines. Echoing an announcement in the Portland *Oregonian*,[136] the *Pendleton East Oregonian* stated on October 30, 1888 that:

> Several mammoth locomotives, 40 tons heavier than the passenger engines now in use, will (soon) arrive in Pendleton and will be used solely for the purpose of hauling trains over the summit between here and La Grande. They are dubbed "Moguls" by railroaders and are worthy of the name.[137]

The first of five such engines arrived that very week, for on November 6, 1888 the *East Oregonian* announced with fitting awe that:

> A "Mogul" engine was seen at the Pendleton yards Sunday on its way to the summit between Pendleton and the Grande Ronde Valley. It is a monster specimen of locomotive building and loomed up immensely as it glided along the rails.[138]

Only four of the fabled five were in fact used on the Mountain Division. The fifth went straight to Starbuck to work on the Alto hill and immediately proved itself capable of taking no less than nine loaded cars to the summit unaided.[139] As no one engine had previously taken more than five cars, this was a feat indeed and may well have justified the $11,000 cost of the new locomotive.[140]

For working heavier passenger trains OR&N obtained 13 new 10-wheelers from Rome Locomotive Works late in 1889.[141] These engines superseded earlier, lighter 4-6-0's built by Manchester Locomotive Works, Manchester, New Hampshire, in 1883.[142] A year later Northern Pacific obtained new 10-wheelers from Baldwin Locomotive Works, Philadelphia, Pennsylvania. One of the first such engines to arrive on the Pacific Slope was No. 626, sent new to Missoula, Montana, for use on the run to Hope, Idaho. This engine was entrusted to veteran locomotive engineer James Baillie, who was reported to be "very proud of it."[143]

The locomotive fuel situation in the Pacific Northwest was saved by the opening of the Northern Pacific coal mines at Roslyn, Washington Territory, late in 1886. Within four years, production from these mines rose to no less than 55,200 tons per month, of which the Northern Pacific took 37,400 tons for use as locomotive fuel as far east as Billings, Montana.[144] In the fiscal year 1890-1891 Northern Pacific obtained 39 percent of its fuel from Roslyn

(309,516 out of a total 791,401 tons).[145] The minehead cost to the NPRR was $2.75 per ton, which compared very favorably with $4.70 per ton paid by Union Pacific for Newcastle coal brought by sea from Seattle to Portland.[146] After a disastrous coal famine on the OR&N lines early in 1888,[147] and the failure to find workable coal deposits in eastern Oregon,[148] Union Pacific also turned to Roslyn, and by December 1890 was buying 12,270 tons of that coal per month.

During the 1880s prices in general continued to decline while wages remained constant. The organization of railroad labor continued to be the prerogative of brotherhoods serving the separate interests of individual grades of employees. Locomotive engineers, firemen, conductors, and brakemen all had their own associations, functioning primarily as mutual benefit or friendly societies. Whenever disputes arose with the railway companies, each brotherhood acted alone, and often came out rather badly.[149] Consequently, by 1889 there was already a yearning for greater railroad labor solidarity. When a local of the Brotherhood of Railroad Brakemen[150] was established at La Grande, Oregon, in July 1889, members of all three other organizations turned out in force to hear a keynote address given by Grand Master Brakeman Wilkinson of Galesburg, Illinois.[151] It was perhaps no surprise, therefore, that Eugene V. Debs received immediate and widespread response when he formed the single, great, industry-wide American Railway Union (ARU) during the economic collapse of 1893.

On September 26, 1893, ARU organizers George W. Howard and James Hogan arrived in Pendleton, Oregon, to address the assembled railroad workers. Mr. Howard pointed out that while the brotherhoods, acting independently, could accomplish little, "by a grand union of the army of railroaders a power would be formed with an irresistible force, like that of a mighty river." The *East Oregonian* reported that "his speech took well, and all the railroaders present who had not signed before, promptly became members of the local union formed at Pendleton." The paper added that ARU locals had been established at every point on the Union Pacific between Omaha and Portland.[152]

Chief Homily Local No. 43 of the American Railway Union was at least a social success. At a ball given under its auspices on November 21, 1893 the people of Pendleton showed "their liberal encouragement" by purchasing 90 tickets. According to the *East Oregonian*, Frazers Opera House dance floor was in good condition and "the owners of the many nimble feet that glided merrily over its smooth surface voted the affair one of the most enjoyable they ever attended."[153]

None of those who attended the ball that evening could have foreseen that within 12 months the ARU would be crushed in a wave of repression arising from an attempt to support striking workers at the Pullman Company car manufacturing plant near Chicago. Nor could they have foreseen that their bid for labor solidarity would so quickly lead to a Supreme Court decision providing American employers with the means of nullifying strikes at their outset; a ruling, moreover, that was not reversed until 1932.[154]

Of all the natural hazards faced by the railroads, snow was probably the worst. Although the 1886 invention of the Leslie steam rotary snowplow revolutionized snow removal,[155] the worst winter weather continued to bring trains to a halt for a week or more at a time. The rotaries did well, but there were few of them and they could not tackle mountain snow slides containing fallen trees.[156] In the severe winter weather of January and February 1890, the Union Pacific used both the Leslie rotary and its rival, the Jull snowplow, on its lines in the Columbia Interior.[157] On January 1, a Spokane-bound passenger train became stuck in a 14-foot snowdrift just north of Tekoa. During the following week the Leslie rotary plough used in the Columbia Valley was sent up to clear the road, but encountered a band of horses in a deep cut. The huge machine "chawed up" several of the unfortunate animals, but was damaged in doing so and had to be taken back to Tekoa for repairs. Consequently the Tekoa-Spokane line was not reopened until January 9. On January 11 bad weather hit the Powder River basin of eastern Oregon and six trains became blockaded near Baker City, there to remain for the next week. A passenger who eventually arrived at Spokane on January 21 told the *Review* that

> There were about 300 passengers altogether and three of them died while we were there. I guess we would never have got away from there had it not been for the new fangled plough which was sent out from Omaha. This machine is a new invention and is called the Jull, after its inventor, who came with it.

The plough is a kind of auger, which makes 300 revolutions a minute. It does not throw the snow like a rotary plough, but banks it up at the sides. It is undoubtedly the greatest snowplough ever invented and bored its way through drifts upon which the rotary snowplough had been unable to make any impression. The rotaries could do nothing in the snowsheds (at Pyles Canyon above Union)[158] which were filled with snow, but the Jull went right through.[159]

Before the end of January more bad weather came. Between Tekoa and Latah the cuts were again filled with snow, to depths of 40 feet. The Jull plough was brought north and "worked well as far as it could go." Eventually, however, the line had to be cleared by 400 men with shovels, working in some places in three tiers. This process was not completed and the line reopened until February 27, 1890.[160]

At other times of year OR&N had to contend with drifting sand. Drifts formed at various points in the Columbia Valley east of the Cascades every time there was dry weather and a high wind. The first recorded derailment due to sand occurred in May 1881 when (former OSN) engine No. 5 struck a drift east of The Dalles.[161] Later that year OR&N built eight watch houses in the sandy districts between Umatilla and Celilo to give warning of drifts to train crews.[162] The drifting sand problem was attributed to range cattle eating every stitch of vegetation and leaving the sand loose. By May 1883, OR&N had discovered that raising the track above the general level of the country prevented the sand from collecting on it. Moreover, a weed known as "dock" was found to be stabilizing drifts in low-lying areas beyond the right of way.[163] Optimism, however, was short lived, for on November 23, 1883 severe drifting between Blalock's and Umatilla brought all trains to a halt.[164] The sand problem just would not go away. Every spring and summer brought more reports of trains stranded and engines derailed. On June 30, 1889, The Dalles baseball team was unable to play at Arlington because three trains had been caught in a sandstorm near Grant's and one engine was off the track.[165] Union Pacific built a special sand-removing machine,[166] but the problem eventually had to be solved by preventing the drifts from forming. In 1892 further experiments demonstrated that boards, properly placed about four inches above the ground in critical areas, would keep the sand moving and prevent it from lodging. As of October 1892 no trains had been held up at the point where the boards had been installed, and a solution appeared to be in sight.[167]

The OR&N also had to contend occasionally with drifting material of a third kind. On December 16, 1887 the *Pendleton East Oregonian* reported that

> Not long ago a train was delayed near Milton by tumbleweeds, the wind having piled a cut full of them. When the engine ran into the cut the weeds crowded up to the front of the cow-catcher in a solid mass, bringing the train to a standstill. The only way out was to set fire to the weeds and wait until they were burned up.[168]

Fire was otherwise a constant hazard, both for the railroads and their neighbors. Unfortunately, railway officials, in common with the general public, tended to take precautions after the fact. Early in August 1886 a disastrous fire at LaGrande, Oregon, destroyed railway and other property alike. As a result, in the following year OR&N installed a better water supply and fire protection system, with a pump developing 52 feet of head and 12 hydrants safeguarding the company's buildings.[169]

Locomotives caused many grass fires, especially in dry and windy weather. In country areas section men were responsible for preventing such fires from spreading but their efforts were often inadequate. A fire caused by a locomotive passing Hot Lake, Oregon, in December 1887 spread through the Grande Ronde Valley destroying most of the year's hay.[170] Earlier that season OR&N had laid off many of the section men as an economy measure.[171]

From the railroad point of view roundhouse fires were particularly disastrous. In the early hours of May 18, 1893 fire broke out in the Union Pacific roundhouse at Starbuck, Washington, as a result of an oil lamp explosion. In less than an hour, the roundhouse, oil house, machine shop, commissary, and office had burned to the ground, badly damaging 13 locomotives. The only available engine in steam was employed heroically to draw all the cars on adjoining tracks to safety. At daylight the scene "was one of utter demolition of everything that had existed." Two locomotives had fallen over on their sides due to the pit timbers burning out unevenly beneath them, and all were "practically ruined, the parts being warped and the machinery drawn out of shape." The damaged locomotives included two passenger and two "hog" (i.e., large freight) engines. Several of these were being overhauled in preparation for the coming grain-handling season. The damage also included the shop stationary engine and all the machine tools. Fortunately, no one was hurt.[172] Other destructive roundhouse fires occurred at Albina, Oregon, on January 18, 1888,[173] at Ellensburg, Washington, on April 14, 1890,[174] and at Hope, Idaho, on August 23, 1891.[175]

Crime was a relatively minor hazard for the Interior railroads. Traveling auditors discouraged employee fraud and embezzlement.[176] In December 1885, OR&N dismissed the station agents at La Grande and Kamela, along with several freight conductors, for falsifying way bills and pocketing the takings.[177] Pilfering of freight cars, meanwhile, remained endemic. Burglary occurred at Colfax, Washington, on September 27, 1887 when the depot safe was blown to pieces with explosive and $2,000 taken.[178] The only reported train robbery took place on the Northern Pacific near "the notorious town of Pottsville," Idaho, on November 19, 1891. A pair of armed bandits entered the mail and express car while the train was in motion and forced the messenger, at gun point, to hand over the $2,800 payroll for the Gold Hunter Mine.[179] Potentially more serious was an attempted train wrecking on the OR&N between Meacham and Kamela in 1888. The criminals laid dynamite charges against the rails on a 60-foot-high trestle bridge and fired them under the locomotive of a passenger train. There was a big bang and enough blast to blow out the oil lamps in the engine cab, but the explosion caused no real damage. The would-be wreckers were arrested at Meacham in November 1888.[180]

Mentally deranged persons also caused occasional trouble. In this class was OR&N brakeman Erwin of Walla Walla, who on June 22, 1889 stole a locomotive and set off at full speed for Riparia. When the engine ran out of steam he was arrested and "adjudged insane."[181] Later that year an armed lunatic, apparently fleeing from treatment, held the passengers and crew aboard a Union Pacific express eastbound from Portland in a state of trepidation. Brandishing a large navy revolver he announced loudly that he did not believe in "this double doctor business." The trainmen humored him for 12 hours until he stepped off the cars at

Pendleton, where he was promptly overpowered and taken away. When searched he was found to have another gun and a first class ticket to New York.[182]

Beyond crime and insanity there was also sheer mischief. In September 1893 a raggedly dressed youth flagged down a westbound Union Pacific passenger train somewhere between Meacham and Gibbon, Oregon. As the cars ground to an unscheduled halt the conductor stepped down to the ballast, feeling certain that he was about to meet a young hero who had saved his train from some imminent disaster. As the youth approached, however, he asked the conductor for a chew of tobacco. When the conductor apologized for not having any, the young man jumped on the train and sought out the "news butcher," who likewise could not oblige. In disgust, the youth dropped to the ground and disappeared into the woods, saying out loud as he went that this must be a pretty poor kind of train not to have any tobacco aboard! The conductor, meanwhile, stood speechlessly beside the cars and watched him go.[183]

The number of railway accidents occurring on the various lines in the Columbia Interior increased greatly during the late 1880s. The alarming deterioration in the safety record was due not only to increases in route mileage and traffic density but also to the short life and early failure of the original structures and equipment. The number of reported accidents rose from four in 1885 to no less than thirty in 1888. After 1891 there was a marked improvement on the Northern Pacific and Union Pacific (former OR&N) lines, but the overall picture was marred by three collisions on the newly opened Great Northern Railway. Accidents reported in the press during the years 1887 to 1894 may be classified by cause, as follows:

A) <u>Accidents due to failure of physical plant</u>

Bridge structural collapse	6
Derailment due to defective track	12
Derailment due to defective wheel/axle	10
Unexplained derailment	11
Collision due to coupler failure	4
Subtotal	43

B) Collisions between trains

Head on (butting) collision	18
Rear end collision	6
Runaway on steep grade (other than those caused by coupler failure)	3
Collision in yard area	4
Collision at intersection of railways	1
Unspecified "wreck"	3
Subtotal	35

C) Collisions with obstructions

With cattle or horses, resulting in derailment	10
With rock slides and washouts	9
With road vehicles at crossings	2
With other obstructions	1
Subtotal	22

D) Other derailments

Due to misplaced switch	1
Due to shifting cargo	2
Due to collapse of burning bridge	4
Runaway on Portland/Albina ferry slips	3
Due to icy track	1
During snowplowing operations	3
Subtotal	14

E) Other mishaps

Car steam heater explosion	1
Subtotal	1

GRAND TOTAL	115

As a result of these accidents the reported casualties were:

	Killed	Injured
Railroaders	47	at least 75
Trespassers	11	at least 4
Passengers	3	33
Totals	61	at least 112

Bridge failures were the most significant accidents of the period. The first-generation, timber-trestle bridges remained a liability until they were either "filled" with earth to form embankments or replaced with more substantial structures. By 1894 nine such bridges, built by the Northern Pacific and OR&N in 1881-1882, had collapsed under the weight of trains, four of them after catching fire.

On the Northern Pacific the trestle bridges just west of Spokane were particularly troublesome. The trestle approach to the Hangman Creek bridge saw two derailments, the second of which, occurring on January 20, 1889, resulted in the collapse of the entire structure.[184] Another trestle bridge, nearer to Spokane, failed under a four-car train of livestock, inward bound from the Spokane & Palouse branch on July 13, 1891. Engine No. 270, running at only about 12 mph, sank through the timbers and came to rest upright. During the fall, however, fireman Flaherty was killed. The cars followed the locomotive into the gulch, forming a sickening pile of splintered wood and dying animals. The bridge had been under repair for several days prior to the accident and the workmen had left the scene only an hour before.[185]

On the OR&N Columbia Valley line to Portland, freight trains plunged through burning bridges near Mosier on two separate occasions.[186] Worse still, on February 2, 1890 nine men were killed and twelve others injured near Cascade Locks when the William's Creek bridge, damaged by flood waters, collapsed under a work train.[187]

The Oregon company's most spectacular bridge failure took place near Alto Summit on the line from Bolles Junction to Starbuck at 10:05 a. m. on August 5, 1894. As a freight train crossed the 96-foot-high, 300-foot-long trestle bridge over Jonas Hollow, the timberwork gave way, throwing the tender and 15 cars into the resulting abyss. Locomotive No. 1487, with engineer Jessee and fireman Roddy, was left standing, minus its tender, on the last bent of the bridge. Conductor Watson and brakemen Wright and Harrison, who went down with the train, received serious injuries. The press report stated that the bridge began to sway as the engine came onto it. In an attempt to get across before the worst happened, engineer Jessee opened the throttle wide and succeeded in saving the locomotive. The additional force exerted by the engine's driving wheels, however, only hastened the collapse of the bridge under the cars and the caboose. The result was an immense "windrow" of shattered timber and a great yawning gap in the railway. The structure was said to have been completely overhauled three years before the accident.[188]

Fortunately none of the high bridge failures involved passenger trains. On March 25, 1890, however, the collapse of a culvert on the Northern Pacific main line between Heron and Noxon, Montana, brought serious enough consequences. Eastbound fast passenger train No. 2 was thrown from the track and locomotive No. 438 and seven of ten cars were scattered in various attitudes along an embankment. A fire that began in the telescoped wreckage of the mail and express cars then consumed all but the two first-class cars at the rear end of the train. In spite of the extensive damage, casualties were limited to an express messenger and three trespassers killed and six passengers injured.[189]

The most common form of track defect in those days before the introduction of tie plates was "spreading of the track," or widening of the gauge, caused by lateral forces turning the rails over outwards. As a result, trains frequently derailed. The most serious example of this kind of accident was the derailment of a Northern Pacific passenger train near Teanaway, Washington, on May 22, 1891 in which four cars left the track and nine passengers were injured.[190]

Derailments caused by broken wheels and axles sometimes reached epidemic proportions. In August 1888 no less than three such mishaps, all resulting in extensive damage, occurred within four days. On the 23rd a broken axle sent an eastbound Northern Pacific tea special into the Clark Fork River near Horse Plains, Montana.[191] Two days later a broken wheel derailed nine cars of a northbound OR&N cattle train between Pendleton and Walla Walla. The accident occurred just as the train was about to commence the steep descent to Blue Mountain Station and killed two brakemen and 75 head of cattle.[192] Finally, on the 26th, three cars of OR&N

eastbound passenger train No. 4, running at speed on the descent from Kamela to La Grande, derailed about a mile west of Five Point bridge. The engineer remained unaware of this and the train ran on for over a mile and crossed the bridge before the cars were eventually "ditched." The three passenger cars, the bridge, and more than a mile of track were badly damaged but, incredibly, no one was hurt.[193]

The consequences of coupler failure were often no less serious than those of broken wheels and axles. On April 22, 1890 five cars became detached from a westbound freight train on the steep climb from Easton, Washington, to Stampede Tunnel. The cars came to rest and then ran away downhill in the opposite direction. Brakeman John Simmons heroically remained on the runaways and screwed down the hand brakes, but to no avail. At the foot of the mountain grade the cars collided head-on with a following westbound passenger train, derailing the locomotive and killing Simmons.[194]

During the night of Saturday, August 11, 1888, OR&N westbound freight No. 15 broke in two just west of Barnhardt's, Oregon, both ends of the train continuing to run in the same direction with only slight difference in speed. After proceeding separately for more than two miles, the detached rear end of the train caught up and collided with the front end, destroying 10 cars. The *Pendleton East Oregonian* reported that "a coal car scooped into a carload of horses, just as one would scoop up a shovelful of wheat, and left some of the animals standing on top of the coal uninjured." Four horses and two colts were killed outright and nineteen others suffered more or less serious injuries.[195]

Throughout the period under consideration, stray horses and cattle presented a real hazard to railway operations and sometimes trains were derailed during encounters with them. Early in July 1887 the locomotive of a Northern Pacific extra freight derailed and fell from a trestle bridge after running into a band of horses about a mile east of Spokane Falls, badly injuring the locomotive engineer.[196] Passenger trains were no less at risk, for on September 2, 1889 an eastbound OR&N express ran into cattle two miles west of Hilgard, Oregon, and the locomotive and three cars were "ditched" and badly damaged.[197] A similar accident occurred to westbound train No. 1 near Clarnie, Oregon, on June 27, 1893.[198]

Encounters with road traffic at grade crossings were still a novelty but already earned the railroads adverse comment in the press. On September 11, 1888 the *Pendleton East Oregonian* reported that a wagon belonging to Mr. John F. Harvey had been smashed to pieces on the crossing near Pendleton depot by OR&N freight engine No. 8. Mr. Harvey had driven his six-horse team and two wagons nearly to the track when he heard the locomotive bell ringing some distance away. He attempted to bring his team to a halt but they became frightened and surged ahead across the track. The engineer and fireman were talking and did not see the granger's predicament. Moreover, the speed of the locomotive increased as it approached the crossing. Mr. Harvey jumped clear just before the engine hit the first wagon squarely in the middle and demolished it. According to the *East Oregonian*,

> Parties who were near at hand at the time were loud in their denunciation of this engineer for his almost criminal carelessness which very nearly cost a human life. Mr. Harvey was bruised somewhat.[199]

Mr. Harvey's wagon was no match for engine No. 8. The public had yet to learn that trains had more momentum than road vehicles and could not be stopped so easily. However, the trains occasionally encountered more formidable obstructions at crossings. On June 8, 1891 the engine of an OR&N passenger train was damaged at Oakesdale, Washington, when it ran into a house being moved across the track![200]

Collisions between trains accounted for about 30 percent of all the railway accidents occurring in the Columbia Interior between 1887 and 1894. Without the protection later afforded by automatic block signals, operations were constantly placed in jeopardy by human error and misunderstanding. Bad weather and the long hours worked by dispatchers and train crews, moreover, compounded the risks. As traffic density increased, so did the number of mishaps. By the end of 1887 trains were colliding with alarming frequency.

To describe many of these collisions would be pointless, for the details varied little. Curiously, the number of casualties was never great, even when passenger trains were involved, apparently because train speeds were, in most cases, quite low. Most of the collisions occurred at only 10 to 15 mph. It is noteworthy that on the few occasions when opposing trains encountered each other at 25 mph, the damage and loss of life were much more extensive. Two freight train collisions, indeed, were violent enough to cause the explosion of locomotive boilers. One searches in vain, however, for reports of Pacific Northwest passenger train collisions as catastrophic as the worst disasters occurring at that time in the Eastern states.

Although main line railway operations were already regulated by train order and rule book, vestiges of the old-time interval system remained to influence events. On the evening of December 21, 1887 a westbound OR&N passenger train ran into the rear of a preceding westbound freight about five miles west of Hilgard, Oregon. The engineer of the freight train had orders to run ahead of the passenger to Pendleton, but because he was late leaving La Grande and lost time struggling up the hill toward Kamela in snowy weather, the passenger train caught up with him. Fortunately the collision occurred at quite low speed and caused no great damage.[201]

Safety continued to depend on locomotive engineers having good watches showing the right time. On December 6, 1887 a head-on collision between Northern Pacific freight trains a mile and a half west of Selah, Washington, was caused by the engineer of the eastbound train having a watch eight minutes slow and mistakenly believing that he could reach Selah before the westbound train left there. Both locomotives and 11 cars were badly damaged, but there were no casualties.[202]

Misunderstandings were often caused by running regular trains in several sections. When this procedure was adopted, the first section had to carry flags on the front of the engine to indicate that a second section was following. On May 4, 1888 the crew of the first section of a westbound Northern Pacific freight failed to show flags, thus causing a collision, near Cheney, Washington, between the second section and an extra freight eastbound. Two engines were telescoped and virtually demolished and seven men were injured.[203]

The layout of passing sidings was responsible for at least two of the accidents occurring during the period under review. Many "sidings" were connected to the adjacent main track by only one turnout, and could properly have been called "spurs." Any train "A," proceeding in the direction trailing the switch and going into the siding to clear the main line for another train "B," had to run entirely past the switch, stop, and then set back into the siding. If train "B," running in the opposite direction on the main track, reached the passing point before train "A," it would have to stop and wait on the main track, leaving at least one train length between itself and the switch. In the early hours of September 20, 1889 eastbound Northern Pacific *Atlantic Express* No. 2 had orders to meet westbound freight No. 13 at Trent, Washington. The express reached the passing point first and stopped on the main track a little more than a train length short of the siding turnout. Engineer Hannigan of No. 13, running downgrade on straight track, saw the headlight of No. 2 when he was still a mile away. However, since he wished to minimize delay to the express, and because his locomotive and train were fitted with air brakes (which had just been introduced), he refrained from braking until the last moment. To his horror, however, when at last he pushed the handle of his brake air valve into the application position, nothing happened. Desperately he threw his engine into reverse and whistled for hand brakes, but he was too late. Although the engineer of No. 2 had already begun to back his train away, a collision occurred at about 10 mph and "disabled" both engines. Brakeman Lewis Hagan was killed and engineer Hannigan and a tramp named Brennan (riding on the platform of No. 2's baggage car) were injured.[204]

Where trains had to descend steep grades, crews were given standing instructions to stop at the top of the hill and screw down the hand brakes on a certain proportion of the cars before proceeding. The train would then go down the hill at controlled speed with the brake shoes on every third or fourth car cherry red and smoking. Sometimes, however, insufficient brakes were applied, or those applied proved ineffective, and the train ran away out of control. The 3 percent grade on the OR&N line just west of Colfax, Washington, was the scene of several such runaways. At 1:45 a. m. on November 17, 1888 an eastbound freight train ran away on the hill, entered Colfax yard at high speed, and crashed into the rear end of the (stationary) Moscow freight. The offending locomotive was "denuded of its machinery" and the caboose of the Moscow train was smashed "like an eggshell." Other cars were scattered throughout the yard area, one landing almost on the doorstep of a nearby house. Locomotive fireman Frank Weddels, two other employees, and a lady passenger on the Moscow train were all injured.[205]

The fabled Alto hill between Bolles Junction and Starbuck was ever a likely place for a runaway. At 2:30 p. m. on Sunday December 23, 1888 a northbound freight train, descending the 3 percent grade with all the car brakes set, reached such a high speed that the second car jumped the track. Another nine cars then followed it into Kellogg Creek. One brakeman was killed and another injured.[206]

Just over a year later Alto hill was the scene of a head-on collision between passenger trains, caused by dispatcher's error. Early in the evening on Sunday, March 1, 1891 northbound train No. 5 was ordered to meet southbound train No. 6 at a point further north than that to which No. 6 had been ordered. The result was a "cornfield meet" near Relief, in which the mail clerk on No. 6 and nine passengers were seriously injured.[207]

The head-on collision releasing most kinetic energy seems to have been one between an eastbound extra freight and a westbound work train on the Northern Pacific main line just west of Hope, Idaho, at 11:00 a. m. on Wednesday October 10, 1888.[208] Both trains were said to have been running at 25 mph. The impact was so great that the boiler of the work train locomotive burst and was hurled a distance of 100 feet from the track.[209] Locomotive engineer Craik and fireman Bush of the work train, and fireman William McEvoy of the extra freight, were killed.[210] A coroner's jury found that neither train was given notice of the other and returned a verdict charging train dispatcher John A. Forehand with criminal carelessness. Forehand had been on duty for 16 hours when the collision took place.[211]

Lest it be imagined that James J. Hill's much-applauded style of management rendered the new Great Northern Railway immune from accident, we should note that the contemporary press reported three collisions, two derailments, and one trestle-bridge collapse on the Columbia Interior sections of that road before the end of 1893. The most serious of these was a rear-end collision between a freight train and a stationary passenger train, due to dispatcher's error, at Atlanta, Montana, early in June 1893.[212] The most spectacular was a head-on collision between an eastbound freight and a stationary westbound freight, followed by fire, at Edwall, Washington, on the night of December 7, 1893. In the latter accident locomotive engineer Joseph Shinski and fireman Wallace of Spokane were both killed.[213]

The consequences of railroaders' errors were nearly always irreversible. Moreover, attempts to rectify mistakes sometimes only made matters worse. Consider, as a last example, a collision occurring a few miles west of Missoula, Montana, on June 30, 1892. On that far off mid-summer day, the Northern Pacific divisional train dispatcher at Helena telegraphed Missoula giving orders to hold regular westbound freight No. 57 until the arrival of an extra freight eastbound. Telegraph operator James Corbett, however, did not immediately enter the order in the train book. Train No. 57 arrived at Missoula behind schedule. The conductor therefore made haste to complete the formalities and get the cars rolling westward again. Glancing at the book, he found no entry for opposing trains. As Corbett was engaged at the telegraph key and there was no time to waste, the conductor left the office, gave his engineer the "highball" signal, and climbed into the caboose for the trip westward. As soon as Corbett realized what had happened he telegraphed De Smet to hold the eastbound until No. 57 arrived. The response, however, was unnerving. The extra had already left, and the stage was set for a head-on collision. Corbett, however, was not a man to give up easily. There was still a chance that if he obtained a locomotive and gave chase, he could catch up with the freight and have it stopped before the impending collision. Rushing out of his office and across the tracks, he persuaded the reluctant crew of the yard engine to set off in pursuit of the errant regular freight. Soon they were speeding westward and before long they caught sight of No. 57's caboose. All might yet be well! Putting on more steam they rapidly closed the gap. Then, suddenly, to their horror, they realized that No. 57 was no longer moving and they had insufficient room to stop. The engineer jumped, leaving the locomotive to crash through the caboose and two cars and telescope three others. In so doing, he broke his leg. His fireman also was badly injured. Telegrapher Corbett escaped more or less unhurt. Half stunned, he crawled with difficulty from the wreckage, only to learn that the engine men of No. 57 and the extra eastbound had seen each other's trains when still some distance apart on straight track and had stopped without colliding.[214] Such were the frustrations of railroading!

Chapter Fifteen

The Road to Ruin

In 1893, uncertainty about United States government monetary and tariff policies, along with a serious decline in Treasury gold reserves, undermined an already shaky American business and financial structure, and precipitated economic collapse. Although the breakdown took place quite suddenly, the conditions giving rise to critical instability had been developing for many years. Railway affairs had played a significant part in their evolution, for the growth of the railway system opened up vast opportunity for investment, not only in railways but also in a multitude of related industries. Surges in railway building shaped the cycles of business activity for several decades. Inevitably, if and when there was a decline in new construction, or even a reduction in its rate of expansion, without a compensating rise of activity in some other field of innovation, the economy would suffer. In fact, an absolute decline in railway building, which set in after about 1887, resulted in a marked curtailment of investment opportunity and caused a prolonged economic downswing.[1]

As railway companies expanded their systems and built mutually competing lines into more remote, undeveloped country, their chances for profits diminished. At the same time, the opening up of vast new tracts of arable land, combined with economics generated by the manufacture of goods on a larger scale, brought a continuous decline in prices. Debts incurred when money was easy to obtain in the 1870s had to be repaid with the hard-won dollars of the 1880s. Farmers and others encountered increasing difficulty in meeting mortgage and loan payments, and unrest grew. Widespread popular demand for inflationary measures to ease the burden of debt, and simultaneous sales pressure from expanding mining interests, led to the Sherman Silver Purchase Act of 1890, which brought about an ineffective increase in the supply of domestic silver coinage and caused a damaging loss of foreign confidence in American financial institutions. The final debacle was delayed for two years, largely by receipts from huge exports of agricultural commodities which compensated for crop failures in Europe. Early in 1893, however, matters came to a head. The Philadelphia & Reading Railroad fell first, and the whole house of cards came toppling down after it. Stock prices collapsed and credit dried up. Banks and stores closed, immigration and land sales came to a halt, and further railway construction practically ceased. Among the transcontinental railroads, the Northern Pacific, Union Pacific, and the Atchison, Topeka & Santa Fe all failed.

The Northern Pacific Railroad was heavily laden with debt. In 1883 the construction cost overrun had been offset by a $20 million second mortgage bond issue.[2] Five years later, $12 million worth of third mortgage bonds were sold to pay for the Cascade Branch.[3] By mid-1888, therefore, the bonded debt stood at about $83 million. The company needed still more money, however, for improvements to existing lines and construction of new branches. Late in 1889 Henry Villard launched an ambitious plan to retire the outstanding debt and provide for ongoing capital requirements. This scheme took the form of a $160 million consolidated mortgage, the proceeds of which were to be allocated as follows:

For the retirement of 1st, 2nd and 3rd mortgage bonds	$75 million
For the retirement of branch line bonds	$26 million
For new branch lines	$20 million
For improvements	$20 million
For premiums on bond exchanges	$10 million
For general purposes	$ 9 million

The expected rates of interest, for maturity in 100 years, were to be 5 percent on $57 million, 4.5 percent on $23 million, and 4 percent on $80 million. Villard thus hoped eventually to reduce the company's fixed charges by about $2 million per year.[4]

The mortgage was impressive in magnitude but in the short term it did nothing to ease the burden of interest. To persuade preferred stockholders to ratify the plan, Villard had to promise them dividends. He also had to pay a premium to induce the bondholders to make the exchange. The first bonds issued under the plan, moreover, were for line improvements and new branches, and actually increased the total debt and fixed charges. Characteristically grandiose, Villard's plan in fact boiled down to just another way of bringing in more capital.

In the fiscal years ending in June 1886 and June 1887, when the total bonded debt was about $72 million, the railway earned about $12 million gross and barely broke even. By 1890, when the bonded debt had reached $105 million, and gross earnings were over $22 million, the surplus was still only about $2 million. As Stuart Daggett noted in his book *Railroad Re-organization*, published in 1908:

> The fact was that Northern Pacific was not self-supporting; it had been obliged to issue $20,867,000 bonds of its own and to guarantee $20,981,000 besides, between 1884 and 1889, in order to secure an advance of $2,462,288 in annual net income during a period of rapidly increasing prosperity; and it was now obliged to increase this indebtedness to maintain its solvency for the future.[5]

In 1890 the company's position was made worse, not only by the payment of over $1 million in dividends on preferred stock, but also by losses resulting from the lease of the Wisconsin Central Railroad. The surplus therefore disappeared, leaving nothing to compensate for lower revenues attending an economic downturn. In November 1890 the London financial house of Baring Brothers nearly failed, and money became tight. The Northern Pacific consolidated bonds could then be sold only at an unacceptable discount. In order to remain solvent the company had to take out short-term, high-interest loans. Despite the fact that the preferred stock dividends were withheld after the first quarter of 1892, the situation continued to deteriorate. By the end of that year the floating debt had increased to almost $10 million.[6] Only by accepting the most stringent conditions could the directors secure any relief. In May 1893 they succeeded in placing a $15 million issue of five-year, 6 percent, collateral trust bonds.[7] The proceeds of this loan enabled them to pay the bond interest due at the end of June. As the depression deepened, however, earnings from traffic diminished by nearly half, and the company's position became untenable. On August 15, 1893 the Northern Pacific Railroad was declared insolvent and placed in receivership.[8]

The failure of the Union Pacific was to a greater extent due to causes rooted in its more distant past.[9] To encourage construction of the overland railroad, Union Pacific received a large grant of land and was loaned money raised by United States first mortgage bond sales amounting to $16,000 for every mile of easily constructed road and up to three times that sum for work in difficult mountainous terrain. These inducements, however, proved insufficient to attract private capital. In 1864, therefore, Congress magnanimously decreed that the government bonds need only be secured by a second lien on the property and permitted the company to double the available loan capital by selling its own first mortgage bonds to the public. Subsequent legislation provided that the government would carry the burden of interest until the bonds matured, at which time the whole debt, both principal and interest, would fall due. On January 1, 1899, therefore, Union Pacific would owe the United States over $33 million principal and about $37 million accrued interest. By 1890, only about $17 million had been deposited in a sinking fund providing for the eventual repayment of this debt. Within a few years the company would have to find another $53 million. Widespread doubt about the railroad's ability to produce the money and avoid foreclosure had a very damaging effect upon the company's credit.

The Union Pacific Railroad was built under a scandalous arrangement whereby the proceeds of bond sales were largely converted into construction company profits, with the residual value of the property bearing little relationship to the amount of money subscribed. Matters were made far worse in 1880 when the Union Pacific, Kansas Pacific, and Denver Pacific railroads merged to form the Union Pacific Railway. As a result of this shady deal, Jay Gould made more than $20 million in profit, while Union Pacific footed the bill and assumed responsibility for the large debts of its weaker constituents. Other subsidiaries acquired at nearly the same time also proved to be liabilities and further weakened the parent company. Oregon Railway & Navigation, acquired in 1889, was a valuable asset but the manner of its purchase brought about a large increase in floating debt.

By 1890 Union Pacific Railway was staggering under the financial load, and in order to buy time to work out its problems issued three-year collateral trust notes. If the economy had remained buoyant and high earnings had been maintained, the railroad might have been able to keep its corporate head above water. Even in 1892 results were fairly encouraging, but by the fall of 1893, with earnings diminished and credit exhausted, all hope of remaining solvent was lost. In mid-October 1893 Union Pacific also passed into receivership, and the era of the old railroad companies came to an unfortunate end.

Nowadays, it is difficult to look at the remaining railroads in the Columbia Interior and imagine what important lifelines they once provided. In the days of the old companies the hopes and fortunes of entire communities hung on twin threads of steel. The settlers arrived by train. The railway brought in lumber for their houses and buildings and all their agricultural implements. And every pound of produce went to market on the same two rails. Towns that have not seen a passenger train in the last 30 years and no longer ship or receive freight by rail, once courted rival railroad companies with generous offers of subsidy. To be left without a railway was to be consigned to oblivion.

All that is now history. By the turn of the century the railroads had passed into the hands of New York investment bankers and were widely perceived as monopolies alien to the public interest. Taxes imposed on the reorganized railway companies provided the money to build the first public motor roads. By 1904 "Better Roads" associations were being formed by a growing automotive lobby, and by 1912 the railways were forced to acknowledge an increasing loss of passenger traffic to private motoring. From then on, public awareness of railroads diminished continuously, and so, likewise, did railway traffic. Once the universal carriers, the railroads now provide little more than long-haul transportation of bulk commodities for large industrial corporations. With the exception of passenger services provided by Amtrak, the trains pass the people by.

The railroad personalities of the late 19th century are almost forgotten. Some of their names were given to settlements in the Columbia Interior and remain in daily use: Adams, Cheney, Endicott, and Pullman. Others survive only as fading paint on weathered sign-boards marking remote junctions and sidings: Colby, Mohler, and Villard Junction. Few persons, other than Hermiston and Pasco railroaders, now know where Villard Junction is, and hardly more know who Henry Villard ever was. That is a pity, for Villard had great vision and high ideals, and his achievements were consider-able. That he failed to bring order to railway expansion in the Pa-cific Northwest was unfortunate, for if his plans had been implemented the railroad network would not have been so exten-sively overbuilt. In North America, however, the course of railway expansion was ever less orderly than the state regulated processes adopted in continental Europe. Villard was unable either to impose satisfactory terms on rivals within his own camp or fend off intru-sion by the upstart James J. Hill.

Hill's venture into the Pacific Northwest was a gamble and a race against time. That he was able to weather the financial storm of 1893 was due to the Great Northern being a new company not yet so deeply in debt as the existing Western railroads. For 10 years, however, the Great Northern Railway remained a very slender thread of steel. Haskell's transit of the Salish Mountains of Mon-tana cannot have been an easy line to operate, and the original route over Stevens Pass in the Cascades was a veritable railroader's night-mare. Even after the opening of the first Cascade Tunnel and the abandonment of Haskell's Pass in favor of the Rexford route, the Great Northern remained a difficult line, its gradient profile epito-mized by its mountain goat and pinnacle emblem. The Northern Pacific continued to be the "Mainstreet of the Northwest," and Hill and the house of Morgan fought great legal and financial battles to gain and keep it. Meanwhile, the Great Northern, planted like a sprouting couch grass runner just below the Canadian border, served Hill's $37 million obsession with the mining potential of southern British Columbia. Not until the second Cascade Tunnel was completed in 1929, and many other improvements were made, did his Pacific Extension become more nearly an American high-capacity trunk route.

Today the Great Northern Railway serves as Burlington Northern's main line from Spokane to Seattle, breaching the mountains at less than 2,900 feet above sea level by means of the second Cascade Tunnel. East of Spokane, BN now uses the former

Northern Pacific main line to Sandpoint, Idaho, where many trains revert to the Great Northern by a new connection. Since the flooding of the upper Kootenai Valley in 1970 trains reach Whitefish, Montana, by a new line from Jennings to Stryker, passing through Fisher River, Wolf Prairie, and the seven-mile-long Flathead Tunnel. The Rexford route, born as Hill's branch line to the Crowsnest collieries of British Columbia, lies submerged behind the Libby Dam. The roadbed of the original Haskell's Pass line of 1892, however, has survived nearly intact as a rough-surfaced, cross-country trail from Little Bitterroot Lake to Tamarack, Montana. Adventurous motorists and amateur railway historians can thus drive along the old Great Northern line and imagine themselves on the head end of one of Jim Hill's trains. It is an exhilarating journey westward across the high country to Pleasant Valley, north through the rock cuts along the shore of Island Lake, and down, down the long hill to Wolf Creek. The most evocative point, however, lies just beyond the west portal of the old tunnel, high on the mountainside north of Dahl Lake. There, under the larch trees at the Salish Mountain divide, one imagines the passing of people and trains long ago: Charles Haskell and his two companions on the first reconnaissance, snowshoeing through the bitter winter of 1890; the Twohy brothers and their Irish laborers, loading broken rock in the dark, smoke-filled headings of the tunnel; the steel gang lustily throwing down three miles of track a day in the spring of 1892; the engine men of heavy freight trains hailing each other in the night as their big Brooks eight-coupleds pass at the summit; and the mighty James J. Hill, glimpsed momentarily in the interior lighting of his business car as he travels purposefully eastward to join battle with the other giants of the railway age.

Appendix A

**Railways in the Columbia Interior, 1879-1893.
Distances in Miles and
Elevations in Feet Above Sea Level.**

1.0 Oregon Railway & Navigation Co.

1.1 Lower Cascades, Washington (eastward) to Upper Cascades, Washington. (Built by OSN Co.)

Location	Distance from Lower Cascades	Opened
Lower Cascades, Washington	0	April 20, 1863
Upper Cascades, Washington	6	

Track originally laid to 5 feet 0 inch gauge. Converted to 3 feet 0 inch gauge to facilitate the use of locomotives available from the WW&CR line (1.3).

1.2 The Dalles, Oregon (eastward) to Celilo, Oregon. (Built by OSN Co.)

Location	Distance from The Dalles	Opened
The Dalles, Oregon	0	April 20, 1863
Celilo, Oregon	12	

Track originally laid to 5 feet 0 inch gauge. Converted to standard gauge by OR&N Co. in February 1880 and incorporated into main line (1.6).

1.3 Wallula, Washington (eastward) to Walla Walla, Washington. (Built by Walla Walla & Columbia River Railroad.)

Location	Distance from Wallula	Elevation	Opened
Wallula, Washington	0	350	1874
(1880 junction with 1.6 and 2.1)			
Touchet	16		
Whitman (1879 junction with 1.4)	27		October 23, 1875
Walla Walla, Washington	32	906	
(1881 junction with 1.9)			

Track originally laid to 3 feet 0 inch gauge. Converted to standard gauge by OR&N Co. May 1881.

1.4 Whitman, Washington (southward) to Blue Mountain Station, Oregon

Location	Distance from Whitman	Elevation	Opened
Whitman, Washington (1879 junction with 1.3)	0		
Barrett, Oregon	8	884	September 1879
Blue Mountain Station, Oregon	14	1398	

Track originally laid to 3 feet 0 inch gauge. Barrett to Blue Mountain Station converted to standard gauge in January 1883 to form part of 1.9. Whitman to Barrett then abandoned.

1.5 Walla Walla, Washington (eastward) to Dudley, Washington and to Dixie, Washington. (Built by Mill Creek Railroad.)

Location	Distance from Walla Walla	Opened
Walla Walla, Washington	0	
Junction	3	1881
Dudley, Washington	6	
Junction	3	September 1882
Dixie, Washington	11	

Track originally laid to 3 feet 0 inch gauge. A westward extension was built into the Washington State Penitentiary at Walla Walla in 1887. The railway was sold to OR&N Co. in 1887 and sold again to Northern Pacific Railway in January 1905. The latter company converted the Dudley line to standard gauge and abandoned the remainder.

1.6 Wallula, Washington (westward) to Portland, Oregon

Location	Distance from Wallula	Elevation	Opened
Wallula, Washington (1880 junction with 1.3 and 2.1)	0		November 3, 1880 3 foot 0 inch gauge until April 17, 1881
Umatilla, Oregon (1882 junction with 1.7)	27		April 4, 1881
Coyote	44		
Castle Rock	52		
Willows (1888 junction with 1.14)	63		
Alkali	72	306	
Blalock's	80		
Quinns	87		November 13, 1880
John Day's	96		
Grant's	103		
Des Chutes	110		
Celilo	113		See 1.2
The Dalles	126	116	

Rowena	134	May 21, 1882
Mosier	141	
Hood River	147	
Viento	154	
Wyeth	160	
Cascade Locks	167	
Bonneville	172	————
Oneonta	180	
Rooster Rock	189	
Troutdale	195	
Clarney	203	November 20, 1882
East Portland	210	
(Junction with Oregon & California Railroad)		
Albina	212	————
Portland, Oregon	213	Willamette River
(Junction with NPRR line to Tacoma via Goble, Oregon, and Kalama, Washington.)		bridge opened July 11, 1888

1.7 Umatilla, Oregon (southeastward) to Huntington, Oregon

Location	Distance from Umatilla	Elevation	Opened
Umatilla, Oregon (Junction with 1.6)	0	296	September 1882
Foster	15	592	
Echo	18	639	
Nolin	24		
Barnhardt	36	907	————
Pendleton (1884 junction with 1.9)	43	1069	June 1, 1883
Mikecha	65	1740	————
Laka (later Huron)	87	2913	October 1883
Meacham	93	3680	————
Kamela (summit)	100	4205	July 21, 1884
Hilgard	111	3003	
La Grande (1890 junction with branch east to Elgin)	119	2788	————
(Low point)	130	2703	September 7, 1884
Telocaset (summit)	142	3448	
(Low point)	146	3190	
North Powder	152	3251	
Haines	162	3335	————
Baker City	171	3457	November 25, 1884
Encina (summit)	181	3968	
Pleasant Valley	184	3766	
Unity (later Oxman)	190	3166	
Durkee	198	2657	
Weatherby	207	2405	
Huntington, Oregon (Junction with Oregon Short Line Railway.)	219	2111	

1.8 Palouse Junction (later Connell), Washington (eastward) to Colfax, Washington. (Built by Oregon & Transcontinental Co. for Northern Pacific Railroad, but ceded instead to Oregon Railway & Navigation Co.)

Location	Distance from Palouse Jc.	Elevation	Opened
Palouse Junction (later Connell), Washington (Junction with 2.1)	0	832	
Sulphur	9		
Kahlotus	18		
Washtucna	29	991	November 20, 1883
Hooper	39	1057	
Pampa	48	1339	
La Crosse (1888 junction with 1.9)	53	1473	
Winona (1889 junction with 1.13)	63	1482	
Endicott	69	1594	
Crest	86	2264	
Colfax, Washington (1885 junction with 1.12) (for extension east see 1.9)	88	1945	

1.9 Pendleton, Oregon (north and east) to Spokane, Washington, via Walla Walla, La Crosse, and Colfax, Washington

Location	Distance from Pendleton	Elevation	Opened
Pendleton, Oregon (Junction with 1.7)	0	1069	February 1884
Adams	13	1527	
Centerville (later Athena)	17	1714	
(summit)	20	1823	March 1, 1887
Weston	21	1797	
(summit)	22	1854	
Blue Mountain Station	27	1398	Part of 1.4
Barrett	33	884	
(low point)	34	845	February 7, 1883
Milton, Oregon	36	1003	
(low point)	43	886	
Walla Walla, Washington (Junction with 1.3)	47	906	July 24, 1881
Prescott	68		
Bolles Junction (Junction with 1.10)	72	1166	
Alto (summit)	84	1906	December 1881
Starbuck (1886 junction with 1.11)	95	645	
Grange City	99		
South Texas (later Riparia)	103	550	
Jerita	121	About 1610	September 5, 1888
La Crosse (Junction with 1.8)	127	1473	
Winona (Junction with 1.13)	137	1482	Part of 1.8

Endicott	143	1594	
Crest	160	2264	
Colfax (Junction with 1.12)	162	1945	September 26, 1886
Garfield (Intersection with NPRR 2.2)	180	2497	
(summit)	185	2614	
(low point)		2558	
Farmington	189	2617	mid October, 1888
Seltice (Junction with 1.13)	195	2515	
Tekoa (Junction with 1.15)	201	2574	early November
Latah	208	2428	1888
Fairfield	216	2547	December 7, 1888
Darknell	220	2599	
Rockford	223	2363	
Manito	228	2576	
(summit)	230	2603	
Freeman	231	2580	
Mica	234	2467	
Chester	241	1994	
Dishman	243	1980	
(Intersection with NPRR 2.1)	248	1913	October 7, 1889
(Intersection and Junction with Great Northern Railway 3.1)			
(Intersection with Spokane Falls & Northern Railway)			
Spokane, Washington	250	1867	
(Original Union Depot)			
(Junction with Seattle, Lake Shore and Eastern Railway 2.12)			

1.10 Bolles Junction, Washington (eastward) to Dayton, Washington

Location	Distance from Bolles Jc.	Elevation	Opened
Bolles Junction, Washington (Junction with 1.9)	0	1166	July 24, 1881
Waitsburg	4		
(1889 intersection with Oregon & Washington Territory Railroad)	5		
Dayton, Washington	14	1660	

1.11 Starbuck, Washington (eastward) to Pomeroy, Washington

Location	Distance from Starbuck	Elevation	Opened
Starbuck, Washington (Junction with 1.9)	0	645	June 1, 1886
Pomeroy, Washington	29	About 1810	

1.12 Colfax, Washington (southeast) to Moscow, Idaho

Location	Distance from Colfax	Elevation	Opened
Colfax, Washington (Junction with 1.8/1.9)	0	1945	September 23, 1885
Shawnee	10		
Pullman, Washington (1887 intersection with Northern Pacific Railroad 2.2)	19	About 2350	
Moscow, Idaho	28	2560	

1.13 Winona, Washington (eastward) to Seltice, Washington, via Oakesdale

Location	Distance from Winona	Elevation	Opened
Winona, Washington (Junction with 1.8/1.9)	0	1482	August 15, 1889
Willada	11	1819	
(summit)	16.5	2047	
St. John	18	1964	
(summit)	19.5	2040	
Juno	21	1978	
Thornton	31	2284	
(summit)	35	2560	
Oakesdale (Intersection with Northern Pacific Railroad 2.2)	39	2447	October 1888
Fletcher	43	2396	
Seltice, Washington (Junction with 1.9)	48	2515	

1.14 Willows Junction, Oregon (southward) to Heppner, Oregon

Location	Distance from Willows Jc.	Elevation	Opened
Willows Junction, Oregon (Junction with 1.6)	0		November 26, 1888
Ione	28		
Lexington	36		
Heppner, Oregon	45	About 1910	

1.15 Tekoa, Washington (eastward) to Mullan, Idaho

Location	Distance from Tekoa	Elevation	Opened
Tekoa, Washington (Junction with 1.9)	0	2472	December 23, 1889
Tilma, Idaho	2	2500	
Lowell	7	2570	

Watt's (summit)	12	2938	
Plummer	15	2651	
Chatcolet	22	2122	
Anderson	33	2122	
Lane	45	2123	
Cataldo	57	2129	
Wardner	69	2291	
Osburn	75	2518	
Wallace (Junction with 1.16)	80	2713	March 1890
Mullan, Idaho	87	3261	

1.16 Wallace, Idaho (northward) to Burke, Idaho

Location	Distance from Wallace	Elevation	Opened
Wallace, Idaho (Junction with 1.15)	0	2713	November 18, 1890
Burke, Idaho	7	3734	

2.0 Northern Pacific Railroad Co.

2.1 Wallula, Washington (eastward) to site of last spike ceremony at Gold Creek, Montana

Location	Distance from Wallula	Elevation	Opened
Wallula, Washington (Junction with Oregon Railway and Navigation Co. 1.3 and 1.6)	0		Wallula – South Ainsworth November 1880. Originally 3 ft. gauge. Conv. to std. gauge May 1881.
Hunt's Junction (1888 junction with 2.8)	2		
Ainsworth	12	350	
Pasco (1883 junction with 2.6)	15	370	Snake River Bridge at Ainsworth opened April 20, 1884.
Eltopia	33		
Bluff Wells (later Mesa)	41		
Palouse Junction (later Connell) (1883 junction with Oregon Railway Navigation Co. 1.8)	51		
Twin Wells (later Hatton)	59		May 16, 1881
Cunningham	63	1166	
Providence (summit)	71	1534	
(low point)	78	1337	
Well no. 7 (later Lind)	79		
Ritzville	96	1825	
Sprague	120		
(summit)	143	2400	
Cheney (1888 junction with 2.13)	145	2343	
Marshall (1886 Junction with 2.2)	152	2137	June 25, 1881
Spokane Falls, Washington (later Spokane)	161	now 1931	

(1888 junction with Seattle, Lake Shore & Eastern Railway)			
(Reference point)	162	1907	January 9, 1882
1889 intersection with OR&N	163	1913	
Hauser Junction, Idaho	181	2138	
(1886 junction with 2.5)			
Westwood (later Rathdrum)	188	2216	
(summit)	202	2460	
Dry Lake (later Granite)	207	(2259)	
Cocolalla	217	2231	
Hangtown (or Ventnor)	228	now 2091	March 5, 1882
(at south shore of west arm of Lake Pend d'Oreille)		lake nominal water level now 2063	
Sandpoint	230	now 2092	
Kootenai	234	2122	July 1, 1882
Hope	245	(2100)	
Clark Fork, Idaho	255	(2140)	
Cabinet, Montana	263	2175	
Heron	269		January 1883
Noxon	279	(2189)	
Trout Creek	295	(2362)	
Belknap	310	(2430)	
Thompson's Falls	316	(2420)	
Eddy	326	(2410)	
Weeksville	333	(2460)	April 1883
Horse Plains	342	(2470)	
Paradise	348	2492	
Third Crossing Bridge	356		June 1, 1883
Perma	359	(2500)	
Jocko	374		
Ravalli	381	2701	June 29, 1883
Arlee	390	3040	
Evaro (summit)	401	3908	
De Smet (1890 Junction with 2.14)	411	3176	
Missoula	418	3167	September 8, 1883
Turah			
Wallace			
Bearmouth	456	(3798)	
Gold Creek, Montana	478	4190	
(Site of Last Spike ceremony. To Helena, Montana, 55 miles, to Duluth, Minnesota, 1198 miles.)		(Milw. elev^n)	

Elevations shown in parentheses are approximations from USGS 7-5 minute topographical sheets.

2.2 Marshall, Washington (southward) to Genesee, Idaho

Location	Distance from Marshall	Elevation	Opened
Marshall, Washington (Junction with 2.1)	0	2137	
Spangle	11	2432	September 1886
Rosalia	27	2226	
Oakesdale (Intersection with Oregon Railway & Navigation Co. 1.13)	38	2467	
Belmont (1891 Junction with 2.3)	43	2510	December 1887
Garfield (Intersection with Oregon Railway & Navigation Co. 1.9)	50	2497	
Palouse City	59	2443	
Pullman (Intersection with Oregon Railway & Navigation Co. 1.12)	76	2359	July 1, 1888
Pullman Junction (1891 Junction with 2.4)	77		
Colton	92	2555	
Uniontown, Washington	95	2570	
Genesee, Idaho	105	2674	

2.3 Belmont, Washington (eastward) to Farmington, Washington

Location	Distance from Belmont	Elevation	Opened
Belmont, Washington (Junction with 2.2)	0	2510	January 2, 1891
Farmington, Washington	6	about 2615	

2.4 Pullman Junction, Washington (east and south) to Lewiston, Idaho

Location	Distance from Marshall	Elevation	Opened
Pullman Junction, Washington (Junction with 2.2)	77		
Sunshine, Washington	81	2584	January 1891
Moscow, Idaho	86	2578	
Joel	93	2610	
Howell	97	2737	
Troy	100	2475	
Kendrick	111	1212	
Juliaetta	115	1087	July 1891
Arrow	124	831	September 15, 1898
Spalding	127	815	
Lewiston, Idaho	137	747	

2.5 Hauser Junction, Idaho (southward) to Coeur d'Alene City, Idaho

Location	Distance from Hauser Jc.	Elevation	Opened
Hauser Junction, Idaho (Junction with 2.1)	0	2160	November 9, 1886
Post Falls	5		
Coeur d'Alene City, Idaho	13	2135	

2.6 Pasco, Washington (westward) to Tacoma, Washington

Location	Distance from Pasco	Elevation	Opened
Pasco, Washington (Junction with 2.1)	0	370	
Kennewick	2	370	1884
Badger	17	690	
Kiona	24	550	
Prosser	40	635	
Satus	60	680	
Toppenish	71	765	
Old Yakima	85		
North Yakima	90	1080	April 1886
Selah	94		
Umptanum	115		
Ellensburg	127	1522	December 21, 1886
Teanaway	148		
Cle-elum (Junction with 2.7)	152	1921	
Easton	166	2180	July 3, 1887
Martin (east end of Stampede Tunnel)	175	2820	Switchbacks July 3, 1887 Tunnel May 27, 1888
(West end of Stampede Tunnel)	177*		July 3, 1887
Weston	185		
Sunday Creek	188		1886
Eagle Gorge	205	1248	1885
Cascade Junction	229		1887
South Prairie	230		
Tacoma, Washington	255 nearly sea level		

*For distances via Stampede Pass switchbacks, add 4 miles for locations west of Martin.

2.7 Cle-elum, Washington to Roslyn, Washington

Location	Distance from Cle-elum	Elevation	Opened
Cle-elum, Washington (Junction with 2.6)	0	1921	December 21, 1886
Roslyn, Washington	3.5		

Line later extended a further 2.5 miles to Ronald.

2.8 Hunt's Junction, Washington (southward) to Pendleton, Oregon. (Built by Oregon & Washington Territory Railroad.)

Location	Distance from Hunt's Jc.	Elevation	Opened
Hunt's Junction, Washington (Junction with 2.1)	0	338	1888
Vansycle, Oregon	16	1416	
Stanton Junction (Junction with 2.9)	20	1812	
Summit at Apex	21	1921	
Helix	24	1769	September 12, 1889
Fulton	34	1532	
Pendleton, Oregon	40	1080	

2.9 Stanton Junction, Oregon (eastward) to Centerville, Oregon. (Built by Oregon & Washington Territory Railroad.)

Location	Distance from Stanton Jc.	Elevation	Opened
Stanton Junction, Oregon (Junction with 2.8)	0	1812	April 1888
(Summit)	7	2200	
Centerville (later Athena), Oregon	14	1714	

2.10 Hunt's Junction, Washington (north and east) to Dayton, Washington. (Built by Oregon & Washington Territory Railroad.)

Location	Distance from Hunt's Jc.	Elevation	Opened
Hunt's Junction, Washington (Junction with 2.1)	0	338	
Eureka Junction (Junction with 2.11)	22	1065	March 19, 1889
Lamar	29	833	
Harvey Shaw's	30		
Climax	33	1148	
Dry Creek	45	688	
(Intersection with Oregon Railway & Navigation Co. 1.9)	52		
Walla Walla	53	975	November 28, 1889
Sapolil	59	1273	
Dixie	64	1606	
Minnick (Summit)	69	1925	
Waitsburg	77	1293	
(Intersection with Oregon Railway & Navigation Co. 1.10)	79		
Dayton, Washington	88	1615	

2.11 Eureka Junction, Washington (northeastward) to Estes, Washington. (Built by Oregon & Washington Territory Railroad.)

Location	Distance from Eureka Jc.	Elevation	Opened
Eureka Junction, Washington (Junction with 2.10)	0	1065	1888
Estes (later Pleasant View), Washington	20	1437	

2.12 Spokane, Washington (westward) to Davenport, Washington. (Built by Seattle, Lake Shore & Eastern Railway).

Location	Distance from Spokane (original Union Depot)	Elevation	Opened
Junction with 2.1 (0.25 miles east of 1886 NPRR Spokane Falls Depot.)	1	1907	1888
Spokane, Washington (original Union Depot) (Junction with 1.9 and temporarily with 3.1)	0	1867	
Greenwood	6		
(Windsor Prairie)	10		
Jameson	15		
Medical Lake (Intersection with Northern Pacific Railroad 2.13) (Intersection with Great Northern Railway 3.1)	22	2437 (NPRR elev^n)	
Logan (or Willow Springs)	30		
Denny's	33		
Gravelles	39		
Oman's	43		
Wheatdale	45		October 17, 1889
(Intersection with Northern Pacific Railroad 2.13)	49		
Davenport, Washington	50	2442 (NPRR elev^n)	

2.13 Cheney, Washington (westward) to Coulee City, Washington

Location	Distance from Cheney	Elevation	Opened
Cheney, Washington (Junction with 2.1)	0	2345	
Medical Lake (Intersection with Seattle, Lake Shore & Eastern Railway 2.12) (Intersection with Great Northern Railway 3.1)	11	2437	February 1889
Reardan	27	2510	

Mondovi	34	2522	
(Intersection with Seattle, Lake Shore & Eastern Railway 2.12)			
Davenport	42	2442	1889
Creston	65	2462	
Wilbur	75	2180	
Almira	88	1931	October 1890
Hanson	92	2112	
Hartline	97	1925	
Coulee City, Washington	109	1596	

2.14 De Smet, Montana (westward) to Wallace, Idaho

Location	Distance from De Smet	Elevation	Opened
De Smet, Montana	0	3237	
(Junction with 2.1)			
Grass Valley	1	3181	February 1890
Frenchtown	10	3055	
Huson	15	3034	October 1890
Lothrop	25	2980	
Rivulet	41	2928	
Quartz	45	2892	
Iron Mountain (later Superior)	57	2775	
Spring Gulch	63	2742	
St. Regis	71	2647	August 25, 1891
Saltese, Montana	95	3386	
St. Regis Pass (Summit)	109	4738	
(Montana-Idaho boundary)			
Pottsville, Idaho	117		
Mullan	121	3261	Originally narrow gauge, opened April 22, 1889; changed to std. gauge in 1891
Wallace, Idaho	128	2744	
(Junction with 2.15 and 2.16)			

2.15 (Cataldo) Mission, Idaho (eastward) to Wallace, Idaho. (Built by Coeur d'Alene Railway & Navigation Co.)

Location	Distance from Mission	Elevation	Opened
New (1888) wharf at Hayshed	1		February 1888
Mission, Idaho	0	2129 (UP elev^{n})	July 1887
Kingston			
Wardner Junction	13	2291 (UP elev^{n})	August 22, 1887
Osborn		2518 (UP elev^{n})	November 2, 1887
Wallace, Idaho (Junction with 2.14 and 2.16)	24	2744	

Track laid to 3 feet 0 inch gauge.

2.16 Wallace, Idaho (north) to Burke, Idaho. (Construction completed by Coeur d'Alene Railway & Navigation Co.)

Location	Distance from Wallace	Elevation	Opened
Wallace, Idaho (Junction with 2.14 and 2.15)	0	2744	December 15, 1887
Burke, Idaho	7	3734 (UP elev^n)	

Track originally laid to 3 feet 0 inch gauge.

3.0 Great Northern Railway

3.1 Pacific Junction at Havre, Montana (west) to Everett, Washington, via Haskell's Pass and the Stevens Pass switchbacks

Location	Distance from St. Paul, Minn.	Elevation	Opened
Pacific Junction at Havre, Montana (Junction with line to Great Falls and Helena)	967	2517	Track to Cut Bank January 20, 1891
Cut Bank	1092	3698	Track to Kalispell January 1, 1892
Two Medicine	1140		
Marias Pass (Summit)	1153	5213	
Columbia Falls	1213	3098	
La Salle	1219	2963	
Kalispell	1228	2946	
Batavia	1234		
Sedan	1238		
Athens	1246	3598	
Marion	1251	3934	
Haskell's Pass (Summit)	1258	4134	
Pleasant Valley	1267	3504	
Lake View	1276	3520	
Melbourne	1279	3622	
Atlanta	1285		
Sterling	1291	3070	
Fisher River	1300	2600	East-west track-layers meet at Troy, April 25, 1892
Jennings	1309	2113	
Libby Creek	1321	2055	
Kootenai Falls	1332	1984	
Troy	1339	1881	
Yakt	1346	1845	Track laid eastward, Sandpoint to Troy
Leonia	1354	1807	
Katka, Montana	1361		

Crossport, Idaho	1366	1782	
Bonner's Ferry	1371	1761	Track laid to
Moravia	1376	1836	Bonner's Ferry,
Naples	1382	2019	March 22, 1892
Elmira (Summit)	1390	2162	
Colburn	1397	2137	
Sandpoint	1405	2107	Track Sandpoint
Laclede	1416	2081	to Albany Falls,
Priest River, Idaho	1427	2070	February 20, 1892
Albany Falls (bridge)			Albany Falls
Newport, Washington	1434	2118	bridge completed
Scotia	1442	2040	about May 10,
Camden	1446	1902	1892
Milan	1456	1765	
Chattaroy	1462	1804	
Morse	1470	1888	Track to Spokane
Hillyard	1474	2026	Union Depot,
(Intersection and junction with			June 1, 1892
Oregon Railway & Navigation			
Co. 1.9)			
Spokane (GN Depot)	1479	1876	Train service
(Intersection with Seattle, Lake			inaugurated
Shore & Eastern Railway 2.12)			St. Paul to
Highland	1487	2049	Spokane,
Lyons	1492	2290	August 14, 1892
Galena	1499	2440	Temporary use of
(Intersection with Northern			port of SLS&E Rly.
Pacific Railroad 2.13)			west of Spokane
Espanola	1502	2378	beginning
(Intersection with Seattle, Lake			July 23, 1892
Shore & Eastern Railway 2.12)			
Waukon	1508	2428	
Edwall	1514	2314	
Moscow	1523	2320	
Harrington	1531	2167	
Coal Creek	1537		
Parker	1546	1790	
Odessa	1556	1539	
Irby	1565	1386	
Krupp	1572	1315	Track to mile
Wilson Creek	1579	1267	1589 September 2,
Stratford	1587	1269	1892
Adrian	1594	1222	Train service
Ephrata	1602	1265	Spokane to
Winchester	1612	1273	Wenatchee via
Quincy	1621	1316	ferry at Rock Is.
Trinidad	1628	1008	inaugurated
Columbia River	1637	598	November 13,
Rock Island	1642	605	1892
Malaga	1646	667	Rock Is. bridge

Wenatchee	1653	633	opened May 2,
Old Mission	1664	787	1893
Peshastin	1672	1047	
Leavenworth	1676	1165	Train service west
Chiwaukum	1687	1829	to Leavenworth,
Nason Creek	1694	2153	early May 1893
Merritt	1697	2175	
Berne	1704	2914	
Cascade Tunnel (East Portal)	1709	3375	
Cascade Summit (i.e., summit of Stevens Pass switchback line)	1713	4025	
Wellington (West portal of original Cascade Tunnel 1900)	1721	3093	"Last spike" driven January 6, 1893
(Last spike site)	At or near 1726		
Madison (later Scenic)	1730	2086	
Foss Creek	1741	933	Train service
Berlin	1745	821	inaugurated
Salmon	1748		between St. Paul
Index	1756	516	and Seattle
Gold Bar	1765	191	June 18, 1893
Sultan	1770	104	
Everett, Washington (Junction with line from Seattle to Vancouver, British Columbia.) (33 miles north of Seattle, Washington.)	1794	29	Track laid eastward to mile 1726

The original Cascade Tunnel, opened in 1900, reduced the distance from St. Paul to Wellington and points west by 9 miles. The summit elevation, at the east end of the tunnel, was 3382 feet.

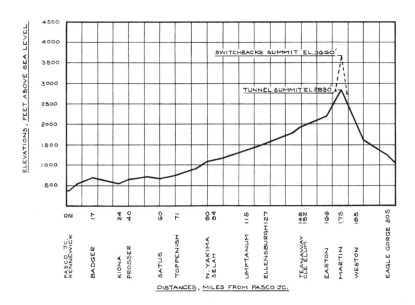

NORTHERN PACIFIC RAILROAD, CASCADE BRANCH, SIMPLIFIED GRADIENT PROFILE, JULY 1888.

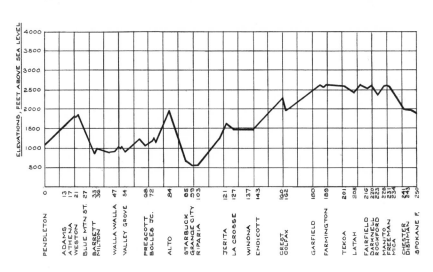

UNION PACIFIC RAILWAY, SIMPLIFIED PROFILE, PENDLETON TO SPOKANE FALLS, OCTOBER 1889

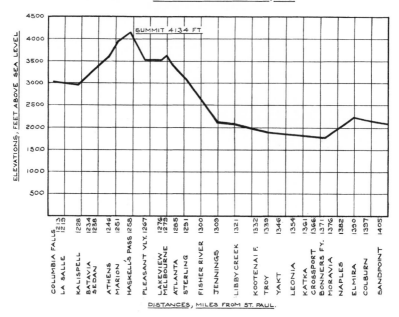

GREAT NORTHERN RAILWAY, SIMPLIFIED PROFILE, COLUMBIA FALLS, MONTANA TO SANDPOINT IDAHO VIA HASKELL'S PASS, 1892.

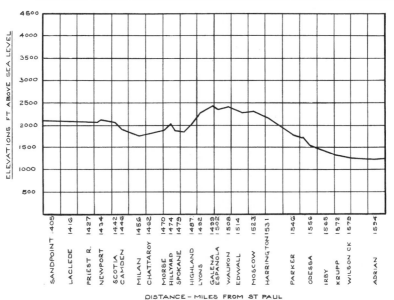

GREAT NORTHERN RAILWAY – SIMPLIFIED PROFILE – SANDPOINT, IDAHO TO ADRIAN, WASH.

GREAT NORTHERN RAILWAY, SIMPLIFIED PROFILE, ADRIAN TO EVERETT, WASHINGTON.
VIA OLD CASCADE TUNNEL 1900

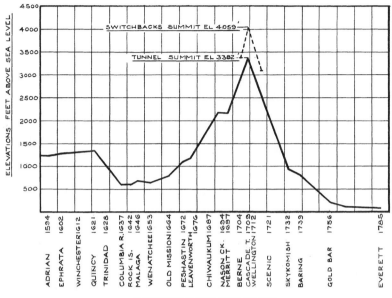

Appendix B

Glossary of Railroad Terms

Contents

1.0 Roadway

1.1   *Alignment* (or *Alinement*)
The horizontal location of a railroad as described by curves and tangents.

1.2   *Branch Line*
A secondary line of railway.

1.3   *Bridge* (See Section 3.0, "Bridges.")

1.4   *Culvert*
A transverse channel of circular, arched, or rectangular cross section, lined with erosion-resistant material, to conduct water under a railway without damaging the roadbed.

1.5   *Curve*
A change in the direction of railway alignment. In North America the rate of curvature is given by the angle subtended at the center of a circular curve by a 100-foot chord, measured in degrees.

1.6   *Cut* (or *Cutting*)
An open excavation above the grade line to remove material below the natural ground surface.

1.7   *Clearing*
The process of removing trees and other obstructions from the natural ground surface before the work of grading commences.

1.8   *Compensation* (of gradient)
The easing of gradient on curves to compensate for the additional resistance encountered by trains due to the curvature.

1.9   *Depot Grounds*
Land required for the accommodation of tracks and buildings at locations where trains stop for the purpose of loading or unloading passengers and/or freight.

1.10   *Embankment* (or *Fill*)
A bank of earth, rock, or other material placed on the natural ground surface to bring the railway roadbed surface up to the grade line.

Fill (see *Embankment*)

1.11   *Grade Line*
The line on the profile representing the tops of embankments and the bottoms of cuttings, forming a roadbed ready to receive ballast and track.

1.12   *Grade* (verb)
To prepare the ground for the reception of ballast and track.

1.13 *Gradient* (or *Grade* [noun])
The rate of inclination of the grade line from the horizontal. Gradient is stated in at least four different ways, thus:

	1.0 / 100	2.2 / 100
Early American	52.8 feet to the mile	116.0 feet to the mile
Recent American	1.00 percent (%)	2.20 percent (%)
British	1 in 100	1 in 45
Continental European	10 mm/m	22 mm/m

1.14 *Grubbing*
The process of removing tree stumps, tree roots, and other organic matter from the right of way prior to grading.

1.15 *Main Line*
A principal line of railway.

1.16 *Right of Way*
Land used or held for railway operations.

1.17 *Rip-rap* (or *Rip-rapping*)
Rock, in large-sized pieces, laid on the slopes of embankments and cuttings to prevent erosion by running water.

1.18 *Roadbed*
A modified ground surface along the right of way, conforming to the desired alignment and grade line of the railway, and made ready to receive ballast and track.

1.19 *Rockwork*
Rock excavations undertaken during the construction of a railway.

1.20 *Ruling Gradient*
The most severe adverse gradient encountered by trains on any given line of railway (except for "momentum gradients" or short hills not consuming all the momentum of trains approaching at given minimum speeds).

1.21 *Slope*
The inclined face of a cutting or embankment.

1.22 *Summit*
Point of reversal of gradient on a railway, from "up-grade" to "down-grade" in either direction of running.

1.23 *Tangent*
Any straight portion of a railway alignment.

1.24 *Tunnel* (see Section 4.0 Tunnels)

1.25 *Vertical Curve*
A curved transition, in a vertical plane, between grade lines at changes or reversals of gradient.

1.26 *Yard*
An extended area accommodating multiple railroad tracks and related facilities. In the railway operating sense, a system of tracks within defined limits, provided for making up trains, storing cars, and other purposes, over which movements not authorized by timetable or train order may be made, subject only to prescribed signals and rules, or special instructions.

1.27 *Unconsolidated Ground*
Ground or earth other than solid rock (i.e., sand, silt, gravel, clay, glacial till, and soils of various types).

2.0 Track

Track is an assembly of rails, crossties, and fastenings, supported in ballast, providing a runway and guidance system for locomotives and rolling stock.

2.1 *Ballast*
Material deposited on the roadbed to:
    transmit and distribute the loads imposed by track and trains;
    provide resistance to movement of the track structure, thus maintaining the correct surface and alignment;
    provide effective drainage;
    reduce frost heaving.
The best ballast material is hard rock or smelter slag, crushed to minus-2 inch size, with carefully regulated particle size distribution. In the late nineteenth century, gravel was the most extensively used railway ballast material.

2.2 *Closure Rail*
In a turnout, those rails connecting the switch points and the frog with each other and with adjacent tracks.

2.3 *Crossties* (or *Ties*)
Transverse members of the track structure, to which rails are spiked or otherwise fastened to maintain the proper railway gauge. Crossties distribute the weight of the rails and the loads imposed by the trains, and transmit these forces into the ballast and the roadbed. In the late nineteenth century, untreated timber was the most commonly used crosstie material. After about 1900, timber crossties were pressure treated with a creosote/gas tar mixture to retard rotting. Reinforced concrete crossties, now extensively used, are a recent innovation.

2.4 *Crossing* (Grade)
A road/railway intersection at rail top level.

2.5 *Crossing* (Track) (or *Diamond Crossing*)
An intersection of two railways at rail top level.

2.6 *Dating Nail*
A special nail, with a two-digit number embossed in the top of the head, driven into a crosstie to indicate the year of installation in the track.

2.7 *Derail*
A retractable device for derailing locomotives and rolling stock in cases of emergency.

2.8 *Elevation* (or *Super-elevation*)
On curves, the vertical distance that the outer rail is above the inner rail. For a given train speed (the "equilibrium speed") the super-elevation is designed to ensure that the resultant of train weight and centrifugal force is perpendicular to the plane of the track.

2.9 *Fastening*
Means of securing rails to crossties. In North America, track spikes have always been the standard type of rail fastening. Other types of fastenings, such as spring clips, are recent innovations.

Fishplate (see *Joint Bar*)

2.10 *Frog*
In a turnout, a frog is used at the intersection of running rails to provide support for the train wheels and clearance for the wheel flanges, thus permitting wheels running on either rail to cross the other rail.

2.11 *Gauge* (or *Gage*)
The gauge of a railway is the transverse distance between the running rails, measured between gauge lines (q.v.). "Standard Gauge," now almost universal in North America, is four feet, eight and a half inches. "Narrow gauge" is any gauge measuring less than standard gauge. In North America, usually three feet, but occasionally in the past, two feet. "Broad Gauge" is any gauge measuring more than standard gauge, such as the Oregon Steam Navigation Company portage railways at the Cascades and The Dalles-Celilo, which were laid to five feet gauge. Broad gauge has disappeared completely from North America, but is still widely used elsewhere in the world.

2.12 *Gauge Line* (or *Gage Line*)
An imaginary line on the inside of the rail head, 0.625 inches below the upper surface.

Grade Crossing (see *Crossing* (Grade))

2.13 *Guard Rail*
An auxiliary rail, laid parallel to a running rail, to prevent train wheels becoming derailed, or to hold train wheels in correct alignment to prevent their flanges from striking the points of frogs at turnouts or crossings.

2.14 *Joint Bar* (also called *Splice Bar* or *Fishplate*)
A steel member embodying beam strength and stiffness in its structural shape; used in pairs for joining rail ends together.

2.15 *Line* (noun)

> **2.15.1** "Line" is loosely used to denote a railway route; i.e., "the Marshall to Pullman line."
> **2.15.2** "Line" also refers to the condition of railway track in regard to uniformity of direction over short distances on tangents, or uniformity of variation in direction over short distances on curves.

2.16 *Line* (verb)
To shift the track laterally to conform with the proper alignment.

2.17 *Main Track*
A track extending through yards and between stations, upon which trains are operated by timetable or train order, or the use of which is governed by block signals.

2.18 *Rails*
Long rolled-steel or wrought-iron members, of special cross section, laid end to end in two parallel lines on crossties. The Rails provide a runway and means of guidance for locomotives and rolling stock with flanged wheels. They also transmit wheel loads to the other components of the track structure (i.e., to the crossties and ballast). In the case of electric railways, the rails may also act as return conductors of electric current used for traction purposes. Since about 1890 rails have also been used as components of track circuits, carrying low electric currents for signal interlocking purposes. Rail weight, and hence relative size, is given in pounds per yard (lb/yard) and has increased from 56 lb/yard in the 1870s to 132 lb/yard today. North American railways have always used flat-bottomed or inverted "T" section rails, referred to in Europe as "Vignoles" type rails, and have never used "bullhead" rails of the British type, carried in cast iron "chairs."

2.19 *Rail Joint*
A fastening designed to unite the abutting ends of contiguous rails; usually consisting of a pair of joint bars (see 2.14) and four, or, more recently, six track bolts (see 2.29).

2.20 *Running Rail*
Ant rail carrying train wheels (as distinct from guard rails).

2.21 *Siding*
A track auxiliary to the main track, enabling trains running in opposite directions to meet and pass each other, or trains running in the same direction to overtake. Sidings now have turnouts at both ends, allowing continuous movement of trains in either direction without reversal. In the 1880s and 1890s, many sidings had a turnout at one end only, and trains had to back either into or out of them.

Splice Bar (see *Joint Bar*)

2.22 *Surface* (noun)
The condition of the track as to vertical evenness or smoothness.

2.23 *Surface* (verb)
To establish or restore satisfactory "surface."

2.24 *Steel Gang*
A group of workmen engaged in laying track.

2.25 *Switch*
Part of a "turnout" (see 2.32). A device used to divert trains from one track to another.

    2.25.1 *Split Switch*
    A switch consisting essentially of a pair of movable tapered "point rails," or "points," with necessary fixtures.
    2.25.2 *Stub Switch*
    An obsolete form of switch, widely used before about 1890, consisting of a pair of full-section running rails which could be lined up butt to butt with the rails of tracks beyond the switch.
    2.25.3 *Spring Switch*
    A switch with an operating mechanism incorporating a spring-loaded device automatically returning the point rails to their original or normal position after the passage of train wheels in the direction "trailing the switch."

2.26 *Switch Rod*
A pull rod connecting the point rails of a switch with the cranked end of the vertical shaft of a (column throw type) switch stand.

2.27 *Switch Stand*
A device for the manual operation of a switch at a turnout. Switch stands in main track are of the high, "column throw" or "horizontal throw," vertical shaft type, complete with target and lamp to indicate the switch position both day and night. The low, "ground throw" or "vertical throw" type switch stands are only used in secondary and industrial track.

Ties (see *Crossties*)

2.28 *Tie Plates*

Steel plates interposed between rails and crossties (two per crosstie) to distribute loads over a wider area, thus protecting the timber material of the crosstie from localized damage. Tie plates have punched holes through which the track spikes can be driven. Shoulders are rolled into the tie plate profile to locate the rail. Modern tie plates are double-shouldered, having shoulders both inside and outside of the rail. "Single-shouldered" tie plates, with a shoulder at the outside of the rail only, are now obsolete. The rail seating of a tie plate is inclined inwards at an angle of about 10 degrees to provide proper rail camber. Tie plates were not generally used until about 1910. Before their introduction, "spreading of the track" caused many derailments.

2.29 *Track Bolt*

A bolt with a button head and oval neck, used with a square nut and a spring washer to fasten together rails and joint bars.

2.30 *Track Circuit*

A low-current electric circuit, using insulated lengths of the running rails as conductors to operate automatic signalling systems regulating the movement of trains. Introduced about 1890 but not in general use until about 1920.

2.31 *Track Spike*

The traditional North American type of rail fastening, still in use with timber crossties.

2.32 *Turnout*

An arrangement consisting of a switch, a frog, and closure rails, by means of which locomotives and rolling stock may be diverted from one track to another. A "lateral turnout" is a turnout in which the diversion is confined to one track only. An "equilateral turnout" is a turnout in which the diversion is shared between the two tracks. The rate of diversion is given by the "turnout number," which is the same as the "frog number" of the frog used in the turnout. For example, in a No. 8 turnout a No. 8 frog is used. In a No. 8 lateral turnout the rate of diversion is 1 in 8. In a No. 8 equilateral turnout the rate of diversion to each track is 1 in 16. In standard gauge track, turnout number has ranged from 5 to 20, depending upon the expected train speed. Nowadays turnouts are commonly Nos. 5, 15, 16, 18, and 20. Speeds of 70 m.p.h. require the use of No. 20 equilateral turnouts in conjunction with 39-foot-long, curved switch points and other refinements.

2.33 *Turntable*

A rotating bridge set in a pit below grade line; used for turning locomotives around through 180 degrees to run in the opposite direction, or through any other angle to provide access to stub tracks in roundhouses and service areas.

2.34 *Turning Wye* (or *Wye*)

A triangular arrangement of tracks on which locomotives and cars may be turned, either singly or as trains.

3.0 Bridges

A bridge is a structure carrying a railway over land or water below the grade line; alternatively, a structure carrying another railway or a road over a railway at a suitable elevation above the grade line.

3.0.1 *Arch Bridge*
A bridge consisting of one or more arch spans (see 3.12.1)
3.0.2 *Cantilever Bridge*
A bridge consisting of one or more cantilever spans (see 3.12.2)
3.0.3 *Deck Girder Bridge*
A bridge with plate girder spans carrying the roadway and the live loads on the upper flanges of the plate girders, the entire structure being below the railway grade line.
3.0.4 *Deck Truss Bridge*
A bridge with truss spans carrying the roadway and live loads on the upper chords of the trusses, the entire structure being below the railway grade line.
3.0.5 *Through Truss Bridge*
A bridge with truss spans, in which the lower chords of the trusses carry the roadway and the live loads with the trains passing between the trusses, inside the structure.
3.0.6 *Trestle Bridge* (or *Trestle*)
A timber bridge consisting of a deck carried on closely spaced vertical frames called "bents," with appropriate bracing, each bent standing on a transverse row of piles driven into the ground or stream bed.

3.1 *Abutment*
Point of span support at the outer end of a bridge.

3.2 *Bent*
One of the multiple vertical support frames of a timber trestle bridge.

3.3 *Brace*
A structural member, often mounted diagonally in relation to other members, imparting rigidity to a structure.

3.4 *Caisson*
A temporary, water-tight compartment, designed to allow men to work on a river bottom during the construction of a bridge pier. In deep water, caissons may be completely enclosed, air-locked, and charged with compressed air to keep the water out.

3.5 *Chord*
The continuous upper or lower main horizontal member of a truss.

3.6   *Deck*

Material placed on a bridge structure to provide a roadway. Often, as in the case of deck girder bridges, closely spaced transverse timbers.

3.6.1 *Ballast Deck*

A bridge deck consisting of a continuous steel pan carrying a layer of ballast in which the railway track is laid in the normal manner.

3.7   *Falsework*

A temporary structure used during the construction of a permanent bridge.

3.8   *Girder*

A main structural component of a bridge span, consisting of a single deep beam, designed to carry bending and shear loads.

3.8.1 *Plate Girder*

A girder built up of steel plate, with a vertical "web" and horizontal "flanges" at top and bottom, with angle iron "stiffening" and "connections," all riveted together into a single unit.

3.9   *Grillage*

A solid assembly of heavy, square timbers, in multiple layers, each layer being at right angles to the adjacent layers. The completed grillage is placed on piles in a submerged position on a river bottom to provide a solid foundation for a bridge pier.

3.10   *Pier*

A vertical support, usually built of masonry or reinforced concrete, erected in a river channel to carry the adjacent ends of two-bridge spans.

3.10.1 *Crib Pier*

A pier consisting of a heavy timber enclosure, filled with broken rock and capped with concrete.

3.10.2 *Pivot Pier*

A pier specially designed to carry a swinging cantilever drawspan at the central pivot of the span. A pivot pier also incorporates a circular runway for the span rollers, and machinery for rotating the drawspan.

3.11   *Piles*

Long timber poles, driven into unconsolidated ground to provide foundations for bridges and other structures.

3.11.1 *Pile Driver*

A device for hammering piles into unconsolidated ground. A pile driver consists of a hammer of given mass, allowed to fall vertically through a known height onto the large diameter end of a pile. When the impacts of the hammer cease to produce a certain minimum penetration of the pile into the ground, the pile is considered to be fully driven, i.e., there is enough friction between the pile and the surrounding ground to ensure that the specified load can be carried on the pile without causing subsequent movement of the pile.

3.12 *Span*
A horizontal structure, supported at its extremities and designed to carry static and dynamic (live) loading at any intermediate point.

> **3.12.1** *Arch Span*
> A bridge span consisting of an arch from which the deck is suspended.
>
> **3.12.2** *Cantilever Span*
> A span consisting of two sub-spans, each supported and restrained at the outer extremity only, and abutting the other sub-span at the mid point of the span or bridge. Each sub-span carries overhanging loads.
>
> **3.12.3** *Drawspan*
> A retractable bridge span providing an open, unobstructed channel for river navigation. In the Columbia Interior of the 1880s and 1890s the existing drawbridges had centrally pivoted drawspans swinging in the horizontal plane.

3.13 *Truss*
A main structural component of a bridge span, consisting of an assembly of horizontal, vertical, and inclined members, some carrying loads in tension and others in compression.

The principal types of trusses used in railway bridges are:

Howe truss:

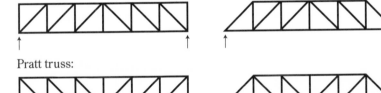

Pratt truss:

4.0 Tunnels

A railway tunnel is an underground excavation made to allow a railway to pass through a hill, ridge, or other landform extending to an elevation far above the desired grade line; or, alternatively, to pass under a river or other intervening body of water.

4.1 *Arch* (or *Back*)
The curved "roof" or upper surface of a tunnel interior.

4.2 *Blasting*
The process of breaking rock by firing explosives loaded into holes drilled into the rock.

4.3 *Breast*
Rock removed during the second part of the tunnel excavation cycle from ground situated below and behind the heading (see 4.7.2).

4.4 *Drilling*
The process of perforating the rock with holes (of about 1.750 to 2.000 inches diameter), later loaded with explosives for blasting (see 4.2).

4.5 *Ground*
The rock or earth material in which a tunnel is excavated.

4.6 *Ground Water*
Water entering a tunnel from the surrounding ground.

4.7 *Heading*
The word "heading" is used in two senses, viz.:

4.7.1 *Heading*
The uncompleted parts of a tunnel during the process of excavation. Headings are driven from the tunnel portals and sometimes also in both directions from the bottoms of intermediate vertical shafts sunk from the ground surface above the tunnel.

4.7.2 *Heading* (or *Pilot Heading*)
Ground removed during the first part of the tunnel excavation cycle from an arched pilot opening at the top of the tunnel cross section, kept ahead of the "breast" (see 4.3).

4.8 *Invert*
The "floor" or lower surface of a tunnel interior.

4.9 *Lining*
Timber, brickwork, or concrete, covering the interior surfaces of a tunnel to retard deterioration of the ground and restrain falls of loose rock.

4.10 *Mucking*
The process of removing broken rock from a tunnel heading as excavation progresses.

4.11 *Portal*
The entry at each end of a tunnel. Designed to provide a vertical face at the tunnel end and to restrain surrounding unconsolidated ground and fractured rock.

4.12 *Refuge Chamber*
An alcove in the side wall of a tunnel, allowing workmen to stand clear of trains passing through the tunnel.

4.13 *Support*
Means of holding up the tunnel arch and side wall in zones of weak or fractured ground. Usually consisting of closely spaced heavy timber frames; nowadays steel frames and/or rockbolts.

4.14 *Ventilation Shaft*
A vertical opening from ground surface to the tunnel axis at an intermediate point in the tunnel. Used during the tunnel drive to provide two more headings at which excavation can proceed. Afterwards used as airways for tunnel ventilation. Not practicable where railroads pass under mountain ranges rising to more than about 500 feet above tunnel elevation.

5.0 Buildings

Backshop (see *Shop*)

5.1 *Depot*
A station building providing the facilities required for handling the arriving and departing of railway passengers. Usually having a ticket office, waiting rooms, a telegraph office, an express company office (handling parcels traffic), and in some cases living quarters for the railroad company agent and his family.

5.1.1 *Union Depot*
A railroad depot used jointly by two or more different railroad companies.

5.2 *Freight House*
A building with railway and road access to the interior, in which goods can be transferred from road vehicles into railroad cars and vice-versa.

5.3 *Roundhouse*
A curved building with rail access by stub tracks radiating from a turntable, with hinged double doors at each track ("stall"). Used to accommodate locomotives idled for servicing or minor repairs.

5.4 *Section House*
A dwelling house on railroad company land, provided for the accommodation of the foreman responsible for maintaining several miles of adjacent roadbed and track.

5.5 *Shop* (or *Backshop*)
A roundhouse annex, or separate building, used for carrying out major repairs or overhauling locomotives.

6.0 Steam Locomotives

A locomotive is a self-propelled tractive vehicle, designed specifically for hauling trains of other rolling stock. The typical American steam locomotive of the late nineteenth century was a two-cylinder, simple expansion, non-superheated machine consisting of a main frame, a boiler, an outside cylinder engine, and running gear, with an auxiliary vehicle, called a "tender," to carry fuel and water.

6.0.1 *Wheel Arrangement—Whyte Notation*

In North America and in Britain, the "Whyte Notation" provided a convenient means of identifying the various types of steam locomotives by their respective wheel arrangements. The Whyte Notation consisted of a series of three numbers corresponding respectively to the number of carrying wheels ahead of the driving wheels, the number of driving wheels, and the number of carrying wheels behind the driving wheels.

Thus:

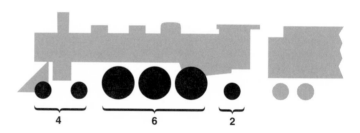

or:

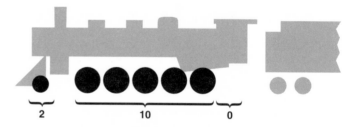

Locomotives were also referred to, loosely, according to the number of their driving wheels, as being "four coupled," "six coupled," "eight coupled," or "ten coupled." Locomotives having two groups of driving wheels, with one group free to move laterally relative to the other, are called "articulated" locomotives.

6.1   *Adhesion Weight*
The weight carried on the driving wheels of a locomotive. About four times the tractive effort developed by the locomotive.

6.2   *"American Type"*
A locomotive of the 4-4-0 wheel arrangement.

6.3   *Air Brake*
A brake actuated by the use of compressed air.

6.3.1 *Automatic Air Brake*
A two-stage air brake system in which changes in compressed-air supply-line pressure are used to control brake application and release at each car in the train. The system is said to be automatic because if the train breaks in two and the train pipe hose connection between cars is severed, the resulting reduction in compressed air supply pressure will apply the brakes.

6.3.2 *Straight Air Brake*
A single-stage air brake system in which compressed air is admitted directly to the brake-actuating cylinders by means of a manually operated valve. Used mainly on locomotives when running alone without trains.

6.4   *Axlebox* (also called *Journal Box* and *Driving Box*)
Axleboxes are wheel/axle bearing assemblies. There are two per axle, transmitting the weight of the locomotive to the rotating axle "journals" just inside each wheel center. In the 1880s and 1890s locomotive axleboxes were of the plain, journal-bearing type, lined with babbitt metal at the semi-cylindrical internal bearing surface, and lubricated with oil picked up by the rotating axle journals from a cloth "packing" installed in a reservoir below the axle.

6.5   *Boiler*
A fired pressure vessel of the shell and tube type, used to generate the high pressure steam required by the locomotive engine. A steam locomotive boiler consists of a water-jacketed "firebox" at the rear end; an intermediate cylindrical "barrel" containing multiple horizontal firetubes surrounded by water; and a cylindrical "smokebox" at the front end, housing the components of the engine exhaust/boiler draft inducing system.

Boiler Tubes (see *Fire Tubes*)

6.6   *Cab*
A shelter on the rear end of a steam locomotive designed to protect the enginemen from the weather.

6.7   *Carrying Wheels*
Locomotive wheels other than driving wheels.

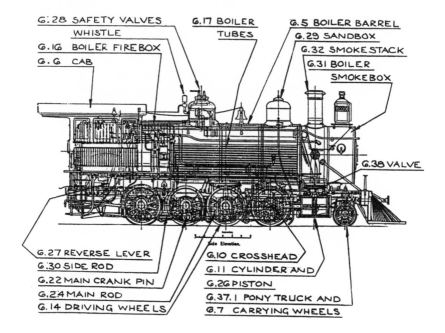

Chimney (see *Smokestack*)

Connecting Rod (see *Main Rod*)

6.8 *"Consolidation"*
A locomotive of the 2-8-0 wheel arrangement.

6.9 *Counter Pressure Brake*
A means of braking whereby atmospheric air can be compressed in the engine cylinders when a train is descending long, steep hills, thus providing continuous retardation without wearing out the brake shoes.

Coupling Rod (see *Side Rod*)

6.10 *Crosshead*
A moving guide block, providing a housing for the wrist pin that links the engine piston rod with the main rod. The crosshead slides backwards and forwards between fixed guide bars that absorb the lateral forces imposed on the piston rod due to the obliquity of the main rod.

6.11 *Cylinders*
The engine cylinders are cylindrical vessels in which the heat of steam is converted into mechanical work in the form of piston thrust. The majority of American locomotives had two cylinders, one on each side of the locomotive ahead of the driving wheels, each with its axis lined up with the center of the main driving axle.

6.12 *Drawbar*
The coupler shank at the rear of the tender, by means of which the locomotive exerts the drawbar pull required to move the train.

6.13 *Drawbar Pull*
The force exerted by a locomotive to haul a train. Drawbar pull does not include the force required to move the locomotive and tender.

Driving Box (see *Axlebox*)

6.14 *Driving Wheels*
Locomotive wheels exerting tangential driving forces against the rails. The driving forces are received from the main rods at the main driving wheel crank pins and distributed to the other pairs of driving wheels by the side rods. The driving wheel radius has to be at least equal to (half piston stroke plus main rod clearance at ground level) and great enough to accommodate the crescent-shaped weights partly counterbalancing the mass of the main and side rods. Locomotives designed to run at high speed had larger driving wheels in order to limit the engine piston speed.

6.15 *Engine Exhaust/Boiler Draft Inducing System*
An ejector nozzle or Venturi arrangement installed in the boiler smokebox, consisting of the convergent nozzle end of the engine exhaust steam pipe and the divergent final exhaust passage provided by the smokestack, separated by a vertical space allowing boiler flue gases to be entrained into the jet flow of exhaust steam. The system functions automatically to draw appropriate quantities of combustion air through the boiler. The harder the engine is worked, the more exhaust steam is produced, the more air is drawn through the boiler, the more fuel can be burned in the firebox, and the more steam is raised. A wonderful self-regulating feature that ensured the success of the steam railway locomotive.

6.16 *Firebox*
A water-jacketed furnace at the rear end of a locomotive boiler, in which fuel is burned to produce the heat required to generate steam for use in the engine cylinders. The floor of the firebox is made up of parallel firebars with intermediate spaces for the passage of combustion air, forming a grate upon which solid fuel is burned. A "firedoor hole" in the firebox back plates, above the level of the grate, allows fuel to be added to the fire. Hot gases produced by combustion are drawn forward through the boiler firetubes by the pumping action of the engine exhaust/boiler draft-inducing system mounted in the smokebox.

6.17 *Fire Tubes* (or *Boiler Tubes*)

Multiple horizontal tubes, about 2 inches in diameter, conducting the hot combustion gases through the cylindrical barrel of the boiler from the firebox to the smokebox. Heat from the gases passes through the tube walls into the water within the boiler barrel, thus raising the water temperature to the boiling point corresponding to the applied steam pressure.

6.18 *Hand Brake*

A manually operated auxiliary means of applying brake shoes to the wheels of the tender. Used generally as a "parking brake."

6.19 *Horsepower*

Horsepower is the rate at which mechanical work is done. Thus, if a locomotive exerts a drawbar pull of 5,000 pounds when running at a speed of 40 mph (58.667 ft/sec) it will be developing:

$$\frac{5000 \text{ lb through } 58.667 \text{ ft/sec}}{550 \text{ ft lb/sec}} = \frac{533 \text{ Drawbar Horsepower}}{\text{(DBHP)}}$$

If an additional force of 1,200 pounds is required to move the locomotive and tender, the tractive effort exerted at the driving wheel/rail interface will be 6,200 pounds, and the locomotive will be developing:

$$\frac{6200 \text{ lb through } 58.667 \text{ ft/sec}}{550 \text{ ft lb/sec}} = 661 \text{ Wheel Horsepower}$$

If the losses within the engine and running gear (including the work done against cylinder back pressure to operate the engine exhaust/boiler draft inducing system) amount to 20 percent, the net power developed in the cylinders will be:

$$\frac{661}{0.8} = \frac{826 \text{ Indicated horse power (IHP)}}{\text{(i.e. cylinder horsepower)}}$$

Given that the indicated horsepower of a steam locomotive may be estimated by dividing the potential rate of steam production (lb/hr) in the boiler by the specific steam consumption (lb/IHP hr) in the engine cylinders, the boiler might have to produce:

826 x 27 = 22,302 lb/hr of steam
and the fireman would have to shovel over a ton of coal per hour into the firebox. If the train was running on straight and level track, and the resistance of the cars was, say, 9.2 lb/ton, the train weight would be:

$$\frac{5000}{9.2} = 543 \text{ tons}$$

or about 15 cars of 25 tons capacity (37 1/2 tons gross). If one then introduced an adverse gradient and curved track, the haulage capacity and/ or speed would diminish rapidly.

6.20 *Injector*
A device with no moving parts, used to force water into the boiler against the pressure inside the boiler.

Johnson Bar (see *Reverse Lever*)

Journal Box (see *Axlebox*)

6.21 *Light Engine*
A locomotive running alone without a train.

6.22 *Main Crank Pin*
The two main crank pins of a steam locomotive are mounted off-center by half a piston stroke and rotationally at 90 degrees to each other in the center castings of the main driving wheels. Each main crank pin carries the "big end" of one main rod, from which it receives the piston thrust developed in the cylinder on that side of the engine.

6.23 *Main Frame*
The main frame is the structural foundation of a locomotive. It consists of two side frames, standing upright, usually inside the wheels, braced by the cylinder castings at the front end, and by the drawhead at the rear end, with other transverse stiffening as required. Designed to carry the boiler and provide attachment points for the suspension springs, engine valve gear, and brake rigging, with jaws or "pedestals" in the lower edges of the side frames to locate the wheel/axle/axlebox assemblies and provide enough vertical clearance for the axleboxes to move up and down as the suspension springs deflect under running conditions.

6.24 *Main Rod* (or *Connecting Rod*)
The two main rods, each articulating at the small (front) end about the crosshead wrist pin, and at the big (rear) end about the main crank pin, convert linear thrust from the pistons into torque at the driving wheels.

6.25 *"Mogul"*
Generally a locomotive of the 2-6-0 wheel arrangement. However, in the Columbia Interior, if not elsewhere, the term was also applied to locomotives of the 2-8-0 wheel arrangement.

6.26 *Piston*
A circular cast iron or steel disc, several inches thick, carrying sealing rings in grooves cut into the periphery, with a long circular section steel "piston rod" integral with or securely fastened into the hub. Each piston reciprocates within one cylinder of the engine and transmits the expansive force of steam to the crosshead, whence it is transmitted, in turn, through the main rod and side rods to the driving wheels.

6.27 *Reverse Lever* (also called *Johnson Bar*)
A large control lever, mounted in the locomotive cab, enabling the locomotive engineer to reverse the direction of travel and to regulate the ratio of steam expansion within the engine cylinders.

6.28 *Safety Valve*
A spring-loaded valve, opening to allow steam to escape from the boiler. Designed to relieve excess steam pressure within the boiler. Each boiler had two, and sometimes three, safety valves.

6.29 *Sanding Gear*
A means of sprinkling or blowing fine sand onto the rails to prevent driving-wheel slippage.

6.30 *Side Rod* (or *Coupling Rod*)
The side rods, carried on the main and subsidiary crank pins set in the driving wheel center bosses at each side of the locomotive, distribute the driving forces to all the driving wheels, thus allowing the engine to develop a maximum tractive effort compatible with the adhesion weight (see 6.1).

6.31 *Smokebox*
The front section of a locomotive boiler, housing the components of the engine exhaust/boiler draft inducing system.

6.32 *Smokestack*
Part of the engine exhaust/boiler draft inducing system, extending through the top of the boiler smokebox to discharge exhaust steam and flue gases to the atmosphere. Wood burning locomotives had smokestacks incorporating spark-arresting devices.

6.33 *"Ten-Wheeler"*
A locomotive of the 4-6-0 wheel arrangement.

6.34 *Tender*
An auxiliary vehicle, coupled directly to the rear of a steam locomotive, to carry fuel and water. Assumed for the purposes of traction calculations to be an integral part of the locomotive.

6.35 *Throttle Lever*
A control lever or crank mounted in a locomotive cab to enable the locomotive engineer to operate the throttle valve controlling the flow of steam from the boiler to the engine cylinders.

6.36 *Tractive Effort*
The net tangential force exerted by a locomotive at the driving wheel rims to move itself and the train. To avoid excessive wheel slippage on the rails the maximum tractive effort was limited to about 28 percent of adhesion weight (see 6.1). It is important to remember that tractive effort is a force, not power.

6.37 *Truck*
A one- or two-axled vehicular sub-assembly designed to carry some of the weight of a locomotive, ahead of or behind the driving wheels, and having some freedom to move laterally relative to the remainder of the

locomotive on curved track. By means of swing-link connections to the locomotive main frame, the lateral movement induces, as a reaction, a centering force, helping the locomotive to negotiate the curve.

6.37.1 *Pony Truck*
A single-axled truck, used in front of locomotive driving wheels.

6.38 *Valve*
A reciprocating device governing the admission and exhaust of steam to and from both ends of an engine cylinder in the proper sequence. In the nineteenth century the "D" type flat slide valve was universally used. Each valve was housed in a "steam chest" located above or alongside the cylinder.

6.39 *Valve Gear* (or *Reversing Gear*)
An engine-driven mechanism imparting reciprocating movement to the slide valves regulating the flow of steam to the engine cylinders. The valve gear was controlled by the reversing lever to select the direction of running and regulate the ratio of steam expansion within the cylinders. In nineteenth century North America Stephenson's twin eccentric "link motion," always accommodated between the main frames, was the universal type of locomotive valve gear.

6.40 *Wheelbase*
A distance between axle centers. Lists of locomotive dimensions usually give "coupled wheelbase" (for the distance from front driving axle to rear driving axle), "locomotive wheelbase," "tender wheelbase," and "total locomotive and tender wheelbase."

7.0 Cars

Cars include passenger cars, freight cars, and service cars (used for purposes internal to the railway company and not for revenue-earning purposes).

7.1 *Axle*
A steel shaft upon which the car wheels are mounted. The axle not only holds the wheels to gauge, but also transmits the load from the journal boxes.

7.2 *Baggage Car*
A passenger train car having wide side doors for the admittance of baggage. May be combined with facilities for handling express, mail, or passengers.

7.3 *Body* (of a car)
That part of a car in or on which the load is placed.

7.4 *Body Bolster*
The transverse members of a car underframe, situated over each truck, to transmit load from the center sill of the underframe to the center plate of each truck.

7.5 *Body Center Plate*
The center plate attached to the underside of the body bolster, mating face to face with the truck bolster center plate.

7.6 *Body Framing*
The framework of the car body. Commonly subdivided into side, end, and roof framing.

7.7 *Bolster Spring*
The main springs of a car, supporting the truck bolster, upon which the weight of the car body rests.

7.8 *Box Car*
An enclosed and roofed freight car with sliding side doors. Used for general service, and especially for lading which has to be protected from the weather.

7.9 *Brake Pipe*
That section of the air brake piping of a car acting as a supply line for the reservoirs, and in the case of the automatic air brake as the sole connecting means by which the car brakes are controlled by the locomotive engineer. The pipe is generally 1.250 inches diameter inside and carries a pressure of 70 lb/sq inch. Flexible hoses provide connections between cars, thus forming a continuous "train line" from the locomotive.

7.10 *Brake Shoe*
Blocks of cast iron or other material forced against the car wheel treads by the action of the brake cylinder through the brake rigging, thus providing a frictional retarding force slowing the train.

7.11 *Business Car*
A car used by railway officials when traveling. Equipped with an office and living accommodations for eating and sleeping.

7.12 *Caboose* or *Caboose Car*
A car attached to the rear of freight trains for the accommodation of the conductor and trainmen. Also used to carry the various stores, tools, etc., required on freight trains. Also called a "way car" or "van."

7.13 *Center Pin*
A long steel bolt or pin passing vertically through the body and truck bolster center plates to locate the truck relative to the car body.

7.14 *Center Sill*
The central longitudinal structural member of a car underframe, transmitting drawbar and buffing forces from one end of the car to the other.

7.15 *Chair Car*
A passenger car equipped with reclining chairs to provide more comfort than the ordinary day car for passengers traveling at night but not desiring to use a sleeping car.

7.16 *Coach* (or *Day Car)*
A passenger car used for day travel and fitted with ordinary (i.e., non-reclining) seats.

7.16.1 *Combination Car*
A passenger car divided into two or more compartments for the accommodation of different classes of passengers.

7.17 *Coupler*
An appliance for coupling cars and/or locomotives together. Before the adoption of automatic couplers between 1880 and 1890 freight car couplers were of the "link and pin" type, while the archaic "Miller" coupler was widely used on passenger cars. Modern automatic couplers, such as the A.A.R. Type "E" coupler, couple automatically upon impact between cars, and can be uncoupled without requiring persons to go between cars. They are therefore much safer than the earlier types of couplers.

Day Car (see *Coach*)

7.18 *Deck*
A term applied to the roof of a car which has a "clerestory" (i.e., a raised central roof section with sliding side lights that can be opened for ventilation purposes). Clerestory car roofs were superseded by continuously arched roofs when air conditioning was applied to railroad passenger cars.

7.19 *Dining Car*
A car in which meals are served to passengers, often incorporating a kitchen and all related appliances and utensils.

7.20 *Draft Gear*
A cushioning device placed between the coupler shank and the center sill of a car to absorb shocks resulting from train movements and the coupling of cars.

End Platform (see *Platform*)

7.21 *Equalizer*
A system of levers and connections designed to equalize the loads carried by the several wheels of a locomotive or car truck.

7.22 *Express Car*
A car operated in passenger trains for carrying express consignments. Often combined with facilities for handling baggage and/or mail.

7.23 *Flat Car*
A freight car having a floor laid over the sills, without any housing or body above.

7.24 *Gondola Car*
A flat-floored freight car with body sides and ends but without a top covering.

7.25 *Hand Brake*
Apparatus enabling the car brakes to be applied manually.

7.26 *Hopper Car*
A freight car with the floor sloping from the ends and sides to one or more hoppers, so that the load can be discharged by gravity through the hopper bottom doors.

7.27 *Hot Box*
An overheated axle journal, caused by excessive friction between the bearing and the journal due to lack of lubricant or the presence of foreign matter.

7.28 *Journal Box*
A metal housing enclosing one rotating journal of a car axle, the stationary journal bearing block, and a retaining wedge. Also containing oil and a device (i.e. oil-soaked packing) for lubricating the journal. There are two journal boxes per axle, located at the outer ends of the axle, outside the wheels, and held within the pedestal jaws of the truck side frames. Nowadays most freight cars are fitted with roller bearings. The old journal bearing is now obsolete.

Mail Car (see *Postal Car*)

7.29 *Ore Car*
A hopper car specially designed for carrying metal ores of high density. Such cars are generally shorter and have less cubic capacity than other hopper cars.

7.30 *Parlor Car*
A luxurious form of day coach, available to passengers upon payment of an extra fare.

7.31 *Platform* (or *End Platform*) [Passenger and Caboose Cars]
A floor at the end of a car, equipped with "platform steps" to facilitate ingress and egress by passengers and trainmen.

7.32 *Platform Hood*
That portion of a passenger car roof extending over an end platform.

7.33 *Postal Car* (or *Mail Car*)
A car used in passenger train service for the purpose of carrying mail. Sometimes also equipped for sorting mail, and for picking up and setting down bags of mail while the train is running at speed.

7.34 *Pressure Retaining Valve*
A device by means of which brake cylinder air pressure may be maintained when a train is descending long downgrades, while, at the same time, the brake pipe pressure is temporarily increased to recharge the car reservoirs.

7.35 *Pullman Car*
A name strictly applicable only to cars operated by the Pullman Company, but, in common usage, often applied to all sleeping, parlor, or drawing-room cars.

7.36 *Railway Service Car*
A car used by a railway company for internal, non-revenue-earning purposes (i.e. ballast cars, supply cars, staff instruction cars, etc.)

7.37 *Refrigerator Car*
A specially built insulated box car used for carrying perishable goods. Originally employing natural air circulation over ice to keep the load cool during transit.

7.38 *Running Board* [Freight cars]
A roof-mounted walkway on a box car, stock car, refrigerator car, or covered hopper car, allowing train men to pass along the train for the purpose of applying the hand brakes.

7.39 *Side Sills*
The outside longitudinal members of a car underframe.

7.40 *Sleeping Car*
A passenger car providing sleeping facilities. The older sleeping cars had open sections with facing seats during the day, which could be made up into berths and curtained off for night service.

7.41 *Stock Car*
A freight car with a roof, slatted sides, and side doors, used for the transportation of livestock. Double-decked for moving sheep, pigs, and smaller animals.

7.42 *Striking Plates* (or *Strikers*)
Cover plates, applied one to each end of a car center sill, with a rectangular aperture in each striking plate for the insertion of the coupler shank and the draft gear. The length of a car is often expressed as the distance "over strikers."

7.43 *Tank Car*
A freight car with a body consisting of an enclosed cylindrical tank with internal baffles, used for carrying liquids. Tank cars originally had separate underframes but now frequently use the tank as a structure replacing the underframe.

7.44 *Triple Valve* [Air Brake System]
A directional control air valve, mounted on each car, to charge the air reservoirs and control the application and release of the air brakes.

7.45 *Truck* [Freight Car]
A two-axled vehicular sub-assembly, designed to carry one end of a freight car. Consisting basically of a transverse bolster between the axles and twin side frames with pedestal jaws at the outer ends to receive the journal boxes. With helical suspension springs between the bolster ends and the bottom chord of each side frame.

7.46 *Truck* [Passenger Car]
A two- or three-axled vehicular sub-assembly designed to carry one end of a passenger car. Compared with freight car trucks, passenger car trucks were fitted with refinements such as swinging bolsters to prevent lateral shocks from being communicated to the car body, and equalizing beams and springs to give better distribution of weight between axles.

7.47 *Underframe*
A structural framework designed to withstand the drawbar and buffing forces imposed on the car and carry the mass of the car body. The underframe includes the center and side sills, bolster, and crossbearers.

7.48 *Wheel Flange*
The projecting edge or rim on the periphery of a car wheel for keeping it on the rail.

8.0 Personnel

8.1 *Agent*
Passenger or freight agent. Person locally responsible for conducting railroad company business transactions with the public.

8.2 *Brakeman* (or *Trainman*)
Person assisting the conductor (see 8.4) on board a train. A brakeman's duties included operating the hand brakes on individual cars, setting switches at passing sidings and in yard areas, and coupling or uncoupling cars during switching operations.

8.3 *Carman*
A person engaged in car repairs.

8.4 *Conductor*
Passenger or freight conductor. Person responsible for the safe operation of a train, receiving train orders from telegraph operators and issuing appropriate instructions to other members of the train crew; taking steps to protect the train from other trains at meeting points or at unscheduled halts beyond yard limits. Passenger train conductors were also responsible for the safety, well-being, and orderly behavior of passengers.

8.5   *Engine Hostler*
A roundhouse hand preparing locomotives for service (i.e., raising steam in boilers) or disposing of locomotives after service (i.e., dropping fires and cleaning out ashpans). Authorized to move locomotives on roundhouse tracks.

8.6   *Locomotive Engineer*
The operator of a locomotive. Responsible to the conductor (see 8.4) in matters concerning train movements. In charge of the locomotive. Responsible for inspecting and lubricating it, reporting defects in its condition, and for supervising the work of the fireman (see 8.7).

8.7   *Locomotive Fireman*
The second man on a locomotive. Responsible for handling fuel, tending the fire, and maintaining water level and steam pressure in the boiler. Charged with taking on enough water to keep the boiler full between stops at water tanks along the railway line. Assisted the locomotive engineer (see 8.6) in looking out along the line ahead for signals, obstructions, etc.

8.8   *Master Mechanic*
Person in charge of a roundhouse and backshop. Responsible for ensuring that locomotives and crews were made available for all trains.

8.9   *"News Butcher"*
A vendor of newspapers, magazines, minor refreshments, and tobacco, working aboard a passenger train for a company franchised by the railway company to sell such items to passengers.

8.10   *Roadmaster*
Person in charge of maintaining roadbed and track on one division of a railroad.

8.11   *Section Foreman*
Person in charge of roadbed and track maintenance on one section of a railroad subdivision.

8.12   *Section Hand*
A workman engaged in the maintenance of railway roadbed and track.

8.13   *Switch Tender*
A person employed to operate a switch at a particular location.

8.14   *Telegraph Operator*
A person employed at a depot or intermediate telegraph office to receive and transcribe train orders and other telegraphed messages from the divisional train dispatcher and deliver such orders and messages in written form to the conductors of trains. Also transmitted outgoing telegraph messages as required.

8.15 *Train Dispatcher*

A person directing movements of trains on one division of a railroad. Responsible for making arrangements for trains to meet and pass, or overtake each other, and for issuing the appropriate instructions to telegraph operators (see 8.14) at points along the railway line.

Trainman (see *Brakeman*)

8.16 *Yard Master*

A person in charge of locomotive and car movements within yard limits at a particular location, i.e., for making up trains, etc.

Notes

Notes for Chapter One

1. *East Oregonian*, May 9, 1884 and November 4, 1884 (Special from New York, October 29, 1884). *Oregonian*, May 9, 1884; July 14, 1884; August 18, 1884; and, especially, September 9, 1884.
2. *Oregonian*, March 14, 1884.
3. *East Oregonian*, September 16, 1884. *Railroad Gazette*, September 19, 1884, p. 692.
4. *Oregonian*, March 1, 1885 and April 12, 1885.
5. *Oregonian*, March 1, 1885 and March 3, 1885.
6. *Oregonian*, March 18, 1885.
7. *Oregonian*, March 19, 1885; April 30, 1885; May 7, 1885; June 4, 1885; July 1, 1885; July 11, 1885; July 28, 1885; August 1, 1885; August 3, 1885; August 4, 1885; and August 16, 1885. *East Oregonian*, March 20, 1885.
8. *Oregonian*, September 22, 1885; September 25, 1885; and October 1, 1885. In both 1884 and 1885 the NP directors elected were: Frederick Billings, Charles B. Wright, Robert Harris (president), J. W. Ellis, August Belmont, J. L. Stackpole, Benjamin P. Cheney, Johnstone Livingstone, John C. Bullitt, Thomas F. Oakes, Rosewell G. Ralston, J. H. Hall, and T. P. Halowell.
9. *Oregonian*, September 18, 1885.
10. Northern Pacific Railroad Company, *Annual Report*, 1886.
11. *Ibid.*
12. *Railroad Gazette*, April 23, 1886, p. 291.
13. *Oregonian*, October 28, 1886. The first American transcontinental railroad link or "Overland Route" was completed by the Union Pacific and Central Pacific companies in 1869. Central Pacific was the creation of California promoters Collis P. Huntington, Leland Stanford, Charles Crocker, and Mark Hopkins, widely known as "The Big Four." In a process of absorption and expansion, these men also took over the Southern Pacific Railroad and extended it east across southern California, reaching the Colorado River at Yuma in 1877. Advancing east across southern Arizona and southwestern New Mexico, the SP arrived at El Paso, Texas, in May 1881. In conjunction with several Texas and Louisiana companies, a through line from El Paso to New Orleans was opened in February 1883. The line from Los Angeles, California, to New Orleans, Louisiana, was always called "The Sunset Route." Its opening gave the California promoters a second outlet to the East, thus

For the full names of newspapers cited in the notes, see the newspapers and periodicals heading in the bibliography.

enabling them to divert traffic away from the Central Pacific and the "Overland Route," leaving Union Pacific high and dry at Ogden, Utah. See Don L. Hofsommer, *The Southern Pacific, 1901-1985* (College Station: Texas A & M University Press, 1986), pp. 4-5.

14. *Oregonian*, October 12, 1886 and November 18, 1886.
15. *Railroad Gazette*, December 17, 1886, p. 880.
16. *Oregonian*, January 6, 1887.
17. *Oregonian*, February 1, 1887.
18. *Oregonian*, February 11, 1887.
19. *Oregonian*, April 24, 1887. *East Oregonian*, April 26, 1887. *Railroad Gazette*, April 29, 1887, p. 294.
20. Stuart Daggett, *Railroad Reorganization* (Boston: Houghton, Mifflin & Co., 1908), p. 237; James Blaine Hedges, *Henry Villard and the Railways of the Northwest* (New Haven, Conn.: Yale University Press, 1930), p. 145; Robert G. Athearn, *Union Pacific Country* (Chicago: Rand McNally, 1971), p. 325. *Railroad Gazette*, April 29, 1887, p. 294. All of these accounts are at variance. I believe Athearn to be the most reliable. For supplementary conditions of the UP lease see *Oregonian*, October 21, 1887.
21. The NPRR line over the Stampede Pass switchbacks was completed June 2, 1887 and opened July 3, 1887.
22. *Oregonian*, March 19, 1887 (O&C leased to SP); *Oregonian*, December 18, 1887 (driving of last spike on O&C previous day).
23. *East Oregonian*, August 2, 1887.
24. Henry Villard, *Memoirs of Henry Villard*, vol. 3 (Boston: Houghton Mifflin & Co., 1904), pp. 321-323. *Railroad Gazette*, September 2, 1887, p. 581. *Oregonian*, September 4, 1887; September 7, 1887; and September 16, 1887.
25. Villard, *Memoirs*, pp. 321-323; Hedges, *Henry Villard* pp. 148-149.
26. Villard, *Memoirs*, pp. 324-325; Hedges, *Henry Villard*, pp. 149-150. *Oregonian*, September 16, 1887; September 20, 1887 (ed.); September 21, 1887; and October 3, 1887. In the fiscal year ending June 30, 1887, NP gross earnings were $12,789, 448; operating expenses $7,173,019; net earnings $5,186,428; other income $424,366; fixed charges $6,025,088; and surplus $65,707. Soon after Villard rejoined NP the company issued $12 million third mortgage bonds, $8 million of which were taken up by Rothschild and Deutsche Bank. Villard, *Memoirs*, p. 325; *Union*, December 3, 1887; *Railroad Gazette*, February 3, 1888, p. 81.
27. Villard's victory was less than resounding. In fact, according to newspaper reports following the election, there was still a majority in favor of the old management. *Union*, October 1, 1887, from *New York Tribune*, September 13, 1887.
28. Hedges, *Henry Villard*, pp. 158-160. *Oregonian*, September 17, 1887 (ed.); October 2, 1887. *Railroad Gazette*, October 7, 1887, p. 658; October 28, 1887, p. 709.
29. *Oregonian*, October 13, 1887.
30. *Oregonian*, January 20, 1888. *East Oregonian*, January 20, 1888.
31. *East Oregonian*, November 22, 1887.
32. *East Oregonian*, December 6, 1887.
33. *Oregonian*, May 7, 1887. The comments were made to Mr. B. Goldsmith, who was interested in the Sierra Nevada and other Coeur d'Alene mines.

34. *Oregonian*, February 14, 1888. Northern Pacific was said to be shipping Coeur d'Alene ore to Wickes, Montana, for 1.34 cents per ton-mile, compared with 2.55 cents to Portland.

35. *Oregonian*, November 3, 1886; January 6, 1887.

36. *Oregonian*, July 22, 1886.

37. *Oregonian*, October 14, 1886; December 25, 1886.

38. T. A. Rickard, *Bunker Hill Enterprise* (San Francisco: Mining & Scientific Press, 1921), p. 75.

39. *Oregonian*, January 19, 1888. (ed.)

40. *Oregonian*, January 23, 1888 (ed.); January 25, 1888. *East Oregonian*, February 10, 1888. *Union*, February 10, 1888; February 11, 1888.

41. *Oregonian*, February 14, 1888; March 1, 1888 (ed.); March 8, 1888 (ed.). *East Oregonian*, February 17, 1888; February 28, 1888. *Railroad Gazette*, March 9, 1888, p. 157.

42. *Oregonian*, March 2, 1888. *Railroad Gazette*, March 9, 1888, p. 163. Athearn, *Union Pacific Country*, p. 326. Van B. De Lashmutt became Mayor of Portland in June 1888. He was interested in the Stemwinder, Honeyman, and Tyler mines in the Coeur d'Alene camp. *Oregonian*, May 7, 1887.

43. Hedges, *Henry Villard*, p. 167.

44. *Oregonian*, March 18, 1888. The six Oregonians who made the trip were C. A. Dolph, Henry Failing, C. H. Lewis, John McCracken, H. W. Scott, and William M. Sibson.

45. Hedges, *Henry Villard*, pp. 168-169.

46. *Oregonian*, March 28, 1888. For similar skeptical assessment of Joint Lease see *East Oregonian*, March 27, 1888.

47. Hedges, *Henry Villard*, pp. 175-182.

48. *Oregonian*, May 16, 1888.

49. *Oregonian*, May 29, 1888. *Railroad Gazette*, June 15, 1888, p. 397.

50. For details of W&I construction, legal difficulties, and plans for extension into Montana see Chapter Nine of this volume.

51. *Oregonian*, July 28, 1888. *East Oregonian*, July 31, 1888. *Railroad Gazette*, August 3, 1888, p. 513. Hedges, *Henry Villard*, p. 185.

52. *Oregonian*, August 6, 1888.

53. *Oregonian*, December 5, 1888.

54. Hedges, *Henry Villard*, pp. 185-190. *Oregonian*, February 22, 1889 and February 23, 1889. *Railroad Gazette*, March 1, 1889, p. 151.

55. *Railroad Gazette*, November 23, 1888, p. 778.

56. Hedges, *Henry Villard*, pp. 190-192.

57. *Railroad Gazette*, March 22, 1889, p. 203.

58. *Oregonian*, April 25, 1889. *Railroad Gazette*, May 3, 1889, p. 302.

59. *Oregonian*, May 14, 1889. Hedges, *Henry Villard*, pp. 195-196.

60. *Oregonian*, May 15, 1889 (ed.).

61. *Oregonian*, May 13, 1889.

62. *Oregonian*, May 18, 1889. Villard, *Memoirs*, p. 331.

63. *Oregonian*, May 19, 1889.

64. *Oregonian*, May 14, 1889; May 15, 1889 (ed.); June 18, 1889.

65. Villard, *Memoirs*, p. 332.

66. *Oregonian*, June 5, 1889. *Railroad Gazette*, June 14, 1889, p. 400. Hedges, *Henry Villard*, pp. 199-200.

67. Villard, *Memoirs*, p. 331. *Oregonian*, June 10, 1889; June 12, 1889; June 13, 1889.
68. *Oregonian*, June 18, 1889. Hedges, *Henry Villard*, p. 202.
69. *Oregonian*, June 22, 1889. No one put forward opposition to the compromise for the OR&N board. The directors elected were: H. W. Corbett, Henry Failing, W. S. Ladd, C. H. Lewis, William H. McIntosh, John McCracken, and W. S. Sibson (all of Portland); and Charles B. Fosdic, V. Mumford Moore, Henry R. Reed, Edmund Smith, Prosper W. Smith, and William P. St. John. On July 1, 1889 Edmund Smith of Philadelphia, a former vice president of the Pennsylvania Railroad, gained election as president to succeed Elijah Smith (no relation), who had been obliged to step down. William S. Ladd became vice president.
70. Villard, *Memoirs*, p. 331.
71. Athearn, *Union Pacific Country*, p. 328.
72. Villard, *Memoirs*, pp. 325-327. *Oregonian*, March 25, 1889; March 29, 1889.
73. *Oregonian*, March 28, 1890.
74. Daggett, *Railroad Reconstruction*, p. 276.
75. *Oregonian*, June 5, 1889.
76. *Oregonian*, June 19, 1889 (from San Francisco *Chronicle*, June 18, 1889).
77. *Oregonian*, September 28, 1889.
78. *Railroad Gazette*, November 22, 1889, p. 779.
79. *Railroad Gazette*, June 26, 1881, p. 458. Union Pacific lost P&PS in the debacle of 1893. The Kalama to Vancouver section was later sold by the receiver to the Northwestern Improvement Company, an auxiliary of the Northern Pacific Railway, and completed for NP in 1903. The Columbia River bridge was started in 1890 by another UP Rly subsidiary set up for that specific purpose. NP later acquired the one stone pier which had been completed, and used it for its own bridge. See Louis Tuck Renz, *History of the Northern Pacific Railroad* (Fairfield, Wash.: Ye Galleon Press, 1980), p. 216.

Notes for Chapter Two

1. *Oregonian*, July 11, 1883.
2. *Oregonian*, December 6, 1883.
3. *Oregonian*, May 29, 1883.
4. *Oregonian*, July 27, 1885 (from Walla Walla *Union*).
5. *Oregonian*, July 25, 1885.
6. Distances as per Union Pacific Railroad Company *Timetable No. 3*, March 9, 1980, and *East Oregonian*, September 25, 1885.
7. Elevations as per Union Pacific Railroad Company, Division Engineer's Office, Portland, Oregon; courtesy of Mr. Jim Reiser, February 1983.
8. *Oregonian*, July 27, 1885.
9. *Oregonian*, September 3, 1885.
10. *Oregonian*, September 16, 1885.
11. *Oregonian*, September 24, 1885.
12. *Weekly Statesman*, August 24, 1879.
13. *Railroad Gazette*, October 28, 1881, p. 601, re OR&N Annual Report.
14. *Oregonian*, October 23, 1885.
15. *Oregonian*, November 5, 1885.

16. *An Illustrated History of South Eastern Washington* (Spokane, Wash.: Western Historical Publishing Co., 1906), p. 516, ff.

17. *Oregonian*, December 13, 1884.

18. *History of South Eastern Washington*, p. 516, ff.

19. *Oregonian*, May 29, 1885.

20. *Oregonian*, June 17, 1885.

21. *Oregonian*, June 20, 1885.

22. *Oregonian*, July 25, 1885.

23. *East Oregonian*, August 4, 1885. *Oregonian*, July 31, 1885. Note that the latter says that the incline was on the Columbia River four miles above Wallula, which appears to have been a mistake.

24. *East Oregonian*, July 19, 1885, says that "From Starbuck to the end of Kellogg Gulch requires two engines to draw fourteen cars."

25. Assuming that, at that time, *John Gates, Spokane, Almota, Annie Faxon*, and *D. S. Baker* were available for use on the Snake River, previous performance of upper river navigation, and correction for Snake River distances, gives 11.3 tons of cargo per vessel net ton per year, which, for an aggregate 3,267 net tons, indicates a probable annual capacity for Riparia to Port Kelly of about 37,000 tons, or about 23,000 tons less than the 60,000-ton crop.

26. *History of South Eastern Washington*, p. 516, ff. In various contemporary accounts, Robert McClellan was also spelled "McClelland."

27. *Ibid.*

28. *Oregonian*, October 16, 1885, says that "The people have offered a freight bonus equivalent to a $150,000 subsidy."

29. *Oregonian*, October 16, 1885.

30. *Oregonian*, October 26, 1885. At that time, Starbuck was "... a thriving burg of about six houses." (*East Oregonian*, July 19, 1885.)

31. *Oregonian*, October 31, 1885.

32. Distance as per Union Pacific Railroad Company *Timetable No. 3*, March 9, 1980.

33. *Oregonian*, October 16, 1885.

34. *Oregonian*, March 18, 1886.

35. *Oregonian*, November 5, 1885.

36. *Oregonian*, December 30, 1885. Note that Hunt had 1,500 acres of land near Corvallis and intended to seed it to grain before spring. He had previously been employed on the Baker City to Huntington section, and more recently on the Oregon Pacific. His name was to loom larger in the railway history of the Interior.

37. *Oregonian*, December 26, 1885.

38. *Oregonian*, December 20, 1885; December 26, 1885.

39. *Oregonian*, December 14, 1885.

40. *Oregonian*, November 5, 1885 and November 28, 1885. *History of South Eastern Washington*, p. 516, ff.

41. *Oregonian*, January 24, 1886.

42. *Oregonian*, February 6, 1886.

43. *Oregonian*, March 18, 1886 (from Starbuck correspondence in Walla Walla *Journal*).

44. *Oregonian*, May 29, 1886.

45. *Oregonian*, July 6, 1886.

46. *Union*, October 9, 1886. *Oregonian*, November 12, 1886.

47. *Oregonian*, December 25, 1886; January 12, 1887. *East Oregonian*, January 15, 1887.
48. *East Oregonian*, January 28, 1887.
49. *Oregonian*, February 24, 1887.
50. *East Oregonian*, February 18, 1887.

Notes for Chapter Three

1. Northern Pacific Railroad Company, *Annual Report*, 1887.
2. *Oregonian*, October 31, 1885; November 3, 1885.
3. *Oregonian*, November 18, 1885. Copy of Articles of Incorporation provided by Archives and Special Collections, Eastern Washington University, Cheney, courtesy of Mr. Charles V. Mutschler.
4. *Oregonian*, February 27, 1886. Copy of supplemental Articles of Incorporation provided by Archives and Special Collections, Eastern Washington University, Cheney, courtesy of Mr. Charles V. Mutschler.
5. *Review*, March 13, 1886.
6. *Review*, March 21, 1886; March 27, 1886.
7. *Railroad Gazette*, April 23, 1886, p. 291.
8. *Oregonian*, April 20, 1886.
9. *Oregonian*, May 5, 1886.
10. *Review*, May 13, 1886.
11. *Review*, May 22, 1886.
12. *Review*, June 11, 1886.
13. *Review*, June 30, 1886. Adna Anderson accompanied Robert Harris to Spangle. Villard blamed Anderson, unfairly, for the NP cost overruns of 1883. Anderson had a good working relationship with Harris and was a respected engineer. After Villard regained control of NP in 1888, Anderson was driven to suicide by Villard's vindictive attitude toward him.
14. *Review*, May 22, 1886.
15. *Review*, September 29, 1886.
16. *Review*, June 6, 1886.
17. *Review*, July 10, 1886. This item says that land sales would be handled by "Wethem & Bolster, the well known real estate agents of Spokane Falls." This seems to be a facetious reference to the Land Department of the NP. It should be noted that the original Articles of Incorporation for the Eastern Washington Railway empowered the company to "purchase, sell, lease, mortgage, and deal in real estate."
18. *Review*, June 30, 1886.
19. *Review*, September 2, 1886.
20. *Railroad Gazette*, October 15, 1886, p. 713. *Oregonian*, October 19, 1886. Northern Pacific *Annual Report*, 1887, says the line was opened November 1, 1886, thus conflicting with local evidence.
21. *Review*, October 23, 1886.

Train No. 18		Train No. 17
6:25 a. m. dep.	Belmont	arr. 6:55 p. m.
11:05 a. m. arr.	Spokane Falls	dep. 2:20 p. m.

22. *Oregonian*, October 28, 1885.
23. *Oregonian*, November 3, 1885.

24. *Oregonian*, November 11, 1885.
25. *Oregonian*, November 26, 1885.
26. *Oregonian*, December 10, 1885.
27. *Union*, December 19, 1885.
28. *Union*, March 6, 1886 (from Palouse *Gazette*).
29. *Oregonian*, March 25, 1886 (from Palouse *Gazette*).
30. *Union*, April 6, 1886.
31. Elevations from Union Pacific Railroad Company, Division Engineer's Office, Portland, Oregon, courtesy of Mr. Jim Reiser. Note that the elevation at Garfield is 2,457 feet. Distances as per Union Pacific Railroad Company *Timetable No. 3*, March 9, 1980.
32. *Oregonian*, May 19, 1886.
33. *Oregonian*, May 27, 1886 (from Albany *Herald*).
34. *Union*, June 12, 1886.
35. *Union*, July 17, 1886. *Oregonian*, August 4, 1886.
36. *Oregonian*, May 29, 1886.
37. *Union*, July 31, 1886. *Oregonian*, August 4, 1886.
38. *Oregonian*, August 31, 1886.
39. *Union*, September 25, 1886.
40. *Oregonian*, December 20, 1886; December 25, 1886. *Review*, December 21, 1886.
41. *Oregonian*, December 31, 1886; January 3, 1887.
42. *Oregonian*, March 28, 1887; April 5, 1887.
43. *East Oregonian*, April 15, 1887 (from Walla Walla *Journal*, April 13, 1887).
44. *Oregonian*, April 12, 1887.
45. *Oregonian*, May 10, 1887.
46. *Oregonian*, May 17, 1887.
47. *Oregonian*, March 21, 1887 and April 5, 1887. Note that OR&N also surveyed lines to Uniontown and Genesee from Colfax, Pullman, and Moscow. The Pullman to Genesee line closely paralleled the S&P. In August 1887 OR&N filed supplemental Articles of Incorporation for the Columbia & Palouse Railway providing a line from Pullman to Genesee (*Union*, August 20, 1887).
48. *Railroad Gazette*, June 3, 1887, p. 376; July 15, 1887, p. 477.
49. *Oregonian*, June 10, 1887.
50. *Union*, July 16, 1887.
51. *Oregonian*, September 13, 1887.
52. *Oregonian*, September 14, 1887.
53. *Union*, December 3, 1887.
54. *Oregonian*, December 15, 1887.
55. *Oregonian*, January 23, 1888.
56. Northern Pacific Railroad Company, *Annual Report*, 1888.

Notes for Chapter Four

1. The lowest pass in the Cascades is Snoqualmie, 3,010 feet above sea level. The original Chicago Milwaukee & Puget Sound line over the top via Laconia, built in 1908, required a 2.75 percent grade for the last 4.37 miles eastbound to the summit. (*Railway Age Gazette*, Vol. 56, No. 22, pp. 1184-1186.) No other lines crossed the Cascade Mountains on surface without switchbacks.

2. Eugene V. Smalley, *History of the Northern Pacific Railroad* (New York: G. P. Putnam's Sons, 1883), pp. 77-84.

3. *Ibid*, pp. 148-153; quotation from p. 152.

4. Northern Pacific Railroad Company, *Annual Report*, 1878.

5. *Oregonian*, December 30, 1885. The surveys were carried out under the general direction of Engineer Virgil B. Bogue.

6. *Weekly Statesman*, January 22, 1881.

7. Engineer Kingsbury appears to have done most of the reconnaissance and preliminary location work in the Yakima Valley.

8. Northern Pacific Railroad Company, *Annual Report*, 1881.

9. *Weekly Statesman*, December 10, 1881.

10. *Oregonian*, May 10, 1883.

11. *Railroad Gazette*, September 7, 1887, p. 397.

12. *Oregonian*, October 26, 1883; November 13, 1883; November 29, 1883.

13. *Railroad Gazette*, January 25, 1884, p. 78. There were several reports that Bennett had been instructed to proceed with a second 25 miles even before Villard resigned. *Oregonian*, January 3, 1884; *Chronicle*, January 3, 1884.

14. *Oregonian*, February 28, 1884.

15. *Oregonian*, May 15, 1884 (from Yakima *Signal*).

16. *Oregonian*, March 19, 1884. *Railroad Gazette*, March 28, 1884, p. 252. One suspects that either Villard or the O&T was trying to embarrass Anderson and delay decisions regarding the Cascade branch.

17. *Oregonian*, May 9, 1884. Kennedy and Chalk were two of the "Mikecha" trinity of OR&N location engineers who had worked on the line over the Blue Mountains.

18. Northern Pacific Railroad Company, *Annual Report*, 1884.

19. *Railroad Gazette*, November 28, 1884, p. 860.

20. For a contemporary description of the line from Kennewick to Yakima see *Oregonian*, December 20, 1884.

21. *Oregonian*, June 16, 1884; June 28, 1884.

22. *Oregonian*, August 23, 1884 (from Yakima *Record*).

23. *Railroad Gazette*, August 22, 1884, p. 628.

24. *Oregonian*, June 16, 1884; July 18, 1884.

25. *Oregonian*, August 23, 1884 (from Yakima *Record*).

26. *Oregonian*, September 24, 1884.

27. *Oregonian*, October 2, 1884.

28. *Oregonian*, December 11, 1884; December 20, 1884.

29. *Oregonian*, February 25, 1885.

30. *East Oregonian*, December 19, 1884.

31. *Oregonian*, February 23, 1885.

32. *Oregonian*, February 25, 1885.

33. *East Oregonian*, March 24, 1885.

34. *Oregonian*, April 13, 1885; May 13, 1885.

35. *East Oregonian*, February 3, 1885. Some work had been done in the Lower Canyon of the Yakima in 1883. *Oregonian*, March 19, 1884.

36. *East Oregonian*, February 10, 1885.

37. *Oregonian*, May 25, 1885; June 2, 1885; June 11, 1885.

38. *Oregonian*, June 30, 1885.

39. *Oregonian*, July 17, 1885; July 23, 1885.

40. Northern Pacific Railroad Company, *Annual Report*, 1886.

41. *Oregonian*, May 14, 1886.
42. Ellensburg was originally spelled "Ellensburgh," in the Scottish manner. The "h" was gradually dropped during the 1880s.
43. *Oregonian*, January 8, 1886. The discrepancy in length is quite evident to the historian. *Chronicle*, June 29, 1881, said the Grange City drawspan was to be 336 feet long while the *Oregonian*, April 24, 1884, reported the length of the Ainsworth drawspan as 346 feet.
44. *Oregonian*, January 8, 1886 and March 18, 1886. Railroad Gazette, November 8, 1889, p. 726.
45. *Oregonian*, February 10, 1886. *Union*, February 13, 1886.
46. *Oregonian*, March 4, 1886.
47. *Oregonian*, March 11, 1886 (from Kittitas *Localizer*).
48. *Oregonian*, April 15, 1886. Northern Pacific Railroad Company, *Annual Report*, 1886, says the first train arrived at Ellensburg March 31, 1886.
49. *Railroad Gazette*, January 24, 1886, p. 84. Northern Pacific Railroad Company, *Annual Report*, 1886.
50. *Oregonian*, March 4, 1886.
51. *Union*, December 12, 1885.
52. *Railroad Gazette*, February 3, 1888, p. 67.
53. *Union*, June 5, 1886. The line was put out for bids in five sections, viz: Section 1: Ellensburg to foot of mountain grade on east side. i. e., miles 125 to 165 from west side of Columbia River. Section 2: mountain grade on east side, i. e., miles 165 to 170.5 from west side of Columbia River. Section 3: the switchback line. Section 4: mountain grade on west side, i. e., miles 70 to 78 from Tacoma. Section 5: Eagle Gorge to foot of mountain grade on west side, i. e., miles 50 to 70 from Tacoma.
54. Northern Pacific Railroad Company, *Annual Report*, 1885. *Union*, May 15, 1886. *Review*, June 8, 1886.
55. Due to the changes at the site of the old Tunnel No. 1 at Cabin Creek, the railway later made two additional crossings of the river. The Milwaukee Road crossed over the NP between these two crossings.
56. *Railroad Gazette*, February 3, 1888, p. 67. 2,830 feet is my own estimation of the summit elevation.
57. There were originally eight tunnels between Pasco and Tacoma. Of these, six were between Easton and Lester. Tunnels Nos. 1 (Cabin Creek), 2 (Dingle's), and 5 and 6 (on the loop), have now been superseded. No. 3 (the Stampede Tunnel) and No. 4 (1 mile west of Stampede Tunnel), remain, and are still numbered 3 and 4.
58. The original line passed underneath the later steel viaduct and extended about 1 mile further up the Green River Valley.
59. *Oregonian*, July 8, 1886.
60. *Oregonian*, August 4, 1886.
61. *Union*, July 31, 1886.
62. *Oregonian*, August 18, 1886.
63. *Oregonian*, September 30, 1886 (from Yakima *Farmer*).
64. *Review*, October 13, 1886 (from Tacoma *Telegraph*).
65. *Oregonian*, July 22, 1886 (from Kittitas *Localizer*).
66. *Union*, August 28, 1886.
67. *Union*, September 11, 1886.
68. *Oregonian*, October 21, 1886.

69. *Ibid.*

70. *Union*, June 5, 1886.

71. *Union*, June 19, 1886.

72. *Oregonian*, October 21, 1886.

73. *Commoner*, December 17, 1886 (from Kittitas *Localizer*).

74. *Oregonian*, December 20, 1886.

75. *Oregonian*, February 14, 1880.

76. *Review*, October 13, 1886 (from Tacoma *Telegraph*).

77. *Ibid.*

78. *Railroad Gazette*, April 23, 1886, p. 291. *Review*, April 22, 1886.

79. Description of switchback line, *Railroad Gazette*, February 3, 1888, p. 67.

80. Route of switchback line: map in *Railroad Gazette*, December 23, 1887. Much of the switchback line was built on trestles and disappeared long ago. The grade can still be seen on the east side of the summit, and the spur line can be traced on the west side thereof. For some distance west of the summit the present gravel road seems to be on the railway roadbed. The most prominent surviving feature is the embankment forming the tail track of the second switchback on the west side.

81. *Oregonian*, January 3, 1887.

82. *Oregonian*, December 15, 1886.

83. *Oregonian*, December 20, 1886.

84. *Oregonian*, December 28, 1886; December 30, 1886. *Ledger*, January 3, 1887.

85. *Ledger*, January 4, 1887; January 18, 1887. *Oregonian*, January 27, 1887.

86. *Railroad Gazette*, December 10, 1886, p. 860. *Oregonian*, December 15, 1886.

87. *Commoner*, December 17, 1886. *Oregonian*, December 30, 1886.

88. *Ledger*, February 1, 1887.

89. *Oregonian*, February 18, 1887.

90. *Oregonian*, April 11, 1887. Ledger, April 11, 1887.

91. *Oregonian*, April 18, 1887. This report gives a hint of how the Chinese laborers were brought to America by the Chinese agents. It relates that "Kwong Tai's manager says that they (the three hundred who quit) were indebted to him altogether to the extent of $4000 and have only worked part of it out."

92. *Ledger*, March 1, 1887.

93. *Oregonian*, March 8, 1887.

94. *Oregonian*, February 17, 1887; March 22, 1887; March 28, 1887.

95. *Oregonian*, May 3, 1887.

96. *Ledger*, April 19, 1887.

97. *Oregonian*, April 4, 1887 (from Yakima *Signal*, April 2, 1887).

98. *East Oregonian*, April 26, 1887. *Oregonian*, May 3, 1887.

99. *Oregonian*, May 12, 1887.

100. *Ledger*, May 3, 1887.

101. *Oregonian*, May 24, 1887.

102. *Ledger*, June 2, 1887. For all its other detail, this article fails to make clear where the ceremony took place. The likelihood, however, is that it was at the west end of the switchback line, and not at the summit. The article says ambiguously that the people gathered "on the extreme top of the switchback, 78 miles from Tacoma." A point 78 miles from Tacoma, however, would have been somewhere near the first switchback on the west side, and probably just about where the tracks actually met. The article, moreover, says that Mrs. Huson "stepped to the front and broke a bottle of champagne OVER

THE TRUE LAST SPIKE." These words suggest that tracklaying had already been completed and the spike that Mrs. Huson and the others afterwards drove was merely ceremonial. The article is also interesting in that it listed as present many of the engineers and foremen whose names recur again and again in the first 15 years of railway construction: Mr. Reardon, J. Jamieson, O. Kimble, and Stephen Aldridge.

103. *Oregonian*, June 14, 1887; June 21, 1887. Some of these were listed as Kennewick, Prosser, Topnish [sic], Yakima, Umptanum [sic], and Ellensburgh [sic].

104. *Railroad Gazette*, January 3, 1888, p. 17.

105. *Review*, November 11, 1886 (reporting first Decapod locomotive passing through Spokane en route to Ellensburg). *Ledger*, July 5, 1887 (complete with illustration of a Decapod engine bearing the number 119). *Oregonian*, August 23, 1887. *Railroad Gazette*, January 3, 1888, p. 17; September 27, 1889 (giving details of the new Consolidation type locomotives and listing the deficiencies of the Decapods); February 3, 1888 (referring to water brakes on the Decapods). The Le Chatelier counter-pressure brake system was widely used in both Continental Europe and America at that time. See Alfred W. Bruce, *The Steam Locomotive in America—Its Development in the Twentieth Century* (New York: Bonanza Books, 1952), p. 268, and Edouard Sauvage *La Locomotive a Vapeur* (Paris: Beranger, 1918), p. 320. The water brake was probably the reason why the Decapods so often blew their cylinder covers (*Oregonian*, August 16, 1887 and April 3, 1888. On the latter occasion both engines were reported to be out of action.)

106. *Union*, August 27, 1887.

107. *Railroad Gazette*, August 5, 1887, p. 517.

108. *Oregonian*, November 29, 1887. *Railroad Gazette*, February 3, 1888, p. 67.

109. *Oregonian*, August 29, 1887. The action was initiated by the General Land Office.

110. *Oregonian*, November 13, 1887.

111. *Oregonian*, October 27, 1887.

112. *Union*, December 31, 1887.

113. *Railroad Gazette*, January 13, 1888, p. 23. For a description of the Leslie Rotary Snow Shovel see *Railroad Gazette*, October 12, 1888, p. 665.

114. *Oregonian*, January 26, 1888. *Railroad Gazette*, February 24, 1888, p. 120.

115. *Oregonian*, April 3, 1888.

116. *Ledger*, July 5, 1887. *Railroad Gazette*, August 5, 1887, p. 519.

117. *Railroad Gazette*, February 3, 1888, p. 67.

118. The switchbacks were a success. Assuming that the 63 cars/day did not include passenger cars, and that half of them were loaded with 10 tons of goods earning $8 per ton, then the daily revenue which the switchback line enabled the company to earn would have been 32 X 10 X 8 = $2,560 per day, or $2,560 X 290 = $740,000, over the whole period the line was operated. Assuming that the traffic required the operation of three freight trains a day over the whole 255 miles between Pasco and Tacoma, and that the cost of operating each train was $1.50 per mile, then operating costs would have amounted to 3 X 255 X 1.5 X 290 = $332,775 over the whole period. Net earnings would then have been 742,400 - 332,775 = $409,625, i. e., more than the cost of building the switchbacks. The indication, therefore, is that the switchback line may well have been worthwhile, certainly from a cash-flow point of view.

Notes for Chapter Five

1. The Northern Pacific directors first authorized the letting of a contract in March 1885 (*Oregonian*, March 26, 1885). The first bids were to have been opened May 12, 1885 (*Oregonian*, May 11, 1885).
2. Northern Pacific Railroad Company, *Annual Report*, 1885.
3. *Railroad Gazette*, January 29, 1886, p. 84. Note that the contract price was then said to be $800,000.
4. *Union*, February 27, 1886.
5. *Oregonian*, March 25, 1886 (from Kittitas *Localizer*).
6. *Oregonian*, March 11, 1886 (from Kittitas *Localizer*).
7. *Oregonian*, March 4, 1886.
8. Northern Pacific Railroad Company, *Annual Report*, 1886.
9. *Ledger*, May 4, 1888.
10. *Oregonian*, March 25, 1886 (from Yakima *Farmer*).
11. *Union*, April 10, 1886.
12. *Union*, May 1, 1886.
13. *Oregonian*, March 25, 1886 (from Yakima *Farmer*).
14. *Union*, May 15, 1886 (from Yakima *Signal*).
15. *Union*, May 1, 1886.
16. *Oregonian*, May 12, 1886 (from Kittitas *Localizer*).
17. *Oregonian*, March 29, 1887.
18. Northern Pacific Railroad Company, *Annual Report*, 1886.
19. *Oregonian*, March 11, 1886 (from Kittitas *Localizer*).
20. *Oregonian*, July 8, 1886 (from Kittitas *Localizer*). It is no longer clear whether they laid a pipe line and found that the pressure drop was too great, or whether the idea was abandoned before reaching that stage.
21. *Oregonian*, August 2, 1886, says that "the smoke is drawn out through the boxing." *Ledger*, May 4, 1888, confirms this, saying "the foul air being carried off through a large wooden flume built along near the top of the tunnel." The normal arrangement nowadays would be to blow air in through the ducting.
22. *Oregonian*, June 10, 1886 (from Kittitas *Localizer*).
23. *Oregonian*, September 6, 1886 (from Kittitas *Localizer*).
24. *Oregonian*, April 7, 1887.
25. *Review*, October 16, 1886. *Oregonian*, October 19, 1886.
26. *Review*, December 16, 1886.
27. *Review*, December 22, 1886 (from Seattle *Times*).
28. *Oregonian*, February 18, 1887.
29. *Oregonian*, September 6, 1886 (from Kittitas *Localizer*).
30. *Oregonian*, March 29, 1887.
31. *Oregonian*, May 24, 1887.
32. *Ledger*, May 8, 1888.
33. *Oregonian*, May 31, 1887.
34. *East Oregonian*, August 9, 1887.
35. *Oregonian*, August 16, 1887; September 8, 1887.
36. *Oregonian*, November 15, 1887.
37. *Oregonian*, June 21, 1887.

38. *Oregonian*, November 21, 1887; January 23, 1888. *Union*, January 21, 1888. *Ledger*, January 25, 1888.
39. *Union*, March 10, 1888. *Railroad Gazette*, March 16, 1888, p. 176.
40. *Oregonian*, March 24, 1888.
41. *East Oregonian*, April 24, 1888 (from Yakima *Signal*).
42. *Ledger*, May 4, 1888.
43. *Ledger*, May 5, 1888.
44. *Ledger*, May 22, 1888 (from Ellensburg *New Era*).
45. *Ledger*, May 8, 1888.
46. *Railroad Gazette*, June 1, 1888, p. 359. Northern Pacific Railroad Company, *Annual Report*, 1888.
47. *Union*, June 23, 1888.
48. *Railroad Gazette*, October 12, 1888, p. 663.
49. *Ibid.*
50. *Ledger*, May 8, 1888.
51. Northern Pacific Railroad Company, *Annual Report*, 1888.
52. Northern Pacific Railroad Company, *Annual Report*, 1889.
53. *Oregonian*, July 13, 1888 (from Yakima *Signal*).
54. *Union*, June 29, 1889.
55. Personal observation, October 1983. Although the tunnel remains unused, Burlington Northern has retained ownership to prevent it from falling into other hands.

Notes for Chapter Six

1. *Railroad Gazette*, November 6, 1889, p. 726.
2. *Oregonian*, November 5, 1887.
3. *Oregonian*, December 20, 1886.
4. *Oregonian*, April 19, 1887.
5. *Oregonian*, May 10, 1887.
6. *Oregonian*, May 31, 1887. *Ledger*, June 1, 1887.
7. *Oregonian*, August 1, 1887.
8. *Oregonian*, November 5, 1887.
9. *Oregonian*, November 26, 1887.
10. *Union*, December 10, 1887.
11. *Oregonian*, January 7, 1888. *Union*, January 14, 1888.
12. *Union*, January 21, 1888.
13. *Union*, February 4, 1888.
14. *Oregonian*, July 20, 1888.
15. *Oregonian*, January 17, 1888.
16. *Ledger*, January 18, 1888.
17. *Oregonian*, April 27, 1888. *Union*, April 28, 1888. Northern Pacific Railroad Company, *Annual Report*, 1888, states that the temporary bridge was re-opened on April 13, but this seems erroneous.
18. *Ledger*, May 6, 1888.
19. *Oregonian*, June 18, 1888.
20. *Oregonian*, July 20, 1888.
21. Northern Pacific Railroad Company, *Annual Report*, 1888.

Notes for Chapter Seven

1. *Oregonian*, March 9, 1886. *Railroad Gazette*, March 26, 1886, p. 223.
2. *East Oregonian*, April 15, 1887, notes that "These are the same officials which have served since the incorporation of the company."
3. *Oregonian*, May 20, 1886 (from Pendleton *East Oregonian*). *Union*, June 19, 1886 (from Pendleton *Laborer*).
4. *East Oregonian*, March 4, 1887.
5. *East Oregonian*, March 15, 1887; March 29, 1887; May 3, 1887.
6. *East Oregonian*, May 17, 1887.
7. E. Z. Ripley *Railroads—Finance and Organization*, (New York: Longmans Green & Co., 1915), pp. 13-18.
8. *East Oregonian*, April 15, 1887; May 17, 1887; May 20, 1887. The original officers of the company were Jacob Frazer, president; W. S. Byers, vice president and treasurer; H. L. Marston, second vice president; H. W. Wheeler, secretary; and W. T. Chalk, chief engineer. By May 17, 1887, F. W. Griffith was vice president and W. S. Byers was only treasurer.
9. *East Oregonian*, May 31, 1887.
10. *Oregonian*, May 31, 1887.
11. *East Oregonian*, October, 25, 1887.
12. *Railroad Gazette*, March 1, 1889, p. 151.
13. *Union*, May 25, 1889.
14. The present two-span steel through-truss bridge dates from 1902. *East Oregonian*, February 3, 1902.
15. *East Oregonian*, June 7, 1887. *Oregonian*, June 10, 1887 (from Pendleton *Tribune*).
16. *East Oregonian*, July 8, 1887.
17. *Oregonian*, August 11, 1887.
18. *East Oregonian*, October 25, 1887.
19. *East Oregonian*, July 12, 1887; September 27, 1887.
20. *East Oregonian*, September 2, 1887. *Oregonian*, September 10, 1887. A first switch had been put into NP track near Wallula on August 13, 1887. *East Oregonian*, August 16, 1887.
21. *East Oregonian*, September 27, 1887.
22. *East Oregonian*, October 25, 1887, says there were 28 bridges between Wallula and Stanton Junction.
23. *Oregonian*, November 14, 1887, refers to "the missing spikes and bolts." The track, therefore, did not reach Killian's until early in December. See *East Oregonian*, December 6, 1887.
24. *East Oregonian*, December 27, 1887.
25. *East Oregonian*, August 26, 1887.
26. *East Oregonian*, December 6, 1887.
27. *East Oregonian*, February 24, 1888.
28. *Oregonian*, February 8, 1889.
29. *Union*, November 5, 1887.
30. *East Oregonian*, June 29, 1888.
31. *East Oregonian*, August 16, 1887; September 2, 1887; September 16, 1887; September 23, 1887.
32. *East Oregonian*, January 27, 1888.
33. *East Oregonian*, February 17, 1888.

34. *East Oregonian*, March 18, 1888.

35. *Union*, March 24, 1888.

36. *Union*, April 21, 1888. *Railroad Gazette*, May 11, 1888, p. 247.

37. *Oregonian*, September 27, 1887.

38. *Union*, April 21, 1888.

39. *East Oregonian*, July 27, 1888.

40. *East Oregonian*, August 31, 1888.

41. *East Oregonian*, September 4, 1888.

42. *East Oregonian*, August 21, 1888.

43. *East Oregonian*, August 28, 1888.

44. *Oregonian*, September 15, 1888.

45. *East Oregonian*, November 27, 1888.

46. *Oregonian*, January 1, 1889.

47. *Union*, January 19, 1889.

48. *Oregonian*, February 13, 1889.

49. *Union*, May 4, 1889; May 11, 1889. *Oregonian*, May 7, 1889. *Railroad Gazette*, May 24, 1889, p. 350.

50. *Union*, May 11, 1889 and May 25, 1889.

51. *Union*, July 13, 1889.

52. *Oregonian*, August 19, 1889, says that trains would cross the river by Thursday (August 22, 1889).

53. Heppner *Gazette*, September 5, 1889 (from Pendleton, *East Oregonian*).

54. *Union*, September 14, 1889.

55. Note that OW&T filed supplemental articles of incorporation for an extension from Pendleton to Heppner. *Union*, April 21, 1888. Locating surveys were in fact carried out for such a line. *Railroad Gazette*, September 27, 1889, p. 638; Heppner *Gazette*, July 18, 1889 and January 23, 1890. Hunt may have had the Morrow County coal deposits in mind.

56. *Union*, October 24, 1885.

57. *Oregonian*, May 20, 1886.

58. *Union*, June 5, 1886.

59. *Union*, August 7, 1886. The incorporators were H. P. A. Isaacs, Max Baumeister, C. Ennis, R. R. Rees, W. R. Hamm, H. E. Homes, B. E. Johnson, and F. Dement.

60. *Railroad Gazette*, December 31, 1886, p. 975. *Oregonian*, March 8, 1887.

61. *Oregonian*, April 4, 1887.

62. *Oregonian*, May 7, 1887.

63. *Union*, May 26, 1887, which claimed to have been "reliably informed that the Pendleton and Centerville line will be extended to Walla Walla next year, and that this scheme originates with the backers of the road who are said to be heavy Northern Pacific stockholders."

64. *Union*, September 3, 1887; October 8, 1887.

65. *Union*, March 17, 1888.

66. *Oregonian*, March 23, 1888.

67. *Union*, March 31, 1888.

68. *Union*, April 7, 1888. *East Oregonian*, April 10, 1888.

69. *East Oregonian*, April 20, 1888.

70. *Union*, March 31, 1888. The engineers were M. C. Shaw and F. Riffle.

71. *Union*, April 21, 1888; April 28, 1888; and May 5, 1888.

72. *Railroad Gazette*, March 1, 1889, p. 151.

73. *Union*, January 12, 1889; January 19, 1889. East 2nd Street now appears to be called Sumach St.
74. *Oregonian*, June 20, 1888.
75. *East Oregonian*, June 29, 1888.
76. *Union*, September 8, 1888.
77. *East Oregonian*, July 27, 1888. Union, July 28, 1888.
78. *Union*, July 28, 1888.
79. *Union*, October 27, 1888.
80. *Oregonian*, October 19, 1888 and November 15, 1888.
81. *Oregonian*, December 1, 1888. *East Oregonian*, December 4, 1888. OW&T had powers to extend the Eureka Flat branch to Grange City and came under local pressure to do so. W. D. Wallace of Starbuck attempted in May 1889 to persuade Hunt to extend it another three miles to the head of Field's Gulch. *Oregonian*, May 28, 1889; *Union*, June 1, 1889. Locating surveys were in fact made for an extension to the Snake River, another 13 miles. *Railroad Gazette*, September 27, 1889, p. 638, but no such line was ever built.
82. *Union*, December 22, 1888.
83. *Union*, January 12, 1889.
84. *Union*, March 16, 1889. Passengers may have travelled on other trains before this date.
85. *Union*, March 9, 1889 and April 6, 1889. *Oregonian*, April 9, 1889.
86. *Union*, May 18, 1889.
87. *Union*, January 19, 1889.
88. *Union*, September 8, 1888; April 27, 1889; May 18, 1889. *Oregonian*, March 11, 1889.
89. *East Oregonian*, March 18, 1888. *Oregonian*, June 18, 1888.
90. *History of South Eastern Washington*, pp. 329-333.
91. *Union*, April 28, 1888.
92. *East Oregonian*, December 4, 1888.
93. *Oregonian*, December 14, 1888.
94. Dayton *Chronicle* comment, from *History of South Eastern Washington*.
95. *Union*, January 26, 1889.
96. Whetstone Hollow was first mentioned in a report on OW&T survey activity. *East Oregonian*, December 4, 1888. Hunt apparently first proposed to extend O&WT there at a meeting in Dayton on January 26, 1889. *History of South Eastern Washington*, pp. 331.
97. *Union*, February 2, 1889.
98. *Union*, May 11, 1889. Prescott people at first sued out an injunction against Walla Walla County issuing warrants. They did not withdraw it until Hunt agreed to build a branch line eastward up the Touchet from Harvey Shaw's to Prescott. *Union*, May 11, 1889. The branch was never built.
99. *Oregonian*, May 16, 1889.
100. *Union*, May 25, 1889.
101. *Oregonian*, June 25, 1889.
102. As of June 14, 1938, Union Pacific trains began to use the NP (O&WT) line over the 7.7 miles from Waitsburg Junction to Dayton Junction, and UP abandoned their own (OR&N) line. This was done in return for UP granting NP trackage rights between Wallace and Burke, Idaho. James L. Ehernberger and Francis G. Gschwind, *Union Pacific Steam—Northwestern District* (Callaway, Neb.: EG Publications, 1968), p. 86.

103. *Railroad Gazette*, March 1, 1889, p. 151.
104. Hunt established a construction and supply yard about two miles east of Walla Walla to which track was laid by the end of July 1889. *Union*, July 20, 1889.
105. *Union*, August 24, 1889.
106. *Railroad Gazette*, November 1, 1889, p. 724. *Oregonian*, November 4, 1889.
107. *Union*, October 19, 1889.
108. *Oregonian*, November 14, 1889. *Union*, November 16, 1889.
109. *Union*, November 23, 1889.
110. *History of South Eastern Washington*, p. 333.
111. *Union*, December 21, 1889. *Railroad Gazette*, January 24, 1890, p. 54.
112. *Oregonian*, September 11, 1888.
113. *Oregonian*, January 23, 1889.
114. *Oregonian*, January 26, 1889.
115. *Oregonian*, March 3, 1889 and March 9, 1889.
116. *Oregonian*, March 26, 1889. Union, March 30, 1889.
117. *Oregonian*, April 2, 1889.
118. *Oregonian*, April 9, 1889.
119. *Oregonian*, April 14, 1889.
120. *Union*, December 7, 1889.
121. *Oregonian*, April 27, 1889.
122. *Oregonian*, August 21, 1889, noted that one survey ran directly in front of Governor Miles C. Moore's handsome suburban residence "and if the road is built it will cause a decided inconvenience to that gentleman who claims that if it is built it will be through spite because he opposed the Walla Walla subsidy."
123. *Railroad Gazette*, August 15, 1890, p. 577.
124. *Union*, December 7, 1889.
125. *Oregonian*, February 27, 1890. *Railroad Gazette*, March 28, 1890, p. 223.
126. *Oregonian*, April 25, 1890 (from Union *Scout*).
127. *Railroad Gazette*, August 15, 1890, p. 577.
128. *Oregonian*, January 23, 1889.
129. *Railroad Gazette*, February 1 , 1889, p. 87.
130. *Oregonian*, March 3, 1889.
131. *Oregonian*, March 26, 1889; April 2, 1889; April 27, 1889. *Railroad Gazette*, August 15, 1890, p. 577.
132. *Oregonian*, February 16, 1890; February 21, 1890.
133. *Oregonian*, March 7, 1890. *Railroad Gazette*, March 28, 1890, p. 223.
134. *Oregonian*, March 18, 1890 (from Waitsburg *Times*).
135. *Oregonian*, March 7, 1890 (ed.).
136. *Oregonian*, April 11, 1890. The deal was to be completed by April 20, 1890. The price was $26,000 per mile. NP planned a terminus at Ocosta. Heppner *Gazette*, August 21, 1890.
137. *Railroad Gazette*, June 6, 1890, p. 407.
138. *Railroad Gazette*, January 30, 1891, p. 87. *Review*, February 26, 1891.
139. *Review*, December 24, 1890.
140. *East Oregonian*, February 21, 1894.
141. *Railroad Gazette*, March 6, 1891, p. 173. *Review*, March 3, 1891. The property was not apparently conveyed until the end of April. *Review*, May 1, 1891.
142. *Railroad Gazette*, December 4, 1891, p. 870.

143. Daggett, *Railroad Reorganization*, pp. 286-287, quoting Villard, *Memoirs*, pp. 359-360.
144. *History of South Eastern Washington*, p. 333.
145. *East Oregonian*, March 22, 1895; May 9, 1895; May 24, 1895.
146. Northern Pacific Railway Company, *Annual Report*, 1904.
147. The Eureka Flat branch was formally abandoned and the track removed in 1981. For a long time before that, however, the last eight miles between Clyde and Pleasant View had lain disused. Personal observation.

Notes for Chapter Eight

1. Heppner *Gazette*, December 27, 1888.
2. *East Oregonian*, March 23, 1888. Col. W. Parson and W. S. Shiach, *An illustrated History of Umatilla County and of Morrow County* (Pendleton, Ore.: W. H. Lever, 1902), p. 296.
3. *Oregonian*, September 27, 1887.
4. *Union*, October 27, 1888.
5. Heppner *Gazette*, April 5, 1888.
6. *Ibid.*
7. *Oregonian*, April 15, 1888.
8. *Oregonian*, April 24, 1888.
9. *East Oregonian*, May 15, 1888.
10. *Oregonian*, August 17, 1888.
11. *East Oregonian*, June 27, 1888.
12. *Oregonian*, October 20, 1888.
13. *East Oregonian*, November 13, 1888.
14. *Oregonian*, November 27, 1888 (including quotation). Heppner *Gazette*, November 29, 1888.
15. *East Oregonian*, November 16, 1888. Heppner *Gazette*, December 27, 1888.
16. *Oregonian*, March 29, 1889.
17. Dispute with Larsen noted in Heppner *Gazette*, August 16, 1888 (from Arlington *Times*, August 10, 1888); April 18, 1889; May 2, 1889; June 30, 1889.
18. Parson and Shiach, *History of Umatilla County and of Morrow County*, p. 312. *East Oregonian*, November 11, 1884. Heppner *Gazette*, August 2, 1888 and June 4, 1891.
19. *East Oregonian*, July 14, 1882 and July 25, 1882.
20. *East Oregonian*, September 21, 1888; October 9, 1888. *Oregonian*, August 26, 1889.
21. Heppner *Gazette*, September 25, 1889 (from Pendleton *East Oregonian*).
22. Heppner *Gazette*, March 13, 1890.
23. *Railroad Gazette*, September 19, 1890, p. 657.
24. Heppner *Gazette*, March 12, 1891 and April 30, 1891.
25. For a geological background to the Morrow County coal deposits, see Oregon State Department of Geology and Mineral Industries report of August 15, 1947, by John Allen Elliot, and report of May 20, 1939, by J. E. Morrison. See also United States, Department of the Interior, Geological Survey, Circular No. 362, 1955, *Coal Resources of Oregon*.

Notes for Chapter Nine

1. D. E. Livingston-Little, "Discovery and Development of the Coeur d'Alene Mines," *Journal of the West* (July 3, 1964): 318-322.
2. Rickard, *Bunker Hill*, pp. 16-23.
3. Ruby El Hult, *Steamboats in the Timber* (Portland: Binsford and Mort, 1952), p. 28.
4. *Oregonian*, November 23, 1883.
5. *Oregonian*, February 1, 1884; March 5, 1884; March 27, 1884. E. W. Wright, ed., *Lewis and Dryden's Marine History of the Pacific Northwest* (1895; rprnt., New York: Antiquarian Press, 1961), p. 232. Another steamer, called *General Sherman*, was placed in service by James Monaghan and associates and competed with the *Coeur d'Alene*. See Hult, *Steamboats in Timber*, p. 31.
6. *Review*, April 3, 1886 (from St. Paul *Pioneer Press*). *Review*, February 10, 1887, announcing Amendment of Idaho Law.
7. *Oregonian*, February 27, 1884, reported the application to Congress for a charter for SF & CdARR Co. Incorporation of S&CdA Rly. Co. as per copy of Articles of Incorporation from Archives & Special Collections, Eastern Washington University, Cheney, courtesy of Charles V. Mutschler. *Review*, April 3, 1886, noted that the House Committee on Pacific Railroads had reported favourably on the matter.
8. *Review*, April 3, 1886. Rickard, *Bunker Hill*, p. 23.
9. *Review*, March 27, 1886 (from Helena *Herald*, March 26, 1886).
10. D. C. Corbin, "Recollections of a Pioneer Railroad Builder," *Washington Historical Quarterly*, 1:2 (1907): 43-46.
11. *Review*, April 25, 1886 (from Helena *Independent*). Northern Pacific Railroad Company, *Annual Report*, 1886.
12. *Review*, June 9, 1886, says "It is understood that J. J. Browne of this city will be president of the proposed Spokane and Coeur d'Alene branch. He will push the project when he is clothed with the necessary authority." Evidently Browne was upset by Corbin's intrusion.
13. *Union*, June 5, 1886. *Review*, July 27, 1886. Northern Pacific Railroad Company, *Annual Report*, 1886.
14. *Oregonian*, May 28, 1886.
15. *Review*, July 9, 1886 (from Helena *Independent*).
16. *Review*, October 24, 1886. *Oregonian*, December 2, 1886. Copy of Articles of Incorporation, courtesy of Archives & Special Collections, Eastern Washington University. Other directors were: General Adna Anderson (chief engineer of the Northern Pacific Railroad); J. M. Buckley (Northern Pacific assistant general manager); and Paul F. Mohr (Chief engineer of the Spokane & Palouse Railway). Spokane entrepreneur J. J. Browne and mining man S. S. Glidden, both active in the original Spokane Falls & Coeur d'Alene Railway scheme, took no part in the compromise promotion.
17. *Review*, August 5, 1886.
18. *Review*, September 2, 1886. *Oregonian*, September 2, 1886.
19. *Oregonian*, October 5, 1886.
20. *Review*, October 7, 1886; October 24, 1886.
21. *Review*, November 12, 1886 (from Helena *Independent*).
22. *Free Press*, March 9, 1889.
23. *Review*, July 9, 1886 (from Helena *Independent*). *Union*, July 10, 1886.

24. *Review*, August 5, 1886.

25. *Review*, August 26, 1886.

26. *Review*, November 12, 1886 (from Helena *Independent*) and November 25, 1886 (from Wardner *News*).

27. Charles R. Wood, *The Northern Pacific: Main Street of the Northwest* (Seattle: Superior Publishing Co., 1968), Appendix B.

28. *Oregonian*, December 25, 1886 (from Spokane Falls *Review*, December 22, 1886).

29. Corbin later sued the contractor, Spaulding, for deficiencies in the quantities of earth moved. *Free Press*, November 19, 1887.

30. *Review*, December 27, 1886; February 25, 1887. *Oregonian*, January 27, 1887; February 10, 1887; February 17, 1887.

31. *Oregonian*, February 17, 1887. The price was reported as "$50,000 to $60,000."

32. *Review*, March 10, 1887. *Oregonian*, March 22, 1887.

33. *Review*, June 7, 1887.

34. *Oregonian*, July 22, 1886.

35. *Oregonian*, April 12, 1887.

36. *Oregonian*, October 14, 1886 (from Walla Walla *Union*) and December 25, 1886.

37. *Review*, October 12, 1886. *Oregonian*, October 19, 1886.

38. *Review*, August 17, 1887.

39. *Free Press*, September 10, 1887. Wood, *Northern Pacific*, p. 75, says that Glidden signed an agreement with Corbin September 5, 1887. Renz, *Northern Pacific*, p. 151, says that Corbin finally bought the Canyon Creek Railroad from Glidden for $41,620 on August 29, 1888, but gives no source.

40. *Free Press*, July 9, 1887; July 16, 1887.

41. *Oregonian*, August 16, 1887. *Free Press*, August 20, 1887.

42. *Oregonian*, March 31, 1887. *Review*, April 5, 1887.

43. *Free Press*, July 2, 1887; July 9, 1887; August 13, 1887. Osborn was also called Osborn's in contemporary newspaper reports.

44. *Free Press*, August 20, 1887; August 27, 1887.

45. *Free Press*, October 1, 1887.

46. *Free Press*, September 17, 1887; October 22, 1887.

47. *Free Press*, November 5, 1887.

48. *Free Press*, September 17, 1887.

49. *Free Press*, November 5, 1887.

50. *Free Press*, December 1, 1887; December 17, 1887.

51. *Free Press*, December 31, 1887.

52. *Free Press*, January 7, 1888.

53. *Free Press*, December 10, 1887.

54. *Oregonian*, January 9, 1888.

55. *Free Press*, February 11, 1888.

56. *Oregonian*, September 22, 1888.

57. *Free Press*, December 10, 1887; April 14, 1888; September 8, 1888; December 15, 1888.

58. *Review*, April 7, 1888. *Free Press*, March 9, 1889.

59. Northern Pacific Railroad Company, *Annual Report*, 1890.

60. *Oregonian*, June 11, 1887.

61. *Free Press*, July 16, 1887.
62. *Union*, July 30, 1887.
63. *Railroad Gazette*, February 10, 1888, p. 97.
64. *Oregonian*, May 16, 1888. *Free Press*, May 19, 1888.
65. *Oregonian*, May 31, 1888; June 2, 1888.
66. *Oregonian*, August 15, 1888.
67. *Oregonian*, August 27, 1888.
68. *Review*, August 18, 1888.
69. *Oregonian*, October 24, 1888; October 25, 1888. *Review*, October 24, 1888.
70. *Oregonian*, November 26, 1888.
71. *Railroad Gazette*, December 14, 1888, p. 827.
72. *Review*, August 29, 1888.
73. *Free Press*, January 26, 1889. *Railroad Gazette*, February 8, 1889, p. 103.
74. *Free Press*, June 23, 1888. The line was to have started at a wye one mile north of Coeur d'Alene City and would have required a summit tunnel almost a mile long. *Free Press*, August 18, 1888.
75. *Review*, July 16, 1888; August 15, 1888.
76. *Review*, July 8, 1888 (from Coeur d'Alene *Sun*). *Railroad Gazette*, July 27, 1888.
77. *Free Press*, August 4, 1888.
78. *Free Press*, July 28, 1888.
79. *Free Press*, August 18, 1888; August 25, 1888.
80. *Oregonian*, August 15, 1888. *Free Press*, September 1, 1888. *Railroad Gazette*, September 14, 1888, p. 613. *Review*, October 9, 1888; October 13, 1888. Northern Pacific Railroad Company, *Annual Report*, 1889.
81. *Free Press*, November 17, 1888.
82. *Free Press*, November 22, 1888.
83. *Free Press*, January 5, 1889.
84. *Free Press*, March 9, 1889; March 30, 1889. Heppner *Gazette*, April 4, 1889.
85. *Free Press*, April 27, 1889.
86. *Free Press*, March 9, 1889.
87. Livingston-Little, "Discovery of Coeur d'Alene Mines," p. 329.
88. Ehrenberger and Gschwind, *Union Pacific Steam*, p. 84.
89. *Oregonian*, June 2, 1888. *Railroad Gazette*, June 15, 1888, p. 398.
90. *Oregonian*, July 16, 1888.
91. *Free Press*, August 18, 1888.
92. *Oregonian*, November 6, 1888.
93. *Oregonian*, November 28, 1888. *Railroad Gazette*, December 14, 1888, p. 827.
94. *Oregonian*, April 5, 1889.
95. *Oregonian*, July 16, 1889.
96. *Free Press*, August 24, 1889.
97. *Oregonian*, October 9, 1889 (from Wallace *Free Press*).
98. *Free Press*, December 14, 1889.
99. *Free Press*, December 28, 1889.
100. *Free Press*, March 8, 1890; March 22, 1890.
101. *Oregonian*, February 24, 1887; July 26, 1887.
102. *Free Press*, August 20, 1887; September 10, 1887.
103. *Review*, July 14, 1888. *Oregonian*, August 15, 1888.
104. *Railroad Gazette*, July 20, 1888, p. 482.

105. *Review*, July 31, 1888; August 7, 1888. *Free Press*, October 13, 1888; February 9, 1889.
106. *Review*, September 12, 1888. *Oregonian*, September 18, 1888. W&I also filed Articles of Incorporation in Montana. *Railroad Gazette*, September 27, 1889, p. 638.
107. *Railroad Gazette*, September 13, 1889, p. 606.
108. *Oregonian*, October 5, 1889.
109. Heppner *Gazette*, November 14, 1889.
110. *Review*, November 7, 1889.
111. *Review*, November 14, 1889.
112. *Free Press*, May 31, 1890; June 21, 1890. Ehernberger and Gschwind, *Union Pacific Steam*, p. 84.
113. Wood, *Northern Pacific*, p. 77.
114. Northern Pacific Railroad Company, *Annual Report*, 1889.
115. *Railroad Gazette*, October 4, 1889, p. 654.
116. The short tunnel is on the upper limb of the loop west of Taft and can still be seen by persons driving west on Interstate Highway 90.
117. Renz, *Northern Pacific*, p. 152.
118. *Free Press*, February 21, 1890.
119. *Railroad Gazette*, August 29, 1890, p. 611.
120. *Railroad Gazette*, October 10, 1890, p. 709.
121. *Railroad Gazette*, December 5, 1890, p. 849.
122. *Review*, December 23, 1890.
123. *Railroad Gazette*, January 3, 1891, p. 18.
124. *Review*, August 1, says that "Yesterday forenoon a party of ladies and gentlemen made their first trip [from Mullan] to Wallace and returned over the broad gauge of track of the NPRR, the work of widening the track having been completed on the previous day."
125. *Railroad Gazette*, August 21, 1891, p. 588, reports the line opened but says the opening "will be celebrated" by an excursion from Wallace to Missoula.
126. *Ibid.*
127. *Free Press*, August 4, 1888; August 25, 1888; September 1, 1888.
128. *Free Press*, April 19, 1890.
129. *Railroad Gazette*, May 1, 1891, p. 313.
130. Wood, *Northern Pacific*, p. 92.
131. *Northwest Mines Handbook*, 1918, p. 16. The *Northwest Mines Handbook* was an annually published compendium of information about mining companies. No publisher was given.
132. Rickard, *Bunker Hill*, p. 90.
133. Livingston-Little, "Discovery of Coeur d'Alene Mines, pp. 327-334.
134. The St. Regis Pass tunnel was never driven, even though McClain & Jansing advertised for men and prepared to start work. *Free Press*, March 8, 1890, confuses NP work with W&I work.
135. Daggett, *Railroad Reorganization*, pp. 286-287.
136. Villard, *Memoirs*, pp. 359-360.

Notes for Chapter Ten

1. *Union*, June 5, 1886.
2. *Oregonian*, December 26, 1886. The terminus was to have been in section 27, Township 10, Range 34 E, at Bowman's Ranch.

3. Robert G. Bailey, *River of No Return: A Century of Central Idaho and Eastern Washington History and Development* (Lewiston, Id.: 1941).

4. *Oregonian*, April 12, 1887; April 21, 1887; April 25, 1887; July 19, 1887 (from Weiser *Leader*). General T. A. Clark worked northwards along the Weiser and Little Salmon rivers and met C. C. Van Arsdol working southwards from Lewiston at White Bird. Clark reported that Van Arsdol and his men "had a rough time of it but looked healthy." The survey found the distance from Weiser to Lewiston was 280 miles, and from Burnt River to Lewiston (apparently surveyed by Van Arsdol's party alone) was 186 miles. The article reported that, "From Salmon River on to Lewiston the route surveyed is terribly rough," the estimated cost being $300,000 per mile, and that "There is probably 21 miles down the Snake River which would cost $200,000 per mile."

5. *Oregonian*, April 25, 1887; May 7, 1887; May 10, 1887 (from Farmington Post). The latter reported that while others had estimated that a 3 percent grade would be required to cross Alpowai Ridge, Stevens claimed to have located a line reducing the grade to 2 percent. See also *Oregonian*, May 31, 1887.

6. *Union*, September 17, 1887, reporting OR&N surveyors making a final location.

7. Hedges, *Henry Villard*, p. 159.

8. *Union*, October 1, 1887; October 15, 1887. Watt was only able to procure land by appealing to the courts for condemnation. *Union*, April 7, 1888; April 14, 1888; May 12, 1888.

9. Hedges, *Henry Villard*, pp. 172-175.

10. *Union*, May 19, 1888, says that Corey Bros. were instructed on Wednesday (May 16, 1888) to quit work on Eureka Flat. This was the day after the U. S. Congress passed the W&I Right of Way Bill. Corey Bros. re-loaded their equipment at Prescott on Monday, May 28, 1888. *Union*, June 2, 1888.

11. Union Pacific Railroad Company, *Timetable No. 3*, 1980. Although the Riparia-La Crosse line still appeared in this timetable, it must have been unofficially closed and partially dismantled some years earlier. In May 1983 about six miles at the Riparia end were used for storing box cars. The remainder of the track had been lifted. Personal observation.

12. USGS 1/62500 map N4630W 11800/15, 1948 "Starbuck, Washington."

13. Union Pacific Railroad Company, Division Engineer's Office, Portland, Oregon, courtesy of Mr. Jim Reiser.

14. *Review*, June 15, 1888 (from Colfax *Gazette*).

15. *Union*, July 7, 1888.

16. *Union*, August 18, 1888.

17. *Oregonian*, August 25, 1888.

18. *Oregonian*, April 17, 1888.

19. *Union*, May 5, 1888.

20. *Union*, July 28, 1888.

21. *Union*, August 25, 1888.

22. *Union*, September 8, 1888.

23. *Oregonian*, November 1, 1888.

24. *Oregonian*, September 11, 1888.

25. *Union*, October 27, 1888; November 17, 1888.

26. *Union*, December 1, 1888. *Review*, December 11, 1888.

27. *Oregonian*, February 19, 1889.

28. Heppner *Gazette*, April 4, 1889.

29. *East Oregonian*, September 4, 1888.
30. *Union*, August 4, 1888. *Oregonian*, February 7, 1889.
31. *Review*, January 22, 1889.
32. *Oregonian*, April 9, 1889.
33. *Oregonian*, April 4, 1889.
34. *Oregonian*, August 30, 1888. *Review*, October 20, 1888.
35. *Oregonian*, July 7, 1889.
36. *Oregonian*, July 30, 1889.
37. *Oregonian*, September 14, 1889.
38. Preliminary surveys to Spokane: *Review*, December 8, 1886; December 15, 1886; *Oregonian*, January 1, 1887. Location surveys to Spokane *Review*, May 13, 1887; *Oregonian*, June 14, 1887 and July 10, 1887.
39. *Review*, August 15, 1888.
40. *Oregonian*, September 19, 1888.
41. *Review*, October 17, 1888.
42. *Review*, November 10, 1888.
43. *Review*, December 14, 1888.
44. *Oregonian*, March 15, 1889.
45. *Review*, August 11, 1888.
46. Copy of articles of incorporation, provided by Archives & Special Collections, Library, Eastern Washington University, Cheney. Courtesy of Charles V. Mutschler. *Oregonian*, May 4, 1889. *Review*, May 9, 1889.
47. *Oregonian*, July 3, 1889. *Railroad Gazette*, June 14, 1889, p. 400.
48. *Oregonian*, June 28, 1889. *Railroad Gazette*, August 16, 1889, p. 354.
49. *Review*, September 5, 1889.
50. *Oregonian*, September 20, 1889. *Review*, September 26, 1889. The leading attorneys and engineers were John H. Mitchell (NP attorney), H. S. Huson (NP Assistant Chief Engineer), W. B. Heyburn (W&I attorney) and W. H. Kennedy (OR&N Chief Engineer).
51. *Oregonian*, October 5, 1889.
52. *Oregonian*, October 8, 1889. *Review*, October 10, 1889.
53. *Union*, August 10, 1889.
54. Copy of articles of incorporation provided by Archives & Special Collections, Library, Eastern Washington University, Cheney. Courtesy of Charles V. Mutschler. *Oregonian*, July 24, 1889.
55. *Review*, April 20, 1890.
56. *Review*, May 10, 1890.

Notes for Chapter Eleven

1. *Weekly Statesman*, July 29, 1882.
2. *Oregonian*, November 25, 1886; December 20, 1886; December 30, 1886. *History of the Big Bend Country* (Spokane: Western Historical Publishing Co., 1904), p. 84.
3. Robert C. Nesbit, *He Built Seattle: A Biography of Judge Thomas Burke* (Seattle: University of Washington Press, 1961), pp. 90-105. Renz, *Northern Pacific*, p. 127. Sol H. Lewis, "A History of Railroads in Washington," *Washington Historical Quarterly*, 3 (July 1912): 191. Hedges, *Henry Villard*, p. 203.

4. Nesbit, *He Built Seattle*, pp. 105-106. Hedges, *Henry Villard*, p. 203, fn.
5. Nesbit, *He Built Seattle*, pp. 108-109.
6. *Railroad Gazette*, August 20, 1886, p. 587.
7. *Oregonian*, December 30, 1886.
8. *Oregonian*, January 3, 1887.
9. *Oregonian*, March 29, 1888; May 18, 1888; May 22, 1888.
10. *Railroad Gazette*, April 1, 1887, p. 225.
11. *Railroad Gazette*, November 4, 1887, p. 725.
12. *Review*, March 25, 1888. *Oregonian*, March 27, 1888 (from Davenport *Times*, March 23, 1888).
13. *Review*, April 8, 1888; April 11, 1888.
14. *Review*, April 21, 1888.
15. *Oregonian*, April 28, 1888.
16. *Review*, May 6, 1888; May 11, 1888.
17. *Oregonian*, October 1, 1888. *Review*, November 21, 1888.
18. *Oregonian*, May 18, 1888.
19. *Oregonian*, May 29, 1888; April 13, 1889.
20. *Oregonian*, December 27, 1887. *Review*, January 3, 1888. *History of the Big Bend Country*, p. 85.
21. *Review*, January 3, 1888.
22. *Oregonian*, March 27, 1888.
23. *Oregonian*, June 23, 1888; June 25, 1888; July 15, 1888; July 19, 1888; July 31, 1888. *Railroad Gazette*, July 27, 1888, p. 497. *History of the Big Bend Country*, pp. 546-547.
24. *Review*, July 21, 1888. *Oregonian*, July 25, 1888; July 27, 1888; July 31, 1888; August 1, 1888; August 4, 1888; August 7, 1888; August 9, 1888.
25. *Oregonian*, June 25, 1888; July 3, 1888; August 4, 1888. *Review*, July 21, 1888; August 8, 1888.
26. *Oregonian*, June 25, 1888; September 27, 1888; October 1, 1888. *Review*, June 26, 1888; November 4, 1888 (details of bridge).
27. *Review*, August 8, 1888; September 21, 1888. The SLS&E engines had names; one of the Spokane engines was named *A. M. Cannon. Review*, November 4, 1888.
28. *Oregonian*, September 27, 1888; October 1, 1888. *Review*, November 21, 1888. *Railroad Gazette*, December 7, 1888, p. 811. *History of the Big Bend Country*, p. 86.
29. *Review*, August 13, 1888. *Oregonian*, August 28, 1888.
30. *Railroad Gazette*, October 5, 1888, p. 661.
31. *Oregonian*, January 21, 1889.
32. *Railroad Gazette*, April 19, 1889, p. 270.
33. Renz, *Northern Pacific*, p. 142.
34. *Railroad Gazette*, July 27, 1888, p. 497.
35. *Union*, May 4, 1889. *Oregonian*, May 22, 1889.
36. *History of the Big Bend Country*, pp. 93-94.
37. *Oregonian*, August 28, 1888; September 11, 1888; June 28, 1889; July 15, 1889. *Review*, September 25, 1888; February 28, 1889; June 6, 1889; July 11, 1889. *Railroad Gazette*, April 5, 1889, p. 235. Northern Pacific Railway Company, *Annual Reports*, 1888, 1889, and 1890. *History of the Big Bend Country*, pp. 85, 86, 88, 93-94.

38. Northern Pacific Railroad Company, *Annual Report*, 1889, p. 43, says that five miles of the roadbed were graded there in June 1888. These earthworks can still be seen. Personal observation 1980.
39. *History of the Big Bend Country*, p. 88.
40. *Review*, September 5, 1889. *Railroad Gazette*, September 6, 1889, p. 592. *Oregonian*, September 11, 1889; September 14, 1889; October 5, 1889.
41. *History of the Big Bend Country*, p. 89.
42. *Review*, October 17, 1889.
43. *Review*, October 28, 1889.
44. *Review*, January 15, 1890.
45. *Review*, January 25, 1890.
46. *Review*, March 9, 1890.
47. *Review*, March 22, 1890.
48. Nesbit, *He Built Seattle*, pp. 147-150.
49. *Ibid*, p. 155.
50. *Oregonian*, March 8, 1890.
51. *Review*, June 11, 1890. *Railroad Gazette*, June 13, 1890, p. 427.
52. *Review*, July 22, 1890. *History of the Big Bend Country*, p. 90.
53. *Railroad Gazette*, September 18, 1890, p. 658 and September 26, 1890, p. 674. *Review*, September 24, 1890.
54. *Review*, March 15, 1892.
55. Renz, *Northern Pacific*, pp. 192, 195, 197. *History of the Big Bend Country*, pp. 106, 112.
56. Washington Water Power Company, *Annual Report*, 1904.
57. Burlington Northern Inc., *Timetable No. 13*, 1978.
58. Personal observation, 1983.
59. *Railroad Gazette*, April 5, 1889, p. 235; August 1, 1890, p. 549; March 20, 1891, p. 205. *Review*, July 10, 1890; February 1, 1891. Northern Pacific Railroad Company, *Annual Report*, 1889.
60. *Review*, March 19, 1891.
61. *Railroad Gazette*, May 11, 1888, p. 312 and June 1, 1888, p. 360. *Oregonian*, August 1, 1888.
62. *Union*, January 19, 1889; March 16, 1889. *Oregonian*, March 12, 1889; March 13, 1889; May 27, 1889; October 17, 1889. *Railroad Gazette*, September 27, 1889, p. 637; October 4, 1889, p. 653; November 22, 1889, p. 779; February 28, 1890, p. 151; March 21, 1890, p. 204. *Review*, September 5, 1889.

Notes for Chapter Twelve

1. For events prior to 1887 I have relied heavily upon Albro Martin, *James J. Hill and the Opening of the Northwest* (New York: Oxford University Press, 1976) and Pierre Berton, *The National Dream* (Toronto: McClelland & Stewart, 1970).
2. *Review*, May 15, 1886.
3. *Review*, December 11, 1891.
4. *Review*, April 6, 1890.
5. Martin, *James J. Hill*, p. 377. *Oregonian*, October 5, 1889.
6. *Review*, June 20, 1890.
7. *Railroad Gazette*, July 31, 1891, p. 539.

8. *Oregonian*, October 23, 1889. *Review*, October 24, 1889.
9. *Engineering News-Record*, May 9, 1935.
10. Daniel C. Haskell, *On Reconnaissance for the Great Northern: Letters of C. F. B. Haskell* (New York: reprint from Bulletin of the New York Public Library, 1948).
11. *Review*, February 5, 1890, in which a correspondent writing from Egan, Montana, states that he "has long been aware that the route was a feasible one for a railroad."
12. Personal observation.
13. *Interlake*, January 3, 1890.
14. John F. Stevens, "An Engineer's Recollections," *Engineering News-Record* (May 9, 1935): 672-676.
15. *Interlake*, February 11, 1890.
16. *Interlake*, January 17, 1890.
17. *Review*, March 18, 1892.
18. *Interlake*, June 27, 1890.
19. *Interlake*, July 18, 1890.
20. *Review*, August 25, 1892.
21. *Interlake*, March 14, 1890.
22. *Interlake*, March 28, 1890.
23. *Oregonian*, February 20, 1890.
24. *Oregonian*, March 8, 1890.
25. *Oregonian*, March 14, 1890.
26. In fact the supplies were brought by CPR to Sumas, then by Bellingham Bay & British Columbia to Bellingham, then turned over to Fairhaven & Southern. *Review*, January 31, 1892. The New Westminster Southern was apparently not used for that purpose because of heavy gradients. Discussion with Mr. Dave Wilkie, Victoria B. C., February 9, 1985.
27. *Review*, March 18, 1892; August 25, 1892. *Interlake*, April 11, 1890; June 27, 1890.
28. *Review*, April 19, 1890; June 7, 1890.
29. *Review*, December 11, 1891. *Interlake*, August 8, 1890.
30. *Railroad Gazette*, August 15, 1890, p. 577.
31. *Railroad Gazette*, September 25, 1891, p. 679. Based on my own extrapolations on USGS 7.5 Minute Series Map "Pleasant Valley Mountain." I believe 1,425 feet is the correct length, and not the 1,900 feet given in the *Railroad Gazette*, February 5, 1892, p. 110. On September 19, 1982, I found the east portal blocked and the west end open but collapsing and quite dangerous.
32. *Railroad Gazette*, August 5, 1892, p. 589.
33. *Interlake*, October 3, 1890.
34. *Interlake*, November 14, 1890.
35. *Interlake*, January 2, 1891.
36. *Interlake*, December 5, 1890.
37. *Interlake*, February 6, 1891.
38. *Interlake*, March 20, 1891.
39. *Interlake*, April 10, 1891.
40. *Columbian*, September 16, 1891.
41. *Interlake*, October 2, 1891.
42. *Interlake*, December 4, 1891.
43. *Columbian*, December 10, 1891.

44. *Columbian*, December 24, 1891.
45. *Review*, January 2, 1892.
46. *Railroad Gazette*, May 29, 1891, p. 378.
47. *Review*, August 6, 1891.
48. *Review*, January 27, 1891; February 3, 1891.
49. *Herald*, October 10, 1891.
50. *Railroad Gazette*, July 17, 1891, p. 505.
51. *Railroad Gazette*, September 4, 1891, p. 624. *Review*, November 15, 1891.
52. *Herald*, November 7, 1891.
53. *Railroad Gazette*, February 5, 1892, p. 110.
54. *Ibid.*
55. *Herald*, November 7, 1891.
56. *Ibid.*
57. *Railroad Gazette*, September 4, 1891, p. 624.
58. *Review*, April 8, 1891.
59. *Interlake*, June 5, 1891.
60. *Review*, May 22, 1891.
61. *Review*, July 4, 1891. Rev. Jonathan Edwards, *An Illustrated History of Spokane County, State of Washington* (Spokane: W. H. Lever, 1900).
62. *Review*, March 15, 1891. *Interlake*, June 5, 1891.
63. Discussion with Mr. L. E. Shawver, Spokane, Washington.
64. *Review*, August 6, 1891.
65. *Herald*, November 7, 1891.
66. *Ibid.* Review, November 8, 1891.
67. *Review*, December 13, 1891.
68. *Herald*, January 2, 1892.
69. *Review*, January 12, 1892.
70. *Herald*, January 16, 1892.
71. *Columbian*, February 25, 1892.
72. *Herald*, March 4, 1892.
73. *Review*, March 24, 1892.
74. *Herald*, March 18, 1892.
75. *Review*, January 29, 1892.
76. *Railroad Gazette*, February 5, 1892, p. 110; February 26, 1892, p. 165.
77. *Herald*, April 8, 1892.
78. *Columbian*, April 28, 1892.
79. *Review*, May 16, 1890.
80. *Review*, September 28, 1890.
81. Stevens, "Engineer's Recollections," *Engineering News-Record* (May 23, 1935): 749-751.
82. *Review*, December 4, 1890.
83. *Review*, May 3, 1891.
84. *Review*, December 12, 1890.
85. *Review*, May 16, 1891.
86. *Review*, December 8, 1891.
87. *History of the Big Bend Country*, p. 98. The engineer involved was almost certainly Thompson, who surveyed the Coulee City route (*Review*, July 1, 1891) and was working on the left bank of the Columbia above the mouth of Moses Coulee at that time (*Interlake*, November 20, 1891; *Review*, December 3; December 5, 1891). There is also a hint given in Haskell, *On Reconnaissance*,

that Haskell was also involved in land speculation. The definition of the Crab Creek route seems to have been spearheaded by Stevens (*Review*, January 10, 1892) in spite of opposition from Beckler, who was said to favor the more northerly route (*Review*, December 3, 1891). The close relationship between Stevens and Hill may date from that time.

88. *Review*, February 12, 1892.
89. *Review*, February 13, 1892.
90. *Review*, February 19, 1892.
91. *Review*, December 11, 1891.
92. *Herald*, April 8, 1892. *Railroad Gazette*, May 13, 1892, p. 358.
93. *Review*, May 29, 1892.
94. *Railroad Gazette*, June 10, 1892, p. 437.
95. *Review*, June 28, 1892; July 15, 1892; July 19, 1892.
96. *Review*, July 22, 1892.
97. *Review*, February 8, 1893; April 7, 1893.
98. *Review*, December 4, 1892.
99. Station names and distances given in this account are based on Great Northern Railway timetable, August 14, 1893, courtesy of Mr. Dave Walter, Montana Historical Society, Helena, Montana, and on the list of stations given in *Review*, January 13, 1893. These station names replaced the siding numbers used during the construction period. Some of them were never commonly used and were soon replaced by others. Note that Berne was originally spelled Byrne. Elevations are those given in GNR timetable 1912, courtesy of Mr. L. E. Shawver, Spokane, Washington.
100. Switchback gradients: *Review*, September 15, 1892. Tailtracks: *Review*, January 13, 1892. Elevation at summit: *Review*, May 12, 1893.
101. *The Great Northern Railway Electrification*, special publication no. 1857 (East Pittsburgh, Penn.: Westinghouse Electric & Manufacturing Co., 1929), pp. 5-6.
102. *Review*, October 13, 1891.
103. *Railroad Gazette*, December 11, 1891, p. 889.
104. *Review*, January 31, 1892.
105. *Review*, November 26, 1891.
106. *Railroad Gazette*, June 24, 1892, p. 483.
107. *Review*, July 24, 1892.
108. *Railroad Gazette*, April 1, 1892, p. 257.
109. *Railroad Gazette*, August 5, 1892, p. 589.
110. *Review*, September 2, 1892.
111. *Review*, July 28, 1892.
112. *Review*, August 25, 1892.
113. *Review*, September 21, 1892.
114. *Review*, October 6, 1892.
115. *Review*, October 25, 1892.
116. *Railroad Gazette*, November 4, 1892, p. 833.
117. *Review*, December 11, 1892.
118. *Review*, December 12, 1892.
119. *Review*, December 19, 1892.
120. *Review*, January 5, 1892.
121. *Review*, January 7, 1893.
122. *Railroad Gazette*, June 24, 1892, p. 483.

123. *Review,* January 7, 1893.
124. *Review,* May 3, 1893.
125. *Herald,* April 22, 1892.
126. *Herald,* April 29, 1892.
127. *Herald,* July 1, 1892.
128. *Review,* September 11, 1892. Ad.
129. *Review,* August 18, 1892.
130. *Review,* November 12, 1892.
131. *Columbian,* February 2, 1893.
132. *Review,* May 4, 1893.
133. *Review,* June 19, 1893.

Notes for Chapter Thirteen

1. *Review,* February 26, 1890.
2. *Oregonian,* March 18, 1890.
3. *Review,* April 8, 1890; April 26, 1890.
4. *Review,* June 20, 1890. *Railroad Gazette,* June 13, 1890, p. 427.
5. *Review,* May 13, 1890. *Railroad Gazette,* July 11, 1890, p. 501.
6. *Railroad Gazette,* August 29, 1890, p. 611.
7. *Review,* August 23, 1890, which added that "Mrs. C. C. Van Arsdol, wife of the resident engineer in charge of the Lewiston extension, gave him a very pleasant surprise on his birthday August 19th by preparing a toothsome repast and social reception."
8. *Review,* October 18, 1890.
9. *Review,* January 21, 1891.
10. *Railroad Gazette,* October 3, 1890, p. 691.
11. *Review,* January 4, 1891.
12. *Review,* June 5, 1891; August 13, 1891.
13. In 1906 the Lewiston & South Eastern Electric Railroad made plans to build on the Tammany Creek and Lake Waha route to Grangeville with a branch to Nez Perce, and carried out some grading. Taking over the partially completed roadbed the Nez Perce & Idaho Railroad laid track 11 miles to Tammany in 1913, but the line was operated only spasmodically until 1928.
14. *Review,* July 15, 1890.
15. *Review,* November 20, 1890.
16. *Review,* January 9, 1891.
17. *Review,* July 24, 1892.
18. *Ibid.*

Notes for Chapter Fourteen

1. *Oregonian,* October 23, 1885.
2. *Oregonian,* February 24, 1887.
3. *Oregonian,* September 6, 1886. *Railroad Gazette,* April 26, 1889, pp. 272-273. The O'Keefe bridge was 112 feet high and 1,000 feet long. Marent Gulch bridge was 226 feet high and 860 feet long. Smalley *Northern Pacific,* p. 419.
4. *Review,* November 20, 1886.

5. *Review*, July 6, 1890. Other Northern Pacific bridges rebuilt during this period included the Natches River bridge just west of North Yakima, replaced in 1891 at a cost of $36,000. *Railroad Gazette*, September 11, 1891, p. 640.
6. *Oregonian*, October 7, 1881; March 23, 1883.
7. *Oregonian*, June 4, 1883.
8. *Oregonian*, September 25, 1883.
9. *Oregonian*, August 15, 1886.
10. *Railroad Gazette*, April 19, 1889, pp. 260-261.
11. *Oregonian*, January 15, 1887.
12. *Oregonian*, February 3, 1887.
13. *Oregonian*, February 10, 1887.
14. *Oregonian*, February 14, 1887.
15. *Railroad Gazette*, May 27, 1887, p. 358.
16. *Oregonian*, June 16, 1887.
17. *Oregonian*, July 27, 1887. *Railroad Gazette*, July 29, 1887, p. 505.
18. *Oregonian*, October 31, 1887.
19. *Oregonian*, December 27, 1887.
20. *Oregonian*, February 7, 1888.
21. *Oregonian*, March 13, 1888.
22. *Oregonian*, March 31, 1888.
23. *Oregonian*, June 2, 1888.
24. *Oregonian*, July 11, 1888.
25. *Oregonian*, July 12, 1888.
26. *Oregonian*, July 16, 1888 and July 20, 1888.
27. *Oregonian*, September 26, 1888.
28. *Oregonian*, July 20, 1888. For a description of the Portland Union Depot, as first proposed, refer to *Oregonian*, September 25, 1883.
29. By mid-October 1889, 10,000 cubic yards of earth had been deposited, and the Union Freight Depot, 800 feet long, had been built upon it. *Oregonian*, October 20, 1889.
30. Verbal information provided by Oregon Historical Society.
31. The entire work in the Kootenai-Granite area covered 17 miles of line. This must have included trestle-filling between Kootenai and Sandpoint. The Granite cut-off was said to be nine miles long, and the re-location between Algoma and Cocolalla five miles. In November 1891 a work train was reported to be engaged in filling trestles between Kootenai and Sandpoint and this would account for the other four miles. At that time a decision had not yet been made to abandon the Pack River trestle and the "scenic" route via Sunnyside. The latter work was not undertaken until after the depression of the 1890s.
32. The west end of the Granite cut-off was at Stone's Spur, just east of Eight Mile Prairie on the original line, and just west of Athol on the new line.
33. *Review*, January 7, 1892.
34. *Review*, November 21, 1891.
35. *Railroad Gazette*, October 30, 1891, p. 773. Thomas Olsen's foreman in charge of the work between Kootenai and Algoma was H. D. Culver, whose name is perpetuated in a settlement northeast of Sandpoint.
36. *Herald*, October 17, 1891.

37. *Railroad Gazette,* July 29, 1892, reported the work practically completed, the only task outstanding being the Granite viaduct, which would soon be completed.

38. The original 1881 alignment may be found by taking U. S. Highway 395 to Athol, Idaho, turning east toward Bayview, then taking the first road to the left (northeast), then following this road (which was probably built partly on the old railway roadbed) around to the east, then proceeding east for almost a mile, then turning left (north) and following a bush road for about 0.4 miles. This trail crosses the old NPRR roadbed at a cut just west of the apex curve on the original easterly loop. The alignment is now somewhat difficult to follow because there are gaps in the embankments where the trestles used to be. Note that the second (1892) alignment was replaced by the present line in 1965.

39. *Oregonian,* April 10, 1888.

40. *East Oregonian,* June 27, 1888.

41. *Railroad Gazette,* August 8, 1890, p. 564.

42. *Review,* July 12, 1888.

43. *Review,* October 28, 1886.

44. *Review,* April 9, 1887.

45. *Union,* August 10, 1889.

46. *Review,* June 6, 1890.

47. *Review,* January 4, 1891. This report states that the NP depot "will be occupied in a fortnight."

48. *Review,* April 23, 1890. The new freight house was completed in April 1893. *Review,* May 1, 1893.

49. Northern Pacific Railroad Company, *Annual Report,* 1889.

50. Late in 1889 or early in 1890.

51. *Traveller's Official Guide of the Railway and Steam Navigation Lines in the United States and Canada,* June 1893 edition. Courtesy of Association of American Railroads Library, Washington, D. C.

52. Trains Nos. 2 and 3 were the winter remnant of a fast service first inaugurated between St. Paul and the "Pacific Coast" on November 20, 1887 (*Free Press,* November 19, 1887). This service was abandoned a year later (*Review,* November 9, 1888), resurrected and extended to Chicago in June 1890 (*Review,* June 11, 1890), and apparently operated on a "summer only" basis thereafter (*Review,* January 9, 1891).

53. *Traveller's Official Guide* gives every indication that as of October 31, 1892, Burke was still served by narrow gauge trains. Early in March 1893, however, a standard gauge rotary snowplow ran through to Burke (*Review* March 6, 1893; from Wallace *American*). The gauge, therefore, appears to have been changed in the intervening period.

54. This junction has, at various times, been called Stanton Jc., Killian's Jc., and more recently Smeltz.

55. Walla Walla cars had previously been incorporated into the Northern Pacific Atlantic and Pacific expresses between Portland and Wallula. *Union,* February 4, 1888.

56. As noted elsewhere herein, in 1890 there were two trains each way daily on the Spokane line.

57. In 1890 these trains were billed as *Coeur d'Alene Express* in advertisements appearing in the Spokane newspapers (i. e., *Review,* June 6, 1890).

58. After the completion of new buildings at Willows Junction in February 1894 the Heppner trains ceased to run along the main line between Willows and Arlington. *East Oregonian*, February 20, 1894.

59. *East Oregonian*, November 27, 1888.

60. Sometimes enginemen, in regaining lost time, made remarkable runs. On June 6, 1887 an NPRR westbound passenger train covered the 161 miles from Spokane Falls to Wallula in 3 hours 45 minutes (including a 20 minute stop at Sprague), thus sustaining an average running speed of 47.1 m. p. h. *Review*, June 9, 1887.

61. The Heppner branch locomotive was driven by J. A. Patterson and fired by Jack Hayes. The latter was killed in a head-on collision with a westbound freight train between Arlington and Willows Jc. on January 4, 1890. *Gazette*, January 9, 1890.

62. *Review*, August 21, 1892.

63. *Gazette*, May 15, 1890.

64. *Review*, August 10, 1886.

65. *Oregonian*, May 11, 1887.

66. *East Oregonian*, August 3, 1888.

67. *East Oregonian*, September 21, 1888.

68. *Union*, September 28, 1888.

69. *Oregonian*, May 5, 1886; May 8, 1886.

70. *Oregonian*, August 23, 1889.

71. *Oregonian*, August 12, 1886.

72. *Review*, February 28, 1889.

73. *Oregonian*, January 13, 1886.

74. *Union*, July 24, 1886. The new building was erected 30 rods north of the old hotel.

75. *Review*, December 3, 1886.

76. *Oregonian*, March 12, 1883.

77. *Oregonian*, March 10, 1885.

78. *Oregonian*, June 12, 1885. At that time it was suggested that the building be used for city or county offices.

79. *Oregonian*, December 10, 1887.

80. *Oregonian*, April 26, 1888.

81. *Oregonian*, April 8, 1890.

82. In the grain growing areas flouring mills were established at early dates. Examples are:
    - the Byers mill at Pendleton, Oregon, beginning operations at 50 barrels per day in 1874 and increasing production to 300 barrels per day by the time the original mill burned down in 1897 (Umatilla County Historical Society *Pioneer Trails*, 8: 3 (Spring/Summer 1984);
    - the Preston & Powell mill at Waitsburg, Washington, that shipped $27,300 worth of flour to Liverpool, England in 1881 (*Weekly Statesman*, August 6, 1881);
    - the H. P. Isaacs mill at Prescott, Washington, erected in 1883 at a cost of $75,000 to produce 300 barrels per day (*Oregonian*, January 13, 1883).

83. *Oregonian*, May 22, 1886.

84. Northern Pacific Railroad Company, *Annual Report*, 1888.

85. *Review*, August 21, 1887.

86. *Union*, December 3, 1887.

87. Northern Pacific Railroad Company, *Annual Report*, 1888.
88. *Union*, September 24, 1887. *Oregonian*, November 14, 1887. At that time OR&N began to run freight trains on Sundays.
89. *Union*, February 18, 1888. In 1888-1889 OR&N bought 600 new air-brake-fitted box cars from the Pullman Car Company, Chicago, Illinois. *Oregonian*, June 19, 1888 and December 15, 1888; *Railroad Gazette*, January 4, 1889, p. 11).
90. *Union*, October 1, 1887.
91. *Union*, November 5, 1887.
92. *Oregonian*, April 11, 1888 (from Pomeroy *Washingtonian*).
93. *Oregonian*, April 19, 1888.
94. *Review*, November 29, 1890.
95. *Oregonian*, February 4, 1889. The stations mentioned were: Pendleton, Adams, Milton, Valley Grove, Dayton, Diamond, Farmington, Pullman, Biggs, Truax, Barnhardt, Centerville, Spofford, Waitsburg, Alto, Colfax, Oakesdale, Grants, Moscow, Weston, Walla Walla, La Grande, Garfield, Guy, The Dalles, Pomeroy, Wallace, Eastland, Latah; to be built in 1889. Future construction was to be at: Blalocks, Endicott, Mockanema, Seltice, Zumwalt, Glenwood, and Tekoa.
96. *Oregonian*, September 2, 1889.
97. *Oregonian*, October 4, 1889. The elevator at Portland was to be 68 feet wide x 325 feet long, of timber construction, requiring 1.5 million board feet of lumber. It was to be covered all over with corrugated iron to reduce the fire hazard, and have mercurial fire alarms and electric lighting.
98. *Oregonian*, September 19, 1889. Mr. Peavey was at that time visiting Portland to inspect the big elevator.
99. Northern Pacific Railroad Company, *Annual Report*, 1889.
100. *Review*, December 23, 1890.
101. Northern Pacific Railroad Company, *Annual Report*, 1891.
102. Frank B. Gill, "Oregon's First Railway," *Quarterly of the Oregon Historical Society*, 25: 3 (September 1924): 233-234.
103. Wright, *Marine History of the Pacific Northwest*, p. 382.
104. *Review*, July 11, 1891.
105. *Railroad Gazette*, October 10, 1890, p. 709; May 8, 1891, pp. 317-318. The latter article stated that the company had previously been called the Farmer's Railway, Navigation, & Steamboat Portage Company, and later the Farmer's Transportation Company. By May 1891, $500,000 had been expended on rock work over a distance of 10 miles. The total cost of the portage railway and the steamers was to have been approximately $2.5 million. The work included one tunnel 250 feet long and a bridge 400 feet long over a tributary of the Columbia.
106. *Railroad Gazette*, August 7, 1891, p. 554.
107. *Review*, January 31, 1893; February 2, 1893.
108. *East Oregonian*, August 17, 1888. The Boat Railway was to have consisted of tracks 9,000 feet long at The Dalles, and 4,500 feet long at Celilo. Maximum grade was to have been 213.84 feet/mile. The vehicles were to have been 196 feet long x 48 feet wide, capable of carrying 714 tons. The cost at Celilo was estimated to be $350,000 for the track, the car, and the machinery. At The Dalles, $662,000. With rock excavations the total cost was estimated at $1,373,000.

109. *East Oregonian*, September 12, 1893. The Corps of Engineers estimated the cost of the portage railway at $454,390.
110. *Railroad Gazette*, December 15, 1899. Plans were also announced for a railway from Spokane to the Columbia River (near the mouth of the Yakima River). In 1906 the Spokane & Columbia River Railway & Navigation Co. was sold to the North Coast Railroad, a pseudo-independent subsidiary of Union Pacific. (The S&CR R&N Co. seems likely to have been the successor to the CR&N Co.). At that time there was said to be 18 miles of completed grade (*Railway Age Gazette*, July 20, 1906) between Connell and Fletcher (near Lyons Ferry) and was part of a line from Ringold Bar to Spokane (*Railway Age Gazette*, April 20, 1906).
111. *The Railway Age*, August 7, 1903, p. 176. For this work, the Oregon Legislature, despite the Corps of Engineers estimate, optimistically appropriated a mere $165,000, a sum soon found to be insufficient. *The Railway Age*, December 11, 1903.
112. *The Railway Age*, September 4, 1903, p. 299; October 9, 1903, p. 48.
113. *Oregonian*, May 4, 1886, and May 7, 1886.
114. *Oregonian*, June 17, 1889.
115. *Oregonian*, September 30, 1886.
116. Parson and Shiach, *History of Umatilla County and of Morrow County*, p. 164.
117. *Oregonian*, May 10, 1887.
118. *Gazette*, May 9, 1889.
119. *Oregonian*, May 27, 1886.
120. There were already some quite large sawmills in production in eastern Washington. At Palouse City, for example, six million board feet of lumber were sawn in 1888, at which time the population of that town was about 850. Most of the lumber produced there, however, would probably have been sold within the Columbia Interior. Not until 1906 was the Potlatch mill (for example) opened to produce lumber for large scale shipment to the east.
121. *Oregonian*, April 22, 1888.
122. *Union*, August 8, 1885.
123. *Oregonian*, July 1, 1889.
124. *Oregonian*, April 18, 1889.
125. *Oregonian*, June 17, 1889. The president of the Grande Ronde Lumber Company was Mr. Stanley, of the Chippewa (Wisconsin) Land & Lumber Company. He was joined in the venture by Mr. Bartlett from Eau Claire. The mill was to have 300 HP machinery and employ 250 men. Eventually the Grande Ronde Lumber Company had a narrow gauge logging railway extending all the way over the Blue Mountain divide to Ukiah.
126. *Oregonian*, April 4, 1890.
127. *Railroad Gazette*, September 26, 1890, p. 673.
128. *Railroad Gazette*, September 4, 1891, reported tracklaying nearly finished.
129. *Review*, September 25, 1890. The live fish were shipped from the Smithsonian Institute for stocking Loon and Deer lakes, north of Spokane.
130. *Review*, September 28, 1890. Over 100 carloads of watermelons were shipped from Yakima in 1890. The reference to Jamaica Ginger was probably humorous.
131. *Review*, September 12, 1889.
132. *Review*, September 23, 1890.

133. *Railway Age Gazette*, early in 1909.
134. In June 1886 Northern Pacific had 386 locomotives, and in 1888, 412. North Pacific Railroad Company, *Annual Reports*.
135. Ehernberger and Gschwind, *Union Pacific Steam*, p. 111. These engines received OR&N Nos. 160-164.
136. *Oregonian*, September 18, 1888.
137. *East Oregonian*, October 30, 1888.
138. *East Oregonian*, November 6, 1888.
139. *Union*, November 24, 1888.
140. *Oregonian*, December 15, 1888.
141. *Union*, August 17, 1889.
142. Ehernberger and Gschwind, *Union Pacific Steam*, p. 110.
143. *Interlake*, December 26, 1890.
144. *Review*, January 10, 1891. This expansion of production was achieved in spite of a fire that destroyed the entire town of Roslyn (*Oregonian*, July 24, 1888) and a bitter strike (*Oregonian*, August 22, 1888). The latter was a result of the Northern Pacific Coal Company wanting to operate Mine No. 3 at lower wages than Mines Nos. 1 and 2. Negro strike breakers were brought in at that time (*Oregonian*, August 24, 1888).
145. Northern Pacific Railroad Company, *Annual Report*, 1891.
146. *Free Press*, May 12, 1888. The total cost of running an eight-car passenger train was said to be $1.00 to $1.25 per mile, of which the locomotive cost was 17.5 cents per mile. Engines consumed 58 pounds of coal and 0.61 pints of lubricating oil per mile. *East Oregonian*, June 24, 1884. Coal cost on NPRR would thus have been eight cents per mile, or nearly half of total locomotive cost.
147. *Oregonian*, November 26, 1887 noted that "OR&N is still using wood on all its engines," and *Oregonian*, January 18, 1888 stated that "Owing to the fuel famine OR&N have abandoned all freight trains."
148. The UP search for coal deposits was not confined to eastern Oregon. In 1888 a geologist named Gager was sent to the Queen Charlotte Islands, off the British Columbia coast, to investigate an anthracite deposit. *Review*, August 2, 1892.
149. For example, OR&N locomotive engineers suffered a reduction in wages when they went onto payment by the mile instead of by the month. *Oregonian*, March 12, 1889.
150. The Brotherhood of Railroad Brakemen became the Brotherhood of Railway Trainmen on January 1, 1890.
151. *Oregonian*, July 12, 1889. Note that Grande Ronde Division No. 362 of the BLE was organized on September 5, 1887. Officials were J. R. Carson, Al. Bailey, and W. O. Moon. *Oregonian*, September 12, 1887.
152. *East Oregonian*, September 28, 1893.
153. *East Oregonian*, November 23, 1893.
154. Richard Hofstadter, William Miller, and Daniel Aaron, *The United States: The History of a Republic* (Englewood Cliffs, N. J.: Prentice Hall, 1957), pp. 537-538. Blanket injunctions, introduced "in re Debs" in May 1895, were finally outlawed by the Norris-La Guardia anti-injunction act of 1932.
155. *Railroad Gazette*, February 19, 1886, p. 135. The prototype of the Leslie rotary snowplow, on the Chicago & North Western Railroad, cut through a 20,810-foot length of three- to ten-foot deep drifts in 3 hours 25 minutes, at an average rate of 100 feet per minute. Some 15 miles of road, blocked for 10 days, was cleared in 9 hours.

156. *Review,* March 6, 1893 (from Wallace *American*). The first trip of an NPRR Leslie rotary snowplow to Burke, Idaho, ended with "6 broken cogs out of the gearwheel" and a trip to Missoula for repairs after the blades hit "a stick of cordwood."

157. The first Leslie rotary snowplow for OR&N arrived in the Columbia Valley in January 1888 (*Oregonian,* January 22, 1888). "It did in three days what 300 men with shovels could not have accomplished in as many weeks" (*Oregonian,* January 24, 1888).

158. The Pyle's Canyon snowsheds were built in 1885. There was one 960 feet long and another 500 feet long. The lumber was obtained "in the Cascades."

159. This report indicates that in eastern Oregon the Jull rotary snowplow performed fairly well. At any rate, well enough to be given a second trial. On April 16-18, 1890 it was tested in competition with a Leslie machine on the Alpine Pass section of the narrow gauge Denver, South Park, & Pacific Railroad (by that time a UP subsidiary). In the frozen snow, however, it worked poorly and derailed frequently. The design was not perpetuated. *Colorado Rail Annual No. 12,* pp. 85-87.

160. *Review,* February 28, 1890. Meanwhile, west of Spokane, the NPRR Central Washington branch remained blocked west of Davenport for more than a month. On January 8, 1890 there was a serious snowplowing accident about four miles west of Wilbur, derailing two locomotives and a wedge-type snowplow, and resulting in the death of two Sprague enginemen. *Review,* January 10, 1890.

161. *Oregonian,* May 26, 1881.

162. *Weekly Statesman,* August 13, 1881.

163. *Oregonian,* September 25, 1883.

164. *Oregonian,* November 24, 1883.

165. *Oregonian,* July 1, 1889.

166. *Review,* May 3, 1891. The sand removing machine was built at Albina Shops. It was designed and patented by C. A. Cameron, the UP Superintendent of Bridges and Buildings.

167. *Review,* October 11, 1892.

168. *East Oregonian,* December 16, 1887.

169. *Oregonian,* May 3, 1887.

170. *Oregonian,* December 3, 1887.

171. *Oregonian,* June 14, 1887 (from La Grande *Gazette*).

172. *Review,* May 19, 1893. This was not the first fire at Starbuck. In August 1887 the depot and adjoining private property were destroyed. By 1890, Starbuck had a seven-stall roundhouse and 79 railway employees. *History of South Eastern Washington,* p. 370.

173. *Oregonian,* January 18, 1888.

174. *Review,* April 15, 1890.

175. *Review,* August 26, 1891.

176. *East Oregonian,* July 27, 1888. This news item reported that Mr. McKenzie, the OR&N traveling auditor, passed through Pendleton on "yesterday morning's freight."

177. *East Oregonian,* December 29, 1885. One of the conductors dismissed was the genial "Shorty" Lash, a well-known and popular figure in Pendleton.

178. *Union,* October 1, 1887.

179. *Review,* November 22, 1891.

180. *East Oregonian,* November 13, 1888.

181. *Oregonian*, June 25, 1889.
182. *Gazette*, December 5, 1889.
183. *East Oregonian*, September 25, 1893.
184. *Review*, September 1, 1888; January 22, 1889. *Oregonian*, January 21, 1889.
185. *Review*, July 14, 1891; *Railroad Gazette*, August 28, 1891, p. 598.
186. *East Oregonian*, September 18, 1888. *Oregonian*, September 15, 1888. *Review*, July 4, 1890.
187. *Review*, February 5, 1890. *Railroad Gazette*, March 21, 1890, p. 194.
188. *Herald*, August 11, 1894. *History of South Eastern Washington*, p. 337.
189. *Oregonian*, March 26, 1890. *Review*, March 27, 1890.
190. *Review*, May 23, 1891. *Railroad Gazette*, July 3, 1891, p. 465.
191. *East Oregonian*, August 24, 1888. *Oregonian*, August 24, 1888; August 30, 1888.
192. *East Oregonian*, August 28, 1888.
193. *East Oregonian*, August 28, 1888.
194. *Review*, April 24, 1890.
195. *East Oregonian*, August 14, 1888.
196. *Oregonian*, July 6, 1887.
197. *Oregonian*, September 3, 1889.
198. *East Oregonian*, June 27, 1893.
199. *East Oregonian*, September 18, 1888.
200. *Railroad Gazette*, July 31, 1891, p. 526.
201. *East Oregonian*, December 27, 1887.
202. *Oregonian*, December 7, 1887.
203. *Union*, May 5, 1888. *Railroad Gazette*, June 29, 1888, p. 426.
204. *Oregonian*, September 21, 1889.
205. *East Oregonian*, November 23, 1888.
206. *Union*, December 29, 1888.
207. *Review*, March 3, 1891.
208. *Review*, October 11, 1888.
209. *Review*, October 12, 1888.
210. *Oregonian*, October 11, 1888.
211. *East Oregonian*, October 19, 1888.
212. *Interlake*, June 9, 1893.
213. *East Oregonian*, December 9, 1893. Shinski had been a founding member of the Spokane GN and SF&N local of the Brotherhood of Locomotive Firemen.
214. *Review*, July 1, 1892.

Notes for Chapter Fifteen

1. Alvin H. Hanson, *Business Cycles and the National Income* (New York: W. G. Norton and Co., 1964).
2. Daggett, *Railroad Reorganization*, p. 274. Hedges, *Henry Villard*, p. 110. Julius Grodinsky, *Transcontinental Railway Strategy, 1869-1893* (Philadelphia: University of Pennsylvania Press, 1962), p. 206.
3. *Union*, December 3, 1887. *Railroad Gazette*, February 3, 1888, p. 81. Daggett, *Railroad Reorganization*, p. 276. Villard, *Memoirs*, p. 325.
4. Daggett, *Railroad Reorganization*, pp. 278-283. Villard, *Memoirs*, pp. 332-334. Grodinsky, *Transcontinental Railway*, pp. 404-405.

5. Daggett, *Railroad Reorganization*, pp. 282-283.

6. *Ibid.*, p. 287. E. G. Campbell, *The Re-organization of the American Railroad System, 1893-1900* (New York: Bonanza Books, 1952), p. 43.

7. Daggett, *Railroad Reorganization*, pp. 288-289; Campbell, *American Railroad System*, pp. 45-46.

8. *East Oregonian*, August 15, 1893. *Herald*, August 19, 1893.

9. Daggett, *Railroad Reorganization*, pp. 220-241. Campbell, *American Railroad System*, pp. 83-90.

Bibliography

Newspapers and Periodicals

Chronicle, Spokane Falls, Washington, 1881.
Columbian, Columbia Falls, Montana, 1891-1893.
Commoner, Colfax, Washington, 1886.
East Oregonian, Pendleton, Oregon, 1884-1885, 1887-1888, 1893-1894.
Free Press, Wallace, Idaho, 1887-1890.
Gazette, Heppner, Oregon, 1888-1890.
Herald, Kootenai and Bonners Ferry, Idaho, 1891-1893.
Interlake, Demersville and Kalispell, Montana, 1890-1891, 1893.
Ledger, Tacoma, Washington, 1886-1887.
Oregonian, Portland, Oregon, 1885-1889.
Railroad Gazette, New York, New York, 1886-1892.
Railway Age Gazette, New York, New York, 1914.
Review, Spokane, Washington, 1886-1893.
Union, Walla Walla, Washington, 1885-1889.
Weekly Statesman, Walla Walla, Washington, 1879, 1882.

Published Sources

Anonymous. *An Illustrated History of South Eastern Washington.* Spokane, Wash: Western Historical Publishing Company, 1906.
_____. *Coal Resources of Oregon (Circular No. 362).* Washington, D. C.: United States Department of the Interior, Geological Survey, 1955.
_____. *The Great Northern Railway Electrification.* East Pittsburgh, Penn.: Westinghouse Electric & Manufacturing Company, Special Publication No. 1857, September 1929.
_____. *History of the Big Bend Country.* Spokane, Wash: Western Historical Publishing Company, 1904.
Athearn, Robert G. *Union Pacific Country.* Chicago, Ill.: Rand McNally, 1971.
Berton, Pierre. *The National Dream.* Toronto, Ontario: McClelland & Stewart, 1970.
Bruce, Alfred W. *The Steam Locomotive in America—Its Development in the Twentieth Century.* New York, N. Y.: Bonanza Books, 1952.
Bailey, Robert G. *River of No Return: A Century of Central Idaho and Eastern Washington History and Development.* Lewiston, Id.: 1941.
Campbell, E. G. *The Reorganization of the American Railroad System, 1893-1900.* New York, N. Y.: AMS Press, 1938.
Corbin, D. C. "Recollections of a Pioneer Railroad Builder. *Washington Historical Quarterly,* 1:2 (1907): 43-46.
Daggett, Stuart. *Railroad Reorganization.* Boston, Mass: Houghton Mifflin & Company, 1908.
Edwards, Rev. Jonathan. *Illustrated History of Spokane County, State of Washington.* Spokane, Wash: W. H. Lever, 1900.
Ehernberger, James L. and Francis G. Gschwind. *Union Pacific Steam—Northwestern District.* Callaway, Neb.: EG Publications, 1968.

Grodinsky, Julius. *Transcontinental Railway Strategy 1869-1893*. Philadelphia, Penn.: University of Pennsylvania Press, 1962.

Hanson, Alvin H. *Business Cycles and the National Income*. New York, N. Y.: W. G. Norton & Company, 1964.

Haskell, Daniel C. *On Reconnaissance for the Great Northern: Letters of C. F. B. Haskell*. New York, N. Y.: Reprint from Bulletin of the New York Public Library, 1948.

Hedges, James Blaine. *Henry Villard and the Railways of the Northwest*. New Haven, Conn.: Yale University Press, 1930.

Hult, Ruby El. *Steamboats in the Timber*. Portland, Ore.: Binsford and Mort, 1952.

Hofstadter, Richard, William Miller, and Daniel Aaron. *The United States: The History of a Republic*. Englewood Cliffs, N. J.: Prentice Hall, Inc., 1957.

Kindleberger, Charles P. *Manias, Panics, and Crashes: A History of Financial Crises*. New York, N. Y.: Basic Books, Inc., 1978.

Lewis, Sol H. "A History of Railroads in Washington. *Washington Historical Quarterly*, 3 (July 1912): 186-197.

Livingston-Little, D. E. "Discovery and Development of the Coeur d'Alene Mines." *Journal of the West* (July 3, 1964).

Malone, Michael P. and Richard B. Roeder. *Montana: A History of Two Centuries*. Seattle, Wash.: University of Washington Press, 1976.

Meinig, Donald W. *The Great Columbia Plain: A Historical Geography 1805-1910*. Seattle, Wash.: University of Washington Press, 1968.

Martin, Albro. *James J. Hill and the Opening of the Northwest*. New York, N. Y.: Oxford University Press, 1976.

Modelski, Andrew M. *Railroad Maps of North America: The First Hundred Years*. Washington, D. C.: Library of Congress, 1984.

Nesbit, Robert C. *He Built Seattle: A Biography of Judge Thomas Burke*. Seattle, Wash.: University of Washington Press, 1961.

Parson, Col W. and W. S. Shiach. *An Illustrated History of Umatilla County and of Morrow County*. Pendleton, Ore.: W. H. Lever, 1902.

Pelling, Henry. *American Labor*. Chicago, Ill.: University of Chicago Press, 1960.

Renz, Louis Tuck. *History of the Northern Pacific Railroad*. Fairfield, Wash.: Ye Galleon Press, 1980.

Richard, T. A. *Bunker Hill Enterprise*. San Francisco, Calif.: Mining & Scientific Press, 1921.

Ripley, E. Z. *Railroads: Rates and Regulation*. New York, N. Y.: Longmans, Green & Company, 1912.

————. *Railroads: Finance and Organization*. New York, N. Y.: Longmans, Green & Company, 1915.

Smalley, Eugene V. *History of the Northern Pacific Railroad*. New York, N. Y.: G. P. Putnam's Sons, 1883.

Sauvage, Edouard. *La Locomotive a Vapeur*. Paris, France: Beranger, 1918.

Stevens, John F. "An Engineer's Recollections." *Engineering News—Record,* between March 21, 1935 and November 28, 1935.

Villard, Henry. *Memoirs of Henry Villard, Volume II*. Boston, Mass.: Houghton Mifflin & Company, 1904.

Wood, Charles R. *The Northern Pacific—Main Street of the Northwest*. Seattle, Wash.: Superior Publishing Company, 1968.

Wood, John V. *Railroads Through the Coeur d'Alenes*. Caldwell, Id.: Caxton Printers, 1983.

Wright, E. W. (ed.) *Lewis and Dryden's Marine History of the Pacific Northwest.* New York, N. Y.: Reprint by Antiquarian Press, 1961; originally published 1895.

Reports, Etc.

Northern Pacific Railroad Company. *Annual Reports,* 1884-1894.
Oregon State Department of Geology & Mineral Industries.Reports by: John Allen Elliot, August 15, 1947; J. E. Morrison, May 20, 1939.
Washington Water Power Company. *Annual Report,* 1904.

Documents

Archives and Special Collections. Eastern Washington University. Cheney, Washington. Articles of Incorporation for:

> Eastern Washington Railway, November 15, 1885.
> Spokane & Palouse Railway, February 6, 1886.
> Spokane & Coeur d'Alene Railway, January 3, 1886.
> Spokane Falls & Idaho Railway, October 23, 1886.
> Spokane Falls & Rockford Railroad, May 3, 1889.
> Union Depot Company of Spokane Falls, July 9, 1889.

Timetables

Montana Historical Society; Helena, Montana. Great Northern Railway *Timetable,* August 14, 1893.
Mr. Lawrence E. Shawver, Spokane, Washington. Great Northern Railway and Northern Pacific Railway timetables, 1912.
Personal. Union Pacific Railroad, *Timetable No. 3,* March 9, 1980.
Burlington Northern, Inc., *Timetable No. 13,* January 8, 1978.

Index